# Mastering Spanish Business Vocabulary

## A Thematic Approach

Elena Meliveo
Edgar Knerr
Javier Cremades
Hermann Josef Knipper

BARRON'S

*All inquiries should be addressed to:*
Barron's Educational Series, Inc.
250 Wireless Boulevard
Hauppauge, New York 11788

*Library of Congress Catalog Card No. 96-78917*

International Standard Book Number 0-8120-9826-9

Printed in the United States of America
9 8 7 6 5 4 3 2 1

# Contents

# List of Abbreviations

| | |
|---|---|
| *u/c* | alguna cosa |
| *Ud.* | usted |
| *Uds.* | ustedes |

# Foreword

## 1. For whom was *Mastering Spanish Business Vocabulary* written?

This book is intended for people who have a Spanish vocabulary of at least 3,600 words and good knowledge of grammar. It is geared toward:

— those studying Romance languages and economics
— foreign language secretaries
— foreign language correspondents
— business translators and interpreters
— foreign trade officials
— export salespeople
— businesspeople
— those taking part in bilingual training programs
— those taking part in job-related exchange programs

## 2. What is the purpose of this book?

*Mastering Spanish Business Vocabulary* allows learners to build up and better retain their business vocabulary systematically by thematic areas. It serves as a study guide in preparing for examinations for foreign language correspondents, business translators, business interpreters, export salespeople and foreign trade officials.

## 3. Where can this book be used?

The book can be used in business schools, high schools and colleges, in adult and continuing education programs, and for self-learning. It is compatible with relevant Spanish language textbooks, any course format, and any instructional method.

## 4. What does this book contain?

*Mastering Spanish Business Vocabulary* is organized according to themes. It consists of 27 subject areas, each subdivided into chapters dealing with the individual aspects of the area. The entries in a chapter are divided into basic and continuing vocabulary and are listed according to thematic associations to provide a meaningful context. The entire vocabulary consists of 4,493 entries, of which 2,465 constitute the basic vocabulary and 2,028 the continuing vocabulary.

The organization makes possible theme-oriented learning in small, easily assimilated units that enable learners to express themselves in a specific thematic context, even before they have worked their way through the whole book. Furthermore, the thematic arrangement makes selection possible: Learners can begin with themes that are important to them, related to a particular learning plan or subject or themes that are meaningfully related, and can omit the other themes or consult them later.

## 5. What makes this book user-friendly and easy to learn from?

— The thematic construction and the concept of small, meaningful learning units.
— The wide choice of themes and comprehensive treatment of the individual thematic areas.
— The understanding of meanings of words through model sentences, dialogues, and corresponding idiomatic English expressions.
— The explanation of important business terms through informative model sentences.
— An alphabetical index of all the Spanish entries. The basic vocabulary entries appear in boldface in the index, those of the continuing vocabulary in lightface.

## 6. What are the sources for the compilation of this book?

The choice of entries was made on the basis of numerous sources:

— technical dictionaries
— word lists from the most-used textbooks of business Spanish
— word lists of adult education organizations
— original Spanish business texts

The words from the sources mentioned were evaluated according to frequency of use, usage, and usefulness. The list thus obtained was then expanded by theme-related additions that appeared necessary for coherence of subject matter.

## 7. How are the basic and continuing business Spanish vocabularies presented?

— Each chapter consists of a basic and a continuing vocabulary list. The basic vocabulary is introduced first; then the continuing vocabulary follows right after it and is clearly indicated by a gray background.
— The Spanish entries are printed in boldface on the left-hand side, while the English terms appear in lightface in the right-hand column. If there is no English expression for an entry, an explanation is given (in italics).

— Explanations in parentheses and italics explain terms that are peculiar to Spain.
— The gender of nouns is indicated by the corresponding masculine or feminine article, *el* or *la*, or their plurals *los* or *las*.
— Feminine forms are given throughout, in the complete form for nouns, by the addition of the corresponding feminine ending for adjectives.
— The 2,100 model sentences include typical colloquial phrases, idiomatic expressions, and grammatical peculiarities.

## 8. How can you best learn with *Mastering Spanish Business Vocabulary*?

You should work through the vocabulary by thematic areas, but the order of the themes is optional.

Generally, it is recommended that you learn in the order established within a chapter, since the entries are arranged in a logical sequence. Master the basic vocabulary first, before turning to the continuing vocabulary. Sections that you have mastered should be repeated regularly to establish them firmly. Daily vocabulary practice is advisable, with quota and speed established according to individual preference or learning goal.

Authors and editors

## The Job Market

el **mercado laboral**
La competencia en el mercado laboral es cada vez mayor.

the labor market
Competition in the labor market is getting tougher and tougher.

la **reforma laboral**
La reforma laboral de 1994 tiene como objetivo flexibilizar el rígido mercado de trabajo y fomentar la contratación.

labor market reform
An object of the labor market reform of 1994 is to make the rigid labor market more flexible and to encourage hiring.

**rígido (a)**

rigid; strict

la **contratación**

employment; hiring; contracting

el **asalariado**, la **asalariada**
Al disminuir el número de asalariados y aumentar el de jubilados, en el futuro habrá dificultades para pagar las pensiones.

wage earner; employee
As the number of employees decreases and the number of retirees increases, it will be difficult to pay pensions in the future.

**buscar trabajo, buscar empleo**
Carlos buscará su primer empleo después de acabar la carrera.

to look for work
After graduation, Carlos will be looking for his first job.

el **puesto de trabajo**

position; post; job

el **empleo fijo**
Con la reforma laboral de los 90 ha aumentado el número de contratos de trabajo temporales disminuyendo los contratos fijos.

permanent position
With the labor market reform of the nineties, the number of fixed-term employment contracts has increased, whereas contracts for permanent positions have declined.

el **centro de trabajo**
En los contratos laborales siempre debe figurar el centro de trabajo.

work site; plant
The work site must always be mentioned in employment contracts.

**laboral**

pertaining to employment

**cambiar**
No es recomendable cambiar de empleo muy a menudo.

to change
It is not recommended to change jobs too often.

**desempeñar**
En su puesto de trabajo desempeña
tareas de mucha responsabilidad.

to perform; carry out
She/he performs very responsible
tasks at her/his job.

**ejercer**
Carmen ejerce de abogada en un
bufete céntrico desde hace un año.

to be employed as
For a year Carmen has been
employed as a lawyer in a down-
town law office.

la **demanda de empleo**

job application; situations-wanted
advertisement

Durante 1993, la demanda de empleo
superó a la oferta.

During 1993 the number of job
applications exceeded the number
of jobs available.

Rechazaron su demanda de empleo.

They rejected his job application.

**rechazar**

to reject; refuse

**superar**

to exceed

la **oferta de trabajo**
Ya existen periódicos especializados
en ofertas de trabajo.

positions open; jobs available
Newspapers specializing in help
wanted ads already exist.

el **permiso de trabajo**
Si un extranjero desea trabajar en
España, deberá solicitar un permiso
de trabajo.

working papers, work permit
If a foreigner wants to work in
Spain, she (he) must first apply for
a work permit.

la **jornada laboral**

work day; working hours; work time

la **jornada semanal**
Habitualmente la jornada semanal es
de 40 horas.

working hours per week
Normally, a weekly work period is
40 hours.

la **jornada reducida**
En verano muchas empresas españolas
tienen jornada reducida, lo que supone,
aproximadamente, 2 horas diarias
menos de trabajo.

reduced work time
In the summer, many Spanish
businesses reduce working time by
approximately two hours.

la **jornada partida**
(En España,) la mayoría de los
trabajadores de los pequeños
comercios tienen jornada partida.
Por ejemplo: de 9 a 13:30 y de
17:00 a 20:30 horas.

interrupted work time
(In Spain,) most employees in
small business are on an interrupted
workday, e.g. from 9 to 13:30
(1:30 P.M.) hours and from 17:00
to 20:30 hours (5–8:30 P.M.).

la **inestabilidad laboral**
La inestabilidad laboral reinante es
una de las mayores preocupaciones
de los sindicatos.

unstable labor market; job insecurity
The prevailing instability of the
labor market is one of the major
concerns of the unions.

**acceder**
Hay que estar realmente bien preparado
para acceder a puestos directivos.

to accede; reach; attain
To attain executive positions one
must be very well prepared.

la **bolsa de trabajo**
La mayoría de las academias y centros de enseñanza tienen una bolsa de trabajo para facilitarle a sus alumnos posibles empleos.

job referral/procurement service
Most private schools and educational institutions have a job referral service to help their students find possible employment.

**facilitar**

to help; facilitate

la **agencia de colocaciones**
En 1994 se han legalizado en España las agencias privadas de colocación.

employment agency
In 1994 private employment agencies were legalized in Spain.

el **Instituto Nacional de Empleo (INEM)**
Pocas personas encuentran trabajo a través del INEM. (España)

National Institute of Employment (Spain)
Few people find a job through the INEM. (Spain)

el **fomento**
El propósito más importante de la reforma laboral es el fomento del empleo.

encouragment; promotion
The most important goal of the labor market reform is the promotion of employment.

la **movilidad geográfica**
Uno de los requisitos cada vez más valorados en el candidato es la movilidad geográfica.

geographic mobility
One of the increasingly important requirements for the job applicant is geographic mobility.

**precisar**
Para el puesto se precisan personas con poca experiencia.

to specify
To fill the position, they're asking for people with minimal experience.

**por cuenta ajena**
Todo trabajador de una empresa es un trabajador por cuenta ajena.

on someone else's account/behalf
Everyone working for a company is working for someone else.

**por cuenta propia**
Los profesionales liberales trabajan por cuenta propia.

on one's own account/behalf
Free-lance professionals work for themselves.

el **trabajo estacional**
En el sector turístico y en la agricultura es donde más abundan los trabajos estacionales.

seasonal work
Tourism and agriculture are the sectors with the largest share of seasonal work.

el **nivel salarial**
Muchas empresas extranjeras piensan que el nivel salarial en España es relativamente alto.

wage level
Many foreign firms think that the wage level in Spain is relatively high.

| | |
|---|---|
| **salarial** | wage-related |
| la **colocación**<br>La finalidad de los contratos de aprendizaje es la colocación de jóvenes sin formación en el mundo laboral. | insertion; placing<br>The goal of training contracts is the placing of unskilled young people into the labor market. |
| la **finalidad** | goal; purpose |
| el **pluriempleo**<br><br>Para financiar los estudios de sus hijos, tuvo que recurrir al pluriempleo durante algunos años. | holding more than one job; moonlighting<br>To pay for his children's studies he had to work at more than one job for some years. |
| la **población activa**<br>La Encuesta sobre Población Activa es el estudio más completo que se publica sobre el mercado de trabajo en España. | the working population<br>The Inquiry into the Working Population is the most complete study published on the labor market in Spain. |

## ▬▬▬ Applying for a Job and Getting Hired ▬▬▬

el **candidato,** la **candidata**
No se harán públicos los nombres de los candidatos al puesto de maestro.

applicant; candidate
The names of the applicants for the teaching position will not be disclosed.

la **entrevista de trabajo**
Existen numerosos libros con consejos para prepararse ante una entrevista de trabajo.

job interview
There are numerous books that give tips on how to prepare for a job interview.

el **currículo**

resumé

el **curriculum vitae**
Muchos jefes de personal exigen que el currículo sea escrito a mano.

curriculum vitae
Many personnel directors insist on a handwritten curriculum vitae.

**escrito a mano**

handwritten

los **datos personales**
En cualquier solicitud de empleo lo primero que hay que rellenar son los datos personales.

personal data/information
Personal data must be filled out first on every job application form.

el **estado civil**
A menudo el estado civil del candidato influye a la hora de la contratación.

civil/marital status
A candidate's marital status often has an influence on whether the applicant is hired.

la **fecha de nacimiento**
La fecha de nacimiento debe figurar siempre entre los datos personales en el curriculum vitae.

date of birth
The date of birth must always be included with personal data on the curriculum vitae.

**reunir las condiciones**
Se ruega a aquellas personas que reúnan las condiciones exigidas se personen el lunes en nuestras oficinas.

meet the conditions; qualify
Those who qualify are asked to come to our offices on Monday.

**personarse**

to appear personally

la **selección**
La selección de candidatos se realiza en función de sus aptitudes.

selection
Candidates are selected according to their qualifications.

**en función de**

according to

la **solicitud**
El plazo de presentación de solicitudes finaliza el próximo mes de mayo.

application
The period (term) for the submission of job applications will end next May.

la **presentación**

submission

**contratar**
Muchas empresas reciben ayuda económica del Estado por contratar personal difícil de colocar.

to hire; engage
Many firms receive economic help from the government if they hire persons difficult to employ.

la **ayuda económica**

economic aid/assistance/help

el **requisito**
Conviene leer con atención los requisitos que se exigen antes de contestar a una oferta de empleo.

requirement; qualification
It is advisable to carefully read the qualifications required before replying to a job offer.

la **experiencia laboral**
Para la mayoría de los trabajos es indispensable tener experiencia laboral.

job experience
For most positions job experience is indispensable.

la **falta de experiencia**

lack of experience

la **igualdad de oportunidades**
Debe existir igualdad de oportunidades entre los candidatos a un puesto de trabajo.

equal opportunity
All applicants for a position should be granted equal opportunity.

el **perfil del candidato**
El perfil del candidato es el conjunto de requisitos que éste debe reunir para el puesto.

candidate's (job) profile
The candidate's job profile consists of all the qualifications he should have for the job.

las **nociones**
Uno de los requisitos para el puesto era que el candidato tuviera nociones de contabilidad general.

ideas (of); familiarity with
One of the requirements for the job was that the applicant have some familiarity with general accounting.

las **referencias**
Cuando se busca empleo es importante poder aportar referencias sobre trabajos anteriores.

references
When looking for a job it is important to provide references concerning prior employment.

**aportar**

to bring along

**discriminatorio (a)**
Muchas mujeres sufren un trato discriminatorio en el trabajo.

discriminatory
Many women are subjected to discriminatory treatment on the job.

el **trato**

treatment

la **colocación**
Los trabajadores mayores de 45 años tienen más dificultades para encontrar una colocación.

hiring; placing
Workers over 45 have more difficulty finding employment.

**capacitado (a)**
Según el jefe, Lucía no estaba capacitada para el puesto.

qualified
According to the boss, Lucia wasn't qualified for the job.

**idóneo (a)**
La dirección vio en Marcos a la persona idónea para el cargo de asesor jurídico.

suitable
Management thought Marcos was suitable for the position of legal adviser.

la **incorporación**
Normalmente, una vez elegidos los candidatos, la incorporación es inmediata.

employment
Once selected, candidates normally start to work immediately.

**ingresar**
El año pasado ingresaron en la plantilla de la empresa tan sólo cinco nuevos trabajadores.

to enter; join
Last year only five new employees were entered on the firm's payroll.

**valorar**
Como tener conocimientos de inglés hoy en día se ha convertido en un requisito casi imprescindible para encontrar empleo, cada vez se valora más un buen nivel de alemán.

to estimate
Since a knowledge of English has become an almost indispensable requirement in finding employment, a good knowledge of German is becoming increasingly desirable.

la **valía**
En casi todos los puestos de trabajo, la retribución se fija en función de la valía del candidato.

value; evaluation
The salary level for most jobs is determined by the evaluation of the candidate's qualifications.

# Job Advertisements

la **persona de contacto**
Todos los interesados deberán concertar una entrevista con nuestra persona de contacto en el número de teléfono abajo indicado.

contact person
All persons interested should arrange for an interview with our contact person at the telephone number indicated below.

la **confidencialidad**

confidentiality

la **reserva absoluta**
Durante el proceso de selección se garantiza absoluta confidencialidad.

non-disclosure agreement
During the selection process absolute confidentiality is guaranteed.

**absoluto (a)**

absolute

**requerirse**
Se requieren cinco azafatas de congreso con buena presencia y dominio del inglés para la semana del 1 al 7 de abril.

to be required/needed
Five personable convention hostesses with an excellent knowledge of English are needed for the week of April 1–7.

la **azafata de congreso**

convention hostess

la **buena presencia**

attractive personal appearance

**variado (a)**
Empresa líder en el sector de máquinas para la fabricación de herramientas busca candidato idóneo para desempeñar una variada actividad en un agradable entorno laboral.

varied
A leading firm in the manufacture of tool-making machinery is looking for a suitable candidate to perform a variety of functions in pleasant working conditions.

la **empresa líder**

leading business

el **entorno**

environment, surroundings

el **interesado,** la **interesada**
Los interesados deberán enviar amplio historial profesional a nuestra sede en Madrid.

person interested
Persons interested should send their full professional history to our offices in Madrid.

el **historial profesional**

professional history

**acorde con**
La retribución será acorde con la experiencia y valía del candidato.

in accord with; commensurate with
Salary will be commensurate with the candidate's experience and qualifications.

la **capacidad organizativa**
El perfil del candidato debe reflejar una marcada capacidad organizativa y un claro carácter comercial.

organizing ability
The candidate's job profile should reflect a strong ability to organize and a well-defined commercial talent.

**marcado (a)**

marked; strong

**reflejar**

to reflect

la **iniciativa propia**
Se busca un profesional de la venta, dinámico, con iniciativa propia y cartera de clientes.

individual initiative
Looking for a dynamic sales professional with individual initiative and a file of private customers.

el, la **profesional**

professional

la **experiencia**
El aspirante deberá acreditar experiencia en puesto similar por un período no inferior a dos años.

experience
The applicant must show proof of experience in a similar position for not less than two years.

el, la **aspirante**
Los aspirantes a director comercial tuvieron que someterse a varias pruebas psicológicas.

candidate; applicant; aspirant
The candidates for the position of commercial director had to submit to various psychological tests.

**acreditar**

to prove

la **cualificación**
Cualificación exigida: graduado escolar o Formación Profesional.

qualification
Qualification required: high school graduate or professional training.

**indispensable**
Un requisito indispensable es el dominio hablado y escrito del idioma inglés.

indispensable
An indispensable requirement is mastery of written and spoken English.

el **dominio**

mastery

**motivado (a)**
Si Ud. es una persona motivada y tiene verdadero afán de superación le damos la bienvenida a nuestro nuevo equipo.

motivated
If you are highly motivated and eager to surpass yourself, we welcome you to our new team.

el **afán de superación**

eagerness to surpass oneself

el **espíritu emprendedor**

Valoraremos muy positivamente el espíritu emprendedor y la iniciativa propia.

entrepreneurial spirit; get-up-and-go personality
We will particularly appreciate an entrepreneurial spirit and individual initiative.

**identificarse**
Buscamos un nuevo compañero que, al igual que nosotros, se identifique totalmente con los objetivos de la empresa y esté dispuesto a integrarse.

to identify oneself
We are looking for a new colleague who, like us, will identify himself completely with the goals of the firm and be ready to fit in.

**intregarse**

to integrate oneself; fit in

**de renombre**
Empresa de gran renombre y en plena expansión necesita cinco comerciales con vehículo propio para su oficina en Barcelona.

renowned; very well-known
Very well-known firm in full expansion needs five sales persons with their own cars for its Barcelona office.

el, la **comercial**

sales person

**imponerse**
Buscamos a la persona que compagine una notable capacidad negociadora con el saber imponerse.

to assert oneself
We are looking for someone who combines outstanding negotiation skills with an assertive manner.

**compaginar**

to combine; reconcile

la **capacidad negociadora**

negotiating skill

la **habilidad negociadora**

negotiating ability

**a nivel de usuario**
Se busca administrativo con conocimientos de inglés e informática a nivel de usuario.

at the user level
Seeking management person with knowledge of English and electronic communication skills at the user level.

el **administrativo,**
la **administrativa**

white-collar worker; office-worker

**llevar a la práctica**
Tendremos muy en cuenta su cualificación académica y si además sabe llevar a la práctica lo aprendido, mejor que mejor.

to put into practice
We will give much weight to your academic qualifications and if, in addition, you know how to put into practice what you've learned, so much the better.

**dispuesto (a)**
Buscamos un profesional con dotes de mando dispuesto a asumir la responsabilidad de la ampliación de nuestra red de distribución.

prepared to
We are looking for a professional with leadership ability ready to assume responsibility for the expansion of our distribution system.

las **dotes de mando**

command skills; leadership ability

| | |
|---|---|
| **asumir responsabilidad** | to assume responsibility |
| el **desarrollo profesional** | professional development; advancement |
| Si tiene clara vocación para la venta, le ofrecemos posibilidades reales de desarrollo profesional. | If you are definitely committed to a career in sales, we offer you solid chances for professional advancement. |
| la **vocación** | vocation; career commitment |
| la **retribución competitiva** | competitive salary |
| Se trata de un trabajo muy exigente con una retribución altamente competitiva. | At issue is a very demanding job with a highly competitive salary. |
| **recompensar** | to remunerate; to pay |
| **exigente** | demanding |

## ▬▬ **Training and Further Education** ▬▬

| | |
|---|---|
| la **enseñanza** | education, teaching |
| La enseñanza asistida por ordenador tiene cada día más importancia en la formación. | Computer assisted instruction is becoming increasingly important in education. |
| **adquirir** | to acquire |
| El objetivo de toda formación es adquirir los conocimientos necesarios para poder trabajar en un futuro. | The object of all education is to acquire the knowledge necessary for work in the future. |
| el **objetivo** | goal; objective |
| **aprender** | to learn |
| En las escuelas taller, los alumnos tienen la oportunidad de aprender un oficio que corre peligro de desaparecer. | In vocational schools, students have the opportunity to learn a trade that is in danger of disappearing. |
| **tener la oportunidad** | to have the opportunity |
| la **beca** | scholarship |
| El ICEX (Instituto de Comercio Exterior) (España) ofrece cada año numerosas becas de estudios en el extranjero. | The Institute of Foreign Trade (Spain) offers numerous scholarships every year for study abroad. |
| **ofrecer** | to offer |

la **carrera profesional**
Cada vez menos empleados desarrollan
su carrera profesional en una sola
empresa.

professional career
Fewer and fewer employees are
spending their entire professional
career with one single company.

la **cultura general**
El hecho de que la gente cada vez
lea menos influye negativamente en
su cultura general.

general knowledge
The fact that people are reading
less and less has a negative influence on their general knowledge.

el **certificado de estudios**
Mario tuvo que traducir su certificado
de estudios para poder solicitar una
beca en los Estados Unidos.

diploma; scholastic certificate
Mario had to translate his diploma
in order to apply for a scholarship
in the United States.

el **diploma**
(En España,) los diplomas de muchas
academias privadas no tienen validez
al no estar reconocidos oficialmente
por el Ministerio de Educación y
Ciencia (M.E.C.)

diploma
(In Spain,) diplomas from many
private schools are worthless
because they are not officially
recognized by the Department of
Education.

**oficialmente**

officially

el **diplomado,** la **diplomada**
En el hospital de Palma de Mallorca
necesitan cinco diplomados/as en
enfermería.

graduate with a degree/diploma
For the hospital in Palma de
Mallorca five people with a
degree in nursing are needed.

**lectivo (a)**
La Asociación Española de Dirección
de Empresas (AEEDE) (España)
quiere imponer un mínimo de 800
horas lectivas para obtener un título
de Master.

school
The Spanish Management Association (Spain) would like to impose
a minimum of 800 credit hours for
the earning of a Master's degree.

la **Formación Profesional (F.P.)**

Professional Training; Professional
School

(En España,) el índice de personas
que no acaban la Formación
Profesional es muy elevado.

(In Spain,) the percentage of people
who drop out of the Professional
Training program is very high.

el **graduado escolar,**
la **graduada escolar**

secondary school graduate

**progresar**
Para poder progresar profesionalmente
es necesario una formación contínua.

to progress; advance
Continuing education is necessary
for professional advancement.

el **seminario**
El mes pasado asistí a un seminario
de técnicas de estudio.

seminar
Last month I attended a seminar
on study techniques.

**familiarizarse**
No le fue difícil familiarizarse con su nuevo puesto de trabajo.

to familiarize oneself; adjust to
He had no difficulty adjusting to his new job.

**profundizar**
Manuel asiste a un curso de Derecho Laboral para profundizar sus conocimientos en este campo.

to deepen
Manuel is taking a course in labor law to gain more knowledge in this field.

**iniciar**
Un compañero se encargará de iniciar a Carlos en su nueva actividad en la empresa.
Hace tan sólo un mes que la empresa ha iniciado sus nuevas actividades en el sector de las comunicaciones.

to initiate; begin
A colleague will be responsible for initiating Carlos into his new job at the firm.
Only a month ago the firm began its new activities in the communications sector.

la **aptitud**
En selección de personal se emplean cada vez más pruebas de aptitud diseñadas por la propia empresa.

aptitude; ability
More and more aptitude tests, devised by the companies themselves, are being used when hiring.

la **calificación académica**
Unas buenas calificaciones académicas no garantizan actualmente un puesto de trabajo.

academic qualification
Nowadays, academic qualifications are no guarantee of a job.

la **capacitación**
Debido al elevado número de parados con formación universitaria, el nivel de capacitación exigido es cada vez mayor.

qualification; training
Due to the large number of unemployed university graduates, higher and higher levels of qualification are being asked for.

la **readaptación profesional**

El INEM (España) organiza numerosos cursos de capacitación en el marco de la readaptación profesional.

re-training; professional development
INEM (Spain) organizes numerous re-training courses for professional development.

el **Curso de Orientación Universitaria (C.O.U.)**
El C.O.U. (España) es un curso de preparación al examen de selectividad e ingreso a la Universidad.

Preparatory Course for University Study
The C.O.U. (Spain) is a prepartory course for the university admissions examination.

la **preparación**

preparation

la **selectividad**
Cada año miles de jóvenes realizan el examen de selectividad para poder acceder a la Universidad.

selection
Every year thousands of young people take the university admissions examination.

el **perfeccionamiento**

continuing education; further training

Las grandes empresas tienen sus propios centros de enseñanza donde se imparten cursos de perfeccionamiento.

Big firms have their own teaching centers where courses in continuing education are given.

el **centro de enseñanza**

teaching, training center

**impartir**

to impart; give courses

la **instrucción permanente**

continuing education

Muchas profesiones precisan, hoy en día, una instrucción permanente debido al contínuo avance tecnológico.

Due to ongoing technological advances, nowadays many professions require continuing education.

la **escuela taller**

vocational school

Las escuelas taller, donde se enseñan oficios tradicionales, pretenden ser una alternativa práctica para jóvenes en paro.

Vocational schools, where traditional trades are taught, claim to be a practical alternative for unemployed young people.

el **oficio**

trade; profession

la **homologación**

official recognition

(En España,) el Ministerio de Eduación y Ciencia (M.E.C.) a veces dificulta la homologación de títulos académicos obtenidos en el extranjero.

(In Spain,) the Department of Education is sometimes reluctant to recognize academic credits and diplomas earned abroad.

el **titulado universitario,** la **titulada universitaria**

university graduate

**imprescindible**

indispensable

Para muchos puestos de trabajo son imprescindibles buenos conocimientos de uno o más idiomas extranjeros.

For many jobs a good knowledge of one or more foreign languages is indispensable.

la **orientación profesional**

professional counselling

La orientación profesional tiene como objetivo asesorar sobre la elección de la profesión.

The goal of professional counselling is to provide assistance on career selection.

la **elección de la profesión**

career selection

la **ponencia**

lecture

En el Instituto Alemán de Madrid (España) se organizan interesantes ponencias sobre temas culturales.

The German Institute in Madrid (Spain) arranges for many interesting lectures on cultural themes.

# Unemployment

el **desempleo**
En 1994, por primera vez, la Unión Europea ha dedicado una cumbre al problema del desempleo.

unemployment
In 1994 the European Union, for the first time, devoted a summit conference to the problem of unemployment.

el **desempleado,**
la **desempleada**
El elevado número de desempleados es un problema que preocupa a todos los países industrializados.

unemployed person

The large number of unemployed is a problem that concerns all industrialized countries.

el **despido**
(En España,) en caso de despido de un trabajador, la dirección debe consultar previamente con el Comité de Empresa.

discharge; letting go; firing
(In Spain,) when a worker is discharged, management should first consult with the (factory) works committee.

**estar en paro**
En España, en 1994, había casi un millón de familias en las que todos sus miembros en edad de trabajar estaban en paro.

to be unemployed
In Spain, in 1994, there were almost a million families in which all the members of working age were unemployed.

**quedarse en paro**
Quedarse en paro no sólo significa un grave problema económico, sino también un problema psicológico para los afectados.

to remain unemployed
Long-term unemployment is not only a grave economic problem but also a psychological problem for those affected.

el **beneficiario,** la **beneficiaria**
Podrán ser beneficiarios de la prestación por desempleo todos aquellos trabajadores por cuenta ajena que se hayan quedado en paro y hayan cotizado durante el período mínimo exigido.

beneficiary; claimant
All non free-lance workers who become unemployed and who have paid contributions during the minimum period required, can claim unemployment insurance payments.

la **causa del despido**

cause of discharge

el **motivo del despido**
Repetidas faltas de asistencia injustificadas pueden ser causa de despido.

reason for dismissal
Repeated unjustifiable failure to report for work can be a cause for discharge.

la **falta de asistencia**

failure to show up; absence

**inscrito (a)**
Para poder percibir la prestación por desempleo se debe estar inscrito en el Instituto Nacional de Empleo (INEM) (España).

enrolled; registered
In order to collect unemployment insurance payments one must be registered with INEM (Spain).

el **recorte**
En los años 90 los sindicatos han convocado numerosas manifestaciones en contra de los nuevos recortes de las prestaciones por desempleo.

cutback; cut
In the 90's the unions called for numerous demonstrations against new cutbacks in unemployment insurance payments.

la **reducción**
Para muchas familias, la reducción del subsidio por desempleo supone un verdadero problema económico.

reduction
For many families the reduction of unemployment compensation poses a real economic problem.

la **prestación por desempleo**

unemployment compensation payment

el **subsidio por desempleo**

unemployment insurance benefits

**reducir**
Para mantener en competencia muchas empresas se han visto obligadas a reducir sus plantillas.

to reduce
To maintain competitiveness many firms have been compelled to reduce their payroll.

el **ritmo**
El ritmo de crecimiento del paro ha llegado a superar las expectativas más pesimistas.

rhythm; rate
The rate of growth in unemployment has surpassed the most pessimistic expectations.

**ascender**
En 1993, el número de parados ascendió a casi 3 millones.

to mount; be promoted; amount to
In 1993 the number of unemployed rose to almost 3 million.

el, **la solicitante**
El solicitante de la prestación por desempleo tiene que presentar la documentación necesaria durante los 15 días siguientes a la extinción del contrato.

claimant
Anyone making a claim for unemployment compensation has to present the necessary documentation within 15 days after termination of his employment contract.

la **documentación**

documentation; supporting documents

**constituir**
Los parados de larga duración constituyen el grupo con más dificultades a la hora de buscar trabajo.

to constitute
Long-term unemployed are the group with the most problems when seeking employment.

la **carga familiar**

(En España,) para los parados con cargas familiares está garantizada una prestación mínima igual al 100% del Salario Mínimo.

dependent; family member with no income
(In Spain,) for the unemployed with dependents, a minimum payment equal to 100% of the minimum wage is guaranteed.

la **cuantía**
(En España,) la cuantía de la prestación por desempleo se fija en función de los ingresos durante los últimos 180 días trabajados.

sum; amount
(In Spain,) the amount of the unemployment payment is determined according to earnings during the last 180 days of employment.

el **desempleo estructural**
El desempleo estructural afecta a sectores industriales en crisis como por ejemplo, en España, la industria metalúrgica.

structural unemployment
Structural unemployment affects industrial sectors in crisis, such as e.g. the metal industry.

el **despido colectivo**
Se considera despido colectivo cuando afecta a más del 10% de la plantilla de una empresa con menos de 300 trabajadores y necesita autorización administrativa.

mass firing
It is considered mass firing when more than 10% of the work force of a firm with less than 300 workers is affected and when official authorization is required.

la **autorización administrativa**

official authorization

el **despido improcedente**
En caso de despido improcedente, el trabajador tiene derecho a ser readmitido o bien al pago de una indemnización.

improper, unjustifiable dismissal
In the event of improper dismissal, the worker has the right to be reinstated or to receive a cash settlement.

**readmitir**

to readmit; rehire; reinstate

**nulo (a)**
El juez consideró que el empresario no había cumplido los requisitos formales y declaró nulo el despido de Pablo.

void; invalid
The judge ruled that the entrepreneur had not complied with formal requirements and invalidated Pablo's dismissal.

**incompatible**
Percibir la prestación por desempleo y tener al mismo tiempo otro tipo de ingresos es incompatible y se sanciona con la extinción de la prestación.

incompatible
To collect unemployment insurance and simultaneously have another source of income is incompatible and is punished by termination of payments.

**sancionar**

to punish; sanction

el **paro estacional**
Siempre, cuando termina la temporada turística, aumenta el desempleo y se considera paro estacional.

seasonal unemployment
Always, when the tourist season is over, unemployment rises and is considered seasonal unemployment.

**percibir**
Como mínimo hay que cotizar durante un año a la Seguridad Social para tener derecho a percibir la prestación por desempleo.

to receive; collect
As a basic minimum, it is necessary to pay in to Social Security for a year in order to be entitled to collect unemployment insurance.

la **tasa de desempleo**
La tasa de desempleo en la Unión
Europea (UE) a finales de 1993
ascendía al 10,6% de la población
activa.

percentage; rate; ratio
The unemployment rate in the
European Union (UE) at the end
of 1993 rose to 10.6% of the
working population.

el **expediente de regulación
de empleo**
SEAT ha presentado un expediente
de regulación de empleo de 10 meses
que afecta a 800 trabajadores.

job adjustment plan

SEAT has proposed a job adjustment plan (for work reduction)
that affects 800 workers for a
period of 10 months.

la **jornada reducida**
Debido a la caída de la demanda,
algunas empresas automovilísticas
han introducido la jornada reducida.

reduced work time; part-time
Because of the drop in demand,
some automobile companies have
introduced a reduced work week.

**introducir**

to introduce

━━━━━ **Social Aspects of Labor** ━━━━━

**estar de baja**

Pedro estuvo casi tres meses de baja
por un accidente de trabajo.

to be on the sick list; be reported
sick
Pedro was on the sick list for
almost three months because of
an accident on the job.

**dar de alta**
Alberto pidió al médico que le diera
de alta porque quería ir a trabajar lo
antes posible.

to declare fit to work
Alberto asked the doctor to
declare him fit to work because he
wanted to return to work as soon
as possible.

**dar de baja**
A muchos empresarios les parece
que los médicos a menudo dan de
baja a los trabajadores con demasiada
facilidad.

to declare unfit to work
Many employers think that doctors
are often too quick to declare
workers unfit to work.

el **derecho**
A través de las cotizaciones a la
Seguridad Social, el trabajador
adquiere el derecho a cobrar
posteriormente la prestación por
desempleo.

right; law; fee
By paying into Social Security, the
worker acquires the right to collect
unemployment insurance later.

la **pensión**
(En España,) el Gobierno estudia la
posibilidad de elevar el número de
años cotizados—actualmente 15—
para poder cobrar una pensión.

retirement; pension
(In Spain,) the government is
studying the possibility of increasing the required number of pay-in
years, presently 15, before being
able to collect a pension.

el **perceptor,** la **perceptora**
Los perceptores de la prestación por
desempleo deben personarse cada
tres meses en las oficinas del INEM
(España).

receiver; collector
Unemployment insurance collec-
tors should report in person every
three months at the unemployment
office.

**jubilar**
Muchas empresas jubilan anticipada-
mente a algunos de sus trabajadores
para, así, reducir plantilla.

to retire
Many companies are retiring some
of their workers early in order to
reduce their work force.

**jubilarse**
La edad normal para jubilarse es a
los 65 años.

to take retirement
The normal retirement age is 65.

**cotizar**
(En España,) el trabajador cotiza a la
Seguridad Social.

to pay in
(In Spain,) the worker pays into
Social Security.

la **cotización**
(En España,) para incentivar la
contratación de parados mayores de
45 años y de larga duración, el Estado
pagará las cotizaciones a la Seguridad
Social durante un período de 1 y 3
años.

paying in contributions
(In Spain,) to encourage hiring
long-time unemployed persons
over 45 the government assumes
Social Security payments for a
period of 1 to 3 years.

la **Seguridad Social**

Social Security

la **jubilación anticipada**

early retirement

la **pensión de invalidez**
Le concedieron la pensión de invalidez
después de haber sufrido un grave
accidente de trabajo.

disability pension
They granted him a disability
pension after he suffered a serious
job-related accident.

la **pensión de viudedad**
Pilar se ve obligada a hacer pequeños
trabajos porque no puede vivir con
la pensión de viudedad.

widow's pension
Pilar is obliged to take little jobs
because she can't live on her
widow's pension.

la **prestaciones sociales**
En España se han recortado algunas
prestaciones sociales, tales como
las sanitarias y la prestación por
desempleo.

social welfare payments
In Spain, some social welfare
payments, such as health care
and unemployment, have been
cut back.

**recortar**

to cut back; trim

la **suplencia**
A través de una agencia de colocación,
la empresa encontró a la persona que
hace la suplencia de maternidad de
Inés.

substitution; replacement
Through an employment agency,
the company found someone to
replace Inés while she was away
on maternity leave.

**dar de baja**
(En España,) al solicitar el subsidio por desempleo, el solicitante deberá presentar un justificante de que la empresa le ha dado de baja en la Seguridad Social.

to lay off; remove from the list
(In Spain,) when applying for unemployment insurance, the applicant must present a certificate attesting that the company has laid him off.

el **justificante**

certificate

la **incapacidad laboral transitoria (I.L.T.)**
La incapacidad laboral transitoria puede durar hasta 18 meses.

temporary inability to work

Temporary inability to work can last as long as 18 months.

el **parte de baja**

sick leave

la **baja por maternidad**
La baja por maternidad oscila entre 16 y 18 semanas.

maternity leave
Maternity leave varies between 16 and 18 weeks.

## Collective Bargaining Partners

el **afiliado,** la **afiliada**
Muchas empresas no contratan a personas afiliadas a un sindicato.

member
Many companies don't hire union members.

la **central sindical**
En España hay dos grandes centrales sindicales: la UGT (Unión General de Trabajadores) y CCOO (Comisiones Obreras).

trade union association
In Spain there are two large unions: the UGT (General Trade Union Organization) and CCOO (Labor Commissions).

la **clase trabajadora**
El PSOE (Partido Socialista Obrero Español) (España) se ha distanciado bastante de sus orígenes que estaban, sobre todo, en la clase trabajadora.

working class
The PSOE (Spanish Socialist Labor Party) (Spain) has moved rather far away from its origins, which were primarily working class.

el **conflicto laboral**
Con la actual crisis económica, los conflictos laborales se centran ante todo en mantener los puestos de trabajo.

labor conflict
Because of the present economic crisis, labor conflicts are chiefly about maintaining jobs.

**centrarse**

to be concentrated/centered

**convocar una huelga**
En RENFE se ha convocado una huelga de dos días en los trenes de cercanías.

to call a strike
RENFE called a two-day strike of suburban trains.

**descontar**
Como no acudió a trabajar el día de la huelga general, se lo han descontado de su sueldo.

to deduct
Because he didn't show up for work on the day of the general strike, they deducted a day's pay from his salary.

**acudir**

to appear; report; come

**en beneficio de**
Los sindicatos actúan en beneficio de los trabajadores.

on behalf of
The unions act on behalf of the workers.

**en perjuicio de**

to the detriment of

**estar de acuerdo**
En la mayoría de los casos, la patronal y las centrales sindicales no están de acuerdo en las cuestiones más importantes.

to agree
In most cases management and organized labor don't agree on the most important issues.

el **estatuto de los trabajadores**
El Estatuto de los Trabajadores (España) es la ley que regula todos los aspectos legales del mercado laboral.

workers' statute
The Workers' Statute (Spain) is the law that regulates all legal issues in the labor market.

**regular**

to regulate

el **aspecto**

aspect; feature

la **negativa**
La negativa del Gobierno a modificar ciertos aspectos de la reforma laboral originó la huelga general.

refusal
The government's refusal to modify certain features of the labor reform triggered the general strike.

**originar**

to cause; trigger

la **negociación**
Las recientes negociaciones entre Gobierno y sindicatos han sido un auténtico fracaso.

negotiation
Recent negotiations between the government and the unions have been a real disaster.

la **negociación colectiva**
La negociación colectiva determinará la política salarial para el año próximo.

collective bargaining
Collective bargaining will determine wage policy for next year.

**determinar**

to determine

la **patronal**
La patronal más importante en España se llama CEOE (Confederación Española de Organizaciones Empresariales) (España).

employers' association
The most important employers' association in Spain is the CEOE (Spain).

la **reivindicación**
Una de las reivindicaciones habituales de los sindicatos es el ajuste de los salarios al coste de la vida.

demand; claim
One of the most customary union demands is a salary adjustment for the cost of living.

el **ajuste** — adjustment

**reivindicar** — to demand; claim

las **partes contratantes de un convenio colectivo** — labor and management as collective bargainers

Las partes contratantes del convenio colectivo llevan más de un año sin ponerse de acuerdo. — Labor and management have been engaged in collective bargaining for more than a year without coming to an agreement.

el **convenio colectivo** — collective bargaining agreement

**ponerse de acuerdo** — to come to an agreement

las **tensiones sociales** — social tensions

A mucha gente le extraña que, a pesar del alto índice de paro, no haya más tensiones sociales. — Many people are surprised there aren't more social tensions, despite (given) the high rate of unemployment.

el **comité de empresa** — employees' council; works (factory) committee

(En España,) para poder constituir un comité de empresa, ésta debe tener como mínimo 50 trabajadores. — (In Spain,) in order to form an employees' council, the factory must employ at least 50 workers.

**declararse en huelga** — to go on strike

Los trabajadores se declararon en huelga para protestar contra el expediente de regulación de empleo. — The workers went on strike to protest the job adjustment (reduction) plan.

la **huelga de advertencia** — warning strike

En la industria metalúrgica se han convocado huelgas de advertencia de dos horas diarias para presionar a la patronal. — In the metal-processing industry, daily two-hour warning strikes were called to put pressure on management.

**presionar** — to apply pressure

la **huelga de celo** — slowdown strike

En la frontera hispano-francesa se formó una larga cola de camiones debido a la huelga de celo de los aduaneros. — A big backup of trucks formed at the Spanish-French frontier because of a slowdown strike by customs officials.

la **huelga espontánea**
la **huelga salvaje** — wildcat strike

La huelga salvaje no está autorizada por los sindicatos. — A wildcat strike is one not authorized by the unions.

la **huelga general** — general strike

En 12 años de gobierno socialista ha habido dos huelgas generales. — There were two general strikes during the 12 years the socialists were in power.

el **cierre patronal** — lock out

El cierre patronal es una contramedida de la patronal ante la huelga. — The lock out is anti-strike counter-action taken by management.

la **contramedida**

countermeasure

el **piquete de huelga**

picket

En varios puntos de la ciudad se reunieron los piquetes de huelga que intentaron impedir el acceso de los empleados a sus puestos de trabajo.

At various points in the city picket lines were formed and attempted to prevent employees from gaining access to their job sites.

el **acceso**

access

**reanudar**

to resume

Después de dos meses de acusaciones mutuas, se reanudaron las conversaciones entre sindicatos y patronal.

After two months of mutual accusations, conversations between labor and management resumed.

la **acusación**

accusation

**mutuo (a), recíproco (a)**

mutual; reciprocal

la **reclamación**

demand

La dirección de la empresa consideró excesivas las reclamaciones de incrementos salariales por parte de los sindicatos.

The company's management considered excessive the wage hike demands made by the unions.

la **mejora salarial**

raise in salary/wages

Los funcionarios se tienen que conformar con una mejora salarial del 1% durante dos años.

For two years, officials will have to make do with a salary increase of 1%.

**conformarse**

to be content with; to make do with

la **ronda de negociaciones**

negatiation round

A pesar de los últimos fracasos, el martes pasado se concertó una nueva ronda de negociaciones que comenzará el mes que viene.

Despite recent deadlocks, last Tuesday a new round of negotiations to begin next month was agreed on.

la **conciliación**

reconciliation; amicable settlement

Como resultó imposible una conciliación, ambas partes tuvieron que someterse al arbitraje del Ministerio de Trabajo.

Since an amicable settlement was impossible, both parties had to submit to the arbitration of the Department of Labor.

**someterse a**

to submit to

el **arbitraje**

arbitration

**recurrir**

to have recourse to

Como el sindicato consideró improcedente el despido de uno de sus afiliados, recurrieron a los tribunales.

Since the union considered the firing of one of its members improper, they took legal action.

# ▬▬▬ Contracts and Compensation ▬▬▬

el **contrato de trabajo,**
el **contrato laboral**
El contrato de trabajo regula las
relaciones de la empresa con sus
trabajadores.

employment contract

The employment contract regulates
relations between the company
and its workers.

**renovar**
(En España,) una empresa sólo podrá
renovar el contrato temporal un
máximo de 3 veces.

to renew
(In Spain,) a company can only
renew a fixed-time contract a
maximum of three times.

la **duración**
(En España,) la duración máxima de
un contrato de aprendizaje asciende
a 3 años.

duration
(In Spain,) maximum contract life
for a training contract runs to 3
years.

la **extinción de un contrato**

En los nuevos contratos de aprendizaje,
después de la extinción del contrato,
no se tiene derecho al subsidio por
desempleo.

contract termination; expiration of
a contract
In the new training contracts, after
expiration of the contract there
is no claim to unemployment
insurance.

la **suspensión del contrato**
Como la empresa atravesaba
dificultades económicas, se procedió
a la suspensión de los contratos de
la mitad de la plantilla durante dos
meses.

suspension of the contract
Since the company was going
through economic difficulties,
management suspended half the
work force's employment contract
for two months.

**proceder**

to proceed

**cobrar**
En la empresa de Marta se suele
cobrar entre el 15 y el 20 de cada
mes.

to collect a salary
In Marta's firm it is customary to
be paid between the 15th and 20th
of each month.

**soler**

to be customary

el **anticipo**
Para poder pagar la reparación del
coche, Daniel tuvo que pedir un
anticipo sobre su sueldo.

advance
In order to pay for repairs to his
car, Daniel had to ask for an
advance on his salary.

la **nómina**
En la nómina siempre debe figurar
la antiguedad del trabajador en la
empresa.

payroll
The employee's seniority in the
firm must always be listed in
payroll.

el **salario base**                           basic salary

el **sueldo**                                 wages

la **paga**                                   pay

las **condiciones de trabajo**               working conditions

**paga extra**                                supplementary wages; extra pay
En la banca los salarios suelen ser           Bank salaries are usually relatively
relativamente bajos pero se compensa          low but are compensated for by 5
con 5 pagas extras.                           salary supplements.

**compensar**                                 to compensate

la **hora extraordinaria**                    overtime
Para mantener puestos de trabajo,             To maintain jobs many companies
muchas empresas reducen el número             reduce their workers' overtime
de horas extraordinarias realizadas           hours.
por sus trabajadores.

la **indemnización**                          indemnization; settlement
Cuando lo despidieron, después de             When they let him go, after more
más de 15 años en la empresa, le              than 15 years in the firm, they
dieron casi 7 millones de pesetas             gave him a settlement of almost
de indemnización.                             7 million pesetas.

la **antiguedad**                             seniority
Al ser el trabajador con más                  Since he was the most senior
antiguedad en la empresa, fue el              employee, he had first choice of
primero en elegir sus vacaciones.             vacation time.

el **finiquito,** la **liquidación**          final accounting; settlement;
                                              closing
Después de la extinción de un contrato        After the expiration of a contract
y con la firma del finiquito, el              and the signing of the final settle-
empleado y la empresa renuncian a             ment, the employee and the
posteriores reivindicaciones                  company renounce any further
económicas.                                   financial claim.

la **gratificación**                          bonus
Este año, la gratificación de Navidad         This year's Christmas bonus
no fue tan generosa como se esperaba.         wasn't as generous as hoped for.

el **plus**                                   supplemental/extra pay
Alvaro reclamó el plus que le corres-         Alvaro asked for extra pay due
pondía por trabajar en días festivos.         him for having worked on holidays.

el **complemento salarial**                   supplemental wages
En muchas empresas los trabajadores           In many companies, workers have
han aceptado una reducción de sus             accepted a reduction in their
complementos salariales a cambio              supplemental wages in exchange
de mantener sus puestos de trabajo.           for keeping their jobs.

la **subida**
El ministro de Economía (España) insistió en que las subidas salariales no deben ser superiores a la tasa de inflación.

raise; increase
The Minister of Economics (Spain) insisted that wage raises should not exceed the rate of inflation.

**salarial**

wage-related

el **horario de trabajo**
(En España,) normalmente el horario de trabajo en las oficinas es de 8 de la mañana a 5 de la tarde.

work time/day
(In Spain,) the normal office work day is from 8 A.M. to 5 P.M.

la **categoría**
El sueldo de todo funcionario se fija en función de su categoría profesional.

category; rank; position
Every official's salary is set according to his professional rank.

la **pretensión**
En las entrevistas personales a menudo se pregunta por las pretensiones económicas del candidato.

claim; demand
During initial interviews, the candidate is often asked what salary he/she has in mind.

la **retribución**
Las retribuciones se fijan de acuerdo con las aptitudes del empleado.

salary
Salaries are commensurate with the employee's skills.

**rescindir**
Si un empleado rescinde el contrato por propia voluntad no tendrá derecho a percibir la prestación por desempleo.

to rescind; cancel; annul
If an employee cancels the contract of his own free will, he will have no right to collect unemployment insurance.

el **plazo de preaviso**
El plazo de preaviso será como mínimo de un mes si la antiguedad del trabajador en la empresa no es superior a un año.

termination notice
If the employee's seniority is less than one year with the firm, his termination notice will be a minimum of one month.

el **contrato a tiempo parcial**
Ella quería que le hicieran un contrato a tiempo parcial para tener las tardes libres y poder cuidar a su hijo.

part-time work contract
She wanted them to give her a part-time work contract so that she could have afternoons free to take care of her son.

el **contrato de aprendizaje**

Los sindicatos rechazan los nuevos contratos de aprendizaje por que las retribuciones varían entre el 70 y el 90% del Salario Mínimo Interprofesional (S.M.I.).

training contract; articles of apprenticeship
The unions reject the new training contracts because the salaries are between 70 and 90% of the minimum wage.

el **Salario Mínimo Interprofesional (S.M.I.)**
El S.M.I. es el salario mínimo fijado por el Estado para todo trabajador por cuenta ajena no importa su profesión.

minimum wage

S.M.I. is the minimum wage set by the government for all non free-lance workers, whatever their profession.

el **contrato de trabajo temporal**

fixed-term contract; limited/ temporary contract

el **contrato de trabajo indefinido**, el **contrato fijo**

open-ended contract

el **contrato por obra**, el **contrato por servicio determinado**

work for hire contract; specific project contract

Los contratos por obra o servicio determinado tienen por objeto la realización trabajos concretos con autonomía y de duración incierta.

Project or service contracts are intended for the independent completion of specific projects within a non-specified time frame.

la **realización**

completion

**incierto (a)**

uncertain

la **prórroga**

prolongation; extension

En los contratos de aprendizaje se pueden acordar hasta dos prórrogas del contrato. Cada una de ellas no podrá ser inferior a 6 meses.

Training contracts can be extended twice. Each extension cannot be less than 6 months.

**prorrogar un contrato**

extend a contract

el **período de prueba**

trial period

Durante el período de prueba cualquiera de las partes podrá rescindir el contrato laboral sin plazo de preaviso.

During the trial period either party can cancel the employment contract without notice.

**irreprochable**

irreproachable

Silvia mostró una conducta irreprochable durante el período de prueba.

During the trial period Silvia's conduct was irreproachable.

**vacante**

empty; vacant

Le contrataron para una plaza que había quedado vacante.

They hired him to fill a vacant position.

**ganarse la vida**

to earn one's living

Con los numerosos despidos mucha gente debe recurrir a su imaginación para ganarse la vida.

What with extensive firing, many people have to be inventive to earn their living.

el **suplemento por turnos**

extra pay for working different shifts

Teresa no puede prescindir del suplemento por turnos, aunque el contínuo cambio de horario influye negativamente en su vida familiar.

Teresa can't do without the extra pay for working different shifts although the constant change in work hours has adversely affected her family life.

la **compensación económica**

monetary compensation; payment

Con la extinción de un contrato de trabajo temporal, el trabajador debe percibir una compensación económica de 12 días de salario por año trabajado.

With the expiration of a contract for temporary work, the worker can collect a monetary compensation of 12 salary days per year worked.

### las **retenciones**

En la nómina de Andrés, las retenciones a cuenta del Impuesto sobre la Renta de las Personas Físicas (IRPF) ascienden al 17% de su salario.

deductions
On Andrés' payroll record, income tax deductions amount to 17% of his salary.

### la **excedencia**

Matías solicitó una excedencia de dos años para poder dedicarse a la educación de su hija.

unpaid leave longer than one year
Matías asked for a two-year unpaid leave in order to devote himself to his daughter's education.

## Primary Sector

el **sector primario**
En el sector primario se incluyen la agricultura, la pesca, la minería y la industria forestal.

primary sector
Agriculture, fishing, mining and forestry are included in the primary sector.

el **sector agrícola**
La importancia del sector agrícola ha ido disminuyendo a lo largo del siglo XX.

agricultural sector
The importance of the agricultural sector has declined in the course of the twentieth century.

las **faenas del campo**
La mecanización facilita mucho las faenas del campo.

field work
Mechanization makes field work much easier.

la **mecanización**

mechanization

la **tierra de cultivo**

land under cultivation

la **superficie cultivable**

workable land

el **cultivo de regadío**
Los árabes introdujeron el sistema del cultivo de regadío en España.

planting with irrigation
The Arabs introduced the irrigation system into Spain.

los **productos de la huerta**

products of vegetable gardens

los **productos hortícolas**

horticultural products

el **cultivo de secano**
En las regiones con escasez de agua, los cultivos de secano han adquirido una gran importancia.

dry farming; hydroponics
In regions where water is scarce, hydroponics has become very important.

los **cítricos**
La mayor parte de los cítricos españoles se destina a la exportación.

citrus fruits
Most Spanish citrus fruits are earmarked for export.

la **abundancia**
La abundancia de un producto agrícolahace bajar los precios en el mercado.

abundance; oversupply
Oversupply of an agricultural product causes its market price to decline.

la **explotación ganadera**
En el norte de España, las explotaciones ganaderas son, en su mayoría, empresas familiares.

cattle-raising operations
In the North of Spain cattle-raising is for the most part a family business.

la **ganadería**
La trashumancia—el traslado de las ovejas a aquellas regiones donde hay pastos frescos—es una actividad muy tradicional de la ganadería española.

cattle-raising
Migratory pasturing—moving sheep to regions where there are fresh pastures—has a long tradition in Spain.

la **trashumancia**

seasonal migration

el **pasto**

pasture

el **jornalero**
Como no abunda el trabajo, la mayoría de los jornaleros sobreviven gracias a las ayudas del PER (Plan de Empleo Rural) (España).

day laborer
Since jobs are scarce, most day laborers survive thanks to the help of the PER (Rural Employment Plan) (Spain).

**abundar**

to be abundant

**productor (ora)**
España es uno de los países más importantes en producción de cítricos.

producer
Spain is one of the most important citrus fruit producing countries.

**forestal**
La actual política forestal defiende la repoblación con especies autóctonas.

pertaining to the forest
Current forestry policy advocates reforestation with indigenous species.

la **especie autóctona**

indigenous species

la **pesca de altura**
En las negociaciones de adhesión de Noruega a la UE, el tema de la pesca de altura ha sido uno de los puntos más espinosos.

deep-sea fishing
Deep-sea fishing was one of the thorniest issues in the negotiations for the admission of Norway to the European Union.

la **pesca de bajura**

coastal fishing

la **flota pesquera**
Las flotas pesqueras españolas y franc-cesas se enfrentaron en el Cantábrico ya que los franceses no respetaron la cuota de pesca establecida por la UE.

fishing fleet
There were confrontations between Spanish and French fishing fleets in the Bay of Biscay because the French did not respect the fishing quota set by the EU.

**pesquero (a)**

fishing

el **minero**
El alto índice de paro en Asturias se debe, principalmente, al desempleo que afecta a los mineros.

miner
The high rate of unemployment in Asturias is due chiefly to unemployment among miners.

el **yacimiento**
La industrialización del norte de
España se basó, en gran parte, en los
ricos yacimientos de carbón de la zona.

deposit
The industrialization of the North
of Spain was based to a large degree
on the rich coal deposits in the area.

**basarse en**

to be based on

**extraer**
Las técnicas para extraer carbón han
experimentado grandes avances
tecnológicos.

to extract
Techniques for coal extraction
have been greatly perfected.

la **recolección**
Casi todo el pueblo participa en la
recolección de la patata.

harvest
Almost the entire village takes
part in the potato harvest.

el **cultivo de la vid**
La reciente ola de frío ha causado
grandes pérdidas en los cultivos de
la vid.

viniculture; wine growing; vineyards
The recent cold spell caused great
losses in the vineyards.

la **producción ecológica**
En España, las producciones ecológicas más importantes se obtienen en
los sectores de frutas y hortalizas.

organic cultivation
In Spain, the chief organically
produced products are fruits and
vegetables.

la **hortaliza**

vegetables

**lácteo (a)**
La mayoría de las grandes empresas
del sector lácteo cosechan fuertes
pérdidas.

dairy
Most large companies in the dairy
sector are showing strong losses.

**cosechar**

to harvest; bring in; show

el **éxodo rural**
El éxodo rural andaluz ha hecho que
barrios enteros de Barcelona estén
habitados casi exclusivamente por
emigrantes andaluces.

rural exodus
As a result of the rural exodus from
Andalucia whole districts of Barcelona are inhabited almost exclusively by emigrant Andalucians.

**hacer que**

to result in; lead to

**padecer**
Muchos pozos de agua en Almería
padecen los efectos de la explotación
de los campos de invernaderos y
están comenzando a salinizarse.

to suffer
Many water wells in Almería are
suffering from the effects of agricultural use of fields and green-
houses and are beginning to salify.

**salinizarse**

to salify; become salty/saline

la **escasez**
La escasez de lluvias en años pasados
ha hecho que en muchas regiones
hubiera cortes en el abastecimiento
de agua corriente.

shortage; scarcity
Lack of rain in earlier years has
resulted in cutbacks in the water
supply in many regions.

la **repoblación forestal**
Los numerosos incendios forestales hacen necesarias serias medidas de repoblación forestal.

reforestation
The numerous forest fires make reforestation measures necessary.

la **deforestación**
La alarmante deforestación de la selva amazónica pone en peligro el equilibrio ecológico mundial.

deforestation
The alarming deforestation of the Amazon rain forest endangers the world's ecological balance.

el **corcho**
Extremadura cuenta con una importante industria del corcho que explota los abundantes bosques de alcornoques de la región.

cork
Extremadura has an important cork industry which makes use of the abundant cork oak woods in the region.

el **vivero**
Los viveros españoles se enfrentan a la fuerte competencia holandesa.

nursery
Spanish nurseries face stiff competition from Dutch nurseries.

las **aguas territoriales**
A menudo, barcos pesqueros españoles han sido detenidos por pescar en las aguas territoriales marroquíes.

territorial waters
Spanish fishing boats have frequently been detained for fishing in Moroccan territorial waters.

la **ostricultura**
La ostricultura se está convirtiendo en una industria muy pujante en Galicia.

oyster farming
Oyster farming is becoming a strong industry in Galicia.

**pujante**

vigorous; strong

la **acuicultura**

aquaculture

la **piscifactoría**
En el norte de Castilla hay numerosas piscifactorías de truchas.

fish farming
In Northern Castile there are numerous trout farms.

la **explotación a cielo abierto**
Las explotaciones a cielo abierto modifican radicalmente el paisaje.

open shaft (pit) mining
Open shaft mining radically changes the landscape.

la **extracción**

extraction

la **cantera**
Las casas de Mallorca se han construido con piedras extraídas de las canteras de la isla.

quarry
Mallorcan houses were built with stones quarried on the island.

# Energy Sector

**energético (a)**
El sector energético registra uno de los beneficios más altos de la economía española.

energy related
The energy sector is showing one of the largest profits in the Spanish economy.

**hidrológico (a)**
El Plan Hidrológico Nacional (PHN) (España) responde a la necesidad de una estrategia nacional en materia de utilización de aguas.

hydrological
The National Hydrological Plan (Spain) addresses itself to the need for a nationwide strategy for water use.

el **abastecimiento**

supply

el **suministro**
España ha firmado un contrato de suministro con Argelia que le garantiza el abastecimiento de gas natural.

delivery
Spain has signed a delivery contract with Algeria which guarantees the supply of natural gas.

el **suministro de electricidad**
Le concedemos un último plazo para saldar sus deudas con nosotros. En caso contrario procederemos al corte del suministro de electricidad.

electricity supply
We are allowing you a final pay period to settle the amounts due us. Otherwise, we'll shut off your electricity.

**proceder a**

to proceed to; move to

la **hulla,** el **carbón de piedra**
La extracción de hulla o carbón de piedra ha estado vinculada tradicionalmente al norte de España.

white coal; hard coal
Hard coal mining has traditionally been associated with the North of Spain.

el **gas natural**

natural gas

la **central nuclear**
Las centrales nucleares deben cumplir estrictas normas en materia de seguridad.

nuclear power plant
Nuclear power plants must comply with strict security measures.

la **central hidroeléctrica**
La abundancia de agua en el norte de España favorece la instalación de centrales hidroeléctricas.

hydroelectric power plant
The abundance of water in Northern Spain encourages the setting up of hydroelectric power plants.

la **central térmica**
El grupo español INITEC va a construir varias centrales térmicas en China.

thermal power plant
The Spanish concern INITEC will build several thermal power plants in China.

el **parque eólico**
El parque eólico de Tarifa tiene una capacidad anual de 30 megavatios, suficiente para abastecer el consumo doméstico de electricidad de 25.000 viviendas.

wind power installation
The wind power installation in Tarifa has a yearly capacity of 30 mega watts, enough to cover the local electricity consumption needs of 25,000 households.

# Secondary Sector

el **sector secundario**
En el sector secundario se produce la transformación de las materias primas procedentes del sector primario.

secondary sector
The processing of raw materials from the primary sector takes place in the secondary sector.

la **transformación**

transformation; processing

la **industria**

industry

**manufacturero (a)**
La industria del calzado es uno de los sectores manufactureros más importantes de España.

manufacturing
The shoe industry is one of the most important manufacturing sectors in Spain.

la **industria del calzado**

shoe industry

la **artesanía**
La artesanía ha experimentado una automatización en su producción debido al elevado coste de la mano de obra.

hand craft; trade
Hand crafts have automated their production due to the high cost of labor.

el **taller artesanal**

hand crafts workshop

**automovilístico (a)**
Las exportaciones del sector automovilístico español tienen un efecto positivo sobre la balanza de pagos.

automobile related
Exports from the Spanish automobile sector have a positive effect on the balance of payments.

el **vehículo**

vehicle

el **utilitario**

commercial vehicle

la **industria del carbón y del acero**
La industria europea del carbón y del acero se enfrenta a la fuerte competencia de los países en vías de industrialización.

coal and steel industry

The European coal and steel industry must deal with strong competition from industrially developing countries.

**siderúrgico (a)**
La Comisión Europea ha urgido a las empresas siderúrgicas a que recorten su producción.

iron and steel industry
The European Commission has urged iron and steel companies to curtail their production.

**urgir**

to urge

**metalúrgico (a)**
La industria metalúrgica española ha experimentado un declive alarmante durante los últimos años.

metal processing
The Spanish metal processing industry has undergone an alarming decline in recent years.

| | |
|---|---|
| el **declive** | decline |
| **alarmante** | alarming |
| la **construcción naval** | ship building |

La provincia de La Coruña cuenta con importantes empresas dedicadas a la construcción naval.

The province of La Coruña has many important ship building firms.

| | |
|---|---|
| la **industria química** | chemical industry |
| **petroquímico (a)** | petrochemical |

Las industrias petroquímicas se suelen instalar en la costa para asegurarse un suministro rápido y directo de las refinerías.

Petrochemical industries are usually situated on the coast to assure a rapid and direct supply to the refineries.

| | |
|---|---|
| la **refinería** | refinery |
| el **ramo de la construcción** | the construction industry |
| la **industria clave** | key industry |

El sector textil fue la industria clave en la Cataluña de primeros de siglo XX.

The textile industry was the key industry in Catalonia at the beginning of the 20th century.

| | |
|---|---|
| **textil** | textile |
| la **industria alimentaria** | food industry |
| el **sector alimenticio** | food sector |
| la **planta siderúrgica** | steel mill |

Una solución para la crisis de las plantas siderúrgicas estaría en una orientación más definida hacia la exportación.

One solution to the steel mill crisis would be a more definite export-oriented outlook.

| | |
|---|---|
| la **orientación** | orientation |
| el **alto horno** | blast furnace |

En el norte de España se han tenido que desmantelar la mayoría de los altos hornos a pesar de ser algunos de los más modernos de Europa.

In Northern Spain it was necessary to shut down most blast furnaces despite their being among the most modern in Europe.

| | |
|---|---|
| **desmantelar** | to dismantle; shut down |
| el **astillero** | shipyard |

Los recortes en los presupuestos de defensa han tenido un efecto negativo sobre la actividad de los astilleros.

Cuts in the defense budget have had a negative effect on shipyard production.

| | |
|---|---|
| la **cerámica** | ceramics |

La cerámica es una de las manifestaciones más ricas y variadas de la artesanía española.

Ceramics is one of the richest and most varied expressions of Spanish hand crafts.

| | |
|---|---|
| la **manifestación** | manifestation; expression |
| la **marroquinería** | leather wear; leather goods industry |

**cárnico (a)**　　　　　　　　　　　meat related
Algunas de las más importantes empresas españolas de productos cárnicos se han instalado ya en Rusia.

Some of the most important Spanish meat processing companies have already established themselves in Russia.

la **industria conservera**　　　　the canning industry

el **sector maquinaria**　　　　　machinery manufacturing sector
la **maquinaria**

la **industria electrónica**　　　electronic industry

la **industria farmacéutica**　　pharmaceutical industry

el **tejido industrial**　　　　　industrial network/structure
Muchos expertos opinan que se ha descuidado mucho el tejido industrial español, al dar preferencia al fomento de las inversiones extranjeras.

Many experts believe Spain's industrial structure was seriously neglected because of preference given to the encouragement of foreign investment.

la **preferencia**　　　　　　　　preference

la **región deprimida**　　　　　depressed area
Algunas regiones del sur de Madrid van a recibir ayudas económicas del programa FEDER (España) al ser catalogadas como regiones deprimidas.

Some regions in the south of the province of Madrid will receive economic assistance from the FEDER (Spain) program because they've been declared depressed areas.

**catalogar**　　　　　　　　　　to catalogue; classify

el **hundimiento**　　　　　　　collapse
Para escaparse del hundimiento económico que afectó al sector, la marca de motocicletas española DERBI ha trasladado la producción a Malasia.

To escape the economic collapse that befell the industry, the Spanish motorcycle firm DERBI moved its production to Malaysia.

**trasladar**　　　　　　　　　　to move

la **reconversión**　　　　　　　reconversion; restructuring
El sector metalúrgico europeo ha sido objeto de una gran reconversión.

The European metal processing industry was the subject of considerable restructuring.

| | |
|---|---|
| la **economía sumergida** | hidden economy |
| Sin la existencia de una economía sumergida, muy extendida en el sector secundario, el problema del paro sería aún mucho más grave. | Without the existence of a hidden economy, which is widespread in the secondary sector, the problem of unemployment would be even more serious. |

## Tertiary Sector

| | |
|---|---|
| el **sector terciario** | tertiary sector |
| El sector terciario comprende el comercio y otros servicios, tales como los ofrecidos por bancos, compañías de seguros, transportes, etc. | The tertiary sector includes business and other services, such as those offered by banks, insurance companies, transport companies, etc. |
| el **sector servicios** | service industry |
| Mientras la actividad de los sectores primario y secundario está en pleno retroceso, en todos los países gana cada vez más importancia el sector servicios. | While activities in the primary and secondary sectors are declining notably, in all countries service industries are growing rapidly. |
| el **retroceso** | recession; cut back |
| **pleno (a)** | full |
| el **servicio** | service |
| la **prestación de servicios** | performance of services |
| Una de las operaciones de prestación de servicios que más ha proliferado en los años 80 y 90 es la de arrendadora o alquiler con opción de compra. | One of the services that has become very widespread in the eighties and nineties is leasing or renting with an option to buy. |
| **proliferar** | to spread; proliferate |
| el **leasing** | leasing |
| el **alquiler con opción de compra** | renting with an option to buy |
| **hotelero (a)** | hotel related |
| El sector hotelero español está en pleno auge, como demuestra el hecho de que la cadena española de hoteles SOL vaya a construir 60 hoteles en Alemania. | The Spanish hotel industry is booming, as evidenced by the fact that the Spanish hotel chain SOL is going to build 60 hotels in Germany. |
| la **cadena de hoteles** | hotel chain |
| el **auge** | boom; upward movement |

el **turismo**

tourism

la **profesión liberal**
En el sector servicios es donde se
concentran la mayoría de las
profesiones liberales.

free-lance professional activity
Most free-lance professionals are
concentrated in the service sector.

la **fuente de ingresos**
El turismo es una de las fuentes de
ingresos más importantes de España.

source of income
Tourism is one of Spain's most
important sources of income.

la **sector de la informática**

data processing; computer science

la **hostelería**
Los empleados de hostelería mejor
capacitados suelen salir de las
escuelas universitarias de turismo.

hotel business
The best trained employees in the
hotel business are usually university
graduates with a specialty in
tourism.

la **gastronomía**

gastronomy

el **bufete de abogados**
Al incorporarse al bufete de abogados,
Miguel tuvo que aportar su cartera
de clientes.

law firm
When Miguel joined the law firm
he had to bring with him his file of
personal clients.

la **gestoría**
La mayoría de la gente deja en manos
de una gestoría la tramitación de
todo el papeleo burocrático.

agency; business rep
Most people leave all the
bureaucratic paperwork to an
agency.

la **tramitación**

transaction; procedure; steps;
negotiation

el **papeleo burocrático**

bureaucratic red tape

la **consultoría**
Para mejorar su estructura y gestión,
la empresa encargó un estudio a una
consultoría internacional.

consulting firm
To improve its structure and
management, the company
commissioned an international
consulting firm to do a study.

**encargar**

to entrust; order; commission

la **auditoría**

auditor firm

la **industria del ocio**

leisure industry

el **sector audiovisual**

audiovisual sector

## Types of Corporations

el **derecho mercantil**
El derecho mercantil regula la
actividad empresarial.

mercantile/commercial law
Commercial law regulates business
activity.

**empresarial**

business related; entrepreneurial

la **sociedad mercantil**
La sociedad mercantil compra y
vende merecancia con la intencion
de realizar una empresa con ánimo
de lucro.

trading company
A trading company buys and sells
goods with the intention of
realizing a business that generates
profit.

la **compañía mercantil**
Compañía Mercantil es la
denominación que hace el
Código de Comercio español
de la Sociedad mercantil.

trading company
In the Spanish Code of Commercial
Law a trading company is called
a "Compañía mercantil."

el **empresario,** la **empresaria**

entrepreneur

el, la **comerciante**

salesperson; business person

la **empresa**
Toda empresa tiene un propósito
lucrativo que se traduce en actividades
industriales y mercantiles, o en la
prestación de servicios.

business; company
Every business intends to make
a profit either by engaging in
industry or commerce or by
performing services.

la **empresa familiar**
La empresa familiar española no dura,
por promedio, más de 15 años a
pesar de ser muy competitiva.

family business
Although they're very competitive,
on average, Spanish family
businesses don't last more than
15 years.

el **socio,** la **socia**
Los socios constituyen la sociedad
mediante la aportación de bienes
que conforman el capital.

partner; firm member; associate
The partners found the corporation
by contributing assets which
constitute the ordinary capital.

el **socio gestor,** la **socia gestora**
El socio gestor dirige la empresa.

managing partner
The managing partner directs the
business.

el **socio colectivo,**
la **socia colectiva**
La sociedad que fundamos ayer
tiene socias colectivas.

general partner; personally liable
partner
The corporation we founded
yesterday has general partners.

el **socio comanditario,**
la **socia comanditaria**
El socio comanditario no puede
participar en la gestión de la
sociedad.

silent partner

The silent partner cannot participate
in the direction of the corporation.

la **sociedad civil**
La sociedad civil es una unión
contractual de dos o más personas
que se obligan a poner en común
dinero, bienes o industria, con
ánimo de partir entre sí las ganancias.

general partnership; civil partnership
A general partnership is a contractual union of two or more persons
who pledge to contribute money,
assests or services performed in
order to share the profits with
each other.

el **ánimo**

intention

la **sociedad de capital,**
la **sociedad capitalista**
Las sociedades de capital son la
Sociedad de Responsabilidad
Limitada y la Sociedad Anónima.

capital corporation

Capital corporations are limited
liability companies and (stock)
corporations.

la **sociedad de responsabilidad
limitada (SL),** la **sociedad
limitada**
El capital social mínimo de la sociedad
de responsabilidad limitada es de
500.000 pts.

limited liability corporation

The minimum corporate capital of
the limited liability corporation is
500,000 pesetas.

la **sociedad anónima (SA)**
La más extendida y utilizada forma
de sociedad en España es la sociedad
anónima.
El capital social mínimo de la
sociedad anónima es de 10.000.000
ptas.

(stock) corporation
The most common and most used
corporate form in Spain is the
(stock) corporation.
The minimum corporate capital of
the (stock) corporation is
10,000,000 pesetas.

la **cooperativa**

cooperative

el, la **cooperativista**
Los cooperativistas fundan una
cooperativa con el fin de ayuda
mutua.

member of a cooperative
Members of a cooperative found
a cooperative in order to help
each other.

la **asociación**
La asociación de heladeros de
Málaga es muy prestigiosa e
influyente.

association
Malaga's ice makers association
is very prestigious and influential.

la **corporación**
Una corporación está formada por
un conjunto de bienes.

corporation
A corporation is formed by an
ensemble of assets.

la **institución**
La institución no es una forma jurídica,
sino cualquier entidad pública o
privada sin ánimo de lucro.

institution
The institution is not a legal form
but any public or private non-profit
organization.

la **sociedad matriz**
¿Cuál es la sociedad matriz de esta
compañía?

parent company
Who is the parent company of this
business?

la **sociedad filial**
La sociedad matriz controla la
sociedad filial.

subsidiary
The parent company controls the
subsidiary.

el **consorcio**
Los grandes consorcios transmiten
confianza a los inversores.

consortium
The big consortiums inspire
investor confidence.

el **holding**
Rumasa ha sido uno de los más
importantes holdings de la historia
de España.

holding company
Rumasa was one of the most
important holding companies in
the history of Spain.

la **joint-venture**
Las joint-venture se han multiplicado
en Europa del Este.

joint venture
Joint ventures have proliferated in
Eastern Europe.

el **acreedor,** la **acreedora**

creditor

el **inversor,** la **inversora**

investor

la **empresa individual**

individually owned business

la **empresa líder**
Somos la empresa líder en el sector.

leading business
We are the leading business in the
industry.

la **empresa multinacional**
Una empresa multinacional está
establecida en varios países.

multinational business
A multinational business is
established in various countries.

la **empresa pública,**
la **compañía pública**
La empresa pública es propiedad
del Estado.

state owned business

A state owned business belongs
to the government.

la **empresa privada**
La empresa privada es propiedad
de particulares.

private business
Privately owned businesses belong
to individuals.

la **gran empresa**

major business/company

la **mediana empresa**
La mediana empresa tiene en España una gran implantación, especialmente en el sector turístico.

middle-range business
Middle-range businesses are very widespread in Spain, especially in the tourist sector.

la **pequeña empresa**
¿Quién niega que la pequeña empresa esté en crisis?

small business
Who denies that small businesses are facing a crisis?

la **sociedad irregular**
A la sociedad irregular le faltan los requisitos de constitución de la escritura pública y de la inscripción registral.

unregulated company
Unregulated companies fail to meet the requirements for official authorization and registry.

**registral**

register; pertaining to the Corporate Registry

la **sociedad personalista**
Las sociedades personalistas no suelen tener un capital social muy alto.

general partnership
General partnerships don't usually have extensive corporate capital.

la **sociedad colectiva**
En una sociedad colectiva todos los socios participan en la gestión.

general partnership
In a general partnership all the partners participate in the running of the business.

la **sociedad comanditaria,**
la **sociedad en comandita**
La sociedad comanditaria no se utiliza demasiado en España.

limited partnership

The limited partnership is not widely used in Spain.

la **sociedad comanditaria por acciones**
La sociedad comanditaria por acciones es una mezcla de sociedad personalista y sociedad de capital.

partnership limited by shares

The partnership limited by shares is a mixture of the general partnership and the joint stock company.

la **mutualidad de seguros**
Para que una mutualidad de seguros tenga carácter mercantil debe practicar el seguro a prima fija.

mutual insurance company
For a mutual insurance company to be recognized as a business, it must offer insurance at a fixed premium.

En la mutualidad de seguros, el socio es a la vez asegurado.

In a mutual insurance company the partner is also insured by the company.

la **fundación**
El presidente de la Fundación Ortega y Gasset (España) es el ex-presidente del Gobierno Leopoldo Calvo Sotelo.

founding
The president of the Ortega y Gasset Foundation (Spain) is the former Spanish Prime Minister Leopoldo Calvo Sotelo.

# Establishing a Corporation

**constituir**
Para constituir una Sociedad
Anónima son necesarios tres
socios como mínimo.

to establish
To establish a corporation, a
minimum of three associates is
necessary.

la **constitución**
¿Cuándo se celebrará la constitución
de la compañía?

establishment; founding
When will the company's founding
be celebrated?

**fundar**
Para fundar una Sociedad
Anónima pueden seguirse
varios procedimientos.

to found; establish
To found a corporation various
procedures can be followed.

el **acto preparatorio**
Los actos preparatorios para la
constitución de una sociedad
pueden realizarlos personas
distintas a los fundadores.

preparation
Preparations for founding a
corporation can be undertaken
by persons other than the corporate
founders.

el **fundador,** la **fundadora**
El fundador es el que concurre,
por sí o por representante, al
otorgamiento de la escritura
social, suscribiendo acciones
de la sociedad.

founder
The founder, either personally or
through an agent, is present at the
issuing of the articles of association
by subscribing the corporation's
stocks.

la **escritura social**

articles of association; document
of incorporation

**social**

corporate

el **administrador,**
la **administradora**
El administrador es el gestor de la
sociedad.

adminstrator; chief executive
officer; chairman of the board
The chief executive officer runs
the corporation.

la **escritura pública**
El Código de Comercio exige
escritura pública para constituir
una sociedad.

public document/record
The Registry of Companies requires
a public record when forming a
corporation.

el **Registro Mercantil**
Toda sociedad deberá ser inscrita
en el Registro Mercantil.

Registry of Companies
Every corporation must be
registered with the Registry
of Companies.

**inscrito (a)**

registered

la **aportación**
Los socios se comprometen a
realizar aportaciones.

contribution; investment; share
The partners pledge to invest in
the company.

los **estatutos**
Los estatutos determinan la estructura
y el funcionamiento de una sociedad.

statutes
Statutes determine the corporation's
structure and operations.

la **razón social,**
la **denominación social**
¿Sabes cuál es la razón social de
SOUTHCO SA?

firm name; trade name

Do you know SOUTHCO SA's
trade name?

la **duración**
La mayoría de las sociedades
suelen tener una duración por
tiempo ilimitada.

duration
Most corporations are generally
formed with no time limit.

el **domicilio**
La sociedad de Derecho español se
constituye con un domicilio que
habrá de radicar en territorio español.

domicile
A corporation subject to Spanish
law must have its corporate headquarters on Spanish soil.

el **pacto**
Los pactos que acuerdan los socios
pueden constar en el contrato social.

pact; agreement
The agreements made by the
partners, can be listed in the
articles of association.

la **denominación**
La denominación de la sociedad que
constituyó el Sr. López Lozano es
Ley y Mercado, una sociedad de
consultoría integrada.

name; designation
The name of the corporation
formed by Mr. López Lozano is
"Law and Market" an integrated
consulting firm.

el **objeto social**
El objeto social señala las actividades
a que se va a dedicar la sociedad.

corporate object/purpose
The corporate purpose indicates
the activities the corporation will
be engaged in.

el **capital**

capital

**desembolsar**
Mañana iremos al banco para
desembolsar el capital suscrito.

pay out; take out; withdraw
Tomorrow we're going to the bank
to withdraw the subscribed capital.

el **capital suscrito**

subscribed capital

la **acción**
El capital social de una Sociedad
Anónima se divide en acciones.

stock
The corporate capital of a corporation is divided into stocks.

el, la **accionista**
El accionista tiene derecho a asistir
a la junta general.

shareholder; stock owner
The shareholder is entitled to
attend the general meeting.

la **fundación sucesiva**

La fundación sucesiva únicamente se permite para la constitución de la sociedad anónima.

phase-out; succession, establishment of future activities
Description of all phase-out or succession activity is permitted only at the time of the corporation's founding.

la **fundación simultánea,**
la **fundación por convenio**

La fundación simultánea se realiza mediante la suscripción de las acciones.

simultaneous establishment/founding

Simultaneous founding is done by stock subscription.

la **suscripción**

subscription

el **socio originario,**
la **socia originaria**

founding partner

la **sociedad en formación**

La sociedad en formación es la que se encuentra en trámites de constitución.

newly formed company
A newly formed company is often in the midst of incorporation.

el **promotor,** la **promotora**

El promotor es la persona que promueve la constitución de la sociedad en el procedimiento de fundación sucesiva.

entrepreneur
The entrepreneur is the person actively engaged in formation of the business as detailed in the plan for future activities.

**promover**

to promote

la **escritura de constitución**

La escritura de constitución de la sociedad debe recoger el nombre, apellidos, nacionalidad y domicilios de los socios, la denominación o razón social, el objeto de la sociedad y su duración, el domicilio social, la aportación de cada socio, los administradores y la forma de adoptar acuerdos sociales.

document of incorporation
The corporation's document of incorporation should include first and last names, nationality and residence of the partners, the firm name, the corporation's purpose and its duration, site of corporate headquarters, each partner's share, the managing directors, and the form for implementing corporate decisions.

**otorgar escritura pública**

El notario es el único que puede otorgar escritura pública.

to authorize/execute a public document
The notary (legal representative) is the only one who can execute a document of public record.

**constar**

En una escritura debe constar siempre la firma del notario.

to appear; be included
The notary's signature should always appear on a document.

la **inscripción**
En las sociedades de capital, la
sociedad adquiere personalidad
jurídica en el momento de su
inscripción en el Registro Mercantil.

registry
In capital corporations, the corporation becomes a legal person the
moment it is registered in the
Commercial Registry.

la **aportación de industria**
La aportación de industria consiste
en que el socio se compromete a
una actividad personal.

contribution of work
The contribution of work consists
in the partner's pledging to be
personally active.

la **capacidad**
Tienen una capacidad para celebrar
un contrato de sociedad mercantil
las personas físicas, mayores de
edad y no incapacitadas legalmente.

capacity
Natural persons who are of age
and not declared legally incompe-
tent are capable of entering into
the contractual obligations of a
trading company.

el **contrato de sociedad**
En toda sociedad mercantil el contrato
de sociedad debe constar en escritura
pública.

corporate contract
In every trading company the
corporate contract must be made
public by a document of record.

**desembolsado (a)**
En los estatutos también deberá
constar el capital social no
desembolsado.
No todo el capital suscrito debe ser
necesariamente desembolsado.

paid in
Non paid-in corporate capital must
also be specified in the statutes.

Not all subscribed capital must
necessarily be paid in.

el **acta**
El contenido de las reuniones del
Consejo de Administración debe
constar en acta.

file; document; record
Written records of board meetings
must be kept.

**levantar acta**

El Secretario del Consejo de
Administración es el encargado
de levantar acta.

keep the minutes; enter into the
record
The secretary of the board is
responsible for keeping the
minutes.

la **acción al portador**
Hoy en día casi todas las acciones
son al portador.
El titular de una acción al portador
es su poseedor.

bearer stock/share
Nowadays almost all stocks are
bearer stocks.
The owner of a bearer stock is the
one who has it.

la **acción nominativa**
La acción nominativa no puede
transmitirse como la acción al
portador.

registered stock
Registered stocks are not transferable, like bearer stock.

la **acción ordinaria**

common stock

la **acción privilegiada**
La creación de acciones privilegiadas no exige especiales requisitos y puede obedecer a muy diversas causas de orden económico.

preferred stock
The creation of preferred stock requires no special conditions and can be due to many diverse economic causes.

el **valor nominal**
El valor nominal es el importe aritmético, submúltiplo de la cifra del capital, de las acciones.

face vaule; par value
Face value is determined by the division of capital by the outstanding stocks.

la **prima de emisión**
La prima de emisión debe ser satisfecha íntegramente en el momento de la suscripción de las acciones.

issue premium
The issue premium must be paid out entirely at the time of subscription of the shares.

el **bono de disfrute**
Cuando redujeron el capital de mi sociedad mis acciones fueron amortizadas, pero me entregaron bonos de disfrute.

certificate of ownership
When they reduced my corporation's capital, my stocks were amortized, but they gave me ownership certificates.

la **acción sin voto**
Los titulares de acciones sin voto tienen un derecho preferente al reparto de beneficios.

non-voting stock
Non-voting stock owners have preferential rights when profits are distributed.

**aportar**

to bring to; pay into; invest

la **aportación no dineraria,**
la **aportación en especie**
La aportación no dineraria puede ser, por ejemplo, un inmueble.

non-monetary investment
investment in kind
Non-monetary investment can be, for example, real property.

la **aportación dineraria**

monetary contribution/investment

la **aportación de capital**
Las aportaciones de capital son necesarias para la operatividad de una sociedad.

monetary investment
Capital investments are necessary for corporate activities.

el **desembolso de capital**

paying in/out of capital

el **fondo de reserva**
La Ley de Sociedades Anónimas obliga a las sociedades que obtienen beneficios a la dotación de un fondo de reserva.

reserve fund; reserves
Corporate law requires corporations that make a profit to establish a reserve fund.

la **dotación**

endowment; allocation

# Corporate Expansion

| | |
|---|---|
| la **absorción** | take-over |
| la **actividad** | activity |
| la **actividad empresarial**<br>En el País Vasco hay mucha actividad empresarial. | entrepreneurial activity<br>In the Basque provinces there is much entrepreneurial activity. |
| la **adquisición de acciones**<br>La compañía aérea Iberia ha adquirido un gran paquete de acciones de Aerolíneas Argentinas. | acquisition of stocks<br>Iberia Air Lines has acquired a large share of Aerolíneas Argentinas stock. |
| la **ampliación de capital,**<br>el **aumento de capital**<br>La corporación bancaria Argentaria realizó en 1993 una importante ampliación de capital. | increase of capital<br><br>The banking corporation Argentaria succeeded in significantly increasing capital in 1993. |
| **asociarse**<br><br>Los Bancos y las Cajas de Ahorro tienden a asociarse para sobrevivir en el mercado único. | to join together; associate; consolidate<br>Banks and savings banks are trying to merge in order to survive in the domestic market. |
| **asociarse con alguien**<br><br>La cadena de televisión por cable PTV va a asociarse con el Grupo Bradley. | to merge/consolidate/combine with someone<br>The cable television chain PTV is going to combine with the Bradley Group. |
| la **adquisición** | acquisition |
| la **fusión**<br>La fusión ha sido una de las más grandes en el sector. | merger<br>The merger has been one of the biggest in the industry. |
| **transferir** | to transfer |
| el **proceso de fusión**<br>Procono, SL está envuelta en un proceso de fusión. | merger process/proceeding<br>Procono, SL is involved in merger negotiations. |
| **canjear** | to exchange |
| **asumir**<br>¿Quién va a asumir la responsabilidad de la empresa? | to assume, take over<br>Who is going to assume responsibility for the company? |

el **beneficio**
Este año los beneficios crecieron
un 22%.

profit
This year, profits grew 22%.

la **cifra de negocios**
El sector de las telecomunicaciones
está alcanzando cifras de negocios
muy altas.

sales
The telecommunications industry
is showing very high sales.

el **volumen de negocios**
El volumen de negocios no es lo
suficientemente alto, ¡ojo!

sales volume
Warning! Sales volume isn't high
enough yet!

la **concentración**
En el sector bancario se ha experimentado un fuerte proceso de
concentraciones.

concentration; consolidation
In the banking sector there has
been much consolidating activity.

**concluir un negocio**
Finalmente hemos podido concluir
este importante negocio.

close a deal
Finally we were able to close this
important deal.

la **conclusión**
La conclusión de este contrato será
muy importante para ambas partes.

conclusion; end
The conclusion of this important
contract will be very important to
both parties.

**desarrollar relaciones
comerciales**
Para crecer es necesario desarrollar
relaciones comerciales.

to develop/foster commercial
relations
To grow it is necessary to develop
commercial relations.

**emprender**
Están pensando en emprender nuevos
negocios.

undertake
They're thinking of undertaking
new business activities.

la **expansión**
Los de Pizzafax sólo piensan en la
expansión.

expansion
All that the people at Pizzafax
think about is expansion.

la **expectativa**
Tienen muy buenas expectativas
para el próximo año.

prospect; expectation
They have very good prospects for
next year.

**extenderse**

to expand

el **gasto de adquisición**

acquisition costs

el **volumen**

volume

la **agrupación**

formation of groups; consolidation

**agrupado (a)**
Las empresas del grupo ZZZ han
sido agrupadas en un nuevo holding.

grouped
The ZZZ group companies have
been grouped in a new holding
company.

el **balance de fusión**
El balance de fusión lo preparan los
administradores de una sociedad.

merger balance
The managing directors of a
corporation prepare the merger
balance.

la **fusión por absorción**
En la fusión por absorción una
sociedad anónima ya existente
absorbe a una o más sociedades.

merger by take-over
In a merger by take-over an already
existing corporation absorbs one
or more corporations.

la **fusión por integración,**
la **fusión por unión**
La fusión por unión de dos sociedades,
implica la extinción de cada una de
ellas y la transmisión en bloque de
los respectivos patrimonios sociales
a la nueva sociedad que se crea.

merger by integration

Merger by integration of two
corporations means the dissolution
of each one and the total turnover
of their respective corporate assets
to the new corporation created.

el **acuerdo de fusión**
El acuerdo de fusión debe ser aprobado
por unanimidad.

merger agreement
The merger agreement must be
approved unanimously.

el **proyecto de fusión**
El proyecto de fusión es necesario
cuando se trata de Sociedades
Anónimas.

merger plan, proposal
A merger plan is required when
corporations are at issue.

la **sociedad absorbente**

the corporation that takes over,
takeover corporation

La sociedad absorbente en una fusión
puede ser de cualquier clase.

The corporate form of the takeover
corporation may be of any kind.

el **canje de acciones**
En las fusiones suele producirse un
canje de acciones.

exchange of stocks
An exchange of stocks usually
occurs in mergers.

la **oferta pública de adquisición
de acciones (OPA)**
En general una oferta pública de
adquisición de acciones tiene como
objetivo alterar la distribución del
poder de decisión dentro de una
sociedad o de un grupo de sociedades.

public stock acquisition offer

In general, the purpose of a public
stock acquisition offer is to change
the executive structure of a corporation or group of corporations.

| la **transformación** | transformation |
|---|---|
| En la transformación se conserva la misma personalidad jurídica. | In a transformation the same legal status is retained. |

el **acuerdo de transformación**
El acuerdo de transformación debe constar en escritura pública.

transformation agreement
The transformation agreement should appear as a public document.

el **beneficio neto**
¿A cuánto asciende el beneficio neto del primer trimestre?

net profit
How high is the net profit in the first quarter?

el **trimestre**

quarter

la **desconcentración**

deconcentration

la **domiciliación**

domicile (e.g. of a bank draft)

**establecerse**
A los grandes despachos de abogados les gusta establecerse en las capitales importantes.

to become established
Large law firms like to establish themselves in important capital cities.

**establecer**
Quieren establecer una sucursal en Nueva York.

to establish
They want to open a branch in New York.

el **establecimiento**
¿Cómo ves la rentabilidad futura de éste establecimiento?

establishment; business
How do you see the future profitability of this business?

## Corporations in Crisis

la **escisión**
La escisión es un proceso inverso a la fusión.

split; separation; division
A split is the opposite of a merger.

la **rescisión del contrato de sociedad**
La rescisión del contrato social implica la extinción de la sociedad.

annulation of the corporate contract

Annulation of the corporate contractmeans the dissolution of the corporation.

la **insolvencia**

insolvency

las **deudas**
Las deudas de la sociedad obligaron al juez a decretar su quiebra.

debts
The corporation's debts compelled the judge to issue a decree of bankruptcy.

**quebrar**
No es inusual ver quebrar hoy empresas que ayer parecían muy sólidas.

to go bankrupt
Today it is not unusual to see corporations go bankrupt that yesterday appeared solid.

la **quiebra**

bankruptcy

la **bancarrota**
Como siga así, este gerente nos va a llevar a la bancarrota.

bankruptcy
If things go on like this, that managing director is going to lead us to bankruptcy.

la **suspensión de pagos**
La suspensión de pagos es un estado legal que debe ser declarado por el juez a solicitud del empresario provisionalmente insolvente.

suspension of payment
Suspension of payments is a legal state declared by a judge at the request of a temporarily insolvent entrepreneur.

la **liquidación**
Todas las sociedades continúan existiendo mientras dure la liquidación de su patrimonio.

liquidation
All corporations continue to exist as long as the liquidation of corporate assets is in process.

el **liquidador**
Los liquidadores son los encargados de repartir el patrimonio social entre los accionistas, previa satisfacción de los acreedores.

liquidator; receiver
Receivers are charged with distributing the corporation's assets among the shareholders, after having first satisfied the creditors.

el **inventario**
Los liquidadores deberán confeccionar el inventario.

inventory
The receivers must draw up an inventory.

el **balance final**
El balance final debe ser elaborado una vez terminada la liquidación.

final balance
The final balance must be compiled once liquidation is complete.

la **disolución**
La inscripción de la disolución de una sociedad en el Registro Mercantil deberá realizarse mediante la presentación de escritura pública en la que conste el consentimiento de todos los socios.

dissolution
Registry of a corporation's dissolution in the Registry of Companies should be done by submission of a public document containing the assent of all the partners.

**cancelar**
En el Registro Mercantil se cancelan los asientos relativos a la sociedad extinguida.

to cancel; erase; remove
In the Registry of Companies, entries concerning the dissolved corporation are removed.

**concluir**
Las actividades de la empresa han concluido.

to conclude
The firm's activities have come to an end.

**la extinción**
Con la extinción se acaba la personalidad jurídica.

dissolution; termination; end
With dissolution the legal status is terminated.

**la insolvencia**

insolvency

**insolvente**
Pretende que el juez le declare insolvente para no pagar.

insolvent
To avoid paying, he intends to have the judge declare him insolvent.

**la reducción de capital**
El Consejo de Administración ha decidido efectuar una reducción de capital.

capital reduction
The Administrative Council has decided to undertake a reduction in capital.

**la segregación**

segregation

**la escisión propia**
En la escisión propia se extingue necesariamente la sociedad escindida.

true split
In a true split the corporation must necessarily be terminated.

**extinguir**

to extinguish

**escindido (a)**

split; divided

**la escisión parcial**
En la escisión parcial la parte del patrimonio social que se divida deberá formar una unidad económica.

partial split/division
In a partial split that part of the corporate assets which is to be divided must constitute an economic unity.

**la causa de disolución**
La existencia de una causa de disolución es el primer paso de todo el proceso.

cause of dissolution
The existence of a cause of dissolution is the first step in the entire process.

**el proyecto de escisión**
El proyecto de escisión es redactado y firmado por los administradores de las distintas sociedades que intervengan en la escisión.

plan for division/splitting
The plan for splitting is drawn up and signed by the managing directors of the various corporations concerned in the division.

**el balance de escisión**
El balance de escisión deberá ser verificado por los auditores y aprobado por la junta general que delibere sobre la escisión.

balance at the time of splitting
The balance at the time of splitting must be checked by the auditors and approved by the general shareholders' meeting which will decide on the split.

**deliberar**

to deliberate; decide on

la **quiebra fraudulenta**
Salvo prueba en contrario, se presumirá como quiebra fraudulenta la del empresario cuya verdadera situación no pueda deducirse de sus libros de contabilidad.

fraudulent bankruptcy
Unless proved otherwise, a bankruptcy is considered fraudulent if an entrepreneur's true financial situation cannot be determined from the books.

la **declaración de quiebra**
La declaración de quiebra se realiza mediante una resolución judicial.

declaration of bankruptcy
The declaration of bankruptcy is effected by court order.

la **masa de la quiebra**
El reparto de la masa de la quiebra se efectúa entre los acreedores.

bankrupt's assets
The bankrupt's assets are distributed among the creditors.

el **balance inicial**
El balance inicial refleja la relación de saldos deudores y acreedores de todas clases.

initial, opening balance
The initial balance indicates the ratio of debit and credit balances of every kind.

el **dividendo pasivo**


Los dividendos pasivos pendientes deben ser cobrados por los liquidadores.

passive dividend; further call; contribution in excess of original share
Pending passive dividends should be collected by the receivers.

el **concierto de transacciones y compromisos**

agreement on transactions and obligations

el **crédito vencido**
Los créditos vencidos serán satisfechos sin sujeción a orden ni prelación alguna.

credit due; payable credit
Credits due will be paid without respect to any order or precedence.

la **prelación**

precedence; preference

el **crédito no vencido**
Deben asegurarse los pagos de los créditos no vencidos.

current credit; non-due credit
The paying off of current credit must be assured.

el **interventor**


Un interventor fiscaliza las operaciones de liquidación.

chartered accountant; auditor; comptroller
An auditor checks the procedures involved in receivership.

**fiscalizar**

verify; check

| | |
|---|---|
| el **sindicato de obligacionistas** | consortium/association of debenture holders |
| El sindicato de obligacionistas puede nombrar un interventor. | The debenture holders' association can name an auditor. |
| la **cuota de activo** | share of assets |
| A cada acción le corresponde una cuota de activo. | Every share of stock is a share in assets. |
| la **cuota de liquidación** | receivership share |
| la **dificultad de pago** | difficulty in payment |
| El Ayuntamiento de Málaga est atravesando serias dificultades de pago. | The Municipality of Málaga is experiencing serious difficulties in meeting payment obligations. |
| la **falta de recursos** | lack of resources/liquidity |
| Nuestra falta de recursos es obvia. | Our lack of resourses is obvious. |
| **obvio (a)** | obvious |
| **subastar** | to auction |
| Estos bienes se van a subastar para poder pagar las deudas. | These assets will be auctioned off to pay debts. |
| el **plan de viabilidad** | restructuring; reorganization plan |
| La junta general de accionistas realizó la evaluación del plan de viabilidad propuesto por los administradores. | The shareholders' general meeting assessed the restructuring proposed by the managing directors. |
| la **evaluación** | evaluation |

## The Organization Chart

el **organigrama**

organization chart; plan; position plan

La expansión de la empresa supone cambios en el organigrama de la misma.

The firm's expansion means changes in its organization chart.

**suponer**

to suppose; mean

la **estructura de la empresa**

structure of the business

Las últimas modificaciones en la estructura de las empresas apuntan a una mayor independencia de cada uno de sus departamentos.

The last changes in the structure of the businesses aim at greater independence for each of its departments.

**apuntar**

to envision; aim at

el **departamento**

department

el **departamento de contabilidad**

accounting department

La reciente informatización del departamento de contabilidad ha reducido el número de personas que trabajaban en él.

The recent computerization of the accounting department has reduced the number of people working in it.

el **departamento de personal**

personnel department

El nuevo jefe del departamento de personal se distingue por su don de gentes y capacidad conciliadora.

The new personnel chief is personable and has the ability to settle quarrels amicably.

**don de gentes**

pleasing way with people; personable; crowd-pleaser

los **recursos humanos**

human resources

Las últimas tendencias en la gestión de recursos humanos quieren dejar atrás la mera administración de personal prestando más atención a los aspectos formativos.

The latest tendencies in human resources management seek to leave behind mere personnel administration and to pay more attention to further training.

**formativo (a)**

formative; training related

el **departamento de compras**

purchasing

el **departamento de ventas**

sales

las **relaciones públicas**
Para mejorar su imagen, muchas grandes empresas han creado un departamento especial de relaciones públicas.

public relations
To improve their image, many big firms have created a special public relations department.

el **ejecutivo,** la **ejecutiva**
Cada vez más empresas alemanas instaladas en España ponen al frente de sus departamentos a ejecutivos españoles.

executive; manager
More and more German firms operating in Spain are putting Spanish executives in charge of their departments.

el **cargo**

position; office

los **altos cargos**
Para atraer a altos cargos cualificados, algunos bancos y empresas públicas han ofrecido contratos con una cláusula de indemnización en caso de una eventual rescisión.

high-level management/executives
To attract high-level executives, some banks and government-owned enterprises have offered contracts with an indemnification clause in case of possible future dismissal.

la **rescisión de un contrato**

contract annulment

**nombrar**
La empresa aún no ha nombrado al nuevo consejero delegado.

to name
The firm still hasn't named the new managing director.

los **mandos intermedios**
Con la reestructuración de muchas empresas, se han eliminado numerosos mandos intermedios.

middle management
After the restructuring of many businesses, numerous middle management positions were eliminated.

la **reestructuración**

restructuring

el **sucesor,** la **sucesora**
Para encontrar el sucesor del director saliente, recurrieron a una empresa de selección de personal.

successor
To find the departing director's successor, they went to an agency specializing in personnel selection.

**saliente**

leaving; departing

el **director,** la **directora**

director

**estar al cargo**
El director adjunto está a cargo del proyecto de ampliar la red de sucursales en el extranjero.

to be in charge
The assistant director is in charge of the plan to amplify the network of branches abroad.

el **director adjunto,** la **directora adjunta,** el **subdirector,** la **subdirectora**

assistant director; deputy director; sub-director

Cuando el director está de viaje, todos los documentos que salen de la empresa deben llevar la firma del subdirector.

When the director is away, all the company's official documents must bear the deputy director's signature.

el **director comercial,** la **directora comercial**

sales director

La directora comercial proyectará la nueva política de venta, encargándose también de la ampliación de los canales de distribución.

The sales director will work out the new sales policy and will also assume responsibility for the establishment of distribution channels.

el **director financiero,** la **directora financiera**

financial director; accounting director

La primera decisión del recién nombrado director financiero fue la de encargar una auditoría interna.

The first decision made by the recently appointed financial director was to commission an internal audit.

la **ejecutiva**

executive board

la **búsqueda de ejecutivos**

executive search

En el campo de la búsqueda de ejecutivos cada vez ganan más terreno las firmas con proyección internacional.

In the field of executive search, firms with an international orientation are gaining more and more ground.

el **Consejo de Administración**

Administrative Council

La duración del cargo de los miembros del Consejo de Administración de una empresa española está limitada a cinco años.

The term of office for members of the Administrative Council of a Spanish firm is limited to five years.

la **dirección**

management

La dirección de la empresa ha aplicado innovadoras medidas en la gestión.

The company's management has employed innovative measures in its conduct of the firm.

el **director general,** la **directora general**

general director

el **subordinado,** la **subordinada**

subordinate

El nuevo director general goza de gran prestigio entre sus subordinados.

The new general director enjoys great prestige with his subordinates.

el **superior**

superior

Las nuevas estrategias de gestión apuestan por una mayor compenetración entre superiores y subordinados.

New management strategies are setting their hopes on more communicative interaction between superiors and subordinates.

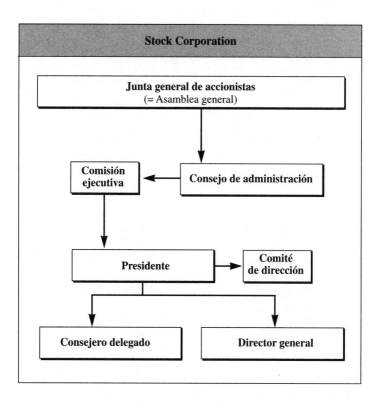

**Stock Corporation**

Junta general de accionistas
(= Asamblea general)

Comisión ejecutiva

Consejo de administración

Presidente

Comité de dirección

Consejero delegado

Director general

| | |
|---|---|
| la **compenetración** | mutual understanding; communicative interaction |
| la **asamblea general** | general assembly |
| la **junta general (de accionistas)** | shareholders' general meeting |
| La junta general de accionistas es convocada por el Consejo de Administración y toma decisiones en cuanto al aumento y reducción de capital, distribución de beneficios, modificación de estatutos, etc. | The shareholders' general meeting is called by the Administrative Council and makes decisions concerning capital increase and decrease, profit distribution, changes in the statutes, etc. |
| la **junta directiva** | board of directors |
| La composición de la junta directiva es un fiel reflejo del reparto de poderes en el grupo. | The composition of the board of directors is a faithful reflection of the group's power structure. |
| **ser un fiel reflejo** | to be a faithful reflection |
| la **posición clave** | key position |
| Por su flexibilidad y excelentes relaciones con sus superiores, se ha hecho con una posición clave. | Thanks to his/her flexibility and excellent relations with his/her superiors (s)he attained a key position. |
| el **nombramiento** | naming, appointing |
| El nombramiento del nuevo consejero delegado no ha sido bien acogido por parte del comité de empresa. | The appointment of the executive member of the board was not well received by the workers' committee. |
| **acoger** | to welcome |
| el **consejero delegado,** la **consejera delegada** | executive member of the board |
| El consejero delegado es un miembro del Consejo de Administración. | The executive member of the board is a member of the Administrative Council. |
| el **presidente de la junta directiva,** la **presidenta de la junta directiva** | chairman of the board of directors |
| El Sr. Moreno es el presidente de la junta directiva más joven que ha tenido la empresa. | Mr. Moreno is the youngest board chairman the company has ever had. |
| el **presidente vitaliciola,** la **presidenta vitalicia** | president for life |
| Al retirarse de sus obligaciones diarias, y en reconocimiento a sus méritos, fue nombrado presidente vitalicio. | When he retired from daily business obligations, and in recognition of his services, he was named president for life. |
| **retirarse** | to retire |

| | |
|---|---|
| **dar lugar a** | to cause; lead to |
| La venta de la empresa a un grupo extranjero dio lugar a profundos cambios en su equipo gestor. | The firm's sale to a foreign group led to major changes in its management team. |
| el **equipo gestor** | management team |
| la **descentralización** | decentralization |
| En el marco de la descentralización de la empresa se concedió mayor autonomía a los diferentes departamentos. | Within the framework of the firm's decentralization, greater autonomy was granted to the different departments. |
| el, la **representante legal** | legal representative |
| Los representantes legales de una empresa están autorizados para actuar en nombre de la misma. | A firm's legal representatives are authorized to act in its name. |

## Personnel

el **asesor,** la **asesora**
adviser; councillor

el **consultor,** la **consultora**
consultant

**consultar**
to consult
El presidente consulta sus asesores antes de elaborar el plan estratégico anual.
The president consults his advisers before working out the annual strategy plan.

el **colaborador,** la **colaboradora**
co-worker; colleague; collaborator
El director saliente propuso a uno de sus colaboradores como su sucesor.
The departing director proposed one of his colleagues as his successor.

**designar**
to designate; name; appoint
El Sr. Gil fue designado para el puesto.
Mr. Gil was appointed to the position.

el **antecesor,** la **antecesora**
predecessor

**destacar**
to stand out; be outstanding
Andrés, que siempre se destacó por sus cualidades comerciales, se convirtió hace dos meses en el nuevo jefe de ventas.
Andrés, whose business sense was always outstanding, became the new sales chief two months ago.

la **calidad**
quality

**hacerse cargo**
to take over; perform
Cuando Fernando asistió al curso de perfeccionamiento, Pedro se hizo cargo, temporalmente, de su trabajo.
When Fernando attended the training course, Pedro took over his job temporarily.

la **gestión**

management

**poner a disposición**

to put at the disposal of

Los consejeros pusieron sus cargos a disposición del presidente de la junta directiva.

The board members put their positions at the disposal of the chairman of the board (i.e. they offered to resign).

el **consejero,** la **consejera**

board member

**permanecer**

to remain

A pesar de las críticas que se vertieron sobre él, el director decidió permanecer en su cargo.

Although the object of much criticism, the director decided to stay at his post.

**verter críticas**

to make criticism

**convocar una junta**

to call a meeting

Con el fin de modificar los estatutos de la compañía, se ha convocado una junta extraordinaria de accionistas para el próximo viernes.

For the purpose of changing the company's statutes, a special shareholders' meeting has been called for next Friday.

la **junta extraordinaria**

extraordinary/special meeting

**celebrar una reunión**

to have a meeting

La reunión semanal de la junta directiva se celebra en la sala de actos.

The board's weekly meeting takes place in the meeting room.

la **sala de actos**

meeting room

**estar reunido (a)**

to be in conference

Para deshacerse del acreedor insistente, la secretaria del jefe de compras tenía orden de decir que éste estaba reunido.

To get rid of the persistent creditor, the head of sales told his secretary to say he was in conference.

el **jefe,** la **jefa**

boss; head; chief

**deshacerse de alguien**

to get rid of someone

**aplazar una reunión, posponer una reunión**

to postpone a meeting

Al no disponer de los últimos datos, la reunión fue aplazada para la próxima semana.

Since the most recent data weren't available, the meeting was postponed till next week.

**suspender una reunión**

cancel a meeting

Para expresar su disconformidad con la marcha de las negociaciones, la delegación extranjera suspendió la reunión prevista.

To express its disagreement with the direction the negotiations were taking, the foreign delegation cancelled the scheduled meeting.

el **acta**

record; file

Debido al caracter reservado de la reunión, se decidió no levantar acta.

Due to the confidential nature of the meeting, it was decided to keep no minutes.

**de caracter reservado**

confidential nature

**pasar a**
Se consideró zanjado el conflicto y
se pudo pasar al siguiente punto del
orden del día.

to proceed to
The disagreement was considered
settled and it was possible to
proceed to the next item on the
agenda.

**zanjar un conflicto**

to settle an issue/disagreement

la **plantilla**
A pesar de la drástica reducción de
la plantilla, se consiguió aumentar
la producción.

payroll
Despite the drastic reduction in
the payroll, it was possible to
increase production.

el **viaje de negocios**
Los avances tecnológicos en
materia de telecomunicaciones
han permitido reducir el número
de viajes de negocios.

business trip
Technological advances in telecommunications have made it
possible to reduce the number of
business trips.

el **ascenso**
Por su carácter tímido e introvertido,
el ascenso de Salvador fue postergado
repetidas veces.

rise; promotion
Because of his shy and introverted
nature, Salvador was passed over
for promotion many times.

**postergar el ascenso de
alguien**

to pass over someone for promotion

el **traslado**
Eloisa ha pedido el traslado a la
nueva oficina de Sevilla para poder
estar más cerca de su familia.

transfer
Eloisa has asked for a transfer to
the new Seville office in order to
be closer to her family.

**optar a un cargo**

Entre las personas que optan al cargo
figuran tres directivos de una misma
empresa.

apply for a position; strive for a
position
Among the people applying for
the position are three directors
of the same firm.

el **directivo,** la **directiva**

director; manager; executive

**asumir**
Nadie quiso asumir la responsabilidad
de la mala gestión durante los últimos
meses.

to assume
Nobody wanted to assume
responsibility for the bad management that prevailed during recent
months.

la **mala gestión**

bad management; mismanagement

**imponerse**
El candidato idóneo debe combinar
capacidad para imponerse en habilidad
negociadora.

to assert oneself
The suitable candidate should
combine a talent for self-assertion
with negotiation skills.

la **capacidad**   capacity; talent

**relevar**   to dismiss
Al salir a la luz su implicación en el caso de corrupción, le relevaron de su cargo inmediatamente.   When his complicity in the corruption affair was revealed, he was dismissed immediately.

**salir a la luz**   to come to light; be revealed; become known

la **implicación**   implication; complicity

**otorgar plenos poderes**   to grant full/plenary power; grant power of attorney
Como condición para aceptar el cargo exigió que se le otorgasen plenos poderes para llevar a cabo una completa reestructuración de la empresa.   He accepted the job on condition that complete power be granted him in order to carry out a total restructuring of the company.

el **ámbito de responsabilidad**   area of authority/responsibility/competence
La dirección recriminó al subdirector por haber sobrepasado su ámbito de responsabilidad.   Management reproached the deputy director for having exceeded his authority.

**sobrepasar, extralimitarse**   to exceed

la **competencia exclusiva**   sole responsibility
El jefe de personal insistió en que la contratación era competencia exclusiva de su departamento.   The head of personnel insisted that hiring was the sole responsibility of his department.

la **toma de decisiones**   decision making
Muchos directivos de edad avanzada encuentran dificultades para adaptarse a la toma de decisiones en equipo.   Many older executives find it difficult to adjust to decision making as members of a team.

**dar órdenes**   to give orders
El responsable de la seguridad de la empresa dio órdenes de no bloquear bajo ningún pretexto las salidas de emergencia.   The company's security officer gave orders that under no circumstances were the emergency exits to be blocked.

el, la **responsable**   person responsible for

el **orden del día**   agenda
¿Alguien desea incluir otro punto en el orden del día para la próxima reunión?   Does anyone wish to include another item on the agenda for the next meeting?

**sin rodeos**   without delay/detour
En la reunión se trató, sin rodeos, de los cambios en la cúpula directiva.   At the meeting, the changes in top management were discussed without delay.

| | |
|---|---|
| la **cúpula directiva** | top management |
| **prolongarse** | to be prolonged |
| Por la urgencia de los asuntos pendientes, la reunión del miércoles se prolongó durante más de cinco horas. | Because of the urgency of the matters pending, Wednesday's meeting lasted more than five hours. |
| la **remuneración** | remuneration; salary |
| En 1994, se han congelado las remuneraciones de muchos ejecutivos españoles. | In 1994, salaries of many Spanish executives were frozen. |
| **congelar** | to freeze |
| el **emolumento** | emolument; income; side income; perquisite; salaries; wages |
| Como muestra de solidaridad, la junta directiva decidió unánimemente no aumentar la cuantía de sus emolumentos. | As a sign of solidarity the board members unanimously decided not to raise their salaries. |
| **unánimemente** | unanimously |

━━━━━ **General Information** ━━━━━

*el financiamiento*

| | |
|---|---|
| la **financiación** | financing |
| Últimamente, los bancos se han mostrado reticentes a la hora de apoyar la financiación de empresas de nueva creación. | Recently banks have been reluctant to finance new businesses. |
| **reticente** | reluctant; reticent |
| la **financiación interna** | internal/individual/private financing |
| la **autofinanciación** | self-financing |
| La financiación interna consiste en financiarse empleando los fondos propios como, p. ej., los beneficios generados en la misma empresa. | Self-financing is financing that makes use of the company's own funds, such as e.g. profits earned by the firm itself. |
| la **financiación propia** | private financing |
| Muchos expertos lamentan la baja proporción de financiación propia de las empresas españolas en comparación con las demás europeas. | Many experts regret the low degree of private financing of Spanish firms compared to other European firms. |
| los **recursos propios** | equity; net asset worth |
| Los recursos propios lo componen las aportaciones iniciales de los socios y las sucesivas ampliaciones de capital. | Equity is comprised of the initial contributions made by the partners and successive capital increases. |
| la **situación financiera** | financial situation/picture |
| Después de un año de fuertes pérdidas, la situación financiera de la empresa ha sido considerada como muy crítica. | After a year of heavy losses, the firm's financial situation has been judged to be very critical. |
| **solvente** | solvent |
| el **plan financiero** | finance plan |
| El plan financiero es un documento que incluye la financiación a largo plazo propiamente dicha, los presupuestos anuales y el llamado presupuesto de tesorería. | The finance plan is a document which includes long term financing as such, the annual budget, and the so-called treasury budget. |
| el **presupuesto** | budget; cost estimate |

la **reducción de gastos**

El informe final de los auditores
reveló la urgente necesidad de
llevar a cabo una drástica reducción
de gastos.

cost/expenses reduction

The auditors' final report revealed
the urgent need to carry out a
drastic reduction in costs.

**drástico (a)**

drastic

**revelar**

to reveal

el **beneficio extraordinario**

Con los beneficios extraordinarios
obtenidos el pasado año, la empresa
ha financiado parcialmente la
instalación de su nueva factoría en
Extremadura.

extraordinary profit

With the extraordinary profits
earned last year, the firm has
partially financed the setting up
of its new factory in Extremadura.

**arrojar beneficios**

Las operaciones comerciales
realizadas en el sector servicios
han arrojado en el primer semestre
del año unos beneficios de 123
millones de pesetas.

to show/earn/yield a profit

Business activities performed in
the service sector have yielded a
profit of 123 million pesetas in the
first half-year.

**generar beneficios**

La estrategia de diversificación ha
generado unos beneficios superiores
a los esperados.

to generate/produce/earn profits

The strategy of diversifying has
produced profits in excess of those
hoped for.

los **beneficios**

profits

**reinvertido (a)**

Parte de los beneficios son reinvertidos
en la propia empresa constituyendo
así un fondo de autofinanciación.

reinvested

A part of the profits are reinvested
in the firm itself thus constituting
a self-financing fund.

la **estrategia**

strategy

las **ganancias**

La enajenación de parte de los terre-
nosedificables propiedad de la
empresa, ha generado ganancias
por un importe de 500 millones
de pesetas.

income; revenues

The selling of a part of the company's constructible real property
has produced income amounting
to 500 million pesetas.

el **terreno edificable**

building lot; constructible land

las **pérdidas**

Las pérdidas generadas por tres años
consecutivos han puesto en peligro la
continuidad de la empresa.

losses

The losses shown three years in
a row have put the company's
existence in jeopardy.

**consecutivo (a)**

consecutive

la **continuidad**

continuation; further existence

la **liquidez**
Cuando los bancos se encuentran con problemas de liquidez a corto plazo, recurren al mercado interbancario para corregir los desequilibrios.

liquidity
When banks have short term liquidity problems, they use the inter-banking market to correct any imbalances.

la **capacidad financiera**
Como los costes de desarrollo del nuevo chip superaban con creces la capacidad financiera individual de las empresas, Apple, Motorola y IBM han unido sus esfuerzos en investigación.

financial capacity
Since development costs for the new chip exceeded by far the individual financial capacity of the firms involved, Apple, Motorola, and IBM combined their research efforts.

**con creces**

by far; amply

**facturar**
Las empresas que facturan más de 1000 millones de pesetas son consideradas grandes empresas.

to bill; to make sales
Companies with sales over 1000 million pesetas are considered big businesses.

la **cifra de ventas**

revenue; return; turnover; sales

la **facturación**
El año pasado, la cifra de ventas se incrementó en un 41%, y asi todo, no causó ningun retraso en la facturación.

billing; invoicing; charging
Last year, sales increased by 41%, and still, there was no delay in the invoicing.

la **recaudación diaria**
A las cinco de la tarde pasa diariamente un camión blindado para recoger la recaudación diaria de la empresa.

daily receipts
Every day at 5:00 P.M. an armored car picks up the company's receipts.

la **auditoría financiera**
La auditoría financiera analiza si los informes financieros y cuentas anuales han sido realizados de acuerdo con lo que marca la ley y si verdaderamente éstos reflejan la realidad económico-financiera de la empresa.

financial audit
The financial audit determines whether the financial reports and annual statements have been done in conformity with the law and whether they do in fact reflect the financial-economic condition of the company.

el **informe financiero**

financial report

la **reserva legal**
(En España,) todas las sociedades anónimas están obligadas a destinar un 10% de sus beneficios a la reserva legal para la compensación de posibles pérdidas.

legal reserves
(In Spain,) all corporations are required to add 10% of their earnings to their legal reserves to cover possible losses.

el **capital propio**
El capital propio lo componen el capital social de la empresa más los beneficios no distribuidos.

equity capital
Equity capital consists of the corporate capital plus retained earnings.

la **estructura financiera**
En la estructura financiera de una empresa se refleja el grado de endeudamiento de la misma, así como el plazo de devolución del capital empleado.

financial structure
A corporation's degree of debt is reflected in its financial structure, as well as the term of investment refunding.

la **confección de un presupuesto**
En la confección del presupuesto para este año se ha tenido en cuenta el incremento de la carga financiera debido al aumento de los intereses.

drawing up of a budget

In drawing up this year's budget attention was given to the increasing financial burden due to the rise in interest rates.

la **carga financiera**

financial burden

**presupuestar**

La empresa ha presupuestado para los próximos tres años unas inversiones por valor de 5.000 millones en América del Sur.

to make a cost estimate; plan for in a budget
The company has planned for investments of 5,000 millions (of pesetas) in South America over the next three years.

el **control presupuestario**
Debido a la mala marcha de los negocios, el consejo de la empresa ha impuesto un férreo control presupuestario para poder reducir gastos.

budget control
Because the business has been doing badly, the executive board has imposed rigorous budgetary controls in order to bring down expenses.

la **marcha de los negocios**

business operations

**férreo (a)**

rigorous

el **ajuste**
Como la rentabilidad de la compañía era escasa, se han llevado a cabo ajustes que han afectado a los gastos superfluos.

adjustment; correction
Since the company's profit margin was slight, corrections affecting superfluous expenses have been implemented.

**superfluo (a)**

superfluous

**ajustarse a**

to adjust to

la **reestructuración financiera**
La reestructuración financiera de la empresa pasa por la reducción de su participación en actividades atípicas.

financial restructuring
The company's financial restructuring will be done by reducing its participation in non-business related activities.

**pasar por**

to go through; be done by

| | |
|---|---|
| **atípico (a)** | atypical |
| la **restricción**<br>Las restricciones en gastos de formación han supuesto la anulación de los cursos de informática impartidos a los empleados. | restriction<br>Cut backs in training expenses led to the cancelling of the telecommunications courses given to employees. |
| la **anulación** | cancellation |
| las **reservas**<br>Las reservas son recursos propios obtenidos de la no distribución de los beneficios de la empresa. | reserves<br>Reserves are corporate resources that represent undistributed earnings of the firm. |
| la **distribución** | distribution |
| las **provisiones**<br>En el caso de las provisiones, y a diferencia de las reservas, se trata de capital destinado a fines concretos. | supply; provision<br>The difference between reserves and provisions is that provisions are earmarked for specific purposes. |
| las **reservas estatutarias**<br>Las reservas estatutarias son aquellas cuya cuantía ya viene fijada por los estatutos de la sociedad y van a cargo del beneficio de la misma. | statutory reserves<br>Statutory reserves are those whose amount has already been established by the corporate statutes and which are deducted from the company's profits. |
| las **reservas voluntarias**<br>Las reservas voluntarias son constituídas libremente por la sociedad, sin que exista obligación legal. | voluntary reserves<br>Voluntary reserves are established at the company's discretion, not in compliance with a legal obligation. |
| las **provisiones para riesgos y gastos**<br>Las provisiones para riesgos y gastos están destinadas principalmente al pago de imprevistos y otros gastos. | provisions for risks and expenses<br>Provisions for risks and expenses are principally intended for contingency and other payments. |
| la **contracción**<br>Como consecuencia de la contracción de los beneficios, muchas empresas adoptan una actitud de extrema cautela en cuanto a contrataciones e inversiones. | contraction; decline<br>Because of shrinking profits, many companies are becoming extremely cautious when hiring and making investments. |
| **adoptar una actitud** | to take an attitude |

| | |
|---|---|
| la **cautela** | caution |

la **capitalización**
Los hoteleros españoles aspiran a la capitalización de las inversiones realizadas en los años anteriores.

capitalization
Spanish hotel keepers are hoping for the capitalization of the investments made in earlier years.

la **nivel de capitalización**
Uno de los objetivos de la fusión fue la consecución de un mayor nivel de capitalización más amplio.

level of capitalization
One of the objectives of the merger was the procurement of a broader capital basis.

la **necesidad de capitalización**
Se estiman en 130.000 millones de pesetas las necesidades de capitalización de Iberia.

capital requirements
Iberia's capital requirements are estimated at 130,000 million pesetas.

la **descapitalización**

decapitalization

la **recapitalización**
Se ha decidido dedicar el 40% de los fondos obtenidos por la venta de Elementos Reunidos S.A. a la recapitalización de la casa matriz.

recapitalization
It was decided to use 40% of the money realized from the sale of Elementos Reunidos S.A for the recapitalization of the parent firm.

el **margen de beneficios**
La presión ejercida por los grandes fabricantes automovilísticos ha reducido considerablemente el margen de beneficios de muchos suministradores.

profit margin
The pressure exerted by the big automobile manufacturers has considerably reduced the profit margin of many supplier firms.

**considerablemente**

considerably

el **umbral de rentabilidad,** el **punto muerto**
El umbral de rentabilidad viene definido por el volumen de ventas necesario para cubrir todos los costes fijos del período y los variables según el propio volumen de ventas.

break-even point

The break-even point is defined as the point at which the volume of sales necessary to cover all the fixed costs of the accounting period and the variable costs corresponding to those sales are covered.

el **trámite burocrático**
La Administración intenta flexibilizar los trámites burocráticos para facilitar a las pequeñas y medianas empresas el acceso a una financiación a medida.

red tape
The administration is trying to cut through red tape to make it easier for small and middle-range businesses to have access to financing tailored to their needs.

| | |
|---|---|
| **flexibilizar** | to make easier/more flexible |
| el **fondo de comercio** <br> El fondo de comercio representa el valor inmaterial que se le atribuye a una empresa en función de su ubicación, clientela, buena imagen, etc. | prestige; goodwill; image; good name <br> A firm's image represents the non-monetary value associated with a company as a result of its location, customers, good reputation, etc. |
| la **ubicación** | location |

# Capital Procurement

la **obtención de capital**
Para facilitar la obtención de capital por parte de las pequeñas y medianas empresas, las cajas de ahorros han abierto una línea de créditos blandos.

obtaining of capital
To facilitate the obtaining of capital by small and medium sized businesses, savings banks have opened a line of easy credit.

el **crédito blando**

easy credit

la **fuente de financiación**
La Administración quiere fomentar las sociedades de capital riesgo como fuente de financiación alternativa para nuevas empresas.

source of financing
The Administration wants to encourage risk capital corporations as an alternative source of financing for new businesses.

**fomentar**

to encourage

**alternativo (a)**

alternative

la **financiación externa**
Entre las formas de financiación externa destacan la financiación mediante créditos y la financiación a través de participaciones.

outside financing
Credit financing and participatory financing are particularly note-worthy forms of outside financing.

la **financiación ajena**
La financiación ajena abarca la obtención de recursos ajenos por los que la empresa deberá pagar un cierto tipo de interés, tales como créditos y empréstitos.

outside financing
Outside financing includes obtaining outside resources for which the company will have to pay a particular rate of interest, as for credits and loans.

los **recursos ajenos,**
el **capital ajeno**

outside capital/resources

el **crédito comercial,**
el **crédito de proveedores**
El crédito de proveedores se produce al conceder el proveedor un período de pago para sus mercancías, que puede ascender a varios meses.

trade credit

In a trade credit, the supplier allows for a payment period for his goods, a period that may be spread over several months.

la **necesidad de liquidez**
Para satisfacer transitorias necesidades de liquidez, la empresa agotó el margen de crédito concedido por el banco.

liquidity necessity
To cover temporary liquidity needs, the company exhausted the credit margin the bank had given it.

**transitorio (a)**

temporary

**satisfacer**

to satisfy; cover

los **números rojos**
La casa matriz amenazó con el cierre si al final del ejercicio las cuentas arrojaban de nuevo números rojos.

to be in the red; suffer losses
The parent company threatened a shutdown if the books again showed losses at the end of the fiscal year.

el **endeudamiento**

debt

el **desequilibrio financiero**
Las repetidas pérdidas de la empresa la condujeron a un desequilibrio financiero de difícil solución.

financial imbalance
The firm's continuing losses brought it to a point of financial instability difficult to correct.

**salir de la situación de pérdidas**
Para salir de la situación de pérdidas, la empresa española recurrió a una ampliación de capital.

get out of a money-losing situation
To get out of its money losing situation, the Spanish company had recourse to capital extension.

**desproporcionado (a)**
Como los bancos consideraron desproporcionada la relación entre los recursos propios y las obligaciones contraídas por la empresa, se negaron a conceder más créditos.

disproportionate; out of balance
Because the banks considered the ratio between the corporation's assets and its contractual obligations to be out of balance, they refused to grant further credits.

**agotar**
La empresa agotó su margen de crédito concertado con los bancos para financiar sus recientes inversiones en el extranjero.

to exhaust
In order to finance its recent foreign investments, the company exhausted the credit margin it had arranged with the banks.

**concertado (a)**

arranged; concluded

la **devolución del préstamo**
Al no poder hacer frente a la devolución del préstamo, la empresa solicitó una refinanciación de la deuda.

repayment of a loan
Because it couldn't keep up the payments on the loan, the company applied for a refinancing of the debt.

la **refinanciación**

refinancing

**cancelar una deuda**
Los españoles argumentaron que
la empresa SEAT había cancelado
todas las deudas antes de pasar a
manos de Volkswagen.

cancel a debt
The Spaniards argued that the
SEAT company had cancelled all
its debts before ownership passed
to Volkswagen.

**pasar a manos de**

transfer of ownership

**estimado (a)**
Como los costes estimados del
proyecto no guardaban relación
con los ingresos potenciales, el
plan no fue aprobado.

estimated
Since the project's cost estimate
bore no relation to the potential
revenues, the plan was not approved.

los **ingresos**

income; revenues; returns

**potencial**

potential

**guardar relación con**

bear relation to

**previsto (a)**
Los gastos inicialmente previstos
para investigación fueron reducidos
en un 12%.

planned; foreseen
The outlays initially allocated for
research were reduced by 12%.

el **beneficio no distribuido**
Los beneficios no distribuidos, es
decir las ganancias del año anterior
no repartidas, forman parte de los
recursos propios de una empresa.

non paid out dividends
Non paid out dividends, i.e. the
prior year's non distributed earnings,
are a part of a corporation's private
resources.

el **beneficio distribuido**

paid out dividends

**destinar a**
Una de las funciones de la Intervención
General del Estado consiste en
comprobar que las ayudas concedidas
a empresas españolas se destinen
realmente a los fines previstos.

to go to; allocate
One of the functions of the State
Auditing Office is to verify that
the subsidies granted to Spanish
companies are really allocated to
purposes intended.

la **Intervención General del
Estado**

State Auditing Office

la **escasez de capital**
La escasez de capital de muchas
empresas es un impedimento de
peso a la hora de realizar nuevas
inversiones.

scarcity of capital; capital crunch
The capital crunch felt by many
corporations is a significant
obstacle to new investment.

**de peso**

significant; weighty

## la **escasez de créditos**
La escasez de créditos ha repercutido negativamente en el consumo y por consiguiente, en las ventas de muchas empresas.

scarcity of credit; credit crunch
The scarcity of credit has had negative repercussions on the consumer and therefore on the sales of many companies.

## la **falta de liquidez,** la **iliquidez**
A pesar de su transitoria falta de liquidez, la empresa sigue siendo considerada solvente.

lack of liquidity; insolvency

Despite its temporary lack of liquidity the company continues to be considered solvent.

## **dispararse**
Como la empresa no se había asegurado frente a las fluctuaciones del mercado de divisas, se dispararon las pérdidas en las operaciones con el exterior.

to explode; go out of control
Since the company had taken no measures to protect itself against fluctuations on the currency market, losses in its foreign operations went out of control.

## las **pérdidas acumuladas**
Las pérdidas acumuladas por la empresa en ejercicios anteriores superan, en la actualidad, su capital social.

accumulated losses
The losses accumulated by the company in earlier business years at present exceed its corporate capital.

## **sustraerse**
Para sustraerse de sus obligaciones de pago, el empresario transfirió parte de su patrimonio a un testaferro.

to get out of; avoid
To avoid meeting his payment obligations, the entrepreneur transferred part of his assets to a front-man.

## el **testaferro,** la **testaferra**

front-man

## el **escándalo financiero**
Los últimos escándalos financieros han puesto en entredicho la credibilidad de la empresa.

financial scandal
The latest financial scandals have cast doubt on the firm's credibility.

## **poner en entredicho**

to cast doubt on

## la **credibilidad**

credibility

## **incurrir en**
Debido a la tardanza del Estado en pagar a sus proveedores, muchas empresas españolas han incurrido en graves dificultades de pago.

to get into; find oneself in
Due to the government's delay in paying its suppliers, many Spanish companies found themselves in serious payment difficulties.

## la **tardanza**

delay

## **conceder una moratoria**
Para evitar la desaparición de 150 puestos de trabajo, los bancos concedieron al grupo una nueva moratoria para el pago de sus deudas.

to grant a delay/moratorium
To avoid the loss of 150 jobs, the banks granted the group a new delay for payment of its debts.

el **crédito puente**
El crédito puente tiene la finalidad de ayudar a superar necesidades financieras transitorias.

bridging loan
The purpose of a bridging loan is to help overcome temporary difficulties in meeting payment obligations.

la **financiación interina**
Debido a la demora en la captación de recursos ajenos, la empresa solicitó del banco una financiación interina del proyecto.

interim financing
Due to the delay in tapping outside resources, the company applied to the bank for interim financing of the project.

la **captación**

tapping; obtaining; receipt

la **prefinanciación**
La prefinanciación es un concepto usado, sobre todo, en el campo de la construcción para superar necesidades iniciales de capital.

pre-financing
Pre-financing is a concept used primarily in the construction industry to overcome initial capital raising problems.

**recurrir a**
La empresa ha tenido que recurrir varias veces a sus reservas para hacer frente a sus imprevistos.

to have recourse to; fall back on
Frequently, the company had to fall back on its reserves to cover unforseen expenses.

los **imprevistos**

unforseen expenses

la **ayuda a fondo perdido**
Como la empresa estaba situada en una región industrial deprimida, le fue concedida una ayuda a fondo perdido que ascendía al 25% del capital solicitado.

non-repayable subsidy
Since the company was situated in a depressed industrial area, it was granted a non-repayable subsidy that amounted to 25% of the capital asked for.

**peticionario (a)**

petitioning; asking for

el **peticionario,** la **peticionaria**

petitioner

el **pliego de condiciones**
Las empresas peticionarias de ayudas a fondo perdido por parte del Ministerio de Industria deberán recoger el pliego de condiciones antes del 24 de junio.

specifications/conditions for receipt
Those companies asking for non-repayable subsidies from the Ministry of Industry must pick up the official list of conditions for receipt of same before June 24.

la **sociedad de capital-riesgo**
Las sociedades de capital-riesgo tienen la finalidad de proporcionar recursos financieros a las pequeñas y medianas empresas, así como asesoramiento.

risk capital corporation
The purpose of risk capital corporations is to provide financial means to small and medium-sized business, as well as to serve them in a consulting capacity.

| | |
|---|---|
| la **asistencia** | help; assistance |
| **captar** <br> Con la ampliación de capital se pretenden captar 570 millones. | to raise/bring in/collect (money) <br> Through capital expansion they're trying to raise 570 million. |
| **cifrarse** <br> Las pérdidas ocasionadas a empresas españolas por la huelga de los controladores aéreos de Marsella se cifran diariamente en varios centenares de millones de pesetas. | to amount to <br> The losses to Spanish companies caused by the air controllers' strike in Marseilles amount to several hundred million pesetas per day. |
| **descartar** <br> Aunque la junta directiva aún no se ha pronunciado al respecto, no se descarta la entrada de nuevos socios en la empresa. | to exclude; rule out <br> Although the board of directors has not yet made any statement concerning the issue, the entry of new partners into the company cannot be ruled out. |

# ■■■ Allocation of Resources ■■■

| | |
|---|---|
| la **asignación de recursos** <br> Es recomendable confeccionar un plan de inversiones para asegurar una óptima asignación de los recursos. | allocation of resources <br> It is advisable to draw up an investment plan to assure optimal allocation of resources. |
| **confeccionar** | to draw up |
| **óptimo (a)** | optimal; best |
| el **plan de inversiones** | investment plan |
| la **inversión** <br> La inversión es el empleo de recursos financieros con el fin de obtener futuros beneficios. | investment <br> Investment is the use of financial means for the purpose of making future profits. |
| el **empleo** | employment; use |
| la **actividad inversora** <br> En tiempos de crisis la actividad inversora se ve afectada por la escasa propensión a la inversión. | investment activity <br> In periods of crisis investment activity is affected by a reluctance to invest. |
| la **propensión a la inversión** | inclination to invest |
| el **clima inversionista** <br> La patronal apela al gobierno para que fomente un clima inversionista favorable a través de la reducción de la carga impositiva. | investment climate <br> Industry calls upon the government to create a climate favorable to investment by reducing the tax burden. |

| | |
|---|---|
| **favorable** | favorable |
| **apelar** | to call upon; appeal to |
| el **proyecto de inversiones** | investment project/intention |
| las **inversiones iniciales** | initial/original/front end investments |

Muchos jóvenes empresarios se encuentran con dificultades a la hora de reunir los medios necesarios para las inversiones iniciales.

Many young business persons have problems when they have to put up the necessary means for the initial investments.

| | |
|---|---|
| **encontrarse con dificultades** | to find oneself in difficulty; have problems |
| las **inversiones de modernización** | modernization investments |

Las inversiones de modernización tienen la finalidad de introducir alguna innovación tecnológica en el proceso productivo de la empresa.

The purpose of modernization investments is the introduction of technological innovations into the company's production process.

las **inversiones de renovación,** las **inversiones de reemplazo**

replacement investments

Las inversiones de renovación están destinadas a la sustitución de elementos del proceso productivo que ya se han quedado obsoletos.

Replacement investments are used for the introduction of technological innovations to replace what has become obsolete in the production process.

| | |
|---|---|
| la **su(b)stitución** | substitution |
| las **inversiones en bienes de equipo** | rolling stock investments |

En los últimos años, muchas empresas han realizado importantes inversiones en bienes de equipo con el fin de aumentar su productividad.

In order to increase their productivity, many businesses have made important investments in rolling stock in recent years.

las **inversiones de expansión**

expansion investments

Las inversiones de expansión se llevan a cabo para aumentar la capacidad productiva de la empresa o ampliar su campo de actuación.

Expansion investments are made to increase the company's productive capacity or to expand its field of operations.

el **campo de actuación**

field of activity/operation

**Investigación y Desarrollo (I+D)**

Research and Development (R&D)

(En España,) el Ministerio de Industria ha diseñado un Plan de Investigación y Desarrollo para el sector aeronáutico que supondrá unas inversiones de 120.000 millones de pesetas.

(In Spain,) the Ministry of Industry has drawn up a plan of Research and Development for the aeronautical sector which calls for the investment of 120,000 million pesetas.

**apostar por**

to commit to; to bet or wager on

Sólo aquellas empresas que apuestan fuertemente por una renovación tecnológica, tendrán posibilidades de sobrevivir.

Only companies strongly committed to technological innovation have a chance to survive.

### incentivar

El Gobierno vasco ha puesto en marcha un plan con el fin de incentivar inversiones estratégicas que, hasta ahora, ha permitido la creación de 2.255 nuevos empleos.

to give incentives to; motivate; stimulate
The Basque government has set in motion a plan to stimulate strategic investments which, so far, has permitted the creation of 2,255 new jobs.

### las **inversiones estratégicas**

strategic investments

### el **coste de la mano de obra,** ellos **gastos de personal coste salarial**

Según la mayoría de los expertos, la competitividad de España pasa por una moderación de los costes salariales.

manpower/labor/wage/personnel costs

According to most experts Spain's competitiveness depends on a reduction in wage costs.

### la **moderación**

moderation; reduction

### los **costes de producción**

Para reducir sus costes de producción, las grandes empresas automovilísticas presionan cada vez más a sus proveedores.

production costs
To reduce their production costs, the big automobile companies are putting more and more pressure on their suppliers.

### presionar

to pressure

### los **gastos corrientes**

Muchas grandes empresas gratifican a aquellos empleados que con sus propuestas ayudan a reducir los gastos corrientes.

current expenses
Many large companies reward those employees whose suggestions help reduce current expenses.

### gratificar

to reward; give a bonus to

### los **gastos de representación**

expense account allowances

### las **dietas**

Las drásticas reducciones de los gastos de representación han repercutido de manera negativa en la facturación de hoteles y restaurantes de lujo.

per diem allowances
Drastic expense account allowance reductions have had a negative effect on the luxury hotel and restaurant trade.

### los **dividendos**

Los dividendos son la parte correspondiente del beneficio neto de una sociedad anónima que se reparte entre sus accionistas.

dividends
Dividends are the corresponding part of a corporation's net profits which is distributed among the shareholders.

### repartir dividendos

to pay out/distribute dividends

### asignar

En los presupuestos del próximo ano, se ha asignado una importante suma al apartado de formación interna.

to assign; allocate; earmark
In next year's budget a significant sum has been allocated to the item "in-house training."

el **apartado**

item; paragraph

la **adquisición**
La adquisición de la empresa automovilística Rover por parte de BMW ha cogido por sorpresa a gran parte del mundo empresarial.

acquisition
BMW's acquisition of the automobile company Rover took much of the business world by surprise.

el **criterio de decisión**

criterion for decision; deciding factor

Uno de los criterios de decisión a la hora de adquirir Rover fue la complementariedad de sus líneas de productos.

One of the deciding factors in acquiring Rover was the complementing of each company's production line.

la **complementariedad**

complementing; extension; filling out

la **proporción**
A la hora de conceder un crédito, los bancos prestan atención a la proporción entre capital propio y deudas.

proportion
When granting credit. banks pay particular attention to the ratio between equity capital and debts.

**prestar atención**

to pay attention

el **plan de viabilidad**

viability plan; rehabilitation plan for restoration to profitability

El gobierno se comprometió a conceder importantes ayudas a condición de que la empresa presentará un plan de viabilidad factible.

The government pledged large contributions on condition that the company submit a practicable rehabilitation plan.

**factible**

practicable

la **desinversión**
Para los trabajadores de SFM (Servicios Ferroviarios de Mallorca), la desinversión llevada a cabo por el gobierno regional ha sido causante del deterioro del servicio.

decline/drying up of investment
According to the employees of SFM (Majorcan Rail Services), the regional government's failure to invest was responsible for a deterioration in services.

el, la **causante**

person responsible for

la **inversión equivocada**
Con el tiempo se ha demostrado que la adquisición del solar cercano a la autopista fue una inversión equivocada.

bad/poor/mistaken investment
After a while it became clear that the acquisition of the land near the highway was a bad investment.

el **saneamiento**

rehabilitation; restoration to profitability

La casa matriz estaba harta de las pérdidas acumuladas por la filial y se negó a elaborar un plan de saneamiento.

The parent firm was fed up with the losses accumulated by the subsidiary and refused to work out a rehabilitation plan.

**elaborar**

to elaborate; work out/up

**diversificar**
Para reducir el riesgo hay que
diversificar las inversiones.

to diversify
To reduce the risk it's necessary
to diversify investments.

la **diversificación**
Ante la crisis del sector, la empresa
optó por la diversificación de sus
actividades.

diversification
Because of the crisis in the industry,
the company decided to diversify
its activities.

**optar por**

to choose; opt for

la **reinversión**
Los sindicatos exigieron una reducción
de los dividendos distribuidos y, en su
lugar, la reinversión de los beneficios.

reinvestment
The unions demanded a reduction
in dividend payments and instead,
a reinvestment of profits.

las **deducciones fiscales
sobre inversiones**
Las deducciones fiscales sobre inversiones son, a menudo, un acicate para
la adquisición de nueva maquinaria.

tax deductions on investments

Tax deductions on investments are
often a stimulus for the acquiring
of new machinery.

el **acicate**

stimulus

la **rentabilidad**
Debido al brusco aumento en los gastos de adquisición de capital, la rentabilidad acusó una fuerte caida.

profitability
Due to the sudden increase in
capital acquisition costs, profitability showed a marked decline.

los **gastos de adquisición de
capital**

capital acquisition costs

**brusco (a)**

brusque; sudden

el **presupuesto de inversiones**
El presupuesto de inversiones
prevé asignar una cantidad aún
mayor que la del año pasado
para modernizar el sistema
informático.

investment budget
The investment budget plans to
make available even more money
than last year for the modernization
of the electronic data processing
system.

el **presupuesto de publicidad**

advertising budget

Durante los primeros años de su
existencia, la empresa destinó
elevadas sumas de dinero a su
presupuesto de publicidad.

During the first years of its
existence, the company allocated
large sums of money to its
advertising budget.

el **desembolso de capital**
La participación del 2% en la entidad
catalana ha supuesto un desembolso
de capital de 200 millones de pesetas.

paying in/contribution of capital
A share of 2% in the Catalonian
company has meant a capital
contribution of 200 million
pesetas.

la **participación**

participation; partnership; share in business

la **entidad**

entity; agency; company

las **inversiones financieras**
Las elevadas posibilidades de obtener beneficios a través de inversiones financieras han repercutido negativamente en las inversiones en plantas industriales.

financial/money market investments
Chances for high profits in money market investments have had negative repercussions on investments in industrial firms.

# Bookkeeping

la **contabilidad**
Todas las empresas tienen la
obligación de llevar la contabilidad
al día.

accounting; bookkeeping
All businesses are obligated to
keep their bookkeeping up to date.

**llevar al día**

to keep up to date

la **contabilidad general**

general accounting

el **asiento**

bookkeeping

ella **anotación apunte**
Toda operación contable debe
reflejarse por medio de un asiento.

entering in the books
All accounting operations should
be entered in the books.

**contable**

pertaining to accounting,
bookkeeping

**cuadrado (a)**
Un saldo está cuadrado si la suma
de los importes en el debe coincide
con la de los importes en el haber.

settled; squared; balanced
A true balance exists when the
sum of the amounts on the debit
side agree with the sum of the
amounts on the credit side.

**descuadrado (a)**

out of balance

**abrir una cuenta**
Para poder registrar las variaciones
que sufre cualquier elemento
patrimonial, hay que abrir primero
una cuenta para ese elemento en
concreto.

to open an account
To show the changes to which any
investments are subject, it is first
necessary to open an account to
show these changes.

el **elemento patrimonial**

investment; asset

**registrar**

to record

el **asiento de apertura**
El asiento de apertura es el primer
apunte que se realiza al abrir un
ejercicio contable y refleja la
situación de las cuentas en ese
momento.

opening/initial book entry
The opening book entry is the
first entry made at the opening of
an accounting year and reflects
the status of the accounts at that
moment.

el **adeudo**

debit entry

el **cargo**
El cargo es una anotación en el
debe de una cuenta.

charge
A charge is a book entry that
debits an account.

**cancelar, anular**
Se cancela una cuenta cuando se traspasa su saldo a otra cuenta, o bien cuando se cierra porque el elemento patrimonial en cuestión ya no existe.

to cancel; annul
An account is cancelled when its balance is transferred to another account, or when it is closed out because the asset in question no longer exists.

**traspasar**

to transfer

**en cuestión**

in question; at issue

la **partida**
Se considera partida cada una de las cuentas que intervienen en un asiento.

posting; item; entry
Every account that appears in the books is considered a posting.

**intervenir**

to appear

**rectificar**
El contable tuvo que rectificar el asiento por que los saldos no cuadraban.

to correct
The accountant had to correct the books because the accounts didn't balance.

**cuadrar**

to balance; be in balance

el **error de cálculo**

calculating error

el **cálculo erróneo**
En la contabilidad informatizada se excluyen los posibles errores de cálculo.

mathematical error
Computerized accounting rules out the possibility of errors in calculation.

la **contabilidad informatizada**

computerized accounting

**falsificar**
Esa empresa fue multada por haber falsificado el balance.

to falsify
That firm was fined for having falsified the balance sheet.

**cerrar las cuentas**
Se considera que se han cerrado las cuentas cuando éstas quedan saldadas, es decir, con saldo cero.

to close the accounts
Accounts are considered closed when they are balanced, i.e. when they have a zero balance.

**saldar**

to balance; close

el **ejercicio contable**

accounting year; fiscal year; business year

En los libros de contabilidad se reflejan todas las operaciones realizadas a lo largo de un ejercicio contable.

The account books show all the business transactions done in the course of an accounting year.

**reflejarse**

to be reflected/mirrored/shown

**contabilizar**
Todas las operaciones comerciales deben ser contabilizadas.

to enter into the books
All business operations should be entered into the books.

el, la **contable**

bookkeeper; accountant

el **debito; deber**
En el debito de una cuenta se registran los movimientos que representan un aumento del activo o una disminución del pasivo.

debit; debit side
Transactions that represent an increase in assets or a reduction of liabilities are registered on the debit side of an account.

el **haber**
En el haber de una cuenta aparecen los movimientos que representan una disminución del activo o un aumento del pasivo.

credit; credit side
Transactions resulting in a reduction of assets or an increase in liabilities appear on the credit side.

el **libro de compras**
Toda empresa o profesional independiente debe registrar en un libro de compras cada una de las adquisiciones realizadas.

purchase book
Every business or free-lance professional should record every acquisition made in a purchase book.

el **libro de ventas**

sales book

el **libro diario**
En el libro diario se registran día a día todas las operaciones que afectan a la actividad de la empresa.

diary; journal
All operations which affect a business's activities are recorded day by day in a diary.

el **libro mayor**
En el libro mayor se registran las operaciones agrupándolas por cuentas.

ledger
Business activities, classified by account, are recorded in the ledger.

**agrupar**

to put into groups; classify; arrange

la **suma y sigue**

carry-over

el **Plan General de Contabilidad (P.G.C.)**
(En España,) el nuevo Plan General de Contabilidad de 1990 ha dado respuesta a la necesidad de una armonización de la terminología contable.

Universal Standard Form of Accounts
(In Spain,) the new 1990 Universal Standard Form of Accounts has responded to the need for a standardizing of accounting terms.

la **terminología**

terminology

la **armonización**

standardization; uniformization

**el Instituto de Contabilidad y Auditoría de Cuentas (ICAC)**
(En España,) el Instituto de Contabilidad y Auditoría de Cuentas es el organismo que se ha encargado de la actualización del PGC adaptándolo a las nuevas necesidades.

Institute for Bookkeeping and Account Auditing
(In Spain,) the Institute for Bookkeeping and Account Auditing is the agency responsible for implementing the General Account Plan and adopting it to new exigencies.

**el organismo**

organism; agency

**la actualización**

actualization; implementation

**el principio contable**
Los principios contables son las normas generales a seguir en la contabilidad.

accounting principle
Accounting principles are the general guidelines that should be followed in accounting.

**la masa patrimonial**

Las masas patrimoniales se agrupan en: activo, pasivo y neto patrimonial.

ensemble of assets/property; wealth; worth; equity
Equity can be divided into: assets, liabilities, and net worth.

**patrimonial**

pertaining to wealth

**el asiento de cierre**
El asiento de cierre es el que se hace al final del proceso contable para saldar todas las cuentas.

closing entry
The closing entry is made at the end of the accounting year to balance all the accounts.

**pasar**
Todos los asientos anotados en el libro diario se deben pasar al libro mayor antes de poder continuar con el proceso contable.

to pass; transfer
All diary entries should be transferred to the ledger before continuing with the bookkeeping process.

**las cuentas anuales**
Según el Plan General de Contabilidad se distinguen las siguientes cuentas anuales: balance de situación, cuenta de pérdidas y ganancias, y la memoria.

annual accounts
According to the General Accounting Plan the following annual accounts are distinguished: balance sheet, profit and loss statement as well as the annual report.

**la auditoría de cuentas**
La auditoría de las cuentas de una empresa no es otra cosa que la verificación por parte de profesionales independientes de la información contable aportada por la empresa.

account auditing
The auditing of a company's accounts is simply outside professional verification of the accounting information supplied by the company.

**la verificación**

verification

| | |
|---|---|
| el **censor de cuentas,** la **censora de cuentas** | chartered/certified accountant |
| el **auditor** La omisión de pasivos obligó al auditor a revisar toda la contabilidad. | auditor The omission of liabilities made it necessary for the auditor to check all the bookkeeping. |
| la **omisión** | omission |
| la **contabilidad de gestión** La contabilidad de gestión analiza las desviaciones que se producen entre las previsiones y lo que realmente va ocurriendo. | business accounting Business accounting analyzes the discrepancies which exist between what was estimated and what is really happening. |
| la **desviación** | difference; discrepancy; deviation |
| la **previsión** | prediction; projection; estimate |
| la **contabilidad por partida doble** En la contabilidad por partida doble toda anotación en el deber de una cuenta debe corresponderse con una anotación en el haber de otra u otras cuentas, y los importes del deber y del haber deben ser iguales. | double-entry bookkeeping In double-entry bookkeeping every entry on the debit side of an account should correspond to an entry on the credit side of another account or accounts, and the credit and debit amounts should be equal. |
| la **memoria** La memoria completa, amplía y comenta la información contenida en el balance y en la cuenta de pérdidas y ganancias. | annual report The annual report complements, extends and comments on the information contained on the balance sheet and in the profit and loss account. |
| **complementar** | to complement |
| el **cuadro de financiación** El cuadro de financiación forma parte de la memoria y recoge información acerca de los orígenes de los recursos del ejercicio y su uso o finalidad. | funds statement (sources and uses of funds) The financial survey is a part of the business report and contains information about the source of the means employed in the accounting period as well as about their use or purpose. |
| las **normas de valoración** Las normas de valoración son el conjunto de criterios que complementan a los principios contables. | valuation techniques The valuation techniques are the criteria which complement accounting principles. |

97

# The Balance Sheet

el **balance**
el **balance de situación**
El balance es una de las tres cuentas anuales y en él se muestra el patrimonio de la empresa.

balance; balance sheet
situation balance
The balance sheet is one of three annual accountings and the company's worth is shown in it.

el **balance abreviado**
Una empresa podrá presentar un balance abreviado cuando el volumen total del activo no supere los 920 millones de pesetas, la cifra anual de negocios sea inferior a 1.920 millones de pesetas, o bien el número de trabajadores no sea superior a 50.

abbreviated/shortened balance sheet
A firm can present an abbreviated balance sheet when the total volume of the assets does not exceed 920 million pesetas, when annual sales are below 1,920 million pesetas, or when not more than 50 workers are employed.

la **cuenta de balance**

Las cuentas de balance son cinco grupos de cuentas que inciden directamente en la elaboración del balance de la empresa.

accounting balance; balance sheet postings/entries
Accounting balances are five accounting groups which have a direct effect on the preparation of the company's balance sheet.

**incidir en**

to have an effect on

la **elaboración**

elaboration; working out; preparation

el **activo**
El activo está integrado por el conjunto de bienes y derechos de una empresa.

assets
The assets are composed of the totality of property and claims of a company.

los **bienes**

properties

los **derechos**
Los derechos de una empresa son todas las deudas que terceras personas tienen frente a dicha empresa.

rights; duties; claims; demands; fees
A company's claims are all the debts third parties have entered into with the company.

el **pasivo**
El pasivo engloba las deudas de la empresa con terceras personas.

liabilities
The liabilites include debts the company has contracted with third parties.

el **patrimonio**
El patrimonio de una empresa está compuesto, por un lado, por el conjunto de bienes y derechos y, por otro, por la suma de las obligaciones contraídas.

wealth; worth; assets; properties
A company's worth is constituted on the one hand by the totality of properties and claims, and on the other by the sum of contracted obligations.

**contraer una obligación**

to contract/assume an obligation

el **neto patrimonial**

net worth

el **pasivo no exigible patrimonio neto**

equity capital

El neto patrimonial comprende el capital social de la empresa.

Net worth comprises the corporation's ordinary capital.

el **capital social**

corporate capital; ordinary capital

El capital social lo componen las aportaciones dinerarias o no dinerarias de cada uno de los socios.

Corporate capital consists of the monetary and non-monetary investments of each of the partners.

**acreedor (a)**

pertaining to credit

Una cuenta es acreedora cuando presenta un saldo al haber. Lógicamente, las cuentas de pasivo deberían tener un saldo final acreedor.

An account is a credit account if it shows a credit balance. Logically, liability accounts should show a final credit balance.

**deudor (a)**

debit; debtor

Al cargar un importe en una cuenta, ésta se convierte en una cuenta deudora.

When an account is debited by a sum, it becomes a debit account.

la **cuenta financiera**

financing account

Las cuentas financieras engloban, entre otros, a los acreedores y deudores por operaciones distintas a la actividad de la empresa.

Financing accounts include, among other things, creditors and debtors from outside the company's operations.

**englobar**

to include

las **existencias**

reserves; stock

Las cuentas de existencias engloban las mercaderías, materias primas, productos semielaborados o elaborados que pertenecen a la empresa.

Reserve accounts include goods, raw materials, semi-finished or finished products that belong to the company.

las **mercaderías**

goods; merchandise

los **proveedores**

supplier obligations

La cuenta de proveedores es una cuenta de pasivo que refleja las deudas con los suministradores de mercancías y bienes.

The supplier obligation account is a liability account which shows debts incurred with suppliers of merchandise and goods.

el **suministrador,** la **suministradora**

supplier

la **depreciación**

depreciation

Algunos elementos del inmovilizado sufren una depreciación económica a causa de los adelantos técnicos.

Because of technological advances some capital asset components are subject to economic depreciation.

el **adelanto técnico**

technological advance

la **amortización contable**
La amortización contable es toda
anotación en los libros de la
contabilidad que refleja la
depreciación sufrida por los
elementos del inmovilizado.

bookkeeping amortization
Bookkeeping amortization is
every entry in the accounting
books that shows depreciation
suffered by the capital asset
components.

la **cuota de amortización**

depletion/depreciation allowance

la **amortización constante**
En la amortización constante, la
cantidad destinada a la amortización
de un elemento o la cuota de
amortización permanece invariable.

straight-line depreciation
In straight-line depreciation the
sum earmarked for depreciation
of an element or the depreciation
allowance remains constant.

**invariable**

invariable; unchanged

**hacer inventario**
Sofía es la encargada de hacer
inventario de las existencias a
final de año.

to take inventory
Sofía is in charge of taking an
inventory of the stock at the end
of the year

el **inventario**

inventory

el **ejercicio contable**

accounting period/year

el **cierre del ejercicio**
El cierre del ejercicio se realiza a
través del asiento de cierre,
quedando, así, todas las cuentas
saldadas y cerradas.

end of year closing
End of year closing is done by
the closing bookkeeping entry, in
which all accounts are balanced
and closed.

el **asiento de cierre**

closing entry

el **balance de comprobación**

trial balance

el **balance de sumas y saldos**
En el balance de comprobación o
de sumas y saldos se hace una
relación de las sumas acreedoras
y deudoras, así como de los
saldos resultantes para cada una
de las cuentas en un momento
determinado.

trial balance
In the trial balance, credit and
debit amounts are listed along
with the balance of each account
at a particular time.

la **relación**

listing

el **balance extracontable**
el **estado de inventario balance de inventario**

inventory list; state of the inventory

Después de hacer inventario de los elementos que componen el patrimonio de una empresa, éste queda reflejado por escrito en un documento llamado estado de inventario.

After making an inventory of the items constituting a company's inventory, these items are identified in a document known as the inventory list.

el **activo fijo**
el **inmovilizado**

capital asset

El activo fijo comprende los elementos del patrimonio que van a servir de forma duradera en la actividad de la empresa.

Capital assets are those assets which will continue to be used in the company's operations.

**duradero (a)**

durable; continuing; permanent

el **activo circulante**

current asset

El activo circulante está formado por el conjunto de elementos del activo que están en continuo cambio, como, por ejemplo, las existencias.

A current asset is formed by the ensemble of asset items which change constantly, as for example, inventory items.

el **inmovilizado material**

fixed assets

El inmovilizado material está compuesto por los elementos patrimoniales materiales, es decir, constituye la estructura física de la empresa.

Fixed assets are composed of material asset items, i.e. those asset items which constitute the physical structure of the business.

el **inmovilizado inmaterial**

non-fixed/non-material asset items

los **gastos de establecimiento**

founding costs

Gastos de establecimiento es una cuenta de activo fijo que comprende los gastos necesarios hasta que la empresa inicie su actividad productiva.

Founding costs is a capital asset accounting item which comprises the expenses necessarily incurred before the business begins its productive operations.

el **pasivo exigible**

outside capital

El pasivo exigible se compone de deudas u obligaciones exigibles a corto y largo plazo.

Outside capital is composed of long-term or short-term due debts or demands.

la **obligación exigible**

due demand/obligation

el **pasivo exigible a corto plazo**

short term obligations

El pasivo exigible a corto plazo lo componen las obligaciones que vencen en un plazo inferior a un año, como, por ejemplo, las deudas con proveedores.

Short term obligations consist of obligations that become due in a term of less than one year, for example obligations to suppliers.

**vencer**

to conquer; become due

el **pasivo exigible a largo plazo**

long term obligations

las **deudas con entidades de crédito**

obligations to credit institutes

La cuenta de deudas con entidades de crédito es una cuenta de balance que figura en el pasivo y que puede pertenecer al pasivo exigible a corto o largo plazo según las propias características de la deuda.

The accounting item "credit institute obligations" is a balance sheet entry which appears in the liabilities and which can belong either with the long or the short term obligations, depending on the nature of the debt.

la **amortización creciente**

progressive depreciation

En la amortización creciente, la cuota de amortización anual va aumentando cada año en una proporción ya establecida.

In progressive depreciation, the annual depreciation rate goes up each year according to a previously established rate.

**establecido (a), fijado (a)**

established; fixed

la **amortización decreciente**

diminishing depreciation

la **amortización acelerada**

accelerated depreciation

la **amortización directa**

direct depreciation

En la amortización directa se anotan las cuotas de amortización en la misma cuenta del elemento que se amortiza, disminuyendo, de esta manera, el valor contable de dicho elemento.

In direct depreciation, depreciation rates are noted in the same accounting entry as the item depreciated, thus diminishing the balance-sheet value of the item.

el **elemento**

element; subject; item

**anotar**

to note; enter; register

**amortizar**

to amortize; depreciate

la **amortización indirecta**

indirect depreciation

los **ajustes de periodificación**

account period adjustments

Los ajustes de periodificación se hacen necesarios para computar en el ejercicio correspondiente los gastos e ingresos cobrados o pagados por anticipado, ya sea total o parcialmente.

Accounting period adjustments are necessary to calculate partial or total expenses paid out or sums received in advance during the corresponding accounting period.

**computar**

to compute

# ■■■■■■ Profit and Loss Accounting ■■■■■■

la **cuenta de pérdidas y ganancias**, profit and loss accounting
la **cuenta de resultados**

La cuenta de pérdidas y ganancias recoge los resultados de explotación, los resultados financieros y los extraordinarios.

Profit and loss accounting shows the results of business operations, the capital results and the out of the ordinary results.

los **ingresos y gastos**
En la cuenta de pérdidas y ganancias se reflejan los ingresos y gastos de una empresa durante un ejercicio contable.

income and expense
Profit and loss accounting shows the company's receipts and expenses during an accounting year.

las **cuentas de gastos**
(En España,) las cuentas de gastos recogen todos los gastos del ejercicio incluídas las pérdidas extraordinarias.

expense account
(In Spain,) the expense account includes all expenses of the accounting year, including extraordinary losses, are shown.

las **cuentas de ingresos**
(En España,) las cuentas de ingresos se recogen todos los ingresos del ejercicio incluídos los beneficios extraordinarios.

sources of income
(In Spain,) all sources of income during the accounting year, including out of the ordinary profits, are shown.

los **ingresos de explotación**
Los ingresos de explotación se producen como consecuencia de la venta de productos o de la prestación de servicios y se registran contablemente en el momento de extender la factura.

operating income
Operating income is produced as a result of the sale of products or the performing of services and is charged to book when invoiced.

el **importe neto de la cifra de negocios**
(En España,) el importe neto de la cifra de negocios registra los ingresos de explotación y los de otras fuentes de ingresos.

net sales

(In Spain,) net sales include revenue from business operations as well as other income sources.

el **cálculo de costes**
El cálculo de costes valora el consumo realizado o previsto para la fabricación de un producto o realización de un trabajo o servicio.

cost accounting
Cost accounting asseses anticipated or already paid out costs for the manufacture of a product or the performance of labor or of a service.

**previsto (a)**

foreseen; prospective

los **servicios exteriores**

services contracted for with third parties

Los servicios exteriores son diferentes servicios contratados por la empresa y que no forman parte del precio de adquisición del inmovilizado, como por ejemplo: transportes, publicidad, reparaciones, etc.

Services contracted for with third parties are the various services contracted for by the company which are not part of the acquisition costs for capital assets, such as, for example, shipments, advertising, repairs, etc.

| | |
|---|---|
| el **precio de adquisición** | acquisition costs |
| los **gastos de personal**<br>En la cuenta de gastos de personal se reflejan, entre otros, las retribuciones al personal y las indemnizaciones. | personnel expenditures<br>Wages and compensation payments to employees, among other things, are shown in personnel expenditures accounting. |
| los **salarios y sueldos** | salaries and wages |
| el **arrendamiento**<br>La cuenta de arrendamientos forma parte de las cuentas de gastos y representa los alquileres de bienes muebles e inmuebles por parte de la empresa. | leasing; renting<br>Leasing and renting accounting are included in cost accounting and show the cost of any chattels or real estate rented by the company. |
| los **bienes muebles** | chattels |
| los **bienes inmuebles** | real estate; real property |
| el **inmueble** | real property; building; lot |
| el **beneficio líquido** | net profit |
| la **ganancia neta**<br>El beneficio líquido neto representa la diferencia positiva entre el total de las ganancias y el total de las pérdidas. | net earnings<br>The net profit is the positive difference between all the earnings and all the losses. |
| el **beneficio bruto** | gross profit |
| la **ganancia bruta**<br>El beneficio bruto recoge la ganancia total sin deducir pérdidas o gastos. | gross earnings<br>Gross profits represent total earnings before deduction of losses or expenses. |
| **deducir** | to deduct |
| la **regularización**<br>La regularización es el conjunto de operaciones contables destinadas a la obtención del resultado del ejercicio, es decir, la diferencia entre los ingresos y gastos en este período. | accounting correction<br>Correction accounting is the totality of accounting operations intended to obtain the result of the accounting year, i.e. the difference between receipts and expenses in that period. |
| el **resultado de la explotación**<br>El resultado de la explotación se calcula restando de los ingresos el coste de las ventas y los gastos del período. | operating profit<br>The operating profit is calculated by deducting sales costs and expenses of the accounting period from receipts. |
| los **rappels**<br>Los rappels son descuentos y similares que se basan en haber alcanzado un determinado volumen de compras o de ventas. | quantity discounts<br>Quantity discounts are price reductions and similar strategies which are employed starting at a determined volume of sales or purchases. |

el **beneficio procedente del inmovilizado material**
Los beneficios procedentes del inmovilizado material forman parte de los beneficios extraordinarios y se producen por la enajenación de inmovilizado material.

profits from fixed/capital assets

Profits from fixed assets are part of non-operating results and include profit or loss from the sale of fixed assets.

la **enajenación**

selling

el **beneficio procedente del inmovilizado inmaterial**

profits from intangibles

el **beneficio antes de impuestos**
Los beneficios antes de impuestos representan la base imponible para determinar el importe del impuesto sobre sociedades y otros impuestos.

profit before taxes
Profits before taxes represent the taxable base used for determining the corporate tax and other taxes.

el **beneficio de explotación**
El beneficio de explotación se obtiene de la diferencia entre todos los ingresos y todos los gastos habidos en el ejercicio.

operating profit
Operating profit is obtained from the difference between all income and expenses in the accounting year.

los **ingresos extraordinarios**
Los ingresos extraordinarios son ingresos de cuantía significativa y que no pueden considerarse periódicos.

non-operating income
Non-operating income is income that cannot be considered periodically recurring income.

los **gastos extraordinarios**

non-operating expense

**significativo (a)**

significant

los **ingresos financieros**
Los ingresos financieros son las rentas del capital, así como los descuentos sobre compras y otros ingresos.

financial/capital revenues
Capital revenues are income on capital, as well as discounts on purchases and other income.

las **rentas del capital**

yield on capital accounts

el **resultados financieros**
(En España,) los resultados financieros se obtienen por la diferencia entre los ingresos y los gastos de carácter financiero, es decir, los que han participado en la financiación de las operaciones comerciales de la empresa.

financial results
(In Spain,) financial results are those obtained from the difference between income and expenses of a financial nature, i.e. those that were involved in the financing of the company's commercial operations.

la **operación comercial**

business operations; commercial activity

el **resultado extraordinario**
El resultado extraordinario se obtiene
por la diferencia entre los ingresos y
gastos extraordinarios procedentes de
operaciones que no tienen que ver
con la actividad propia de la empresa.

non-operating results
Non-operating results are obtained
by the difference between non-
operating income and expenses
from business operations which
are unrelated to the business' usual
activities.

**tener que ver con**

to have to do with; be related to

las **pérdidas de explotación**
Si el resultado de la explotación es
negativo se habla de pérdidas de
explotación.

operating losses
If the result of business operations
is negative one speaks of operations
losses.

las **provisiones**
(En España,) las provisiones son
correcciones de valoración que
ponen de manifiesto pérdidas de
valor o minusvalías.

reserve funds
(In Spain,) reserves are value
corrections which show losses
or depreciation of assets.

**poner de manifiesto**

to show; make evident; reveal

la **minusvalía**

decline/reduction in value;
depreciation

la **conciliación**
(En España,) la conciliación de cuentas
es el proceso mediante el cual se
pretende explicar las diferencias
surgidas en la comparación de los
resultados derivados de dos sistemas
de información contable.

reconciliation
(In Spain,) the reconciliation of
accounts is the process by which
one tries to explain the differences
shown in the comparison of the
results derived from two different
bookkeeping systems.

**derivar**

to derive

las **reservas**
Las reservas son beneficios no
repartidos que se ahorran con la
finalidad de autofinanciar la empresa
y poder hacer frente a posibles
eventualidades futuras.

reserves
Reserves are non-distributed
profits retained for self-financing
of the company and for coping
with possible future exigencies.

la **eventualidad**

eventuality

**hacer frente a**

to cope/deal with; resist

## Production Sites

| | |
|---|---|
| la **factoría** | factory |
| la **planta** | plant; mill |
| Un fabricante japonés de automóviles ha impuesto duras condiciones para mantener abierta su factoría en España. | A Japanese automobile manufacturer has set difficult conditions for keeping its factory in Spain open. |
| **imponer condiciones** | to impose conditions |
| las **instalaciones** | installations; facilities |
| Las nuevas instalaciones de SEAT en Martorell (Barcelona) se encuentran entre las más modernas del mundo. | SEAT's new facilities in Martorell (Barcelona) are among the most modern in the world. |
| el **complejo industrial** | industrial complex; major facility |
| Algunos de los grandes complejos industriales del norte de España han sido desmantelados en los últimos años. | In the last few years some of the great industrial complexes in Northern Spain have been dismantled. |
| **desmantelar** | to dismantle |
| la **ubicación de la planta** | plant location |
| la **emplazamiento de la planta** | plant site |
| Uno de los factores determinantes a la hora de decidir la ubicación de la planta fueron las buenas comunicaciones del polígono industrial. | One of the determining factors in selecting a plant site was the industrial zone's good transportation infrastructure. |
| el **polígono industrial** | industrial zone |
| **determinante** | determining |
| el **terreno industrial** | industrial building site |
| Para apoyar la instalación de nuevas fábricas, la administración pública cede terrenos industriales en condiciones muy favorables. | To encourage the setting up of new factories, the authorities make building sites available under very favorable terms. |
| la **instalación** | installation; setting up |
| **ceder** | to cede; yield; grant; make available |
| la **capacidad productiva** | productive capacity |
| El aumento de la capacidad productiva y la reducción del número de empleados han dejado de ser una contradicción. | The increase in productive capacity and the reduction in the number of employees has ceased to be a contradiction. |

la **contradicción**

contradiction

el **fabricante**
SEAT es el principal fabricante
nacional de automóviles.

manufacturer
SEAT is the chief domestic automobile manufacturer.

**nacional**

national; domestic

la **fabricación**
La próxima primavera se comenzará
con la fabricación en serie del nuevo
modelo de la gama alta.

manufacture
Next spring mass-production of
the new luxury model will begin.

la **gama alta**

high end of the production range;
luxury

la **gama baja**

low end of the production range;
budget; low price

el **equipo productivo**

means of production

el **parque de maquinaria**
Para evitar la pérdida de competitividad, se decidió la renovación
del parque de maquinaria.

machinery
To avoid losing competitiveness,
it was decided to revamp the
machinery.

la **competencia**

competitiveness

el **montaje**
En Cataluña se ha hecho todo lo
posible por evitar que las instalaciones
de SEAT se conviertan en un mero
centro de montaje de vehículos.

assembly; putting together
In Catalonia everything possible
was done to prevent SEAT's
facilities from becoming nothing
more than a center for vehicle
assembly.

**mero (a)**

mere

la **cadena de montaje**
La introducción de la robótica en las
cadenas de montaje ha reducido
considerablemente las necesidades
de personal.

conveyor belt; assembly line
The introduction of robots to
assembly lines has considerably
reduced personnel requirements.

el **componente**
Cada vez con más frecuencia, los
fabricantes de componentes se
asientan en las cercanías de las
grandes fábricas automovilísticas.

component
Increasingly, component manufacturers are setting up in the
vicinity of large automobile
factories.

**asentarse**

to set up; establish; settle

la **máquina-herramienta**
La industria española de máquinas-
herramientas intenta compaginar un
nivel técnico alto con un precio
competitivo.

machine tool
The Spanish machine tool industry
is attempting to combine a high
level of technology with a competitive price.

el **montacargas**
El manejo del montacargas es competencia exclusiva del personal autorizado.

freight elevator
Only authorized personnel are permitted to use the freight elevator.

la **pieza de recambio**

part

la **pieza de repuesto**
Aunque se ha dejado de producir ese modelo, se garantiza el suministro de piezas de recambio originales durante los próximos diez años.

spare part
Even though that model is no longer in production, spare part replacement is guaranteed for the next ten years.

la **inauguración**
El ministro de Industria aprovechó la inauguración de la nueva factoría textil para arremeter contra las exigencias salariales de los sindicatos.

inauguration; opening
The Minister of Industry took advantage of the occasion of the opening of the new textile factory to criticize sharply union wage demands.

**arremeter**

to criticize severely; to attack sharply

**entrar en funcionamiento**
Debido a unos problemas de última hora, la planta no entrará en funcionamiento antes del otoño.

to commence business operations
Due to some last minute problems, the plant will not be operating before autumn.

la **puesta en funcionamiento**

opening of business

el **rendimiento**
Después de superar un bache de actividad, la fábrica está produciendo de nuevo a pleno rendimiento.

performance
After pulling out of a slump, the factory is again producing at full capacity.

el **bache**

slump

**pleno (a)**

full

el **exceso de capacidad**
La tasa de utilización insuficiente ha conducido a un exceso de capacidad con graves consecuencias financieras para la empresa.

excess/over capacity; surplus
Insufficient use of the means of production led to a capacity surplus and serious financial consequences for the company.

la **tasa de utilización**

use/capacity rate

la **infrautilización**

under capacity; use at less than full capacity

La crisis económica de principio de los 90 se ha visto reflejada en una infrautilización de las capacidades de muchas fábricas.

The economic crisis at the beginning of the 90's was mirrored in underutilization of many factories.

| | |
|---|---|
| **verse reflejado (a)** | to be reflected/mirrored in |
| la **tecnología punta** | cutting-edge technology; advanced technology |
| La empresa TALGO (Tren Articulado Ligero Goicoechea Oriol) fabrica trenes de tecnología punta que se exportan a países como Alemania. | The TALGO (Lightweight Articulated Train Goicoechea Oriol) manufactures technologically advanced trains that are exported to countries like Germany. |
| la **vida útil** | durability; shelf-life; life cycle; product life |
| A causa de las vertiginosas innovaciones técnicas en la informática, la vida útil de los ordenadores se ha reducido considerablemente. | Because of breathtaking technological innovations, the product life of computers has been considerably reduced. |
| **vertiginoso (a)** | breathtaking |
| **obsoleto (a)** | obsolete |
| Debido a la tecnología obsoleta de sus fábricas, el grupo textil ya no puede codearse con sus competidores extranjeros. | Due to the obsolete technology of its factories, the textile group could no longer hold its own against its foreign competitors. |
| **codearse con** | mix/hobnob with; keep pace with; hold one's own against |
| el **competidor,** la **competidora** | competitor |
| **quedar fuera de servicio** | to be/remain out of service; to suspend operations |
| Por una fuga de gas, la fábrica de productos químicos quedó fuera de servicio durante dos semanas. | Because of a gas leak, the chemical products plant was out of service for two weeks. |
| la **fuga de gas** | gas leak |
| la **protección contra accidentes** | protection against accidents |
| La insuficiente protección contra accidentes en el sector de la construcción ha causado indignación entre los sindicatos. | Insufficient protection against accidents in the construction industry has provoked outrage among the union members. |
| **causar indignación** | to cause indignation/provoke outrage |
| la **prevención de accidentes** | accident prevention |
| la **siniestralidad** | frequency of accidents; incidence of accidents |
| La alta siniestralidad en el complejo industrial ha puesto de manifiesto la necesidad de adoptar medidas preventivas. | The high rate of accidents in the industrial complex has demonstrated the need to adopt preventive measures. |

**preventivo (a)**                          preventive

el, la **vigilante de seguridad**           security officer; watch person;
                                            watchman

Después de repetidos robos en el            After repeated robberies in the
almacén, la empresa se vió obligada         warehouse, the company was
a contratar un vigilante de seguridad.      obliged to hire a watchman.

el **margen de seguridad**                  safety/security margin
El análisis del accidente por parte de      The analysis of the accident by the
la comisión investigadora demostró          investigating commission showed
que la causa del mismo fue el escaso        that the accident was cause by the
margen de seguridad de la central.          low security margin of the nuclear
                                            energy plant.

# ■■■ Planning and Manufacturing ■■■

el **proceso productivo**                   production process
Los factores que intervienen en el          Factors that figure in the production
proceso productivo son: mano de             process are: work force, machines,
obra, maquinaria, herramientas y            tools, and raw materials.
materias primas.

la **mano de obra**                         manpower; labor; work force

el **factor de producción**                 production factor

la **producción en cadena**                 assembly line production

la **producción en serie**                  series production
A diferencia de la producción por           In contrast to commissioned pro-
encargo, en la producción en serie          duction, series production is
se calcula el volumen de la misma           calculated on the basis of estimated
en función de la previsión de venta.        sales.

la **producción por encargo**               commissioned production

la **producción por pedido**                production on order

la **producción en masa**                   mass production

la **producción en gran escala**            large scale production
La producción en masa ha posibilitado       Mass production has made it
el acceso de sectores amplios de la         possible for broad sections of
población a bienes de consumo de            the population to acquire high
alta calidad.                               quality consumer goods.

**posibilitar**                             to make possible

**amplio (a)**                              broad; comprehensive

**a medida**                                according to measure/specifications
En la producción a medida se puede          In production according to specifi-
seguir a rajatabla la idea del cliente,     cations it is possible to satisfy
aunque a un precio bastante elevado.        client demands very precisely, but
                                            at a rather high price.

111

**a rajatabla**

very precisely; exactly according to specifications

el **trabajo en cadena**
Para paliar los efectos negativos del trabajo en cadena, muchas empresas fomentan el trabajo en pequeños grupos.

assembly line/conveyor belt work
In order to mitigate the negative effects of assembly line work, many companies encourage work in small groups.

**paliar**

to mitigate; alleviate

**a destajo**
En el trabajo a destajo, el trabajador cobra por pieza producida.

piece work
In piece work, the worker is paid according to the number of pieces produced.

la **coordinación**
La coordinación óptima de los factores de producción es una de las tareas de la dirección de una empresa.

coordination
Optimal coordination of production factors is one of the functions of a company's management.

la **tarea**

task; function

la **planificación**
El error de la empresa fue una planificación a corto plazo, buscando la máxima rentabilidad, sin definir un plan de futuro.

planning
The company's error lay in its short term planning, aimed at maximum profitability, without defining a plan for the future.

**máximo (a)**

maximum

**definir**

to define

**proyectar**
El grupo español proyecta abrir dos nuevas empresas manufactureras en Argentina.

to project
The Spanish group is planning to open two new manufacturing businesses in Argentina.

la **definición del puesto de trabajo**
La definición del puesto de trabajo es una descripción de las condiciones y tareas intrínsecas del puesto de trabajo.

job definition

Job definition is a description of the job's conditions and its essential tasks.

**intrínseco (a)**

intrinsic; essential

el **capataz**, la **capataza**
Después de diez años como obrero en la fábrica, le ascendieron a capataz.

foreman; forelady; foreperson
After working ten years as a laborer in the factory they promoted him to foreman.

**poner en marcha**

to set in motion; begin operations; get under way

Una vez que el consejo de administración haya dado el visto bueno, se procederá a poner en marcha la producción del nuevo modelo.

Once the administrative council has given the green light, production of the new model will get under way.

**dar el visto bueno** | to see and approve; give the green light; approve

**manejar una máquina** | operate a machine
Para manejar ciertas máquinas hace falta una buena instrucción previa. | To operate certain machines, thorough previous training is necessary.

la **instrucción** | instruction; training

el **reloj para fichar** | time clock
Con motivo de la introducción del horario flexible en el trabajo, instalaron un reloj para fichar. | When flexible work hours were introduced, they installed a time clock.

**dar abasto** | to provision adequately; keep up with demand
Como la capacidad de producción no daba abasto a los pedidos, se subcontrataron los servicios de otra empresa. | Since production capacity couldn't keep up with demand, the services were subcontracted to another firm.

**subcontratar** | to subcontract

el **exceso de producción** | excess production
Las empresas siderúrgicas se quejan de que el exceso de producción incide negativamente en los precios. | Steel companies are complaining that excess production is having a negative effect on prices.

la **disminución** | diminution; lessening; cutback
La Unión Europea considera que la única solución para el sector siderúrgico es una disminución de la producción. | The European Union is of the opinion that the only solution for the steel industry is a cutback in production.

**restringir** | to limit; restrict
Muchas empresas restringen la producción en su país para trasladarla a otros donde la mano de obra es más barata. | Many companies are limiting production in their own countries and moving to other countries where labor costs are cheaper.

la **suspensión** | suspension
Debido a la estancación del volumen de ventas, se decidió la suspensión temporal de la producción del artículo. | Because of a stagnation in sales volume, it was decided to suspend production of the article temporarily.

la **estancación** | stagnation

el **cese** | suspension; stop
El cese de la producción de SEAT en la Zona Franca de Barcelona ha provocado graves conflictos con los sindicatos. | SEAT's suspension of production in the free zone of Barcelona has caused serious conflicts with the unions.

| | |
|---|---|
| la **chapuza**<br>Debido a las chapuzas en la instalación eléctrica, se produjeron varios apagones en la fábrica. | botched/shoddy piece of work<br>Due to the botched job done when installing the electricity, there were several power outages in the factory. |
| el **apagón** | power interruption/outage |
| el **defecto de material**<br>El fabricante se quejó airadamente de los defectos del material suministrado, y se replanteó la conveniencia de cambiar de proveedor. | material defect<br>The manufacturer angrily complained about defects in the material delivered and again raised the question as to whether it wouldn't be in order to change supplier. |
| **airadamente** | angrily |
| **plantearse** | to raise |
| la **conveniencia** | suitability; advantage; use |
| el **desecho**<br>La gran cantidad de desechos en la producción hizo necesario un conscienzudo control de la calidad. | rejects<br>The large number of rejects in production made rigorous quality control necessary. |
| **concienzudo (a)** | conscientious; rigorous |
| el **defecto de fabricación**<br>El informe pericial demostró que la serie de accidentes obedecía a un gravísimo defecto de fabricación de los coches. | defect in manufacturing<br>The expert report showed that the series of accidents was due to a very serious defect in the manufacture of the automobiles. |
| **obedecer a** | to obey; be due to |

## ■ Optimization; Maintenance and Quality Control ■

| | |
|---|---|
| la **optimización**<br>La optimización de los recursos empleados debe ser objetivo prioritario de toda empresa que se precie de ser competitiva. | optimization<br>The optimization of the means employed should be the top priority of any firm that aspires to be competitive. |
| **preciarse** | to pride oneself; boast; be self-respecting |
| **prioritario (a)** | prioritary |

114

la **modernización**
La remodelación de la fábrica supuso
una modernización que acabó con
estructuras anquilosadas.

modernization
The restructuring of the factory
called for modernizing to put an
end to antiquated structures.

la **remodelación**

remodelling; restructuring

**anquilosado (a)**

encrusted; antiquated

**acabar con**

to put an end to

los **avances tecnológicos**
Los avances tecnológicos han
adquirido dimensiones hasta
hace poco impensables.

technological advances
Technological advances have
assumed dimensions that until
recently were thought inconceivable.

**impensable**

inconceivable

**adquirir dimensiones**

to acquire/take on/assume
dimensions

la **innovación**
Una de las razones de la creciente
saturación del mercado es la escasez
de innovaciones técnicas.

innovation
One reason for increasing market
saturation is the scarcity of technological innovations.

la **mejora**
La mejora permanente de las condiciones laborales repercute positivamente en la productividad.

improvement
The constant improvement in
working conditions has had positive repercussions on productivity.

la **productividad**
A través de la minimización de los
transportes se consiguió un incremento
considerable de la productividad.

productivity
By reducing transportation dis-
tances, a considerable increase in
productivity was achieved.

la **minimización**

minimizing

el **incremento**

increment; increase

la **racionalización**

rationalization; streamlining;
making efficient

La racionalización de la producción
tiene como objetivo aumentar los
rendimientos o reducir los costes
con el mínimo esfuerzo.

Rationalization of production aims
at increasing profitability or
decreasing costs with the least
possible effort.

**tener como objetivo**

to have as objective; aim at

el **esfuerzo**

effort

la **automatización**
El grado más avanzado de automatización en la producción viene dado
por la fabricación en cadena.

automatization
The highest degree of automatization results from assembly line
production.

**venir dado por**      to result from

**economizar**      to economize
Desde su fundación, la política de la compañía siempre ha sido la de economizar recursos.      Ever since its founding, company policy has always been to economize resources.

la **política de la compañía**      company policy

**abaratar costes**      to reduce costs
La gestión de la nueva directiva ha permitido, durante el primer semestre, abaratar los costes en un 23%.      Thanks to the new executive team's management, costs were lowered 23% in the first half year.

el **semestre**      half year

**surtir efecto**      to show results; have an effect
Después de algunos problemas iniciales de adaptación, las medidas de racionalización surtieron efecto.      After some initial adjustment problems the rationalization measures showed results.

**inicial**      initial

la **adaptación**      adaptation

**aprovechar al máximo**      to exploit maximally; make full use of; take best advantage of
El consorcio construyó una nueva fábrica aprovechando al máximo las subvenciones del gobierno regional.      The consortium built a new factory taking full advantage of the subsidies given by the regional government.

**potenciar**      to augment; increase; maximize
Para potenciar los buenos resultados cosechados con la racionalización, contrataron a un especialista en técnicas de producción.      To maximize the good results achieved by rationalization, they engaged a specialist in production techniques.

**distinguirse por**      to distinguish oneself by
La empresa siempre se ha distinguido por su innovadora tecnología puesta al servicio de la producción.      The company has always distinguished itself by its innovative technology from which production benefited.

**poner al servicio de**      to place at the disposal/service of

la **ventaja competitiva**      competitive advantage
Al no escatimar medios en el campo de I+D, la empresa se aseguró con ello ventajas competitivas inalcanzables.      By sparing no effort in the area of research and development, the company secured unbeatable competitive advantages for itself.

**no escatimar medios**

to spare no effort

**inalcanzable**

unattainable; unsurpassable

el **control de calidad**
Los expertos recomendaron integrar
el control de calidad en el proceso
productivo y concienciar a los
diferentes grupos de trabajo.

quality control
Experts recommended including
quality control in the production
process and raising the awareness
level of the various work teams.

**integrar**

to integrate

**concienzar**

to make conscientious; to raise
awareness

el **certificado de calidad**
Sólo después de meticulosos controles
se concede el certificado de calidad.

certificate of quality
The certificate of quality is granted
only after meticulous checks.

**meticuloso (a)**

meticulous; thorough

el **control al azar**
Para reducir el elevado volumen de
artículos defectuosos, se incrementará
el número de controles al azar.

random sample
To reduce the high volume of
defective articles, more random
samples will be taken.

**incrementar**

to increase

**supervisar**
Para supervisar el proceso de producción, se instalaron sofisticados
mecanismos de control.

to supervise
To supervise the production process,
sophisticated control mechanisms
were installed.

**sofisticado (a)**

sophisticated

**instalar**

to install

el **mecanismo de control**

control mechanism

la **medición de tiempos**
En la medición de tiempos se
cronometran los sucesivos pasos
de la producción con el fin de
aumentar la productividad.

time measurement
In time measurement, the successive
stages of production are timed in
order to increase productivity.

**cronometrar**

to time

**sucesivo (a)**

successive

el **paso**

(work)step; stage in the production
process

la **prima de producción**
La concesión de primas de producción
es un estímulo financiero para los
trabajadores.

production bonuses
Granting production bonuses is a
financial stimulus for workers.

117

| | |
|---|---|
| el **trabajo en equipo**<br>El trabajo en equipo pretende reforzar el sentido de responsabilidad propia y, por consiguiente, eliminar fricciones causadas por sistemas jerárquicos. | team work<br>Team work seeks to reinforce a sense of personal responsibility, and consequently to eliminate friction caused by hierarchical structures. |
| **pretender** | to strive; seek |
| **reforzar** | to strengthen; reinforce |
| las **fricciones** | frictions |
| el **reparto de tareas**<br><br>La eliminación de dos niveles jerárquicos ha originado un nuevo reparto de tareas. | distribution/division/delegation of tasks/functions<br>The elimination of hierarchies has led to a new distribution of tasks. |
| el **nivel jerárquico** | hierarchical level |
| la **retroacción** | repercussion |
| la **retroalimentación**<br>Uno de los objetivos de la reorganización fue la intensificación de los canales de retroalimentación entre trabajadores y dirección. | feedback<br>One of the objectives of the reorganization was the reinforcing of feedback channels between workers and management. |
| la **reorganización** | reorganization |
| la **intensificación** | intensification; reinforcement |
| **justo-a-tiempo**<br>El sistema de producción justo-a-tiempo abarata los costes de almacén pero aumenta la vulnerabilidad ante interferencias en sus vías de suministro. | just-in-time<br>The just-in-time production system lowers warehousing costs but increases the risk of disturbances in the supply system. |
| la **vulnerabilidad** | vulnerability |
| la **interferencia** | interference; disturbance; interruption |
| el **tiempo-ciclo,** el **período de circulación**<br>Recortar el tiempo-ciclo es una de las medidas más eficaces para abaratar costes. | processing time; run duration<br><br>Shortening processing time is one of the most effective means for cost reduction. |
| **eficaz** | effective; efficient |

# ■ Warehousing ■

el **almacén**
La fábrica cuenta con un almacén
enorme en un polígono industrial
de las afueras.

warehouse; depot
The factory has at its disposal an
enormous warehouse in an industrial zone on the outskirts of town.

el, la **almacenista**
El almacenista es aquella persona
que se dedica profesionalmente al
almacenaje de mercancías.

warehouser
The warehouser is that person
who devotes him/herself professionally to the storage of merchandise.

el **almacenaje**

warehousing

el **almacenamiento**

storage

**almacenar**
Como se retrasaba el traslado de la
fábrica a su nuevo emplazamiento,
se tuvo que almacenar la maquinaria.

to store; warehouse; put in storage
Since the factory's move to its
new facilities was delayed, the
machinery had to be put in storage.

el **empleado de almacén,** la
**empleada de almacén**
Se busca empleado de almacén con
experiencia en el manejo de géneros
voluminosos.

warehouse employee/worker

A warehouse worker with experience in handling bulky quantities
is wanted.

el **género voluminoso**

bulky quantity

el **manejo**

handling

las **existencias,** el **stock**
Como los gastos de almacenamiento
sobrepasaban lo justificable,
decidieron una drástica reducción
de las existencias.

inventory; stock
Since warehousing costs exceeded
any justifiable amount, they decided
on a drastic reduction in stock.

**justificable**

justifiable

los **gastos de almacenamiento**

warehousing costs

**tener en almacén**
Si no tenemos el artículo en almacén,
lo pediremos a nuestro depósito
central y lo tendrá en quince días.

to hold in storage
If we don't have the article in
stock, we'll ask our central warehouse for it and you'll have it in
two weeks.

el **depósito**

depot; storeroom; warehouse

**liquidar existencias**
Como la empresa pasaba por un mal
momento, decidió liquidar sus existencias a precio de coste.

to liquidate/clear out stock
Since the company was going
through a difficult time, the
company decided to liquidate
its stock at cost.

**reponer existencias**
Después de la informatización del almacén, resultó mucho más fácil saber cuándo había que reponer existencias.

to restock; replenish merchandise
After the warehouse converted to computers, it was much easier to know when to reorder.

la **variación de existencias**
La variación de existencias es registrada diariamente por el ordenador.

change in inventory
Changes in inventory are registered daily by the computer.

el **deterioro debido al almacenamiento**
Para la empresa, los deterioros debidos al almacenamiento han supuesto pérdidas cercanas al 3% de la cifra de ventas.

damage/deterioration due to storage

For the company warehousing damages amount to approximately 3% of turnover.

el **resguardo de almacén,** el **certificado de almacén**
El certificado de almacén es un título-valor pignorable extendido con la promesa de entregar la mercancía almacenada contra presentación del mismo.

warehouse receipt

The warehouse receipt is a negotiable security made out with the promise of handing over the stored merchandise upon presentation of same (the warehouse receipt).

**pignorable**

negotiable; transferable

la **rampa de carga**
En la nueva rampa de carga pueden descargar simultáneamente hasta siete camiones.

loading platform
Up to seven trucks can be unloaded simultaneously on the new loading platform.

**simultáneamente**

simultaneously

la **carretilla elevadora**
El empleo de carretillas elevadoras hace posible un mejor aprovechamiento del espacio, ya que se puede llegar hasta estanterías de gran altura.

fork-lift truck
The use of fork-lift trucks makes it possible to take better advantage of space available, since high-up top shelves can also be reached.

el **aprovechamiento del espacio**

exploitation of space; space utilization

**apilar**
¡Atención! Frágil. No apilar más de cinco unidades.

to pile up; heap; stack
Careful! Fragile! Do not stack more than five items.

la **unidad**

unity; item; piece

el **almacén de productos terminados**
En el almacén de productos terminados se guardan dichos productos antes de su comercialización.

manufactured products warehouse

Before they are marketed, manufactured products are stored in a manufactured products warehouse.

## la **clasificación de artículos**
En la clasificación de artículos
participan cinco operarios.

merchandise sorting
Five workers are employed in the
sorting of the merchandise.

## el **operario,** la **operaria**

worker

## el **control de existencias**
Con la informatización del almacén
se ahorró mucho tiempo en el control
de existencias.

stock/storage control
After the warehouse adopted a
computer system, much time was
saved in inventory control.

## la **recepción**
El horario de recepción de remesas
es de 10:00 a 18:00 horas de lunes
a viernes.

acceptance/receipt
Shipments are received between
10:00 A.M. and 6:00 P.M. Monday
through Friday.

## la **remesa**

shipment

## el **plazo de almacenaje**
Al sobrepasar el plazo de almacenaje
fijado en 15 días se cobrará un recargo
del 10%.

duration/time/length of storage
If the two weeks storage time contracted for is exceeded, a supplement
of 10% is collected.

## **abastecerse**
Abastecerse según el concepto de
justo-a-tiempo implica la reducción
de existencias y de la capacidad de
almacenamiento interno, reduciendo
así, los costes.

to provision/supply oneself
Self-supplying according to the
just-in-time principle causes a
reduction in inventory and in
storage capacity, thus reducing
costs.

## la **reducción de existencias**

reduction of stock/inventory

## la **capacidad de almacena-
miento**

warehousing capacity

## la **rotación de stocks**
La rotación de stocks es la relación
entre la cifra de ventas y el promedio
de existencias en un período de tiempo.

stock turnover
Stock turnover is the ratio between
sales and the average amount of
inventory in a certain time period.

**━━━━━ Products ━━━━━**

el **producto**

product

el **producto manufacturado**

manufactured product

el **producto terminado producto acabado**
El calzado es uno de los productos
manufacturados con mayor peso en
la exportación española.

finished product

Shoes are one of the most important
manufactured products exported
by Spain.

el **producto semielaborado**
Los productos semielaborados no
salen totalmente terminados de la
fábrica, sino que deben ser sometidos
a un tratamiento posterior.

semi-finished product
Semi-finished products never
leave the factory entirely manufactured; they must instead undergo
further processing.

el **tratamiento**

treatment; processing

el **producto perecedero**
La comercialización de productos
perecederos precisa de una sofisticada
infraestructura de conservación y
distribución.

perishable goods
The marketing of perishable goods
requires a sophisticated infrastruc-
ture to take care of food preservation and marketing.

la **conservación**

food preservation; keeping fresh

los **productos de primera
necesidad**

essential/daily use products

los **productos alimenticios**
Los productos alimenticios deben
estar sometidos a estrictos controles
de calidad para no poner en peligro
la salud de los consumidores.

foodstuffs
Foodstuffs should be subject to
strict quality controls to avoid
jeopardizing consumer health.

**estar sometido (a)**

to be subject to

**estricto (a)**

strict

**poner en peligro**

endanger; jeopardize

los **bienes de consumo**
La industria de bienes de consumo
suministra los artículos de primera
necesidad.

consumer goods
The consumer goods industry
supplies essential products.

la **novedad**
Al tratarse de una auténtica novedad en el sector audiovisual, la empresa encargó primero un estudio de mercado.

novelty
Since it was a real novelty in the audiovisual industry, the company commissioned a market study.

**novedoso (a)**

new; of a new type

el **prestigio**
Como el producto gozaba de un gran prestigio a nivel internacional, se exigía una suma considerable por la concesión de licencias.

prestige
Since the product enjoyed great prestige internationally, a substantial sum was demanded for the granting of franchises.

la **concesión de licencias**

franchise granting

la **licencia**

license; franchise

el **concesionario,** la **concesionaria**

concessioner; franchise receiver

El concesionario está autorizado a utilizar el derecho que le otorga la licencia a cambio de una compensación en forma de regalía.

The concessioner is authorized to make use of the entitlement granted in the franchise by paying the franchising fee.

**estar autorizado (a)**

to be authorized

la **regalía**

franchising/licensing fee

**de primera calidad, de alta calidad**

of first/top/prime/high quality

Los productos de primera calidad siempre están muy solicitados independientemente de la actual situación económica.

Top quality products are always much in demand no matter what current economic conditions may be.

**solicitado (a)**

in demand

**independientemente**

independently

el **artículo**

article

**de baja calidad**
Al comprobarse que los artículos eran de muy baja calidad, el distribuidor se vió obligado a retirarlos del mercado.

of low quality; inferior
When it was demonstrated that the articles were of very low quality, the distributor was obliged to withdraw them from the market.

**de calidad inferior**
La campaña publicitaria hizo hincapié en que los productos de la competencia eran de calidad bastante inferior.

of inferior quality
The advertising campaign emphasized that the quality of the competition's products was quite inferior.

**competitivo (a)**
La relación calidad-precio es decisiva para que un producto pueda ser competitivo.

competitive
The price-quality ratio is the chief determinant of a product's competitiveness.

la **relación calidad-precio**

price-quality ratio

**decisivo (a)**

decisive; determining

el **coste medio**
El coste medio de un producto es el
coste total dividido por el número
de unidades producidas.

average cost; unit cost
The average cost of a product is
the total cost divided by the number
of units produced.

el **coste total**

total cost

la **garantía**
A pesar de que se había acabado la
garantía, le arreglaron la máquina
averiada como señal de buena voluntad.

guaranty; warranty
Even though the warranty had
expired, they fixed the broken
machine as a token of goodwill.

**averiado (a)**

broken; not functioning

el **plazo de garantía**
Dentro del plazo de garantía, la
empresa se compromete a correr
con los gastos de desplazamiento,
mano de obra y reposición de
piezas originales.

term of the warranty
During the term of the warranty,
the company promises to assume
transport costs, labor, and the
replacement of spare parts.

la **reposición**

replacement

los **gastos de desplazamiento**

transportation costs

la **responsabilidad**
La empresa asumirá la responsabilidad
de sanear vicios ocultos e inherentes.

responsibility
The company will assume responsibility for the repair of hidden and
intrinsic defects.

**sanear**

to repair; clean up; rehabilitate;
refurbish

el **vicio oculto**

hidden defect

el **defecto oculto**

hidden deficiency

el **vicio inherente**

inherent defect

el **vicio intrínseco**

intrinsic defect

**defectuoso (a)**
Como el fabricante rehusó cambiar
la mercancía defectuosa, la empresa
contrató los servicios de un abogado.

defective
Since the manufacturer refused to
exchange the defective merchandise,
the company hired a lawyer.

la **mercancía**

merchandise

**dañado (a)**
La compañía de seguros se hizo cargo
de los costes de reposición de la
mercancía dañada.

damaged
The insurance company paid the
replacement cost of the damaged
merchandise.

la **merma**
A menudo se producen mermas en los productos alimenticios envasados.

weight loss; shrinkage; settlement
Often, packaged foodstuffs undergo settlement.

**envasar**

to package; bottle

el **embalaje**
Generalmente, los costes de embalaje van incluídos en el precio y corren a cargo del vendedor.

packaging
Generally, packaging costs are included in the price and are charged to the seller.

el **peso bruto**
El peso bruto de un producto incluye el peso del artículo y su embalaje.

gross weight
A product's gross weight includes the weight of the article and its packaging.

la **tara**
Se denomina tara al peso del embalaje.

La última remesa de artículos adoleció de importantes taras que los inutilizaban.

tare, unladen weight; defect
The weight of the packing material is called tare.
The last shipment of goods showed significant defects which rendered them useless.

**adolecer**

to suffer from; to be defective

**inutilizar**

to render useless

**bruto por neto**

gross for net

las **propiedades**
Las propiedades de un producto deben amoldarse continuamente al comportamiento cambiante de los consumidores.

characteristics
Product characteristics must continuously be adopted to changing consumer patterns.

**amoldarse a**

to adopt to

el **acabado**
Se puede elegir entre diferentes acabados de este modelo.

finish; style; design
You can select from different styles for this model.

la **gama de productos**
En nuestras nuevas instalaciones hay una amplia exposición de toda nuestra gama de productos.

product range
In our new facilities there is a comprehensive exhibition of our entire range of products.

la **diversificación**
Mediante la diversificación de los productos se llega a mayor número de segmentos de consumidores en el mercado.

diversification
Through product diversification one can reach a greater number of consumer groups on the market.

la **fase de desarrollo**
El éxito de los fabricantes japoneses de automóviles reside, en gran parte, en fases de desarrollo abreviadas.

development phase
The success of Japanese automobile manufacturers is in large measure due to shortened development phases.

el **lanzamiento**
El lanzamiento del nuevo producto fue, desde el comienzo, objeto de una campaña de acoso y derribo por parte de la competencia.

launching; introduction
The introduction of the new product was, from the very beginning, targeted by a smear campaign on the part of the competition.

la **campaña de acoso y derribo**

campaign of detraction and vilification; smear campaign

**ser objeto de**

to be the object/target of

**afamado (a)**
Aunque nuestros afamados productos están en el mercado desde hace más de 15 años, nunca hemos dejado de mejorarlos.

famous; well-known
Although our famous products have been on the market for more than 15 years, we've never stopped improving them.

**emblemático (a)**
Aún habiendo desarrollado productos de alta tecnología, su producto emblemático sigue siendo el modelo 530 de los años 80.

leading/top of the line
Even though they've developed high technology products, their leading product continues to be model 530 from the 80's.

la **amplitud del surtido**

varied/broad range of selection/assortment

Decidieron restringir la amplitud del surtido para abaratar costes en su colección de invierno.

They decided to limit the range to lower costs for their winter collection.

la **colección**

collection

la **amplitud del número de modelos**
Se decantó por sus productos gracias a la amplitud del número de modelos que ofrecía la marca.

wide range of models

She finally chose their products because of the wide range of models offered by the brand.

**decantarse por algo**

to make up one's mind/decide on/for something

la **ampliación del surtido**
Se acometió una ampliación del surtido como medida adicional a la nueva campaña de captación de clientes.

expansion of selection/stock
They undertook to expand selection as an additional measure in their new campaign to gain customers.

**acometer**

to undertake/tackle

la **innovación de productos**
La innovación de productos supone la incorporación de productos resultantes de logros tecnológicos.

product innovation
Product innovation means including products that result from technological achievements.

el **logro**

success; achievement

la **variación de productos**
A menudo, la variación de productos se limita a modificaciones insignificantes.

product variation
Often, product variation is limited to insignificant changes.

**insignificante**

insignificant

**la difusión de productos**

product diffusion

Para una eficaz difusión de sus productos se hizo necesario remodelar las redes de distribución.

For the efficient diffusion of its products a restructuring of its distribution network became necessary.

**la eliminación de un producto**

elimination of a product

Normalmente se lleva a cabo la eliminación de un producto al disminuir sus ventas.

Usually the elimination of a product is effected when its sales decline.

**el ciclo de duración de un producto**

product life-cycle

El ciclo de duración de un producto comprende las fases: introducción, crecimiento, saturación y degeneración.

A product's life cycle includes the phases: introduction, growth, saturation, decline.

**la marca registrada**

trademark

La marca registrada sirve para la caracterización y diferenciación de los productos de una marca frente a otros.

The trademark serves to characterize and differenciate one brand from others.

**la caracterización**

characterization

**la diferenciación**

differentiation

**la denominación de origen**

designation of origin

En España, la regulación de la denominación de origen certifica la calidad y autenticidad de la procedencia de productos tradicionales de la tierra.

In Spain, regulation of designation of origin certifies the quality and authenticity of provenance of traditional agricultural products.

**la regulación**

regulation

**certificar**

to certify

**la autenticidad**

authenticity

**la protección de marcas**

brand name protection

Después de muchos intentos frustrados, la protección de marcas sigue siendo una asignatura pendiente del comercio internacional.

After many frustrating attempts, brand name protection continues to be a problem which international trade must solve.

**el intento frustrado**

frustrated/frustrating attempt

**la asignatura pendiente**

pending task/problem

**la propiedad industrial**

industrial property/legally protected trade rights

La no observancia de la propiedad industrial va, sobre todo, en detrimento de las pequeñas y medianas empresas.

Failure to respect industrial property has especially detrimental effects on small and medium sized businesses.

| | |
|---|---|
| la **observancia** | observance |
| en **detrimento de** | to the detriment of |
| la **falsificación**<br>En los países asiáticos está muy extendida la falsificación masiva de artículos de marca. | falsification; faking; counterfeiting<br>The massive counterfeiting of brand name articles is very widespread in Asian countries. |
| el **artículo de marca** | brand name article |
| **estar extendido (a)** | to be widespread |
| la **patente**<br>La patente confiere a su titular el derecho de explotación en exclusiva de una invención. | patent<br>The patent confers on its holder the right to exclusive exploitation of an invention. |
| **conferir** | to confer |
| el **derecho de explotación** | right of exploitation |
| la **patente pendiente** | patent pending |

## Product Design

| | |
|---|---|
| el **recipiente**<br>En vista de la creciente concienciación ecológica se han sustituído los recipientes de plástico por otros totalmente reciclables. | container<br>In view of growing ecological awareness, plastic containers have been replaced by totally recyclable ones. |
| **reciclable** | recyclable |
| la **concienciación** | awareness |
| el **envase**<br>A menudo, el envase es decisivo a la hora de decantarse por un producto. | packaging; container<br>Often the packing is the decisive factor in product selection. |
| el **papel de embalaje**<br>Por cinco rollos grandes de papel de embalaje le regalamos 100 m. de cinta adhesiva. | packaging paper<br>For every five large rolls of packing paper we'll make you a present of 100 meters of tape. |
| el **rollo** | roll |
| el **frasco** | bottle; flask |
| el **palet,** la **paleta**<br>Suministramos esta mercancía en paletas. | palette<br>We deliver this merchandise on palettes. |

la **etiqueta**
En la etiqueta de los productos perecederos deberá figurar la fecha de caducidad.

label
The expiration date should appear on the labels of perishable goods.

la **fecha de caducidad**

expiration date; date when best used by

**al dorso**
Para mayor información sobre nuestros productos llame al número de teléfono que aparece al dorso.

on the back/dorsal side
For further information about our products call the telephone number that appears on the back.

las **instrucciones de uso,** las **instrucciones de manejo**
Recomendamos lean atentamente las instrucciones de uso ya que la empresa no se hace responsable de daños por errores de manejo.

directions for use

We recommend that you read the directions for use since the company does not assume responsibility for damages resulting from errors in use.

**hacerse responsable de**

to assume responsibility for

el **código de barras**
Para aligerar el trabajo de las cajeras, el supermercado ha comprado varios lectores de códigos de barras.

price code
To make cashiers' jobs easier, the supermarket has bought several scanners.

**aligerar**

to alleviate; make easier

el **lector**

reader; scanner

el **diseño**

design; pattern

el **diseño industrial**
Algunas de las muestras más geniales del diseño industrial proceden de los años 20.

industrial design
Some of the most brilliant industrial design products date from the 20's.

**genial**

ingenious; brilliant

el **diseño del producto**

product design

el **diseñador,** la **diseñadora**
Conocidas empresas extranjeras encargan el diseño de sus productos a jóvenes diseñadores catalanes.

designer
Well-known foreign companies entrust the design of their products to young Catalan designers.

el **logotipo**
El diseño de un logotipo no debe someterse a modas pasajeras.

logo
A logo's design should not reflect passing fashions.

**pasajero (a)**

passing; transitory

la **imagen de marca**
La absorción de la empresa se efectuó únicamente por la buena imagen de marca de su producto más antiguo.

brand image
The company was taken over solely because of the good image of its oldest product.

la **línea de productos**
Se ha creado una línea de productos realmente innovadora en cosmética que incluye elementos marinos.

product line
A new line of really innovative cosmetic products containing materials from the sea was created.

**innovador (ora)**

innovative

el **prototipo**
En el salón del automóvil de Frankfort se presentará el nuevo prototipo, aunque aún no se ha decidido su fabricación en serie.

prototype
The new prototype will be introduced at the Frankfurt Automobile Show, even though its serial production has not yet been decided upon.

el **surtido**
Uno de los aspectos más destacados de la marca es su amplio surtido y variedad en todas las líneas de productos.

assortment; selection
One of the brand's most distinctive features is its broad assortment and variety in all product lines.

la **variedad**

variety

**destacado (a)**

outstanding

## ■■■■■ Particular Economic Circumstances ■■■■■

la **capacidad de compra**

buying power

el **poder adquisitivo capacidad adquisitiva**

purchasing power

Los sindicatos alegan que hace falta aumentar los sueldos para incrementar la capacidad adquisitiva.

The unions allege that wage increases are necessary for the raising of purchasing power.

**alegar**

to allege

**efectuar una compra**

to make a purchase

Hoy en día, al efectuar una compra, muchos clientes hacen uso de las tarjetas de crédito.

Nowadays, many clients use their credit cards when they buy something.

la **compra a plazos**

installment buying; purchase on credit

Para poder efectuar compras a plazos, el cliente debe demostrar ingresos regulares y un puesto de trabajo fijo.

To be able to buy on credit, the client has to show proof of regular income and a steady job.

**tomar en consideración**

to take into consideration

Antes de comprar algo a plazos, se deben tomar en consideración los elevados costes de financiación.

Before buying on credit, high financing costs should be carefully considered.

**comprar a plazos**

to buy on the installment plan

el **empobrecimiento**

impoverishment; pauperization

El recorte de las prestaciones sociales ha conducido a un empobrecimiento aún mayor de muchas familias.

The reduction in social welfare payments has led to even greater pauperization of many families.

el **recorte de las prestaciones sociales**

cutting of social welfare benefits/payments

el **enriquecimiento**

enrichment

**endeudarse, contraer deudas**

to get/go into debt; incur debts

Muchas familias se endeudaron debido a la facilidad con que los bancos otorgaban créditos personales.

Many families went into debt because of the banks' readiness to grant personal credit.

el **crédito personal**

personal credit/loan

el **grado de endeudamiento**

degree/extent/level of debt

El exceso de deudas contraídas ha llevado a muchas familias a un grado de endeudamiento que incluso ha llegado al embargo de sus bienes.

Many families were so deeply in debt that they finally had to pawn their personal property.

el **exceso de deudas**

excessive debt

los **intereses de usura**
La Unión de Consumidores culpó a los bancos de ser los responsables de aplicar intereses de usura para créditos por descubierto.

usurous interest rates
The Consumer Union accused the banks of being responsible for charging usurous interest rates for overdrawn credits.

el **despilfarro**
El abogado defensor alegó que sólo el afán de notoriedad era lo que había empujado a su cliente al despilfarro del dinero a él confiado.

waste; to squander
The defense attorney alleged that only a pathological desire for recognition had motivated his client to squander the money entrusted to him.

**confiar a alguien**

to entrust/confide something to someone

el **afán de notoriedad**

craving for recognition

**de libre disposición**
Después de haber pagado el alquiler y los otros gastos corrientes, tan sólo le quedaron 30.000 pesetas de libre disposición.

freely available; free and clear
After having paid the rent and other current expenses, all he had left free and clear was 30,000 pesetas.

**al alcance de todos los bolsillos**
La idea que estaba detrás de la producción del SEAT 600 era la de fabricar un utilitario al alcance de todos los bolsillos.

within everyone's price range/pocketbook
The idea behind the production of the SEAT 600 was to produce a utility vehicle everyone could afford.

la **distribución de la renta**
Uno de los cometidos más importantes del Estado debe ser una distribución equitativa de la renta entre la sociedad.

income distribution
One of the government's most important tasks should be the equitable distribution of income in society.

**equitativo (a)**

equitable

la **redistribución de la renta**
Una de las bases del Estado social es la redistribución de la renta a través medidas fiscales.

income redistribution
One of the foundations of the social welfare state is the redistribution of income through taxation policies.

el **Estado social**

social welfare state

la **renta real**
Los sindicatos intentan conseguir un aumento de sueldo que, por lo menos, equivalga a la pérdida de la renta real.

real income
The unions are trying to obtain a wage increase that would at least be equivalent to the drop in real income.

**equivaler**

to be equivalent to; correspond to

| | |
|---|---|
| **pasar de** | to go from |
| La economía ha pasado de unos años de vacas gordas a años de vacas flacas, afectando particularmente a la economía doméstica. | The economy's transition from a few years of prosperity to lean years has primarily affected the domestic economy and the private sector. |
| los **años de vacas gordas** | prosperous years |
| los **años de vacas flacas** | lean years |
| la **economía doméstica** | domestic economy; private sector |
| la **economía familiar** | family budget |
| **afectar** | to affect |
| la **propensión al ahorro** | tendency/propensity/inclination to save |
| En la crisis económica se perfila un aumento de la propensión al ahorro y una disminución de la propensión al consumo. | Periods of economic crisis show an increased tendency to save and a drop in consumption. |
| **perfilarse** | to show; be revealed; become evident |
| la **propensión al consumo** | inclination to consume |
| la **renta per cápita,** la **renta per habitante** | per capita income |
| Todos los indicadores económicos hacen presagiar un incremento de la renta per cápita en las Islas Baleares. | All the economic indicators point to an increase in per capita income on the Balearic Islands. |
| **presagiar** | to predict; point to |
| el **indicador económico** | economic indicator |

## ▬▬▬▬ Consumption and Buying Habits ▬▬▬▬

el **comprador,** la **compradora**
Aunque, teóricamente, el comprador está en el centro de atención, la realidad deja mucho que desear.

the buyer
Although, theoretically, the customer is king, the real state of things leaves much to be desired.

**dejar que desear**

to leave to be desired

el **consumidor,** la **consumidora**
Cada vez más consumidores se adhieren a la UC (Unión de Consumidores) para defender activamente sus intereses.

the consumer
More and more consumers are joining the CU (Consumers' Union) in order to defend their interests vigorously.

la **Unión de Consumidores (UC)**     Consumers' Union

**adherirse a**     to join

el **consumidor final,** la **consumidora final**     consumer
El IVA es un impuesto indirecto a pagar por el consumidor final.     The VAT is an indirect tax that must be paid by the consumer.

el **Impuesto sobre el Valor Añadido (IVA)**     Value Added Tax

el, la **cliente habitual**     steady/regular customer
Los clientes habituales suelen recibir un trato preferente por parte de los comerciantes.     Regular customers are usually given preferential treatment by business people.

el **trato preferente**     preferential treatment

el, la **cliente potencial**     potential client/customer
Los bancos intentan atraer a jóvenes ya que ellos son futuros clientes potenciales.     The banks are trying to attract young people since they are future potential clients.

la **clientela**     clientele
Los expertos recomiendan cuidar la clientela, ya que captar a un nuevo cliente resulta cinco veces más difícil que conservar un cliente habitual.     The experts recommend attentiveness to customers, since winning new customers is five times more difficult than keeping a regular customer.

la **clientela fija**     fixed clientele/customers
La aspiración de los comerciantes es convertir la clientela ocasional en clientela fija.     Business people hope that occasional customers will become regular customers.

la **clientela ocasional**     occasional customers

la **aspiración**     aspiration; hope

el **consumo a gran escala**     large-scale consumption; mass consumption

La variación de los hábitos de consumo ha conducido a un consumo a gran escala de productos precocinados.     Fluctuations in consumer habits have led to large scale consumption of precooked products.

**precocinado (a)**     pre-cooked

los **hábitos de consumo**     consumer habits

el **consumo propio**     personal consumption
Dentro de nuestra oferta especial se pueden llevar cinco botellas destinadas al consumo propio.     As per our special offer, you can take with you five bottles for personal consumption.

la **compra impulsiva**
Los supermercados colocan golosinas junto a las cajas para inducir a la compra impulsiva.

impulse buying
The supermarkets place candies near the cash register to stimulate impulse buying.

**inducir**

to induce; stimulate

las **golosinas**

sweets; candies

el **descontento**
La entrada en vigor de los horarios comerciales prevista en la nueva Ley de Cierre de Comercios (España) ha provocado el descontento de muchos compradores.

discontent; dissatisfaction
When the business hours specified in the new Store Closing Law (Spain) took effect, many buyers expressed dissatisfaction.

la **entrada en vigor**

becoming effective; (time of) taking effect

la **Ley de Cierre de Commercios**

Store Closing Law

el **horario comercial**

business hours

el **consumo per cápita,** el **consumo por habitante**
El comportamiento cambiante de los consumidores respecto a la tradicional dieta mediterránea repercute en el consumo per cápita de los productos de la huerta.

per capita consumption

Changing consumer habits regarding the traditional Mediterranean diet have an effect on per capita consumption of products from vegetable gardens.

el **comportamiento de los consumidores**

consumer habits

el **segmento**

segment

las **compras de acaparamiento**
Los rumores sobre una inminente escasez de productos de primera necesidad han disparado las compras de acaparamiento.

hoarding purchases
Rumors concerning an imminent shortage in essential life-sustaining products set off hoarding.

**disparar**

to trigger; set off

la **abstinencia de consumo**
Las reglas del juego de la sociedad consumista han provocado una abstinencia parcial de consumo por parte de consumidores más conscientes.

consumer abstinence/boycott
The rules of the game in the consumer society have caused a partial consumer boycott by some more aware consumers.

la **sociedad consumista**

consumer society

el **perjuicio**
Los hurtos por parte de los empleados son los que causan mayor perjuicio al propio comercio.

damage; disadvantage
Employee thefts do the greatest damage to the businesses they work for.

| | |
|---|---|
| las **reglas del juego** | the rules of the game |
| el **boicot**<br>El boicot de potitos españoles por parte de consumidores centroeuropeos ha provocado la alarma social en España. | boycott<br>The boycott of Spanish (baby food) jars by central European consumers has led to social unrest in Spain. |
| la **alarma social** | social unrest |
| el **potito** | little jar (of baby food) |
| **encontrar una buena acogida**<br>En los últimos años, los productos naturales han encontrado una muy buena acogida entre consumidores de todas las edades. | to be well received<br>In recent years, natural products have been very well received by consumers of all ages. |
| la **edad** | age |
| la **satisfacción del consumidor**<br>La satisfacción del consumidor es un campo en el que todavía queda mucho camino por recorrer. | consumer satisfaction<br>Consumer satisfaction is a field in which there is still much ground to cover. |
| **recorrer** | to cover (distance/ground) |
| el **hurto de tienda**<br>En casi todos los grandes almacenes existe un dispositivo interno de televisión para prevenir y atajar los numerosos hurtos. | shoplifting<br>In almost all big department stores there is a video surveillance system to prevent and discourage the high incidence of shoplifting. |
| el **dispositivo** | system; appliance; device |
| **atajar** | to head off; block; discourage |

## ■■■■ Market Research and Market Strategies ■■■■

el **mercado**
Por mercado se entiende aquel lugar en el que se realizan operaciones de compra y venta de determinados bienes entre personas relacionadas comercialmente.

market
By market is meant that place in which purchases and sales of certain goods are effected between people relating to each other in a commercial context.

el **marketing,** la **mercadotecnia**
El concepto de marketing abarca todas las actividades del ámbito externo o comercial de la empresa con el fin de optimizar la venta de sus productos.

marketing
The concept of marketing includes all activities in the commercializing and distribution sphere of a company for the purpose of optimizing the sale of its products.

el **análisis de mercado**              market analysis

el **estudio de mercado**              market study/examination
El cometido de los estudios de mercado  The purpose of market studies is
es la obtención de datos acerca de las  to obtain data concerning existing
condiciones existentes en el mercado    market conditions and future
y su comportamiento futuro.             market behavior.

la **investigación de mercado**        market research

la **mercadología prospección**        market research/forecasting
**de mercado**

el **cometido**                        task; duty

**hacer averiguaciones, averiguar**    to do research; investigate; find out
La prospección de mercado hace         Market research investigates
averiguaciones sobre las preferencias  consumer preferences and needs.
y necesidades del consumidor.

las **necesidades**                    necessities; needs

el **cuestionario**                    questionnaire
El número de cuestionarios remitidos   The number of questionnaires
no ha sido suficiente como para poder  received wasn't enough to draw
llegar a una conclusión vinculante.    binding conclusions.

**remitir**                            to remit; transmit

**llegar a una conclusión**            to arrive at a conclusion

**vinculante**                         binding; obligatory

**hacer una encuesta, realizar**       to make a survey; undertake a
**una encuesta**                       survey

**encuestar**                          to survey
El Ministerio de Sanidad y Consumo     The Department of Health has
ha realizado una amplia encuesta para  undertaken a broad survey to find
conocer la evolución de los hábitos    out about the eating habits of the
alimenticios de los españoles.         Spanish people.

la **evolución**                       evolution; development

la **encuesta**                        inquiry; survey

la **encuesta por entrevista**         survey conducted by interview
Se recurre a la encuesta por entrevista One has recourse to the survey
para obtener datos más concluyentes    conducted by interview to obtain
sobre los deseos de los consumidores.  more conclusive data concerning
                                       consumer wants.

137

**concluyente**

conclusive

la **encuesta por muestreo**
En las encuestas por muestreo, los encuestados son elegidos aleatoriamente dentro de grupos de población que reúnen ciertas características comunes.

random sample survey
Those surveyed in random sample surveys are carefully selected to represent groups with certain common traits.

el **encuestado,** la **encuestada**

person surveyed

**aleatoriamente**

by chance; at random

la **encuesta posterior**
Las encuestas posteriores se emplean para realizar un seguimiento periódico de la conducta de los consumidores.

follow-up survey
Follow-up surveys are used to continue tracking consumer behavior over a definite period of time.

el **seguimiento**

follow up; check up

**entrevistar**
Después de entrevistar a más de 3.000 personas, se llegó a la conclusión de que el producto necesitaba ciertas modificaciones.

to interview
After 3,000 people were interviewed, they concluded that the product needed certain changes.

el **sondeo de mercado**
Hoy en día, casi ninguna empresa se arriesga a lanzar un producto al mercado antes de haber realizado un sondeo.

market testing; market research
Nowadays, hardly any firm would risk launching a product on the market without first doing market research.

**arriesgar**

to risk

**lanzar al mercado**

to launch/go on the market

**sondear**

to probe; test; investigate

el **mercado de compradores**
En el mercado de compradores, el vendedor depende del comprador debido al exceso de la oferta.

buyers' market
In a buyers' market, the vendor is dependent on the buyer because of an excess of supply.

el **mercado favorable a los vendedores**
Al existir un exceso de demanda, surge un mercado favorable a los vendedores, es decir, aparece una dependencia de los compradores respecto de los vendedores.

sellers' market

When there is excess demand a market favorable to the seller arises, i.e. the buyers are dependent on the sellers.

el **exceso**

excess; overhang

la **mezcla comercial,** el **marketing-mix**

marketing-mix

El marketing-mix consiste en la acción combinada de varios instrumentos comerciales para alcanzar la mayor eficacia comercial.

A marketing-mix consists of the combined action of various marketing factors in order to achieve greater commercial results.

la **eficacia**

efficiency; effectiveness

el **viaje de prospección de mercados (VIAPRO)**

market research trip

(En España,) el Instituto Español de Comercio Exterior (ICEX) subvenciona viajes de prospección de mercados que realizan los exportadores para evaluar las posibilidades de ventas en el extranjero.

(In Spain,) the Spanish Institute of Foreign Trade subsidizes market research trips taken by exporters to evaluate the chances for selling abroad.

**recoger información, recabar información**

to gather information

Los métodos más frecuentes para recabar información sobre un producto son las entrevistas y los tests con voluntarios.

The most frequently used information gathering methods concerning a product are interviews and tests with volunteers.

el **test**

test

el **tamaño de la muestra**

size of the sample

Se puso en duda la representatividad del estudio debido a que el tamaño de la muestra no superaba las 1.000 personas y no abarcaba todos los grupos de edad.

Doubt was cast on the validity of the study since the size of the sample did not exceed 1,000 people and did not include all age groups.

la **representatividad**

representativeness; validity

la **disparidad**

disparity; gap; deviation; divergence

Debido a la disparidad de criterios, no se pudo realizar una evaluación paralela de ambas encuestas.

Due to the divergence of the criteria, it was not possible to make a comparative evaluation of the two surveys.

la **evaluación**

evaluation

el **potencial en el mercado**

market potential

Para sondear el potencial en el mercado del nuevo producto, encargaron un estudio de mercado.

To investigate the market potential of the new product, they commissioned a market study.

la **estimación de ventas**

sales estimate

Al hacerse públicos los datos corregidos de las variaciones estacionales, se comprobó que las estimaciones de ventas había pecado de optimistas.

When the data, corrected for seasonal variations, appeared, it was clear that sales estimates had been too optimistically calculated.

| | |
|---|---|
| **corregido, a de las variaciones estacionales** | corrected for seasonal variations |
| la **variación estacional** | seasonal variation |
| **pecar de** | to be at fault for |
| **ventas** | sales |
| el **pronóstico de ventas** | sales estimate/forecast |
| La introducción del producto en un mercado de ensayo auguró excelentes pronósticos de ventas. | The introduction of the product to a test market gave promise of excellent sales forecasts. |
| **augurar** | to augur; promise |
| el **mercado de ensayo** | test market |
| el **índice obtenido por muestreo** | random sampling index |
| Como número de partida para el análisis estadístico eligieron el índice obtenido por muestreo. | They took the random sampling index as a starting number for the statistical analysis. |
| **estadístico (a)** | statistically |
| **por término medio** | on average |
| Los resultados obtenidos después de la nueva campaña publicitaria superaron, por término medio, en un 5% los obtenidos el año anterior. | The results obtained after the new advertising campaign surpassed, on average, last years' results by 5%. |
| **alcanzar la cifra de** | to amount to; reach the sum of |
| Las ventas del nuevo modelo alcanzaron la cifra de 45.000 unidades en dos semanas. | Sales of the new model amounted to 45,000 units in two weeks. |
| **situarse en** | to be located in |
| Su agresiva política de ventas le ha permitido situarse entre las primeras empresas del sector. | Their aggressive sales policy is responsible for their status as one of the most important companies in the industry. |
| la **consolidación** | consolidation; securing |
| Aunque su irrupción en el mercado fue espectacular, su consolidación como marca líder tardó varios años. | Although their entry onto the market was spectacular, it took several years before they could consolidate their position as the leading brand. |
| la **irrupción** | break in; dramatic entry |

**espectacular**　　　　　　　　spectacular

**la penetración en el mercado**　　market penetration
Su penetración en el mercado como　Their penetration of the market as
marca independiente vino acompañada　an independent brand was accom-
por un fuerte aumento del consumo　panied by a sharp increase in con-
que redundó en su beneficio.　　　sumption, which worked out very
　　　　　　　　　　　　　　　much to their advantage.

**redundar en beneficio de**　　　to redound to/work out to someone's
　　　　　　　　　　　　　　　advantage

**la implantación**　　　　　　　introduction
A los tres años de la implantación del　Three years after the introduction
producto en el mercado, se había　of the product to the market, it
alcanzado ya una cuota de mercado　had already achieved a market
del 9,5%.　　　　　　　　　　share of 9.5%.

**la cuota del mercado**　　　　　market share

---

# Trade Fairs, Shows

**la exposición**　　　　　　　　exhibition
Las exposiciones o salones se　　　Exhibitions or shows differ from
diferencian de las ferias en que en　trade fairs in that the former
las primeras sólo se exponen los　　merely display products, whereas
productos, mientras que en las　　at trade fairs products are also sold.
segundas también se venden.

**el salón**　　　　　　　　　　show; exhibition
Los más importantes salones y ferias　Madrid's most important exhibi-
de Madrid son FITUR (Feria Interna-　tions and trade fairs are I.T.F.
cional del Turismo), SIMO (Feria de　(International Tourism Fair),
Material Informático) y ARTE (Feria　SIMO (Electronic Media Fair),
de Arte Moderno); en Barcelona, el　and ARTE (Modern Art Fair); in
Salón del Automóvil y el Salón　　Barcelona, the Automobile Show
Náutico, así como en Valencia el　　and Boating Show, and in Valencia,
Salón del Mueble.　　　　　　　the Furniture Fair.

**exponer**　　　　　　　　　　to show; exhibit

**la feria**　　　　　　　　　　trade fair
La Cámara de Comercio edita un　　The Chamber of Commerce pub-
calendario de ferias que ayuda a　　lishes a calendar of trade fairs
evitar coincidencias de fechas.　　that helps avoid any conflict of
　　　　　　　　　　　　　　　dates.

**editar**　　　　　　　　　　　to publish; put out

la **coincidencia**

coincidence; conflict

el **recinto ferial**

fairgrounds

IFEMA en Madrid ha organizado un servicio propio de transporte con el fin de facilitar el acceso de los visitantes de la feria al recinto de la exposición.

IFEMA in Madrid has organized its own transportation service to make it possible for visitors to reach the fairgrounds more easily.

el, la **visitante de la feria**

visitors to the fair

el **pabellón**

pavilion; exhibition hall

El pabellón alemán en la Exposición Mundial de Barcelona 1929 fue construído por Mies van der Rohe.

The German pavilion at the 1929 World's Fair in Barcelona was built by Mies van der Rohe.

la **exposición mundial**

world's fair

la **afluencia del público**

public interest; number of visitors

La afluencia del público, que ha superado con creces las expectativas de los expositores, ha supuesto una cifra récord de visitantes.

Public interest greatly exceeded exhibitor expectations, which led to a record number of visitors.

la **cifra récord**

record number

la **superficie de exposición**

exhibition surface area

Como la superficie de exposición ya no da abasto con el aumento de peticiones de nuevos expositores, se construirán tres nuevos pabellones.

Since the exhibition area is already inadequate, given the increase in would-be exhibitors, three new exhibition halls will be built.

la **petición**

demand; petition

el **expositor,** la **expositora**

exhibitor

**fluctuar**

to fluctuate

Las alteraciones monetarias han hecho que la participación extranjera en la feria haya fluctuado considerablemente.

Currency fluctuations have resulted in considerable fluctuations in the number of foreign participants in the fair.

las **alteraciones monetarias**

currency fluctuations

la **participación**

participation

los **días para profesionales del ramo**

days for visitors from the trade/industry

Normalmente, los dos o tres primeros días de una feria están reservados a profesionales del ramo.

Usually, the fair's first two or three days are reserved for trade reps.

el, la **profesional del ramo**

trade rep

**despertar interés**
Las novedades de la feria de muestras han despertado gran interés entre el numeroso público aisistente.

to awaken interest
The novelties exhibited at the trade fair awakened great interest among the numerous visitors.

la **feria de muestras**

trade fair

la **entrada gratuita**
Para promocionar la primera feria en su categoría, se han distribuido más de 13.000 entradas gratuitas.

free entry; free ticket
To promote the first fair of its kind, more than 13,000 free tickets were distributed.

la **feria monográfica**

theme fair

la **feria especial**
Las ferias monográficas están dedicadas a un único sector industrial o comercial.

specialized fair
Specialized fairs are devoted to a single industrial or commercial sector.

la **feria comercial**
La finalidad de las ferias comerciales es la de promocionar la exportación de productos nacionales.

trade/commercial fair
The purpose of trade fairs is to promote the export of domestic products.

la **feria del libro**
La feria del libro de Madrid, que tiene lugar cada abril en el parque del Retiro, atrae cada año a miles de visitantes.

book fair
Madrid's book fair, which takes place every April in the Retiro park, attracts thousands of visitors every year.

la **feria industrial**
En Bilbao tienen lugar la mayoría de las ferias industriales españolas.

industrial fair
Most Spanish industrial fairs take place in Bilbao.

el **salón del automóvil**
Para anticiparse al lanzamiento del nuevo modelo de la competencia decidieron presentar las novedades apresuradamente en el Salón del Automóvil de Barcelona.

automobile show
To get in ahead of the market appearance of the competition's new model, they decided to exhibit their own innovations early at the Barcelona Automobile Show.

**anticiparse a**

to anticipate; get in ahead of

**apresuradamente**

hurriedly; early

la **presentación**
Las ferias son las citas anuales donde los fabricantes hacen la presentación de sus nuevos productos.

presentation
Fairs are annual occasions at which manufacturers present their new products.

la **cita anual**

annual meeting/appointment

la **exhibición**
Al inaugurar la feria, el ministro hizo mención de la impresionante exhibición de los últimos adelantos tecnológicos.

exhibition; display
When he opened the fair, the minister mentioned the impressive exhibition of the latest technological advances.

143

| | |
|---|---|
| **inaugurar** | to inaugurate; open |
| **hacer mención de** | to make mention of ; mention |
| el **montaje**<br>Para acelerar el montaje y desmontaje de los stands, se sirvieron de un novedoso sistema de ensamblaje. | montage; assembly<br>To hasten the setting up and dismantling of the stands, they used a new assembly system. |
| el **desmontaje** | disassembling; dismantling |
| el **ensamblaje** | joining; assembly |
| el **stand** | stand |
| **clausurar**<br>Al clausurar la feria, todos los expositores expresaron su satisfacción por la buena acogida y desarrollo de la misma. | to close<br>When the fair closed, all the exhibitors expressed their satisfaction at how well the fair was received by the public and how well it was progressing. |
| la **acogida** | welcome; reception |

## General Information

| | |
|---|---|
| la **publicidad** | advertising |
| la **propaganda** | publicity; propaganda |

La publicidad abarca aquellas actividades destinadas a dar a conocer un
producto, aumentar su grado de
divulgación y estimular su demanda.

Advertising includes those activities
intended to make a product known,
to increase its degree of distribution,
and to stimulate demand.

| | |
|---|---|
| **dar a conocer** | to make known |
| el **grado de divulgación** | degree/extent of spread/diffusion/distribution |
| **estimular** | to stimulate |
| **publicitario (a)** | advertising |
| la **agencia de publicidad** | advertising agency |

Al igual que en los demás países, en
España también se ha producido un
despiadado proceso de concentraciones
y absorciones entre las agencias de
publicidad.

As in other countries, in Spain
too, advertising agencies have
been subjected to a no-holds-barred
concentration and takeover process.

| | |
|---|---|
| la **absorción** | absorption; takeover |
| **despiadado (a)** | pitiless |
| el **mensaje publicitario** | advertising message |

El mensaje publicitario es lanzado
para orientar y generar necesidades
ante una saturación del mercado.

The advertising message is dis-
seminated to orientate and to
create demand even if the market
is already saturated.

| | |
|---|---|
| **orientar** | to orientate |
| el **eslogan** | slogan |
| **condicionar** | to condition/manipulate |

Muchos críticos sostienen que la
publicidad condiciona al individuo
ejerciendo una influencia nociva
sobre él.

Many critics allege that advertising
conditions individuals by exercis-
ing a bad influence on them.

| | |
|---|---|
| **sostener** | to allege; maintain |
| **ejercer influencia, influenciar** | to exert influence; influence |
| **nocivo (a)** | bad; noxious |

la **susceptibilidad**
En su famoso libro, "Los secretos
seductores", Packard desveló ya en
los años sesenta la susceptibilidad y
predisposición de los receptores del
mensaje publicitario.

susceptibility
As early as the 60's Packard, in his
famous book, *The Secret Seducers,*
revealed how much the public was
susceptible to and predisposed to
the advertising message.

**desvelar**

to reveal; expose

la **predisposición**

predisposition

el **receptor,** la **receptora**

receptor; receiver

**persuadir**
La publicidad no puede persuadir a
un consumidor indiferente, pero sí
puede hacer que uno indeciso se
incline por una u otra alternativa.

to persuade; convince
Advertising can't convince an
indifferent consumer, but it can
influence an indecisive one in
favor of one or another alternative.

**inclinarse por**

to be inclined to

la **publicidad selectiva**
Para evitar las pérdidas por dispersión,
decidieron apostar por una publicidad
selectiva en medios de difusión
limitada.

selective/targeted advertising
To avoid scattered losses, they
decided to go for selective
advertising in media with limited
diffusion.

las **pérdidas por dispersión**

scattered losses

**cubrir las necesidades**
La pretensión de los creadores
publicitarios es la de cubrir las
necesidades informativas acerca
del producto.

to cover necessities
The claim of advertising agents is
that they provide necessary information about the product.

el **creador publicitario,** la
**creadora publicitaria**

advertising agent/executive/copyist

la **economización de la
publicidad**
La economización de la publicidad
se consigue cuando los medios
empleados guardan relación con el
resultado obtenido.

economic viability in advertising

Economic viability in advertising
is achieved when the deployed
means stay in ratio to the result
obtained.

el **mensaje inequívoco**
Un mensaje inequívoco es imprescindible para diferenciar un producto
de los de la competencia.

unequivocal/unmistakable message
An unmistakable message is indispensable in order to differentiate a
product from its competitors.

la **veracidad publicitaria**
La veracidad publicitaria exige que
no se hagan promesas que no se
puedan mantener a largo plazo.

truth in advertising
Truth in advertising demands that
no long term undeliverable
promises be made.

la **efectividad publicitaria**
Con la creciente insensibilización
frente a los anuncios publicitarios,
la efectividad publicitaria se ha visto
claramente mermada.

advertising effectiveness
Increasing indifference to advertising claims has significantly
lessened advertising effectiveness.

la **insensibilización**

desensitizing; indifference

la **publicidad subliminal**
La publicidad subliminal tiene como
objetivo influenciar al consumidor
sin que aquél se de cuenta de ello.

subliminal advertising
Subliminal advertising aims at
influencing consumers without
their being aware of it.

la **publicidad exagerada**
La publicidad exagerada puede llegar
a tener un efecto boomerang ya que
debido a ella aumenta la resistencia
a la publicidad.

exaggerated (claims) advertising
Advertising that makes exaggerated
claims can have a boomerang effect
since it provokes increased
resistance to advertising.

el **efecto boomerang**

boomerang effect

la **resistencia a la publicidad**

advertising resistance

la **publicidad comparativa**
En los EEUU, la publicidad comparativa es totalmente lícita.

comparative advertising
In the USA, comparative advertising is entirely legal.

**lícito (a)**

licit; permitted; legal

la **publicidad despreciativa**

hostile advertising

el **emplazamiento de producto**
Una de las técnicas implantadas es
el emplazamiento de producto que
consiste en insertar estratégicamente
productos dentro de una película.

product placement
One of the techniques employed is
product placement which means
the stategic insertion of products
into a film.

**implantar**

to use; employ

la **publicidad disimulada**
El intento de insertar publicidad en
un programa televisivo sin consentimiento previo de la emisora es considerado publicidad disimulada.

sneaky advertising
The attempt to insert advertising
into a television program without
the station's prior consent is considered sneaky advertising.

**televisivo (a)**

television

la **publicidad fraudulenta**

fraudulent advertising

la **publicidad desleal publicidad
engañosa**
Si un fabricante publica datos falsos
sobre la naturaleza y procedencia de
los productos o tamaño de la empresa,
se considera publicidad fraudulenta.

misleading advertising; deceptive
advertising
If a manufacturer publishes false
information on the nature and
source of the products, or the size
of the company, that is considered
fraudulent advertising.

# Advertising Media

la **publicidad en prensa**
La publicidad en prensa ofrece la ventaja de que se puede releer tantas veces como se quiera.

printed advertising
Printed advertising has the advantage of being able to be read as many times as one wants.

**releer**

to reread

el **anuncio publicitario**

advertising; ad

**insertar un anuncio, poner un anuncio, anunciar**
Decidieron poner diariamente un anuncio de cuatro módulos en la sección de economía para beneficiarse de las tarifas más bajas para anunciantes regulares.

to insert/run/take out an ad

They decided to take out a quarter page ad in the business section every day to take advantage of the lower rates for regular advertisers.

la **sección de economía**

business section

el **módulo**

module; page-share

la **tarifa (de publicidad)**

(advertising) rate

el, la **anunciante**

advertiser; ad placer

el **espacio fijo**
Vamos a publicar su anuncio en el suplemento del fin de semana pero sin la garantía de que sea en un espacio fijo.

fixed space; set position
We're going to publish your ad in the weekend supplement, but we can't guarantee that it'll be in a set place.

**publicar**

to publish

el **suplemento de fin de semana**

weekend supplement

el **publirreportaje**
Un publirreportaje tiene el aspecto de un reportaje sobre una empresa, pero en realidad es un anuncio publicitario encubierto.

advertising story
An advertising story looks like a story on the company, but in reality it's a hidden advertisement.

**encubierto (a)**

hidden

los **anuncios clasificados,** los **anuncios por palabras**
Las tarifas de los anuncios clasificados se calculan en base al número de palabras empleadas.

classified ads

Classified ad rates are calculated on the basis of the number of words used.

el **encarte**
Un encarte es un folleto publicitario intercalado entre las páginas del periódico.

advertising supplement
An advertising supplement is a prospectus laid into a newspaper.

| | |
|---|---|
| el **folleto publicitario** | advertising prospectus/brochure |
| **intercalar** | to lay/stick in; insert |
| el **recargo** | additional fee; supplement; surcharge |
| Por un anuncio en la contraportada del suplemento se cobra un recargo del 50% sobre su precio. | For an ad on the last page of the supplement a surcharge of 50% above the regular price is charged. |
| la **contraportada** | last printed page |
| la **publicidad televisiva** | television advertising |
| La proliferación de nuevas cadenas de televisión ha hecho que los precios de la publicidad televisiva hayan caído en picado. | The proliferation of new television stations has caused television advertising rates to plummet. |
| la **proliferación** | proliferation; multiplication; increase |
| la **cadena de televisión** | television network/station |
| el **canal de televisión** | television station |
| **caer en picado** | to plummet |
| la **interrupción para publicidad** | commercial interruption |
| la **publicidad sobreimpresa** | blended in advertising/shared screen advertising |
| Una alternativa a las molestas interrupciones del programa para publicidad es la publicidad sobreimpresa, empleada frecuentemente en las retransmisiones deportivas. | One alternative to annoying commercial breaks in programming is shared screen advertising, frequently used during the broadcasting of sports events. |
| la **retransmisión deportiva** | broadcasting of sports' events; "sportscasting" |
| **molesto (a)** | annoying |
| los **medios publicitarios** | advertising media |
| Entre los medios publicitarios se encuentran los anuncios, carteles, películas, etc. | Included in advertising media are advertisements; posters, films, etc. |
| el **soporte publicitario** | advertising carrier |
| Soportes publicitarios son los medios de difusión como, entre otros, periódicos, revistas, radio y televisión. | Advertising carriers are the media of diffusion such as, newspapers, magazines, radio and television. |
| los **medios de difusión** | diffusion/dissemination media |
| el **índice de audiencia** | ratings |
| El índice de audiencia es decisivo a la hora de fijar las tarifas de publicidad. | The ratings are a determinant factor in the setting of advertising rates. |

| | |
|---|---|
| la **Oficina de Justificación de la Difusión (OJD)** | Agency for the Regulation of Newspaper Edition |
| En España, la Oficina de Justificación de la Difusión lleva el control de las tiradas de los diferentes periódicos nacionales. | In Spain, the Agency for the Regulation of Newspaper Publishing supervises the circulation of the various domestic newspapers. |
| la **tirada** | print run; circulation; edition |
| el **patrocinio** | patronage; sponsorship |
| El patrocinio de acontecimientos deportivos—sobre todo en tenis—ha proliferado en el mundo publicitario. | The sponsoring of sports events—especially tennis, has become very widespread in the advertising world. |
| el **acontecimiento deportivo** | sports event |
| **proliferar** | to proliferate; become widespread |
| **patrocinar** | to sponsor |
| El torneo de golf, patrocinado por una conocida empresa automovilística, ha ganado nuevos adeptos para este deporte. | The golf tournament, sponsored by a well-known automobile manufacturer, has won new golfing fans. |
| el **adepto,** la **adepta** | fan; devotee |
| el **patrocinador,** la **patrocinadora** | sponsor; patron |
| el **cupón-respuesta comercial** | advertising reply coupon |
| Los cupones-respuestas comerciales, muy extendidos en todo tipo de revistas, pretenden establecer un contacto directo con los consumidores. | Advertising reply coupons, often found in all kinds of magazines, try to establish direct contact with consumers. |
| la **publicidad directa** | direct advertising |
| Debido a la escasa eficacia de los mailings, la publicidad directa se está desplazando cada vez más hacia la publicidad por teléfono. | Because of the negligible effect of the mailings, direct advertising is moving more and more towards telephone advertising. |
| el **mailing** | mailing |
| **desplazar** | to move |
| la **publicidad por teléfono** | telephone advertising |
| la **publicidad exterior** | outside advertising |
| Está prohibido fijar publicidad exterior en edificios públicos, siendo responsable la empresa anunciadora. | It is prohibited to post advertisements on public buildings, for which the advertising agency is held responsible. |
| la **empresa anunciadora** | advertising agency |

| | |
|---|---|
| la **publicidad en vallas** | advertising by posters/billboards/signs |
| En las autopistas españolas se ha prohibido la instalación de publicidad en vallas para no desviar la atención de los automovilistas. | The setting up of advertisement billboards has been prohibited along Spanish highways to keep drivers from being distracted. |
| **desviar la atención** | to distract one's attention |
| el **cartel publicitario** | advertising poster/bill |
| Con motivo del décimo aniversario de la productora cinematográfica, regalaron reimpresiones de carteles publicitarios de los años 20. | On the occasion of the film company's tenth anniversary, they gave away reproductions of advertising posters from the 20's. |
| **con motivo de** | on the occasion of |
| la **productora cinematográfica** | film company |
| la **reimpresión** | reimpression; reproduction |
| la **publicidad a base de globos** | balloon advertising |
| la **publicidad aerostática** | advertising in the air |
| La publicidad a base de globos se esta abriendo camino en España, alcanzando una facturación de 700 milliones de pesetas en 1993. | Balloon advertising is making its way in Spain, having reached a sales volume of 700 million pesetas in 1993. |
| **abrirse camino, abrirse paso** | to open the path; make one's way |
| el **globo aerostático** | balloon |
| la **publicidad en medios de transporte públicos** | advertising on means of public transport |
| el **itinerario** | itinerary; route |
| Como la empresa pública de autobuses no podía garantizarles un itinerario fijo, prescindieron de poner publicidad en sus vehículos. | Since the publicly owned bus company couldn't guarantee them a regular route, they lost interest in putting advertisements on their vehicles. |
| **prescindir de** | to dispense with; renounce |

## Advertising Campaigns

| | |
|---|---|
| la **campaña de publicidad**, la **campaña publicitaria** | advertising campaign |
| Para combatir la apatía del mercado, se ideó una campaña publicitaria agresiva dirigida a un público mayoritariamente joven. | To combat market apathy, they came up with an aggressive advertising campaign primarily targeted at young people. |

**idearse** — to think up

**mayoritariamente** — primarily

**combatir** — to fight; combat

la **apatía** — apathy

la **campaña de promoción de ventas** — sales promotion campaign

Al quedarse estancada la facturación, la nueva ejecutiva de la empresa decidió poner en marcha una campaña de promoción de ventas por todo lo alto.

When sales stagnated, the new executive board decided to undertake a pressure sales promotion campaign employing all means necessary.

**quedarse estancado (a)** — to slump; stagnate

**por todo lo alto** — with all the trimmings

el **descuento de lanzamiento** — introductory discount

Una manera de hacerse con clientes consiste en ofrecer dentro de la campaña publicitaria un descuento de lanzamiento.

One method for winning over clients is to offer them an introductory discount as part of an advertising campaign.

**hacerse con clientes** — to win customers/clients

la **muestra gratuita** — free sample

Al comprar el champú se le obsequia con una muestra gratuita de hidratante corporal por valor de 400 pts.

When you buy the shampoo you get as a free gift a sample of the body milk lotion worth 400 pesetas.

el **hidratante corporal** — body milk lotion

**por valor de** — worth; with a value of

**reembolsar** — to reimburse

El lema de unos grandes almacenes españoles es que si no queda satisfecho, le reembolsamos su dinero.

The motto of one of the big Spanish department stores is: If you're not satisfied, we refund your money.

el **lema** — motto

**sin compromiso** — without obligation

El centro cultural hispano-alemán "Dialog" ofrece una semana de asistencia a clase sin compromiso.

One can attend classes for a week with no obligation at the Spanish-German cultural center "Dialogue."

la **planificación de medios publicitarios** — advertising media planning

La planificación de medios es el procedimiento sistemático para la elección de los soportes publicitarios idóneos para un determinado producto.

Advertising media planning is the systematic procedure for the selection of advertising carriers suitable for a specific product.

**sistemático (a)**

la **estrategia de medios publicitarios**

En la estrategia de medios publicitarios se distinguen principalmente dos tipos: la vertical y horizontal.

la **estrategia vertical de medios publicitarios**

El objetivo primordial de la estrategia vertical de medios publicitarios es el de alcanzar a las mismas personas el mayor número posible de veces.

la **estrategia horizontal de medios publicitarios**

El objetivo primordial de la estrategia horizontal de medios publicitarios es el de llegar al mayor número posible de personas durante el tiempo de la campaña.

el **grupo-objetivo**

El grupo-objetivo lo componen todas aquellas personas a las que la publicidad se propone alcanzar.

el **área de cobertura publicitaria**

El área de cobertura publicitaria depende del radio de atracción del anunciante.

el **radio de atracción**

systematic

advertising media planning strategy

In media planning there are chiefly two kinds of strategy: the vertical and the horizontal.

vertical strategy in media planning

The chief object of vertical strategy in advertising media is to reach the same people the greatest number of times possible.

horizontal strategy in media planning
The prime goal of horizontal strategy in media planning is to reach the greatest number of people possible during the advertising campaign.

target group
The target group consists of all those people whom the advertising proposes to reach.

advertising area
The advertising area depends on the catchment area of the advertiser.

catchment area

## Distribution and Sales

la **distribución**
La distribución abarca todas las actividades destinadas a proporcionar al cliente bienes o servicios a cambio de una compensación económica.

distribution; sales
Sales includes all activities intended to provide goods or services to the customer in exchange for a material consideration.

la **distribución**
La distribución se puede definir como la realización técnica y organizativa de la comercialización de productos y servicios.

distribution; sales
Distribution can be defined as the technical and organizational implementation of the marketing of products and services.

la **comercialización**

commercialization; marketing

**comercializar**
Apple España comercializó en 1993 37.000 ordenadores.

to commercialize; market; sell
In 1993 Apple Spain sold 37,000 computers.

los **canales de distribución,** las **vías de distribución**
La reestructuración de sus canales de distribución tenía como objetivo reducir el número de intermediarios y minimizar las pérdidas por fricción.

distribution channels/network

The restructuring of their distribution channels was aimed at reducing the number of middlepersons and limiting friction losses.

**minimizar**

to minimize; limit

las **pérdidas por fricción**

friction losses

la **red de distribución**
Uno de los pasos más decisivos para ser dominante en el mercado es la estructuración de una extensa red de distribución.

distribution network
One of the most decisive steps taken towards dominating the market was the setting up of an extensive distribution network.

la **estructuración**

structuring; setting up

**extenso (a)**

extensive

**dominante en el mercado**

dominating the market

el **sistema de distribución**
En los sistemas de distribución diferenciamos entre los sistemas pertenecientes, ligados y ajenos a la empresa.

distribution system
When dealing with distribution systems we differentiate between company-owned, company-connected, and outside distribution systems.

**diferenciar**

to differentiate

**perteneciente a**

belonging to; owned by

**ligado (a)**

attached; connected

**ajeno (a)**

foreign; outside

los **agentes de distribución**

sales agents

En la venta de plantas industriales son los ejecutivos mismos los que, por la complejidad del asunto, actúan de agentes de distribución.

In the sale of industrial facilities, because the deal is so complex, the top executives themselves act as sales agents.

la **complejidad**

complexity

**actuar de**

act as

la **distribución directa**

direct distribution/sales

En la distribución directa, la empresa hace llegar el producto al consumidor final sin la participación de intermediarios.

In direct sales, the company delivers the product directly to the consumer without the intervention of middlepersons.

la **distribución indirecta**

indirect sales

la **franquicia**

franchise; franchising

En la franquicia, un franquiciador vende al franquiciado el derecho de comercializar su producto y utilizar su sistema de ventas y su nombre.

In franchising, a franchiser sells to a franchisee the right to market his product and to use his name and sales system.

el **franquiciador**

franchiser; franchise grantor

el **franquiciado**

franchise receiver; franchisee

**conquistar**

to conquer

Como consecuencia de la floja demanda interna no les quedó otro remedio que conquistar nuevos mercados.

As a result of low domestic demand, they had no other alternative but to conquer new markets.

la **demanda interna**

domestic demand

**flojo (a)**

weak; feeble

**no quedar otro remedio**

to have no other solution

las **operaciones de venta**

sales operations

Las operaciones de venta de menor envergadura se confieren a los empleados del departamento de ventas.

Small-scale sales operations are entrusted to employees in the sales department.

| | |
|---|---|
| la **envergadura** | scale; scope; significance |
| las **operaciones mercantiles** | mercantile/commercial/business operations |
| la **clave de distribución** | distribution key |
| el **baremo de distribución** | distribution calculator |
| Los cambios en la asignación de las claves de distribución por parte de la empresa automovilística significaron la fijación de nuevas cuotas mínimas de ventas para los concesionarios. | Changes in the assigning of distribution keys by the automobile maker meant the setting of new minimum sales quotas for the concessionaries (dealers, licensees). |
| la **fijación** | fixing; establishment; setting |
| el **concesionario** | concessionary; licensed dealer |
| el **distribuidor,** la **distribuidora** | distributor |
| A causa del cierre de nuestra sucursal rogamos diríjanse a nuestro nuevo distribuidor. | Because of the closing of our branch we ask you to please contact our new distributor. |
| la **casa distribuidora** | distribution house/firm |
| el **cierre** | closing |
| la **sucursal** | branch |

## ▬▬▬▬▬ Commercial Business Structures ▬▬▬▬▬

| | |
|---|---|
| el **comercio** | commerce; trade |
| El comercio sirve de vínculo entre el productor y el consumidor final. | Trade serves as a link between the producer and the final consumer. |
| el **vínculo** | link; bond; tie |
| el **comercio al por mayor** | wholesale trade |
| el **comercio mayorista** | wholesaling |
| El comercio al por mayor se dedica al acopio de grandes cantidades para revenderlas posteriormente a consumidores en gran escala. | Wholesale trade engages in the purchase of large quantities for subsequent resale to large consumers. |
| el **acopio** | purchase; buying up |
| **revender** | to resell |
| el **consumidor en gran escala,** la **consumidora en gran escala** | bulk/large consumer |
| el **comerciante al por mayor** | wholesaler |

las **grandes superficies**

large surface area markets; supermarkets; shopping malls

Para acaparar una mayor cuota del mercado, las grandes superficies ensalzan cada vez más la compra como vivencia y satisfacción personal.

To capture a larger market share, shopping centers increasingly extol shopping as an experience and a means of providing personal satisfaction.

**acaparar**

to capture; grab

la **vivencia**

experience

**ensalzar**

to extol; praise; exalt

el **descuento al por mayor**

wholesaler's discount

Para poder concederle un descuento al por mayor, tendrá que afiliarse a nuestra cooperativa de compras al por mayor.

In order to grant you a wholesaler's discount, you'll have to become a member of our wholesalers' purchasing cooperative.

**conceder**

to grant

la **cooperativa de compras al por mayor**

wholesalers' purchasing cooperative

**afiliarse a**

to join; become a member of

**a granel**

loose; in large quantities; unpackaged

Por su reducido volumen, sentimos no poder atender su pedido, ya que nosotros únicamente vendemos a granel.

We regret that because of its small size we are unable to fill your order, since we only sell in large quantities.

**atender un pedido**

to fill an order

el **pequeño comercio**

small business

El pequeño comercio está cediendo cada vez más terreno a las grandes superficies y su única salida es la especialización.

Small business is losing more and more ground to shopping centers and its only way out of difficulty is specialization.

**ceder**

to cede; give way

el **terreno**

ground

la **salida**

exit; way out

la **especialización**

specialization

el **comercio al detalle,** el **comercio minorista comercio al por menor**

retail; retailing; retail trade

El comercio al por menor en España se apoya, en su mayor parte, en estructuras familiares, lo cual impide con frecuencia su modernización.

Retail trade in Spain is based primarily on family structures, which is often a hindrance to its modernization.

los **grandes almacenes**
El Corte Inglés, una cadena de grandes almacenes, considerada como la empresa española modelo, ha abierto en 1995 un nuevo centro en Palma de Mallorca.

big department stores
The Corte Inglés, a large department store chain considered to be a model Spanish business; opened a new branch in Palma de Mallorca in 1995.

la **cadena**

chain

el **modelo**

model

el **hipermercado**
Los hipermercados no pueden ofrecer la variedad de oferta de las grandes superficies, pero están ubicados más cerca de donde viven los consumidores.

consumers market
Consumers markets can't offer the abundant variety found in shopping centers, but they are located closer to consumer residential areas.

el **hiper de bricolaje**

do-it-yourself market; hardware store

la **variedad de oferta**

variety of selection

**estar ubicado (a)**

to be located

la **tienda de ultramarinos**

grocery store; Mom and Pop store

la **tienda de comestibles**
Las tiendas de ultramarinos en los pueblos también tienen una función social como centro de comunicación.

food market
Mom and Pop stores in villages also have a social function as communication centers.

el **anticuario**

antiques dealer

la **casa de ventas por correo**

mail order house

la **casa de ventas por catálogo**
En España, las casas de venta por correo están todavía en sus comienzos y aún está por ver si la venta por catálogo despegará algún día.

catalogue sales firm
In Spain, mail order houses are just starting out and it still remains to be seen whether catalogue sales will someday make a breakthrough.

**estar en sus comienzos**

to be just starting

**estar por ver**

to remain to be seen

**despegar**

to take off; make a breakthrough

la **buhonería**
Hoy en día, la buhonería es una actividad en vías de extinción.

door-to-door sales; peddling
Nowadays, door-to-door sales are becoming extinct.

**en vías de extinción**

to become extinct; be on the way out

el **buhonero,** la **buhonera**

door-to-door salesman; peddler

|  |  |
|---|---|
| el **comercio ambulante** | itinerant sales |
| la **venta callejera** | street sales |
| Los pequeños comerciantes luchan con todos los medios a su alcance contra la venta ambulante. | Small business persons are fighting in every way they can against street sales. |
| la **venta de casa en casa** | house-to-house sales |
| Algunas empresas recurren todavía a la venta de casa en casa, ya que ofrece la ventaja de ser una venta personalizada. | Some companies still make use of house-to-house sales because it offers the advantage of personalized selling. |
| **personalizado (a)** | personalized; direct |
| la **venta a domicilio** | door-to-door sales |
| La venta a domicilio se fundamenta en la capacidad de persuasión de los vendedores para engatusar a los clientes. | Door-to-door sales depend on the salespersons' skill at fast talking their customers. |
| la **capacidad de persuasión** | talent for persuading |
| **engatusar** | to wheedle; get around; coax; fast talk; talk someone into |
| la **empresa de reparto a domicilio** | home delivery business |
| Las empresas de reparto a domicilio que más éxito han tenido son las de venta de pizzas. | The home delivery businesses that have been most successful are those that sell pizzas. |
| la **teletienda** | teleshopping |
| El éxito de la teletienda se debe al impacto visual de la presentación de los artículos. | The success of teleshopping is due to the visual impact of the articles shown. |
| el **impacto visual** | visual impact |

## Middlemen; Intermediaries

|  |  |
|---|---|
| el, la **comercial** | travelling salesperson |
| Buscamos un comercial con coche propio, bien introducido en el ramo de las máquinas de imprimir. | We're looking for a travelling salesperson with (his/her) own car, well-versed in the field of printing presses. |
| la **máquina de imprimir** | printing press |
| el **sueldo fijo** | fixed/set salary |
| Ofrecemos sueldo fijo más comisión y poder para concluir contratos. | We're offering a fixed salary plus commission and the authority to sign contracts. |

| | |
|---|---|
| la **comisión** | commission |
| el **poder para concluir contratos** | authorization to make/enter into/sign contracts |
| **trabajar a comisión** | to work on a commission basis |
| la **especificación de gastos** | account/listing/specification/enumeration/statement of expenses |

En cuanto hayamos recibido su especificación de gastos, pasaremos a su liquidación sin demora. | As soon as we've received your statement of expenses we'll proceed immediately to settle them.

| | |
|---|---|
| la **liquidación de gastos** | settlement/payment of expenses |
| **sin demora** | without delay; immediately |
| el, la **comisionista** | commission agent/merchant |
| el, la **agente comercial** | commercial agent |
| el, la **representante** | independent (trade) representative |

El agente comercial trabaja en nombre y por cuenta ajenos, cobrando una comisión de garantía si se responsabiliza de los pagos de los clientes. | A commercial agent works in someone else's name and for the account of her/his employer, receiving a guarantee commission if she/he assumes responsibility for customers' payments.

| | |
|---|---|
| **en nombre y por cuenta ajenos** | in someone else's name and for someone else's account |
| **en nombre y por cuenta propios** | in one's own name and for one's own account |
| la **comisión de garantía** | guarantee commission; *del credere* commission |
| **responsabilizarse de** | to assume responsibility for |
| el, la **agente comercial independiente** | independent commercial agent |
| el, la **agente comercial multicartera** | commercial agent for multiple firms |
| la **zona de representación** | sales territory |

Para la zona de representación de Baleares buscamos un jefe de zona con contrato de representación exclusiva. | For the Balearic Islands sales area we're looking for a territory director with an exclusive contract.

| | |
|---|---|
| el **jefe de zona,** la **jefa de zona** | territory/regional director |
| el **contrato de representación exclusiva** | exclusive agent contract |
| el, la **corredor de comercio** | commercial broker |

Debido a sus profundos conocimientos del mercado, los corredores de comercio juegan un papel importante en el corretaje de barcos, fletes, seguros, etc. | Due to their extensive knowledge of the market, commercial brokers play an important role in the brokerage of ships, freight, insurance, etc.

| | |
|---|---|
| el **corretaje** | brokerage |
| el **corretaje,** los **derechos de mediación** | brokerage fee; procurement commission |
| el, la **corredor de fincas,** el, la **agente de la propiedad** | real estate agent |
| la **correduría** | broker's office; procurement agency |
| Para obtener la prima de seguros más reducida hemos consultado a varias corredurías. | To receive the lowest insurance premium we have consulted several brokers' offices. |
| **consultar** | to consult |
| el **intermediario,** la **intermediaria** | intermediary; agent; broker |
| Se vende finca rústica con casa señorial y 14.000 m{2Expo} de terreno cerca de Sineu. Abstenerse intermediarios. | For sale: Rural property with manor house and 14,000 square meters near Sineu. No brokers. |
| la **finca rústica** | country estate |
| la **casa señorial** | manor house/domain |
| **abstenerse** | to refrain/abstain |
| la **mediación** | mediation |
| Menos mal que el Sr. Cerró y Garcías ha intervenido en nuestro favor. Sin su hábil mediación nunca se habría cerrado el negocio. | It's a good thing that Mr. Cerró y Garcías intervened on our behalf. Without his skillful mediation the deal would never have been concluded. |
| **intervenir** | to intervene |

## Retail Sales

| | |
|---|---|
| el **escaparate** | show window/display |
| La decoración de los escaparates como gancho para atraer a clientes adquiere cada vez más importancia, y con ello, naturalmente, la función del escaparatista. | Show window decoration, as a customer eye-catcher, is becoming increasingly important, and along with it, of course, the function of the window decorator. |
| el, la **escaparatista** | show window decorator |
| **adquirir importancia** | to acquire importance/become important |

el **gancho**

hook; enticement; eye-catcher

el, la **dependiente**
De la amabilidad de los dependientes de un comercio depende el trato que recibe el cliente.

salesperson
How a business' customers are treated depends on the attitude of the salesperson.

la **amabilidad**

amiability; friendliness

el **mostrador**
Si tiene la amabilidad de pasar por este otro mostrador, le enseñaré los modelos que tenemos.

sales counter
If you would be so kind as to step to the other counter, I'll show you all the models we have.

**enseñar, mostrar**

to show

la **caja**
Para pagar los artículos pase directamente por caja, por favor.

cashier's desk; cash register; cashier
To pay for the articles, please go directly to the cashier.

**directamente**

directly

**hacer caja**

to count/tally the money in the till/cash register

Al final del día, al hacer caja, se dió cuenta de que, nuevamente, faltaban más de diez mil pesetas.

At the end of the day when tallying the cash register, she realized that, once again, more than ten thousand pesetas were missing.

el **dinero suelto**
Lo siento, no llevo dinero suelto, así que le tendré que dar un billete de 10.000 pesetas.

change
I'm sorry, I have no change, so I'll have to give you a 10,000 peseta note.

el **horario de comercio**
Se ha solicitado al Gobierno libertad total de horarios de comercio y la supresión de las limitaciones ahora existentes.

business hours
The Government has been asked to permit total freedom for establishing business hours and to abolish now existing limits.

la **limitación**

limitation; restriction

las **rebajas**
En esta época, en muchas tiendas hay llamativos letreros con la palabra "rebajas" para incitar a los clientes a la compra.

clearance sales
In this season, there are many stores with prominent signs proclaiming "clearance sales" to stimulate customers to buy.

**incitar a la compra**

to incite/stimulate to buy

**llamativo (a)**

striking/conspicuous/prominent

|  |  |
|---|---|
| el **letrero** | sign |
| las **rebajas de agosto**<br>Cada vez se ha ido adelantando más el comienzo de las rebajas de agosto, y ahora es fácil ver comercios que las anuncian en julio. | August/summer sales<br>The August clearance sales have been moved up more and more, and now it's not unusual to see businesses announce them in July. |
| el **comienzo** | beginning |
| las **rebajas de enero** | January/winter clearance sales |
| la **devolución**<br>Para la devolución de artículos, es imprescindible traerlos en la envoltura original. | exchange<br>To exchange articles, it's indispensible to bring them back in their original wrappings. |
| la **envoltura** | wrapping; packaging |
| **original** | original |
| **devolver** | to exchange |
| la **reclamación**<br>No se admitirán reclamaciones sin la presentación del ticket de compra. | complaint<br>No claims will be honored without presentation of the sales slip. |
| el **ticket de compra** | sales slip; cash register receipt |
| **reclamar** | to claim; demand |
| el **artículo en oferta** | sale item |
| la **oferta especial**<br>Los supermercados siempre tienen artículos en oferta que van cambiando cada mes. | special offer<br>The supermarkets always have sales items that vary from month to month. |
| la **atención al cliente,** el **servicio al cliente**<br>Da gusto comprar en esos grandes almacenes porque, aunque son más caros, la atención al cliente es francamente exquisita. | customer service/ attitude towards the customer<br>It's a pleasure to shop in those big department stores, because even though they're more expensive, their attitude towards the customer is simply marvellous. |
| **dar gusto** | to give/be a pleasure |
| **francamente** | frankly; simply |
| **exquisito (a)** | exquisite; marvellous |
| la **caja central**<br>Si quiere que se lo envuelvan en papel de regalo, diríjase por favor a la caja central. | main cashier's desk<br>If you want it gift wrapped please go to the main cashier's desk. |

| | |
|---|---|
| **envolver en papel de regalo** | to gift wrap |
| la **cartera de clientes** | regular clientele |
| la **liquidación por fin de temporada** | season's end sale; seasonal close out sale |
| En la liquidación por fin de temporada a menudo se encuentran artículos de marca a mitad de precio. | In seasonal close out sales, brand name articles can often be found at half price. |
| la **liquidación total** | going out of business sale |
| Si realmente uno busca, en las liquidaciones totales por cierre de negocio se pueden encontrar muchas gangas. | If one really looks hard, one can find many bargains in going out of business sales. |
| el **cierre de negocio** | closing out of business |
| la **ganga** | bargain |
| **rebajado (a)** | reduced |
| Durante las rebajas, en las etiquetas deben aparecer el precio original del artículo y el precio ya rebajado. | In final close out sales, the original price and the earlier reduced price must appear on the label. |
| el **artículo invendible** | unsellable article; white elephant; shelf sitter |
| el **muerto** | deadwood; drug on the market |
| En todas las tiendas hay algunos artículos invendibles que se sacan a la venta temporada tras temporada. | In all stores there are some white elephants that are trotted out for sale season after season. |
| **sacar a la venta, poner a la venta** | to offer for sale; put on sale |
| el **éxito de ventas** | sales success; fast/good selling items |
| Esta nueva lámpara halógena ha sido, por su diseño y calidad, un rotundo éxito de ventas. | Because of its design and quality, this new halogen lamp has been a resounding success. |
| **rotundo (a)** | resounding |
| **venderse como churros** | to sell like hotcakes |
| El nuevo sofá-cama se vende como churros. | The new convertible sofa is selling like hotcakes. |
| **confiar en** | to trust in |
| **obsequiar** | to make a present of/give |
| En compras superiores a 15.000 pesetas, le obsequiaremos con un artículo por valor del 10% de la compra. | For purchases in excess of 15,000 pesetas, we will make you a gift of an item worth 10% of the purchase price. |
| el **obsequio** | gift |
| **regatear** | to haggle |

## Import and Export

la **importación**
La importación abarca la entrada de bienes y servicios procedentes de países extranjeros.

importation; importing
Importing includes the entry of goods and services originating in foreign countries.

**importar**

to import

la **exportación**
El Gobierno Español anima de forma incansable a las empresas nacionales a una mayor proyección internacional.

exportation
The Spanish government tirelessly urges domestic firms to think more strongly in international terms.

la **proyección**

projection

**animar**

to animate; encourage; urge

**incansable**

tireless

el **importador,** la **importadora**
El importador se dedica a introducir géneros extranjeros.

importer
The function of importers is to bring in foreign goods.

**importador (ora)**

import

**dedicarse a**

to devote/dedicate oneself

el **exportador,** la **exportadora**

exporter

el **comercio exterior**
El Instituto Español de Comercio Exterior (ICEX) (España) ofrece asistencia de toda índole a empresas exportadoras españolas para fomentar el comercio exterior.

foreign trade
The Spanish Institute of Foreign Trade (ICEX) (Spain) offers assistance of all kinds to Spanish export firms in order to encourage foreign trade.

el **Instituto Español de Comercio Exterior (ICEX)**

The Spanish Institute of Foreign Trade

**de toda índole**

of all sorts/kinds

la **asistencia**

help; assistance

el **intercambio comercial**
La economía española de los años cuarenta fue de orientación económico-interior con un escaso intercambio comercial con el exterior.

commercial interchange/relations
Spain's economy in the 1940's was oriented to the domestic market and commercial relations with foreign countries were limited.

el **estímulo a la exportación**
El Ministerio de Economía se vió
obligado a intensificar los estímulos
a la exportación para contrarrestar el
debilitamiento de las exportaciones
españolas en los mercados internacionales.

export stimulus
The Department of Commerce felt
it necessary to intensify export
stimuli to counteract the falling off
of Spanish exports on international
markets.

**contrarrestar**

to counteract; check

**promocionar**
La tarea más importante del Ministro
de Economía en su viaje a China fue la
de promocionar la venta de productos
españoles.

to promote
The Department of Commerce's
most important task during a visit
to China was to promote the sale
of Spanish products.

la **promoción del comercio
exterior**

promotion of foreign trade

**operar**
Las actividades comerciales de las
empresas españolas que operan en
mercados internacionales han experimentado un incremento sustancial.

to operate
The commercial activities of
Spanish companies doing business
in international markets have
experienced substantial growth.

**experimentar**

to experience; undergo

**sustancial**

substantial

**colaborar**

to collaborate

la **exportación directa**
La exportación directa se realiza a
través de contactos directos con la
clientela en el extranjero, p. ej.,
mediante una red comercial propia.

direct export
Direct export takes place through
direct contacts with customers
abroad, e.g. by means of the
company's own distribution network.

la **red comercial**

distribution network

el **consignatario,** la
**consignataria**
El consignatario de las mercancías
es la persona determinada por el
remitente para recibir las mercancías
y, a continuación, entregarlas a su
destinatario.

receiver; consignee

The consignee of the merchandise
is the person designated by the
sender to receive the goods and
subsequently to deliver them to
the person intended (addressee).

a **continuación**

subsequently

la **autorización administrativa
de exportación**
La autorización administrativa de
exportación es una licencia de exportación, expedida por la Dirección
General de Transacciones Exteriores
(DGTE) (España), en la cual se
autoriza la realización de expediciones
de mercancía, como, p. ej., en operaciones de compensación.

official export authorization

The official export authorization is
an export license, issued by the
General Board of Foreign Transactions (Spain), which permits the
transport of merchandise, such as,
e.g. in compensation operations.

| | |
|---|---|
| la **licencia de exportación** | export license |
| **expedir** | to issue |
| la **expedición de documentos** | issuing of documents |
| la **expedición de mercancías** | shipment of merchandise |
| **autorizar** | to authorize |
| la **Dirección General de Transacciones Exteriores (DGTE)** | General Board of Foreign Transactions |

(En España,) dependiendo del Ministerio de Economía y Hacienda, la DGTE tiene encomendada la concesión de autorizaciones para transacciones con el exterior.

(In Spain,) the DGTE is subordinate to the Ministry of Economics and Finance and is responsible for the issue of permits for business dealings with foreign countries.

**encomendar** — to entrust; commend

el **libre acceso al mercado** — free access to the market

A pesar de los esfuerzos realizados para facilitar el libre acceso a los mercados extranjeros, las restricciones y barreras comerciales gozan de gran popularidad para proteger la industria autóctona.

Despite the efforts made to facilitate free access to foreign markets, commercial restrictions and barriers enjoy great popularity as protectors of indigenous industry.

la **barrera comercial** — commercial barrier

la **popularidad** — popularity

el **boicot comercial** — commercial boycott

A finales de los años cuarenta, Franco empleó todos los medios a su alcance para conseguir la supresión del boicot comercial, impuesto por los países democráticos.

At the end of the forties, Franco used all the means at his disposal to achieve the lifting of the commercial boycott imposed by the democratic countries.

la **supresión** — suppression; lifting; abolition

el **tráfico de contrabando** — smuggling; contraband traffic

El tráfico de contrabando tradicional dedicado a la importación ilegal de tabaco, se ha visto superado por el tráfico de drogas.

Traditional smuggling that engaged in the illegal importation of tobacco has been largely supplanted by the drug traffic.

el **tráfico de drogas** — drug traffic

la **incautación** — confiscation

A pesar de los espectaculares éxitos cosechados por la policía en la incautación de mercancía de contrabando, las leyes insuficientes permiten a muchos capos salir en libertad.

Despite spectacular police successes in the confiscation of contraband goods, inadequate legislation allows many big crime bosses to go scot-free.

167

| | |
|---|---|
| **cosechar un éxito** | to achieve/reap a success |
| **insuficiente** | insufficient; inadequate |
| la **reimportación** | reimportation |
| La reimportación de automóviles es un negocio redondo para los comerciantes que saben sortear los escollos de las legislaciones nacionales. | The reimportation of automobiles can bring fat profits to those dealers who know how to navigate the reefs of different countries' laws. |
| el **negocio redondo** | lucrative business deal |
| **sortear un escollo** | to avoid the reefs |

## ▬▬▬ Export Financing ▬▬▬

la **financiación del comercio exterior**

foreign trade financing

La financiación del comercio exterior es el conjunto de factores que sirven para fomentar los intercambios comerciales con el exterior.

Foreign trading financing is the ensemble of factors that serve to encourage trade relations with foreign countries.

la **financiación de las importaciones**

financing of imports

En las compraventas con aplazamiento de pago, los importadores españoles pueden recurrir a la financiación de sus importaciones, tanto en divisas como en pesetas.

In deferred payment buying and selling, Spanish importers can finance their imports either in pesetas or in foreign currencies.

la **compraventa**

buying and selling; sale

la **compraventa con aplazamiento de pago**

deferred payment buying and selling; deferred billing

la **financiación a la exportación**

export financing
Export financing is accomplished, usually, by export credits which are different from suppliers' credits and orderer credits.

La financiación a la exportación se lleva a cabo, generalmente, mediante créditos a la exportación, diferenciándose entre créditos comerciales y créditos del ordenante.

el **crédito a la exportación**

export credit

el **crédito comercial,** el **crédito de suministrador**

supplier credit; credit on merchandise
Supplier credit is an easing of credit which the exporter grants his foreign customers by permitting the deferring of the contractual payment obligations.

El crédito comercial es una facilidad crediticia concedida por el exportador a sus clientes extranjeros mediante un aplazamiento en las obligaciones de pago contraídas.

la **facilidad crediticia,** la **facilidad de crédito**

credit easing; preferential credit

el **aplazamiento**

deferring; delay

el **crédito del ordenante,** el **crédito de adquisición**
En el crédito del ordenante, el banco concede un crédito directamente al consignatario extranjero.

customer/orderer credit

In orderer credit, the bank grants a credit directly to the foreign consignee.

el **ordenante**

orderer; accredited customer

el **crédito documentario**
El crédito documentario es la orden—normalmente irrevocable—de un banco, que obra en nombre de un cliente suyo, de pagar, contra entrega de los documentos exigidos, un importe determinado a un tercero a condición de que los términos del crédito se hayan cumplido.

letter of credit
A letter of credit is the normally irrevocable order issued by a bank operating in the name of a client, to pay a specified sum to a third party upon delivery of the required documents, on condition that the terms agreed to in the letter of credit have been fulfilled.

**irrevocable**

irrevocable

**revocable**

revocable

**obrar en nombre de alguien**

to act/operate in someone's name

la **entrega de documentos**

handing over of documents

el **crédito de aceptación contra documentos,** el **crédito de reembolso**
El crédito de aceptación contra documentos es un crédito de aceptación muy popular en la financiación de la importación y exportación. Se paga al exportador a través de un crédito documentario, garantizado por el banco del importador, el cual puede ser descontado.

documentary credit

Documentary credit is an acceptance credit very commonly used in import-export financing. The exporter is paid by a discountable letter of credit guaranteed by the importer's bank.

**descontar**

to discount

el **banco emisor**
El banco emisor es el banco que efectua la apertura de un crédito documentario a favor del beneficiario, sigiuiendo instrucciones del ordenante.

issuing bank; crediting bank
The issuing bank is the bank that arranges for the opening of a documentary credit in favor of the beneficiary, following its client's instructions.

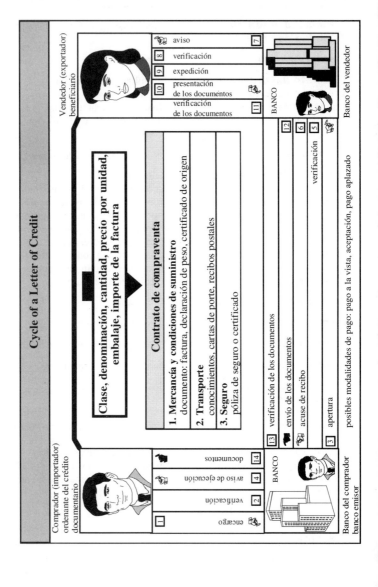

Cycle of a Letter of Credit

Comprador (importador)
ordenante del crédito
documentario

Vendedor (exportador)
beneficiario

Clase, denominación, cantidad, precio por unidad,
embalaje, importe de la factura

**Contrato de compraventa**

1. Mercancía y condiciones de suministro
documento: factura, declaración de peso, certificado de origen

2. Transporte
conocimientos, cartas de porte, recibos postales

3. Seguro
póliza de seguro o certificado

7  aviso
8  verificación
9  expedición
10 presentación de los documentos
11 verificación de los documentos

BANCO

Banco del vendedor

1  encargo
2  verificación
4  aviso de ejecución
14 documentos

BANCO

12 verificación de los documentos
6  envío de los documentos
5  acuse de recibo   verificación
3  apertura

Banco del comprador
banco emisor

posibles modalidades de pago: pago a la vista, aceptación, pago aplazado

el **banco avisador,** el **banco notificador** · advising bank; notifying bank

el **banco confirmador** · confirming bank

los **"Usos y reglas documentarias del crédito documentario"** · "Uniform Rules and Practice for Letters of Credit"

Los "Usos y reglas documentarias del crédito documentario", editados por la Cámara de Comercio Internacional (España), pretenden unificar, al máximo posible, la ejecución de estos créditos documentarios. · The "Uniform Rules and Practice for Letters of Credit" issued by the International Chamber of Commerce (Spain) attempt to standardize, as much as possible, the execution of letters of credit.

la **ejecución** · execution; carrying out

**unificar** · to unify; standardize

el **cobro documentario** · document collection

En el cobro documentario, llevado a cabo por el banco de un exportador, se emplean una serie de documentos como vehículo para transmitir el dominio de la mercancía. · In document collection, which is done by an exporter's bank, a series of documents is employed as a means for the transfer of ownership of the merchandise.

**transmitir** · transfer

la **letra comercial,** el **efecto de comercio** · commercial letter

Las letras comerciales sirven de soporte documentario de los derechos de cobro en una transacción de mercancías. · Commercial letters serve as documentary support for the safeguarding of collection claims in a transaction involving goods.

el **soporte** · support; backup

la **transacción de mercancías** · transaction in merchandise

la **factura proforma** · pro forma invoice

La factura proforma se expide con anterioridad a la entrega de la mercancía. · The pro forma invoice is made out prior to delivery of the merchandise.

**expedir** · to issue; make out

**con anterioridad** · prior; before

**detallar** · to list in detail; detail

En la factura proforma se detallan las condiciones en las que el exportador está dispuesto a vender sus productos. · The conditions on which the exporter is prepared to sell his products are listed in detail on a pro forma invoice.

| | |
|---|---|
| la **factura provisional**<br>La factura provisional se utiliza en aquellos casos en que la cantidad o el volumen de la mercancía a suministrar todavía no han sido fijados, como, p. ej., en productos a granel. | provisional bill<br>The provisional bill is used in those cases in which the quantity or volume of the merchandise to be supplied have not yet been established, as e.g. in bulk goods. |
| la **garantía de riesgo a la exportación (GRE)** | export risk guarantee (comparable to the German government's coverage of German exporters through the Hermes Credit Insurance Co.) |
| La garantía de riesgo a la exportación es una garantía estatal de créditos particulares en operaciones de exportación. | The export risk guarantee is a state guarantee of private credits for export transactions. |
| las **fianzas en operaciones de importación y exportación** | import-export guarantees |
| Las fianzas en operaciones de importación y exportación son afianzamientos a depositar en la Caja General en el caso de transacciones de productos agrarios o pesqueros entre España y los países comunitarios. | Import-export guarantees are sureties to be deposited in the Deposit Bureau for transactions between Spain and the countries of the European Union involving agricultural or maritime products. |
| el **afianzamiento** | guarantee; surety |
| **depositar** | to deposit |
| la **Caja General** | Spanish Government Deposit Bureau |
| el **país comunitario** | country in the European Union |
| el **incumplimiento de contrato** | violation/breech of contract; non-fulfillment of contract |
| Si en un contrato mercantil los sujetos contractuales incumplen las estipulaciones acordadas, hablamos de incumplimiento de contrato; estas desavenencias se pueden solventar por procedimientos judiciales o prevenir mediante la fijación de garantías. | If the contract partners do not comply with the terms of a commercial contract, we speak of violation of contract; these points of contention can be resolved by legal means or be avoided to begin with by the setting of guarantees. |
| el **contrato mercantil** | commercial contract |
| el **sujeto contractual** | contract partner |
| la **desavenencia** | dispute; disagreement; point of contention |
| **solventar** | to resolve |

| | |
|---|---|
| **por procedimiento judicial** | by legal means; through the courts |
| **prevenir** | to prevent |
| el **forfaiting** | forfaiting |
| En operaciones de forfaiting, el exportador vende un documento representativo de la entrega de bienes a un banco especializado en esta clase de transacciones y deshaciéndose así de cualquier riesgo de cobro, aunque a unos costes elevados. | In forfaiting transactions, the exporter sells a document indicating the delivery of goods to a bank specialized in this sort of transaction, and thereby declares himself exempt from any risk of payment, however large the amount may be. |
| el **trueque** | barter |
| La versión moderna del trueque son operaciones de compensación, donde se admite el intercambio de mercancías sin movimiento alguno de fondos. | The modern form of barter operations are compensation transactions in which the transfer of goods is permitted without any monetary funds at all changing hands. |
| la **versión** | version; variation; form |
| las **operaciones de compensación** | compensation transactions |

## Customs

| | |
|---|---|
| la **aduana** | customs office/bureau/authority |
| La aduana es un recinto acotado en aeropuertos, puertos y fronteras donde están ubicados los despachos y almacenes aduaneros. | Customs is a demarcated section in airports, ports, and at frontiers where customs offices and depots are located. |
| **acotar** | to mark off; demarcate |
| **ubicar** | to locate |
| el **despacho aduanero** | customs office |
| el **almacén aduanero** | customs depot |
| el **territorio aduanero** | customs area/zone/territory |
| El territorio aduanero es el área por donde circulan libremente las mercancías sin estar sometidas a control aduanero; no coincide siempre con el territorio nacional, ya que varios países pueden constituir un territorio aduanero. | The customs zone is the area in which goods circulate freely, subject to no customs control; it does not always correspond to national boundaries since various countries can establish a customs area. |
| el **control aduanero** | customs control/surveillance/checking |

el **despacho aduanero,** los **trámites de aduana**
customs formalities

El despacho aduanero es la totalidad de los controles y formalidades aduaneras impuestas a los productos introducidos en un país.
Customs formalities are the sum of checks and surveillance measures imposed on products imported into a country.

la **totalidad**
totality; sum

la **formalidad**
formality

**pagar aduana sobre u/c**
to pay duty on something

Cuando intentaba hacer pasar por desapercibido el ordenador sujeto a aduana, le pillaron y le obligaron a pagar aduana sobre él.
When he surreptitiously tried to bring in the computer without declaring it, he was caught and made to pay duty on it.

**hacer pasar**
to bring in

**por desapercibido**
imperceived; surreptitiously

**sujeto a aduana**
subject to customs duties

**pillar**
to catch

**exento de aduana, exento de aranceles**
duty-free

la **franquicia arancelaria,** la **exención arancelaria**
exemption from customs duty; toll exemption

Si un ciudadano de la UE traslada su domicilio a España, puede reclamar franquicia arancelaria para sus bienes personales.
If a citizen of a country in the EU moves his residence to Spain, he can claim an exemption from customs duties for his personal property.

**trasladar su domicilio**
to move one's residence/domicile

los **bienes personales**
personal property

**declarar en aduana**
to declare and pay duty on

¡Todos aquellos que tengan algo que declarar, que pasen por la puerta roja, por favor!
All those who have anything to declare, please go through the red door!

el **derecho arancelario,** el **arancel aduanero, derecho aduanero**
customs fee/duty/tariff

Los derechos arancelarios son gravámenes que deben soportar los productos a la hora de atravesar una frontera.
Customs duties are taxes collected on products when they are taken across a frontier.

los **aranceles preferenciales**
preferential customs duties

**arancelario (a), aduanero (a)**
customs/tariff related

| | |
|---|---|
| los **aranceles interiores** | domestic tariffs |
| el **certificado de origen** | certificate of origin |
| El certificado de origen es un documento expedido por las cámaras de comercio del país exportador para acreditar que la mercancía es originaria de la nación indicada. | The certificate of origin is a document issued by chambers of commerce in the exporting country to attest that the provenance of the merchandise is from the country indicated. |
| el **país exportador** | exporting country |
| **ser originario (a) de** | to come from |
| el, la **agente de aduana** | customs agent; customs broker |
| ¡Voy a llamar la atención a mi agente de aduanas; por tercera vez consecutiva ha omitido la indicación del país de procedencia! | I'm going to point out to my customs agent that three times in a row he forgot to indicate the country of provenance. |
| **llamar la atención a alguien sobre u/c** | to call something to someone's attention; to point something out to someone |
| el **país de procedencia** | country of provenance |
| el **país de origen** | country of origin |
| la **indicación** | indication |
| **omitir** | to omit |
| la **unión aduanera** | customs union |
| La diferencia entre una zona de libre comercio y una unión aduanera radica en que no sólo se suprimen los aranceles entre sus países miembros, sino que también fijan un arancel exterior común frente a terceros países; p. ej la UE entre sí y el Mercado Común Centroamericano. | The difference between a free trade zone and a customs union is that not only are customs abolished among the member nations but also a common foreign tariff with respect to non-participating nations is established, e.g. the members of the EU and the Central American Common Market. |
| **radicar en** | to be based on; rooted in; consist in |
| la **zona de libre comercio** | free trade zone |
| **suprimir** | to suppress; abolish; do away with |
| el **arancel exterior común** | common tariff for non-participating nations |
| el **país miembro** | member nation |
| el **país tercero** | third country/non-participating country |
| el **Documento Unico Aduanero** | EU Standard Administrative Document |
| El Documento Unico Aduanero— obligatorio desde el 1 de enero 1988— es un documento imprescindible para el intercambio de mercancías entre los países miembros de la UE y con terceros países. | The EU Standard Administrative Document, obligatory since the 1st of January, 1988, is an indispensable document for the exchange of goods between the member nations of the EU and with non-participating nations. |

| | |
|---|---|
| el **certificado de circulación de mercancías** | certificate of exchange of goods |
| el **contingente**<br>La fijación de contingentes es una medida cuantitativa para establecer límites superiores en la importación y exportación de productos; se diferencia entre contingentes arancelarios y no arancelarios. | quota; contingent<br>The fixing of quotas is a quantitative measure undertaken to establish upper limits for the import and export of products; a distinction is made between quotas subject to customs and those exempt from customs. |
| el **límite superior** | upper limit |
| el **contingente arancelario** | customs quota |
| la **restricción cuantitativa,** la **limitación de cupo** | quantity restriction |
| la **vigilancia aduanera**<br>La vigilancia aduanera en Galicia se ha incautado grandes cantidades de mercancía de contrabando. | customs surveillance/control<br>Customs surveillance in Galicia has confiscated large quantities of smuggled goods. |
| **incautarse, requisar** | to confiscate |
| la **mercancía de contrabando** | contraband/smuggled goods |
| el **alijo** | contraband; illegal consignment |
| **precintado (a)**<br>El tráfico de contrabando en camiones precintados está en el punto de mira de la policía. | armored<br>The trade in smuggled armored trucks is a subject of particular police attention. |
| **estar en el punto de mira** | to have one's sights set on; be particularly interested in |
| **bajo precinto aduanero** | under customs seal/sealed by customs |
| el **desarme arancelario** | reduction of customs |
| el **desmantelamiento arancelario**<br>El desarme arancelario es la reducción progresiva y escalonada de aranceles con el propósito final de llegar a la eliminación de las barreras arancelarias. | dismantling of tariff barriers<br>Reduction of customs is the continuing, step-by-step reduction of tariffs with the final goal of eliminating tariff barriers. |
| **progresivo (a)** | progressive; continuing |
| **escalonado (a)** | in phases/stages |
| el **propósito final** | final goal |
| las **barreras arancelarias** | tariff barriers |

# International Business Terms

los **incoterms**

international commercial terms; incoterms

Los incoterms, elaborados en 1928 por la Cámara de Comercio Internacional, son normas internacionales sobre la interpretación de los términos comerciales.

The incoterms, drawn up in 1928 by the International Chamber of Commerce, are international norms for the interpretation of commercial terms.

la **interpretación**

interpretation

en **fábrica**

ex works; at the factory

"En fábrica"—la mínima obligación posible—es una cláusula que indica que el vendedor únicamente es responsable de poner las mercancías a disposición del comprador en la fábrica.

"Ex works"—the least possible obligation—is a clause stating that the seller is responsible only for making the goods available to the purchaser at the factory.

la **cláusula**

clause

**franco en almacén**

free warehouse

**franco transportista (FCA)**

free carrier (FCA)

En la versión de los incoterms del 1.7.1990, los conceptos "franco sobre vagón" y "franco sobre railes" han sido sustituidos por el término "franco transportista" para afrontar las necesidades del transporte moderno con trailers y ferries.

In the July 1, 1990 version of the inco terms, the concepts "free on railroad car" and "free railroad" were replaced by the term "free carrier" to deal with modern transport needs via trailers and ferries.

el **concepto**

concept

**afrontar**

to deal with; take into acount

**franco a bordo (FOB)**

free on board (FOB)

"Franco a bordo" quiere decir que el vendedor ha cumplido con su obligación de entrega una vez que la mercancía haya sobrepasado la borda del buque en el puerto de embarque convenido.

"Free on board" means that the seller has fulfilled his delivery obligation once the merchandise has entered the area of the ship in the port of embarkation agreed upon.

la **obligación de entrega**

obligation to deliver

el **puerto de embarque**

port of embarkation; shipping port

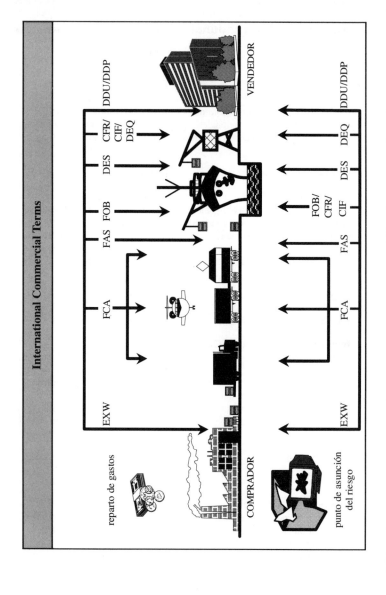

International Commercial Terms

| | |
|---|---|
| **franco al costado del buque (FAS)** | free alongside ship (FAS) |
| **entregada en muelle (DEQ)** | delivered ex quai (delivery duty paid) (DEQ) |
| **entregada sobre buque (DES)** | delivered ex ship (DES) |
| **coste, seguro y flete (CIF)** El vendedor se hace cargo de los gastos, el seguro marítimo y el flete para el envío hasta el puerto de destino. | cost, insurance and freight (CIF) The seller assumes freight, insurance and other diverse expenses for shipment to the port of destination. |
| el **seguro marítimo** | insurance for shipment by sea |
| el **puerto de destino** | port of destination |
| **transporte y seguro pagado hasta** El exportador incluye en el precio exigido el coste, embalaje, importe del flete más el seguro de transporte, pero sólo con cobertura mínima. | shipping and insurance paid/free till The exporter includes in the price demanded, packaging, freight, and shipping insurance costs, but only at minimal coverage. |
| **entregada, derechos pagados (DDP)** El término "entregada, derechos pagados" significa que el vendedor ha cumplido con su deber de asumir todos los gastos, derechos, impuestos y otras cargas, implicando la obligación máxima del vendedor. | delivery duty paid (DDP) The term "delivery duty paid" means that the seller has fulfilled his obligation to assume all expenses, duty fees, taxes and other charges, which constitutes the maximum obligation of the seller. |
| **asumir los gastos** | to assume/bear costs |

## ■■■■■ Request for Information and Offer ■■■■■

| | |
|---|---|
| la **demanda** | demand; inquiry |

el **prospecto**
prospectus/literature
Estamos interesados en sus productos. We are interested in your products.
Por favor, envíennos sus prospectos. Please send us your literature.

el **catálogo**
catalogue

la **muestra**
sample; pattern
¿Tienen Uds. muestras de sus artículos?
Do you have samples of your products?

la **solicitud de oferta,** la **petición de oferta**
written request for a quotation
Frecuentemente, la petición de oferta es el primer paso para iniciar una operación de compraventa.
A written request for a quotation is often the first step towards making a sale.

la **oferta**
offer; selection

la **oferta oral**
oral/verbal offer
Rogamos nos confirmen por escrito la oferta oral hecha por teléfono el día 25 del corriente.
We ask that you confirm in writing the verbal offer made to us by telephone on the 25th of this month.

la **oferta por escrito**
written offer

**hacer saber**
to inform
Al no haber recibido respuesta alguna referente a nuestra carta de fecha 17 de mayo de 1995, rogamos nos hagan saber si nuestra oferta sigue siendo de su interés.
Since we have received no reply in reference to our letter dated May 17, 1995, we ask that you inform us if our offer is still of interest to you.

**hacer llegar**
to have sent
Antes de cursar el pedido, rogamos nos hagan llegar una oferta en firme de la que se puedan desprender todas las informaciones esenciales.
Before we send the order, we ask you to send us a binding offer from which we will be able to gain all essential information.

la **oferta en firme**
firm offer

la **oferta vinculante**
binding offer

**desprender de**

gain/gather from

la **oferta sin compromiso**

offer subject to availability; non-binding offer

la **oferta ventajosa**
En nuestro establecimiento no sólo encontrará numerosas ofertas ventajosas, sino también la más variada selección.

advantageous offer
In our establishment you will not only find numerous advantageous offers but also the most varied selection.

la **selección**

selection

**variado (a)**

varied

el **establecimiento**

establishment; store; firm; business

**en tanto haya existencias**
La oferta es válida hasta agotar existencias.

as long as the supply lasts
The offer is good as long as the supply lasts.

la **cantidad demandada**

the quantity asked for/requested/ordered

Si Uds. consiguen suministrarnos la cantidad demandada en el plazo de tres días, podrán contar con que les compraremos, a partir del mes próximo, cada semana una cantidad fija, de lo contrario tendríamos que echar mano de una oferta nada despreciable de su competencia.

If you can deliver the quantity requested within 3 days, we will continue to buy from you weekly; otherwise, we will accept the offer of your competitor.

**echar mano de**

to fall back on; make use of

la **cantidad fija**

set/fixed quantity

**de lo contrario**

otherwise

**nada despreciable**

not insignificant; competitive, attractive

la **competencia**

competition

**rechazar una oferta, declinar una oferta**

to reject/decline/refuse an offer

Como se desprende de la prensa especializada, su nuevo motor todavía está en pañales y arroja fallos mecánicos; por lo tanto preferimos cubrirnos las espaldas y declinar su oferta.

As can be seen from the trade press, your new motor is still in its infancy and still suffers from mechanical deficiencies; we therefore prefer to play it safe and refuse your offer.

la **prensa especializada**

specialized/trade press

**estar en pañales**

to be in diapers; be in its infancy

| | |
|---|---|
| **arrojar fallos** | to reveal deficiencies; to be defective |
| **tender a** | to tend to |
| **cubrirse las espaldas** | to cover one's back; secure oneself |
| **hacer uso de una oferta**<br>Antes de entablar relaciones comerciales con su empresa y hacer uso de su oferta, rogamos nos mencione personas a las que podamos pedir referencias. | to accept an offer<br>Before entering into a business relationship with your firm and accepting your offer, we ask you to furnish us with the names of people whom we can ask for references. |
| **entablar** | to begin; enter into |
| **mencionar** | to mention |
| **invitar a ofertar** | to invite to make an offer/bids |
| **invitar**<br>Invitamos a todas las empresas interesadas en la subasta pública para el alumbrado de la calle Mayor a retirar el pliego de condiciones y ofertar hasta el día 15 de octubre. | to invite<br>We ask all firms interested in the public invitation of bids for the lighting of the Calle Mayor (Main Street) to pick up terms of the tender invitation and to submit their bids by October 15. |
| la **subasta pública** | public invitation to submit bids/tenders |
| el **alumbrado** | lighting |
| **retirar** | to pick up |
| el **pliego de condiciones** | conditions for the tender invitation |
| la **subasta**<br>Sacaremos a subasta todos los objetos que se encuentren durante más de un año en la oficina de objetos perdidos que no hayan sido retirados hasta la fecha. | auction<br>We will auction off all items which have been in the lost and found bureau for more than a year and have not been claimed by the auction date. |
| **sacar a subasta** | to auction off |
| la **oficina de objetos perdidos** | lost and found bureau |
| la **puja mínima**<br>La puja mínima en la subasta forzada del inmueble sito en la calle del Desengaño n 69 de Madrid, ha sido determinada en 25.900.000 pesetas. | minimum bid<br>The minimum bid in the forced auction sale of the building located at No. 69 on the Calle del Desengaño, in Madrid has been set at 25,900,000 pesetas. |

| la **subasta forzada** | forced auction sale |
| **sito (a)** | situated; located |
| **adjudicar** | to award |
| La casa será adjudicada al mejor postor. | The house will be awarded to the highest bidder. |
| el **mejor postor** | the highest bidder |
| **pujar** | to bid; make a higher bid |

## The Order

| el **pedido,** la **orden** | order |
| El pedido es un acto de voluntad de adquirir una mercancía bajo determinadas condiciones por parte del comprador. | The order is a voluntary act on the part of the buyer to acquire merchandise under predetermined conditions. |
| el **acto de voluntad** | act of will; voluntary act |
| **cursar un pedido, hacer un pedido** | to give an order |
| el **otorgamiento del pedido** | giving of an order |
| Antes del otorgamiento definitivo del pedido vamos a colocar un pedido de prueba. | Before we give you a definite order we are going to request a sample order. |
| **colocar un pedido** | place an order |
| **definitivo (a)** | definite |
| el **pedido de prueba** | sample order |
| la **ejecución de un pedido,** la **realización de un pedido** | filling of an order |
| la **adjudicación del pedido** | placing of an order |
| La adjudicación del pedido al cuñado del ministro ha causado un auténtico revuelo, alimentando las sospechas de corrupción difundidas en círculos empresariales. | The placing of an order with the minister's brother-in-law created a real uproar, lending support to the widespread suspicions of corruption among top businessmen. |
| **alimentar** | to nourish |
| **difundir** | to diffuse; spread |
| **en círculos empresariales** | in entrepreneurial circles; among top businessmen/women |

la **aceptación del pedido**

acceptance of the order

Antes de confirmar la aceptación del pedido, cerciórese de que el cliente ha liquidado la última factura.

Before confirming acceptance of the order, make sure the client has paid the last bill.

**cerciorarse**

to make sure

**confirmar un pedido, acusar recibo de un pedido**

to confirm an order

Rogamos nos confirmen por fax el pedido y detallen las condiciones estipuladas por teléfono.

We ask you to please confirm the order by fax and to list in detail the conditions stipulated by telephone.

**estipular**

to stipulate; to agree contractually

la **cartera de pedidos**

order book; orders on hand

la **entrada de pedidos**

receipt/arrival of orders; volume of orders

Nuestra participación en la feria ha originado una entrada de pedidos nunca vista hasta el momento.

Our participation in the fair led to our receiving more orders than we'd ever seen before.

el **pedido pendiente**

pending order; unfilled/outstanding order

Les pedimos nuestras más sinceras disculpas por el pedido pendiente desde hace tres semanas, sin embargo queremos destacar que se debe a fallos ajenos a nuestra responsabilidad.

Please accept our most sincere apologies for your order which has been pending for three weeks; nevertheless we wish to emphasize that this is due to circumstances beyond our control.

**pedir disculpas**

to apologize

**sincero (a)**

sincere

el **boletín de pedido,** la **nota de pedido**

order form

el **libro de pedidos**

order book

**añadir un pedido, hacer un pedido suplementario**

to add an order; give a supplementary order

**añadir**

to add

Al pedido realizado hace tres días queremos añadir 15 frascos del perfume "Lola Flores".

We would like to add 15 bottles of the perfume "Lola Flores" to the order we placed three days ago.

el **pedido inicial**

first/initial order

En las órdenes de enlace concedemos un plazo de pago de 90 días; en el pedido inicial insistimos en que se pague en efectivo.

For all subsequent orders we allow a 90 day payment period; for the first order we insist on payment in cash.

| | |
|---|---|
| la **orden de enlace** | subsequent order |
| el **pedido consecutivo** | follow-up order |
| la **cancelación de un pedido,** la **anulación de un pedido** | cancelling of an order |
| En caso de anulación de un pedido, Ud. deberá sufragar la tasa de cancelación. | If an order is cancelled, you must pay the cancellation fee. |
| **sufragar** | to pay; make good for |
| la **tasa de cancelación** | cancellation fee |

## The Sales Contract

**negociar**
Estamos reunidos para negociar las modalidades del contrato, pero nos gustaría dejar claro que nuestro margen de negociación es bastante restringido.

to negotiate
We are meeting to negotiate the provisions of the contract, but we should like to make it clear that our room for leeway in negotiation is rather limited.

**restringido (a)**

limited

las **modalidades de un contrato,** las **disposiciones de un contrato,** las **estipulaciones de un contrato**

provisions/terms of a contract

**dejar claro**

to make clear

el **margen de negociación**

negotiation margin; room for leeway in negotiation

el **contrato de compraventa**
En un contrato de compraventa se definen las condiciones de la enajenación de una mercancía o servicio contra pago de un importe determinado.

sales contract
In a sales contract the conditions are defined for the sale of goods or the performance of services for payment at an agreed upon price.

las **condiciones estipuladas**
Las condiciones estipuladas contractualmente en lo que se refiere a la adquisición de la máquina tienen que ser cumplidas al pie de la letra por las partes contratantes.

stipulated/agreed upon conditions
Contractually stipulated conditions referring to the purchase of the machine must be fulfilled to the letter of the law by the contracting parties.

**contractual**

contractual

**al pie de la letra**

literally; to the letter of the law

la **parte contratante**

contract partner/party

| | |
|---|---|
| la **obligación contractual** | contractual obligation |
| el **cierre de un contrato,** la **conclusión de un contrato** | expiration of a contract |
| Los compradores se comprometen a satisfacer el precio de la compraventa al cierre del contrato. | The purchasers pledge to pay the sale price upon expiration of the contract. |
| **capacitado (a) para contratar** | legally competent |
| Las partes contratantes se declaran capacitadas para contratar y se comprometen a cumplir con las condiciones pactadas. | The contracting parties declare that they are legally competent to enter into a contract and obligate themselves to observe the terms agreed upon. |
| **comprometerse a** | to pledge |
| **pactar** | to agree to |
| **cumplir** | to fulfill; keep |
| la **duración del contrato** | duration of the contract |
| La duración prevista del contrato es de 18 meses con una reconducción tácita de un año. | The planned duration of the contract is 18 months with the tacit understanding that it will be extended for a year. |
| **tácitamente** | implicitly; tacitly |
| la **reconducción de un contrato** | contract extension |
| la **cláusula de revocación** | cancellation/revocation clause |
| Les aconsejó incluir en el contrato, como medida cautelar, una cláusula de revocación. | She advised them to include a revocation clause in the contract, as a safeguard. |
| la **medida cautelar** | precautionary measure; safeguard |
| la **cláusula de reserva de propiedad** | right of ownership clause |
| Cada contrato de compra a plazos incluye una cláusula de reserva de propiedad, a saber la mercancía no pasa a ser propiedad del comprador hasta haber satisfecho el último plazo. | Every installment sales contract includes a right of ownership clause declaring that the merchandise does not become the buyer's property until the last installment has been paid. |
| la **cláusula penal** | damages for breech of contract clause; liquidated damages clause |
| Insistimos en la inclusión de una cláusula penal que prevea una pena contractual a determinar por cada día de demora. | We insist on including a damages for breech of contract clause which foresees liquidated damages to be determined for every day delayed. |
| la **inclusión** | inclusion |
| **prever** | to foresee |

| la **pena contractual** | liquidated damages |
| la **demora** | delay |
| el **lugar de jurisdicción** | place of jurisdiction |
| El lugar de jurisdicción será Barcelona. | The place of jurisdiction will be Barcelona. |
| la **infracción de un contrato** | contract infraction/infringement/violation |
| Lamentamos tener que comunicarles que sus repetidas infracciones del contrato nos obligan a rescindir el mismo; el asunto está ahora en manos de nuestros abogados. | We regret to have to inform you that your repeated violations of the contract compel us to proceed to its cancellation; the matter is now in the hands of our lawyers. |

## Price

**fijar el precio**
Estos precios se fijaron en función del tipo de cambio del dólar, así que ahora el artículo le resulta más barato de lo que en realidad vale.

to set the price
These prices were set according to the dollar exchange rate, therefore the article will now cost you less than it's really worth.

**resultar, salir**

to turn out; result

**subir el precio, aumentar el precio**

to increase the price; go up in price

**elevar el precio**
De un mes para otro ha subido el precio de estos artículos porque la demanda es enorme y el fabricante se lo puede permitir.

to raise the price
From one month to the next the price of these goods has gone up because the demand is enormous and the manufacturer can get away with it.

la **demanda**

demand

la **subida de los precios**
A primeros de año siempre hay una subida generalizada de los precios, sobre todo en el sector alimenticio.

price increase
At the beginning of the year there is always a general price increase, especially in the food industry.

la **reducción de los precios**

price reduction

la **disminución de los precios**

lowering of prices

la **revisión de precios**
En vista de la situación actual del mercado, nos hemos visto obligados a considerar una revisión de precios de los artículos en oferta.

price revision; re-pricing
In view of the actual market situation, we have been obliged to consider a revision of the prices for the articles in the offer.

**a mitad de precio**
Todos los artículos están a mitad de precio por liquidación de temporada.

at half-price
Because of the seasonal close-out sale, all merchandise is at half-price.

el **precio irrisorio**

dirt cheap

el **precio de venta al público (PVP)**
En el precio de venta al público que figura en las etiquetas de los artículos ya va incluído el IVA.

list price

The VAT is already included in the list price shown on merchandise labels.

**inasequible**
Esa cadena de supermercados está pensada para gente pudiente, porque los precios son totalmente inasequibles para gente corriente y moliente.

unaffordable
That supermarket chain caters to the affluent, because the prices are totally out of reach for the average consumer.

**pudiente**

affluent; wealthy

la **gente corriente y moliente**

average consumers

**asequible**

affordable; within reach

**inmejorable**
Estamos francamente satisfechos con nuestro nuevo proveedor porque sus precios son ciertamente inmejorables.

unbeatable; unexcelled
We're extremely satisfied with our new supplier because his prices are surely unbeatable.

**ciertamente**

certainly; surely

la **validez**
El presente presupuesto tiene un plazo de validez de dos meses.

validity
The present cost estimate is valid for a period of two months.

**válido (a)**
Esta oferta es válida hasta fin de existencias.

valid
This offer is valid as long as the supply lasts.

el **descuento,** la **rebaja**
Todos los artículos ya llevan incluído en el precio un descuento del 10%, por este motivo no podemos aplicar otra rebaja.

discount
The prices on all the articles already reflect a discount of 10%, therefore we cannot grant any further discount.

el **descuento por cantidad**
A través de nuestro catálogo de productos comprobará que aplicamos un descuento por cantidad del 10%, si el cliente pide más de cinco unidades de cualesquiera de nuestros productos.

quantity discount
You will perceive from our catalogue that we give a 10% quantity discount, if the customer orders more than five items of any one of our products.

**rebajar**
Debido a la mala aceptación que ha
tenido este producto hemos decidido
rebajar el precio al máximo.

to reduce
Due to the poor reception this
product has had, we've decided to
reduce the price to the maximum
extent possible.

la **aceptación**

acceptance; reception

el **regateo**
El regateo es una costumbre muy
extendida en ciertos ámbitos, tales
como mercados semanales, anticua-
rios, etc.

haggling
Haggling is a very widespread
practice in certain areas, such as
weekly markets, antiques, etc.

**regatear**

to haggle

**fulminar los precios**
"¡Durante el mes de agosto fulmina-
mos los precios!" Eslóganes como
éste son cada vez más habituales en la
publicidad de las grandes superficies.

to slash prices
"Prices slashed during the month
of August!" Slogans like this are
increasingly customary in shopping
center advertising.

el **eslógan**

slogan

el **precio competitivo**
Al hacer pedidos a gran escala, los
grandes almacenes compran más
barato de sus proveedores lo que
repercute en el precio; pudiendo, así,
ofrecer a sus clientes precios muy
competitivos en comparación con los
pequeños comerciantes.

competitive price
Through large-scale buying, big
department stores buy more
cheaply from their suppliers and
this is reflected in the price; therefore, compared to small business
people, they are able to offer very
competitive prices.

**repercutir en el precio**

to have an effect on the price

**en comparación con**

in comparison to

**negociable**
En los artículos de segunda mano,
no hay precios fijos, siempre se trata
de precios negociables.

negotiable; transferable
In second hand articles, there are
no fixed prices; the price is always
negotiable.

el **precio fijo**

fixed price

**módico (a)**
Llévese esta moderna aspiradora y
una plancha a vapor por el módico
precio de 7.595.- pesetas.

modest; moderate
Take home with you this modern
vacuum cleaner and a steam iron
for the modest price of 7,595
pesetas.

el **precio de venta al público recomendado**

suggested retail price

En los catálogos, a menudo figuran precios de venta al público recomendados, que no son más que precios orientativos, ya que están sujetos a modificaciones.

Suggested retail prices are often found in catalogues; they are only price guidelines since they are subject to change.

el **precio orientativo**

orientating price; price guideline

la **tarifa de precios,** la **lista de precios**

price list

Rogamos nos manden su tarifa de precios vigentes para esta temporada, ya que en el fax la columna de los precios unitarios es practicamente ilegible.

Please send us your current price list for this season, since the unit prices column on the fax is practically illegible.

el **precio vigente**

currently correct price

la **columna**

column

el **precio unitario**

unit price

el **precio por unidad,** el **precio por pieza**

each price; price per piece; item price

**ilegible**

illegible

**abaratarse**

to make cheaper; fall in price

La reducción de los costes de producción ha abaratado los precios de fábrica.

The reduction in production costs has made the manufacturing cost cheaper.

el **precio de fábrica**

manufacturing cost

el **cálculo**

calculation

## Delivery

**entregar**

to deliver; hand over

Si se firma el contrato de compraventa antes del día 15, podremos servir el pedido inmediatamente y entregar el coche hasta finales de mes.

If the sales contract is signed before the 15th, we'll be able to fill the order immediately and deliver the car by the end of the month.

**servir el pedido**

to fill the order

la **entrega**

delivery

Nos complace su oferta de fecha día 8 de mayo, pero la condición indispensable para otorgar el pedido es la entrega inmediata de la mercancía en el lugar de entrega indicado.

Your offer, dated May 8th appeals to us, but an indispensable condition for our placing the order is the immediate delivery of the merchandise at the delivery site indicated.

el **lugar de entrega**

delivery site

**suministrar**

to supply; deliver

el **suministro**
Esperamos su suministro dentro de 2 meses.

supplying; delivery; shipment
We're expecting your shipment within two months.

el **envío**
En las condiciones de entrega se detallan los gastos de envío y de embalaje.

shipment; delivery
Shipping and handling costs are enumerated in the conditions for delivery.

las **condiciones de entrega**
Perdone, Señora Lopez, pero aquí abajo, en las condiciones de entrega, dice claramente: pagadero a la entrega. Si se niega a pagar, tendremos que llevarnos la mercancía.

conditions for delivery
Pardon us, Mrs. Lopez, but down here in the conditions for delivery it states clearly: payable on delivery. If you refuse to pay, we'll have to take the merchandise back with us.

**pagadero a la entrega**

payable on delivery

el **envío contra reembolso**
En el envío contra reembolso se entrega la mercancía sólo contra pago del importe adeudado.

COD shipment
In a COD shipment the merchandise is handed over only upon payment of the amount owed.

**a porte debido**

unpaid; not free; shipping extra

**a porte pagado**

postpaid; shipping included

**correr a cargo de, ser de cuenta de**
En pedidos por debajo de 150.000 pesetas, los gastos de envío corren al cargo del comprador.

chargeable to

In orders amounting to less than 150,000 pesetas, shipping costs are charged to the buyer.

**listo (a) para el envío**
Podemos confirmarles que la mercancía pedida por Uds. está disponible y ya lista para el envío.

ready for shipment
We can confirm to you that the merchandise you ordered is available and already ready for shipment.

el **aviso de envío**
En el aviso de envío se informa al comprador que la mercancía ha salido ya de la fábrica o del almacén y que está de camino.

shipping notice
In the shipping notice the buyer is informed that the merchandise has left the factory or the warehouse and is on the way.

la **fecha de entrega**
Por la presente les devuelvo la partida de 3.000 huevos de pascua que nos llegaron el día 18 de mayo, lo cual me parece un sustancial retraso en la fecha de entrega.

delivery date
I am returning to you herewith the shipment of 3,000 Easter eggs which we received on the 18th of May, which seems to me a considerable delay in delivery date.

**por la presente**

herewith

el **plazo de entrega**

delivery period/date

el **plazo de suministro**

time within which an article can be supplied

Hemos instalado un programa de facturación que nos avisa automáticamente si no hemos observado el plazo de entrega.

We've installed a billing program that automatically lets us know if we haven't delivered by the date promised.

el **proveedor**

supplier

Lamentamos no poder informarles sobre nuestros proveedores ya que, por principio, no desvelamos nuestras fuentes de suministro.

We regret that we can't let you know who our suppliers are since, as a matter of principle, we do not reveal our supply sources.

**desvelar**

to reveal

**por principio**

on principle

la **fuente de suministro**

supply/delivery source

**suministrable**

deliverable/available

Este artículo no es suministrable de forma inmediata ya que no está en nuestro programa de entrega desde hace dos años y únicamente podemos enviarlo sobre pedido.

This article cannot be delivered immediately, since it hasn't been in our delivery program for more than two years and we can only ship it on special order.

el **programa de entrega**

delivery program

**únicamente**

only; solely

**enviar sobre pedido**

to ship on/by order

el **envío parcial**

partial shipment

Su reclamación referente a un envío incompleto carece de fundamento y por tanto es injustificado, ya que les habíamos informado con antelación que le íbamos a remitir un envío parcial.

Your complaint in reference to an incomplete shipment is without any basis in fact and is therefore unjustified, since we had already informed you in advance that we were going to send you a partial shipment.

**carecer de fundamento**

to be groundless/without basis in fact

**injustificado (a)**

unjustified

**con antelación**

in advance

los **documentos de envío**

shipping documents

Como la agencia de transportes contratada por Uds. no había cumplimentado debidamente los documentos de envío, se produjo un retraso del camión en aduana que nos ha causado importantes pérdidas.

Since the shipper you contracted for did not duly complete the shipping documents, the truck was held up at customs which resulted in significant damages for us.

| | |
|---|---|
| **contratar** | to contract; engage; hire |
| **cumplimentar** | to fill out |
| **debidamente** | duly; properly |
| **causar** | to cause |

el **acuse de recibo**
Tenga la amabilidad de firmar el acuse de recibo aquí abajo para certificarnos la recepción de la mercancía.

confirmation of receipt
Please be so kind as to sign the confirmation of receipt here below to assure us that the goods were received.

el **recibo de entrega,** el **resguardo de entrega,** la **nota de entrega**

delivery receipt/certificate

el **albarán**
El albarán justifica que la mercancía ha sido entregada, pero no es ningún comprobante de pago y debe ser firmado por el cliente en el momento de la entrega.

delivery receipt
The delivery receipt is proof of the merchandise having been delivered, but it in no way shows that it's been paid for and must be signed by the customer when the merchandise is handed over.

el **recibí**
Si es tan amable, firme el albarán en el recuadro donde figura "recibí".

acknowledgement/recipient
Please sign the delivery form in the box where it says acknowledgement.

el **recuadro** — box; grid

---

## Billing

la **factura**
En toda factura deben figurar datos tales como fecha y lugar de expedición de la misma, así como el nombre y el domicilio del cliente y la forma de pago.

bill; invoice
Every bill should provide information such as the date and place it was made out, as well as the customer's name and address and the means of payment.

la **fecha de expedición** — date made out

**facturar**
Por motivos contables, el último pedido realizado por Uds. no se ha incluido en esta factura, sino que se facturará aparte.

to bill; invoice
For bookkeeping reasons, your last order was not included in this bill; it will be billed separately.

el **comprobante de pago**

proof of payment

el **comprobante de compra,** el **justificante de compra**

proof of purchase

Sin justificante de compra no podemos atender su reclamación.

Without proof of purchase we cannot honor your claim.

el **recibo**

receipt

Haré un recibo por el importe que ha pagado y se lo mandaré por correo.

I'll make out a receipt for the amount you paid and send it to you by mail.

**ascender a**

to amount/come to

El importe total de nuestra factura nr. 23/95 asciende a 16.750,- ptas. ya incluido el descuento del 13%.

The total amount of your invoice #23/95 comes to 16,750 pesetas which includes the discount of 13%.

el **importe total**

sum total

el **total de la factura**

entire/total amount of the bill

**liquidar una factura, saldar una factura, pagar una factura**

to pay a bill

Nuestro empleado pasará mañana por sus oficinas para proceder a liquidar la factura que a nuestro pesar aún tenemos pendiente con Uds.

Our employee will call at your offices tomorrow to pay the outstanding bill which, to our regret, we still owe you.

la **modalidad de pago,** la **forma de pago**

means/method of payment

Le participamos que nos es imposible estar de acuerdo con la modalidad de pago aplazado solicitada por Uds. en su escrito de fecha 23.03.95.

We must inform you that it is not possible for us to arrange for the installment payment plan you asked for in your letter of March 23, 1995.

**participar algo a alguien**

to communicate something to someone/inform

las **condiciones de pago**

conditions of payment

Como respuesta a su solicitud, les proponemos las siguientes condiciones de pago: pago por adelantado con un 5% de descuento o bien pago contra reembolso sin descuento alguno.

In reply to your inquiry, we suggest the following conditions of payment: payment in advance with a 5% discount or else payment on delivery with no discount at all.

el **pago por adelantado**

pre-payment

el **pago por anticipado**

payment in advance

el **pago contra reembolso**

payment on delivery

**extender una factura**

to make out/draw up a bill

Haga el favor de extender una factura por el importe total de las compras efectuadas por nuestra empresa durante el mes de julio.

Please make out a bill for the entire amount of all purchases made by our company during the month of July.

**extender un recibo**

to make out a receipt

la **mensualidad**
Nuestra cadena de tiendas ofrece la posibilidad de pagar sus muebles en seis cómodas mensualidades sin entrada alguna.

monthly payment
Our chain of stores offers you the possibility of paying for your furniture in six easy monthly payments with no down payment at all.

la **entrada**

down payment

el **pago inicial**

initial payment

**dejar una señal**

Puede dejar una pequeña señal.

to make a down payment/pay on account
You can make a small down payment.

**por cuenta de**
Los precios que figuran en el catálogo no incluyen gastos de envío que correrán por cuenta del comprador.

charged to; to the account of
The catalogue prices do not include shipping costs which will be charged to the buyer.

los **gastos de envío**

shipping costs

**desglosado (a)**
Necesitaría que me mandara la factura desglosada para poder verificar mejor las diferentes partidas.

broken down (account/bill)
I will need you to send me a breakdown of the bill so that I can better check its different postings.

**verificar**

to check

el **desglose**

breakdown; structuring

la **prórroga de pago**
Como se trata de una oferta especial limitada al mes de abril, sentimos no poder concederles la solicitada prórroga de pago.

postponement; delay in payment
Since it's a special offer limited to the month of April, we regret that we can't accept the delayed payment you propose.

el **pago al contado**
Le comunicamos que nuestra empresa sólo acepta pedidos sobre la base de pagos al contado.

payment in cash
We should like to inform you that our firm only accepts orders on a cash payment basis.

**pasar al cobro**
Le informamos que a partir del día de la fecha únicamente el Sr. Herrero será el encargado de pasar al cobro de los importes aún pendientes.

to collect/receive payments
We wish to inform you that beginning with today's date, only Mr. Herrero will be responsible for collecting any still outstanding sums.

**presentar al cobro**

to cash; hand in for payment

# Complaints

la **reclamación**
En caso de reclamación, diríjanse por escrito a nuestro servicio posventa en el plazo de 20 días a partir de la recepción de la mercancía.

the claim
In case of any claims, please get in touch in writing with our after sales service within 20 days after receipt of the merchandise.

**hacer una reclamación**

to make a claim

**reclamar**

Después de una espera infructuosa de 23 días, nos vemos obligados a reclamar el pedido Nr. 456-16 y manifestamos, al mismo tiempo, nuestra extrañeza por esa tardanza inusual.

to claim; ask for the return of; recall; demand
After waiting in vain for 23 days, we are compelled to ask for the recall of our order #456-16 and we would like to let you know at the same time that we are very put off by this unusual delay.

**infructuoso (a)**

fruitless; useless; in vain

la **espera**

waiting; waiting period

la **extrañeza**

astonishment; annoyance

**inusual**

unusual

**manifestar**
Con esta carta quiero manifestar mi descontento absoluto con la ejecución del último pedido.

to express
With this letter I'd like to express my total dissatisfaction with your handling of my last order.

**quejarse**
En los últimos tiempos nuestros clientes se han venido quejando de sus embalajes.

to complain
Recently, our customers have been complaining about the packaging of articles received from us.

**subsanar**
Por ello, rogamos subsanen esta carencia o, de lo contrario, tendremos que contratar el envío a través de otra empresa.

to remedy; take care of
Therefore, please take care of this problem or else we will have to engage another firm to handle our shipping.

la **carencia**

defect; deficiency; lack

**tomar medidas**
En respuesta a su reclamación de fecha 15 de febrero de 1995, lamentamos las molestias causadas y le aseguramos que tomaremos las medidas pertinentes para que incidentes de esta naturaleza no tengan lugar en un futuro.

to take measures
With reference to your claim dated February 15, 1995, we regret any annoyance caused, and we assure you that we will take all necessary measures to insure that incidents of this kind will not happen again in the future.

|  |  |
|---------|---------|
| la **molestia** | annoyance; disturbance |
| el **incidente** | incident |
| la **índole** | type; kind |
| la **naturaleza** | nature |
| **tener lugar** | to take place |
| el **daño** | damage; harm |
| La falta de hermeticidad del contenedor ha ocasionado daños irreparables en la mercancía, dejándola totalmente inservible. | The fact that the container was not properly sealed resulted in irreparable damage to the merchandise, rendering it entirely useless. |
| la **hermeticidad** | impermeability; seal |
| **irreparable** | irreparable |
| **inservible** | useless |
| **dañado (a)** | damaged |
| el **desperfecto** | defect; damage |
| De las 24 piezas de porcelana suministradas por Uds., 11 han llegado a nuestras manos bastante deterioradas y 5 tienen graves desperfectos. | Of the 24 porcelain pieces supplied by you, 11 arrived in our hands in a quite battered state and 5 of them have serious defects. |
| **deteriorado (a)** | damaged; faulty |
| **llegar a nuestras manos** | to reach us; arrive in our hands |
| el **desperfecto de fabricación** | factory defect |
| el **malestar** | displeasure |
| No tengo más remedio que expresarles mi malestar. | I have nothing more to say except to express my displeasure to you. |
| **cuantioso (a)** | abundant; considerable |
| **por equivocación** | inadvertently; by mistake |
| Por equivocación le hemos enviado un lote de productos que no es el solicitado por Uds., rogamos nos lo devuelvan con cargo a nosotros. | By mistake, we sent you a merchandise item not ordered by you; please return it to us at our expense. |
| el **lote de productos** | merchandise item |
| **con cargo a nosotros** | at our expense; charged to us |
| el **servicio posventa** | customer service desk |
| Para cualquier queja sobre el producto adquirido o reparación en el plazo de garantía se encuentra a su disposición, de 9 a 18 horas ininterrumpidamente, el servicio posventa. | For any complaints about the product you have purchased from us, or for repairs within the warranty period, our customer service desk is open all day, with no break for lunch, from 9:00 A.M. to 6:00 P.M. |

| | |
|---|---|
| la **queja** | complaint |
| **ininterrumpidamente** | uninterruptedly |
| el **fallo de fabricación** | manufacturer's defect; defect in manufacture |
| Sentimos comunicarle que la entrega de su pedido se demorará unas semanas más de lo previsto debido a unas imperfecciones detectadas parcialmente atribuibles a un fallo de fabricación. | We're sorry to have to inform you that the filling of your order will take a few weeks more than planned because of imperfections we have discovered which are partially due to defects in manufacture. |
| **demorarse** | to be delayed |
| la **imperfección** | imperfection |
| **detectar** | to detect; discover |
| **atribuible a** | to be due to |
| **parcialmente** | partially |
| la **devolución** | return; exchange |
| Sin el ticket de compra no se podrán admitir devoluciones de artículos. | Without the sales slip we cannot accept any articles for return or exchange. |
| **admitir** | to permit; accept |
| el **vale** | certificate |
| En cualquier caso, no se reembolsará el dinero, sino que se extenderá un vale por el importe de la compra. | In no case will we refund the money in cash; instead we'll make out a certificate for the amount of the purchase. |

## Collections

| | |
|---|---|
| **a más tardar** | at the latest |
| Que se hayan demorado en los pagos debido a la ausencia por enfermedad de su contable, no es justificación. Así que, a más tardar, el martes esperamos nos hayan transferido los importes pendientes. | Your accountant's absence due to illness is not a valid reason for your falling behind in payments. We will expect you to remit the outstanding amounts to us by next Tuesday at the latest. |
| la **ausencia** | absence |
| la **justificación** | justification |
| **transferir** | to transmit; remit |

| | |
|---|---|
| el **importe** | amount; sum |
| **pendiente** | outstanding; due |
| las **obligaciones de pago,** los **compromisos de pago** | payment obligations |
| Desgraciadamente, nos veremos obligados a romper nuestras relaciones comerciales si Uds. siguen incumpliendo sistemáticamente sus obligaciones de pago con nuestra empresa. | Unfortunately, we shall be compelled to sever our business connections with you if you persist in systematically failing to meet your payment obligations to our company. |
| **romper relaciones comerciales** | to break/sever business relations/connections |
| la **ruptura** | break |
| **incumplir las obligaciones de pago** | to fail to meet payment obligations |
| **sistemáticamente** | systematically |
| **pendiente de pago** | outstanding; in arrears; due |
| Le concedemos un último plazo adicional de 15 días para saldar las cuentas aún pendientes de pago. | We will grant you a final grace period to settle the bills still in arrears. |
| el **departamento jurídico** | legal department |
| De lo contrario, deberá intervenir nuestro departamento jurídico. | Otherwise, we shall have to refer the matter to our legal department. |
| el **retraso en el pago** | payment delay |
| Su retraso en el pago representa una infracción de las condiciones del contrato. | Your delay in payment constitutes a violation of the conditions of the contract. |
| el **recordatorio de pago** | payment reminder; dunning letter |
| **a condición de** | with the condition; on condition that |
| Debido a las malas experiencias anteriores, de ahora en adelante sólo atenderemos sus pedidos a condición de que el pago se haga por adelantado. | Because of prior past experiences, from now on we will fill your orders only on condition that payment be made in advance. |
| **de ahora en adelante** | from now on |
| **atenerse a** | to face |
| Siendo éste el tercer recordatorio de pago que le enviamos, rogamos por última vez cumplan con sus condiciones de pago o se atengan a las consecuencias. | Since this is the third payment reminder we've sent you, we politely ask you for the last time to meet your obligation to pay or to be prepared to accept the consequences. |

**por vía judicial**
Hace ya meses que esperamos el pago de su deuda con nosotros, así que, en vista de lo cual, no nos queda más remedio que recurrir al cobro de la deuda por vía judicial.

by legal means; in the courts
For months we've been waiting for you to pay your debt to us; in consequence thereof, we have no other recourse but to seek collection of the debt in the courts.

**en vista de lo cual**

in consequence thereof

**el requerimiento de pago**
Aún, no sólo no hemos recibido contestación a nuestros repetidos requerimientos de pago, sino que, obviamente, Ud. rehusa el pago de su deuda.

demand for payment
Not only have we failed to receive any reply to our repeated demands for payment, but, furthermore, you obviously refuse to pay what you owe.

**obviamente**

obviously

**rehusar**

to refuse

## Office Equipment

**el despacho**
En su amplio y luminoso despacho tiene muchísimas plantas que, al tiempo que decoran, le dan una nota de color.

office
In his large and airy office he keeps a great many plants that make the office decorative and lend it color.

**luminoso (a)**
luminous; light; airy; bright

**decorar**
to decorate

la **nota de color**
a touch of color

la **mesa de escritorio**
Toda secretaria tiene en su mesa de escritorio un bloc de notas para hacer pequeñas anotaciones.

writing desk
Every secretary has on her desk a writing pad for making small notes.

el **bloc de notas**
note pad; writing pad

la **anotación**
note

el **vade**
blotter

el **clip**
Antes de hacer las fotocopias, no olvide retirar los clips de los originales.

paper clip
Before making the photocopies, don't forget to remove the paper clips from the originals.

la **fotocopia**
photocopy

la **fotocopiadora**
copying machine; photocopier

el **original**
original

la **ampliación**
Con esta fotocopiadora se pueden hacer ampliaciones de DIN A4 a A3 y también fotocopiar en ambas caras.

enlargement
With this copying machine you can make enlargements from DIN A4 to A3 and also photo-copy bothsides.

**en ambas caras**
on both sides

**fotocopiar**
to photocopy

la **reducción**
reduction

el **documento**
Los documentos que deben ser firmados por el jefe se introducen en carpetas que luego se dejan sobre su mesa para que él los firme.

document
The documents to be signed by the boss are placed into folders which are then left on his desk for his signature.

la **carpeta**

folder; portfolio

el **archivador**

file folder

Todos los documentos y facturas que entran en la oficina se guardan en archivadores que normalmente suelen tener varios separadores.

All bills and documents that arrive in the office are kept in file folders which usually have various separators.

el **separador**

separator; separating pages

la **funda de plástico**

plastic wrap

No tires las fundas de plástico, son muy útiles para archivar las transparencias.

Don't throw away the plastic wraps, they're very useful for filing the transparencies (films/slides).

**tirar**

to throw away/out

el **archivo**

file room; file storage area

En su oficina hay una habitación que se usa como archivo donde se almacenan los originales de los documentos durante años.

In his office there's a room that's used as a file room where the originals of documents are stored for years.

el **cesto de los papeles**

waste paper basket

la **papelera**

waste basket

Todas las tardes, la señora de la limpieza se encarga de vaciar las papeleras de los despachos.

Every afternoon, the cleaning lady undertakes the task of emptying the office waste baskets.

la **señora de la limpieza**

cleaning lady

la **grapadora**

stapler

Se equivocaron y compraron unas grapas demasiado pequeñas para la grapadora.

They made a mistake and bought staples too small for the stapler.

la **grapa**

staple

la **taladradora**

file hole puncher

Estoy harto de taladrar cientos de hojas con una taladradora manual, ¿por qué no lo encargamos a una imprenta?

I'm fed up with punching holes in hundreds of sheets with a manual puncher; why don't we get a printing shop to do that?

**taladrar**

to punch file holes

la **imprenta**

printer; printing shop

el **fichero**

file; filing cabinet; filing lists

En el armario de la derecha hay un fichero con todas las direcciones y datos fiscales de los proveedores.

In the cabinet on the right there's a file with all the addresses and financial information on the suppliers.

la **máquina calculadora**

calculating machine

la **calculadora**

calculator

Hoy en día, la calculadora se ha convertido en un instrumento imprescindible en cualquier oficina.

Nowadays the calculator has become an indispensable instrument in every office.

la **calculadora de bolsillo**

pocket calculator

el **sello**
Al pie de todas las facturas emitidas por la empresa figura su sello y la firma de la persona responsable.

stamp; seal
At the foot of all bills sent out by the firm you'll find its seal and the signature of the person responsible.

el **tampón**

stamp pad; ink pad

**emitir**

to send out

el **tablón de anuncios**
En el tablón de anuncios se ponen comunicados importantes de la empresa a sus trabajadores.

bulletin board
The company posts important notices to its employees on the bulletin board.

el **abrecartas**
Uno de los regalos de empresa más frecuentes son abrecartas y pisapapeles.

letter opener
Letter openers and paperweights are frequent presents given by the company.

el **pisapapeles**, el **sujetapapeles**

paperweight

la **balanza para cartas**
Cuando las cartas pesan más de lo normal es muy útil tener a mano una balanza de cartas para saber el franqueo que les corresponde.

scale for weighing letters
When letters are overweight it's very useful to have a scale for weighing letters on hand to ascertain the postage they'll take.

**tener a mano**

to have on hand

la **centralita telefónica**
Una centralita telefónica suele tener varias líneas, allí se reciben todas las llamadas que luego serán pasadas a sus destinatarios.

telephone switchboard
A telephone switchboard usually has several lines on which all calls are received and are then transmitted to the persons for whom they are intended.

la **máquina de escribir automática**
Las máquinas de escribir automáticas ofrecen la ventaja de tener un visor.

electronic typewriter

Electronic typewriters have the advantage of a screen.

el **fallo**

mistake; error

el **visor**
El visor permite ver lo que se está escribiendo y corregir los posibles fallos antes de que se escriba definitivamente sobre el papel.

visor; screen; monitor
The screen permits one to look at what is being written and to correct any errors before final printout on paper.

**definitivamente**

definitely; finally

la **cinta mecanográfica**
Aunque tenía varias cintas mecanográficas, ninguna era la apropiada para el modelo de su máquina de escribir.

color ribbon
Although she had various color ribbons on hand, none was suitable for her typewriter model.

**apropiado (a)**

suitable; appropriate

la **cinta correctora**

correcting ribbon

el **dictáfono**
Su jefe dejó grabado el protocolo en el dictáfono y ella sólo tuvo que ir escribiéndolo a medida que oía la grabación.

dictaphone
Her boss left the minutes on the dictaphone for her and she could only keep typing as long as she heard the recording.

**a medida que**

at the same time as; as long as

la **máquina destructora de documentos**
La directora tiene en su despacho una pequeña máquina destructora de documentos para deshacerse de informes estrictamente confidenciales.

paper/document shredder

In her office the director has a document shredder for the disposing of strictly confidential reports.

**deshacerse de u/c**

to get rid of/dispose of something

la **sala de juntas**
La sala de juntas ha sido recientemente equipada con un proyector de transparencias, un vídeo y una pantalla de proyección de gran tamaño.

meeting room; conference room
The conference room has recently been equipped with a film projector, a video camera, and a large projection screen.

**equipar**

to equip

el **proyector de transparencias,** el **retroproyector**

slide/film projector

la **transparencia**

slide; film; transparency

la **pantalla de proyección**

projection screen

la **secretaría**

secretary's office; department office

El horario de secretaría es, de lunes a jueves, de 9 a 6. Los viernes de 9 a 3.

Office hours are Monday through Thursday from 9:00 to 6:00. Fridays from 9:00 to 3:00.

el **horario**

business hours; office hours

el **fax**
¡Para agilizar las gestiones, mándeme el presupuesto por fax lo antes posible!

fax
To speed up processing, fax me the cost estimate as soon as possible.

| | |
|---|---|
| **agilizar** | to accelerate; speed up |
| la **gestión** | dealing with; processing |
| **mandar un fax** | to send a fax; fax |
| el **interfono** | intercom |
| Para evitar desplazamientos innecesarios, hay un interfono que comunica el despacho de la directora con el de su secretario. | To avoid unnecessary moving around, the director's office is connected with her secretary's office by an intercom system. |

## Office Activities

**archivar**
Para facilitar el trabajo a la hora de buscar un documento, es necesario archivarlo correctamente y por orden alfabético.

to file
To make the task of finding a document easier, it's necessary to file it correctly and in alphabetical order.

**por orden alfabético**

in alphabetical order

**encargarse de**
La secretaria del jefe de dirección se encarga de concertar las citas con los clientes y proveedores.

to undertake a task; take charge of
The managing director's secretary takes charge of making appointments with customers and suppliers.

**concertar una cita, concertar una entrevista**

to coordinate/arrange for/make an appointment/interview

**anular una cita**

to cancel an appointment

**tomar nota**
Generalmente, en todas las juntas se suele tomar nota de los puntos más importantes para luego elaborar un protocolo.

to make/take note
Generally, at all meetings it is customary to take notes on the most important points which are later written up for the record.

el **protocolo**

minutes; record

**elaborar un informe, redactar un informe**
Haga el favor de redactar un informe de la propuesta y mándelo por duplicado al jefe de nuestra delegación en Bilbao.

make/draw up a report; write up a report
Would you please draw up a report on the proposal and send it in duplicate to the head of our Bilbao branch?

**hacer el favor de**

to be so kind as; please; do the favor of

la **delegación**

delegation; branch

**por duplicado**

in duplicate

**por triplicado**

in triplicate

la **propuesta**

proposal

**escribir a máquina**
Necesitamos una secretaria que no sólo sepa escribir a máquina, sino que lo haga, como mínimo, a una velocidad de 200 pulsaciones por minuto.

to type
We need a secretary who not only knows how to type but who is also capable of speed typing at the rate of 200 keystrokes per minute.

las **pulsaciones a máquina**

keystrokes

**equivocarse al escribir a máquina**

to make an error in typing; make a typo

**dictar una carta**
Su jefe le dicta unas cinco cartas al día como término medio.

to dictate a letter
On average, his/her boss dictates about five letters a day to her/him.

**como término medio**

on average

la **corrección**
Después de escribir la carta, siempre conviene releerla para hacer las oportunas correciones estilísticas y ortográficas.

correction
After typing the letter, it's always good to reread it to make any necessary corrections in style and spelling.

**releer**

to reread

**estilístico (a)**

stylistic

**ortográfico (a)**

spelling; orthographic

el **líquido corrector**
Si es por una palabra, tápelo con un poco de líquido corrector y así no tiene que volver a repetir la carta.

correction fluid
If it's for just a word, apply a little correction fluid and you won't have to retype the whole letter.

la **caja menor**
En la oficina existe una caja menor de donde sale el dinero para los pequeños gastos cotidianos.

petty cash box
There's a petty cash box in the office which provides the money for small everyday expenses.

**cotidiano (a)**

daily

el **horario de oficina**
En la puerta de la entrada hay un cartel con la siguiente inscripción: "¡No se atenderán pedidos fuera del horario de oficina!"

office/business hours
There's a sign at the front door that says: "Orders not accepted outside of business hours!"

el **anexo**
En el anexo le adjuntamos la lista de precios de nuestros productos para el nuevo año.

enclosure
In the enclosure you will find a price list of our products for the new year.

la **circular**
En la circular repartida entre los trabajadores figuran los nuevos cambios en la junta directiva.

circular; memo
In the memo sent to employees there is information about the new changes in the board of directors.

el **expediente**
La empresa tiene un expediente de cada trabajador donde figuran, entre otros, sus datos personales, estudios y desarrollo profesional en dicha empresa.

file; dossier
The firm has a file on every worker containing, among other things, her/his personal data, education, and professional development in the firm.

**realizar gestiones**

Por favor realice las gestiones necesarias para organizar nuestra participación en la feria anual.

to take steps/measures; institute proceedings
Please take the necessary steps to organize our participation in the annual trade fair.

**redactar una carta**
Redactar una carta de manera clara y concisa es más difícil de lo que puede parecer a primera vista.

to write/frame/compose a letter
To compose a clear and concise letter is more difficult than it might seem at first sight.

**a primera vista**

at first sight

**conciso (a)**

concise

**recriminar**

Después de su reiterada falta de puntualidad, su jefe se vió obligado a recriminarle por ello.

to reproach; make recriminations; warn
After his repeated failure to be punctual, his boss felt it necessary to warn him about that.

**reiterado (a)**

repeated

la **puntualidad**

punctuality

**verse obligado (a)**

to feel obliged to; feel it necessary to

**hacer caso omiso**

Hicieron caso omiso de sus instrucciones y no le mantuvieron al corriente de la evolución de las negociaciones.

to fail to observe; not bother with; ignore
They ignored his instructions and didn't keep him informed about the progress of negotiations.

**mantener al corriente de**

to keep informed about

**hacerse esperar**
Aunque la secretaria le había citado a las 12 en punto, aún le hicieron esperar casi 15 minutos.

to keep waiting
Although the secretary had told him to be there at 12 o'clock sharp, they still kept him waiting for almost 15 minutes.

la **taquigrafía**
En España, la taquigrafía ha caído totalmente en desuso.

stenography
In Spain, stenography is no longer used at all.

**caer en desuso**

to stop being used; come into disuse

el **registro de entrada**
Todas las cartas que llegan a la oficina son marcadas con el registro de entrada, donde figura fecha y hora de recepción.

record of receipt
All letters that arrive in the office are marked with a record of receipt which includes the date and the time received.

el **registro de salida**

record of mailing; mailing docket

la **copia en papel carbón**
Con el empleo generalizado de ordenadores y fotocopiadoras en las oficinas, ya apenas se emplean copias en papel carbón.

carbon copy
With the widespread use of computers and photocopiers in offices, carbon paper is hardly used any more.

**generalizado (a)**

general; widespread

el **orden del día**
Se han retirado algunos puntos del orden del día para poder incluir otros aspectos que urge discutir.

agenda
Some points have been withdrawn from the agenda so that more urgent matters for discussion could be included.

el **punto del orden del día**

agenda point

**incluir en el orden del día**

to include in the agenda; put on the agenda

**retirar del orden del día**

withdraw from the agenda

**levantar acta, dejar constancia**

to take the minutes; keep a written record

el **empleado encargado de llevar la correspondencia en lengua extranjera,** la **empleada encargada de llevar la correspondencia en lengua extranjera**
Unicamente las grandes empresas tienen empleados encargados de llevar la correspondencia en lenguas extranjeras, en las más pequeñas lo hacen las secretarias con idiomas.

employee in charge of conducting foreign language correspondence


Only major firms employ foreign language correspondence coordinators. In smaller companies, foreign language secretaries perform this task.

| | |
|---|---|
| el **secretario con idiomas,** la **secretaria con idiomas** | foreign language secretary |
| **estar reunido (a), estar en una reunión** | to be in a meeting; be in conference |
| Lo siento, en estos momentos el Sr. Mielgo no le puede atender porque está reunido. | I'm sorry but Mr. Mielgo can't see you now because he's tied up in a meeting. |
| **atender** | to receive; see |
| **atender una llamada** | to take a telephone call |

# ■■■■■■ Electronic Data Processing ■■■■■■

| | |
|---|---|
| la **elaboración electrónica de datos** | electronic data processing |
| La elaboración electrónica de datos ha revolucionado la ofimática de manera inimaginable hasta hace sólo unos pocos años. | Electronic data processing has revolutionized office technology in ways that were inconceivable until just a few years ago. |
| **revolucionar** | to revolutionize |
| **inimaginable** | unimaginable; inconceivable |
| la **ofimática** | office technology; communications technology in the office |
| el **ordenador** | computer |
| el **disco duro** | hard disc |
| ¿Qué necesito para iniciarme en la autoedición?—Le recomiendo un PowerPC con un disco duro de 1000 megas, una memoria de 32 megas de RAM y un monitor con una pantalla de 20 pulgadas. | What do I need to get started in desktop publishing?—I recommend a PowerPC with a 1000 MB hard disc, a 32 MB Ram main memory, and a monitor with a 20 inch screen. |
| **iniciarse** | to get started in |
| la **autoedición** | desktop publishing |
| el **mega(byte)** | megabyte |
| la **memoria** | (main) memory |
| el **monitor** | monitor |
| la **pantalla** | screen |

| | |
|---|---|
| la **pulgada** | inch |
| el **teclado** <br> Para introducir y elaborar datos, se puede usar tanto el teclado como el ratón. | keyboard <br> To feed and edit data either the keyboard or the mouse can be used. |
| **introducir datos** | to introduce; feed in; enter |
| **elaborar datos** | to edit |
| el **ratón** | mouse |
| la **tecla** | key |
| **teclear** | to type in; feed |
| **hacer clic** <br> Para hacer una copia de seguridad, mueva el cursor sobre la carpeta o el fichero, haga clic y arrástrelo sobre el icono del disquete. | to click <br> To make a backup copy, move the cursor to File or Data File, click and drag it to the disc icon. |
| la **copia de seguridad** | safety/backup copy |
| el **cursor** | cursor |
| la **carpeta** | file |
| el **fichero** | data file |
| **arrastrar sobre** | to drag to |
| el **icono** | icon |
| el **disquete** | disc |
| la **base de datos** <br> Estoy muy contento con mi base de datos, ya que guarda automáticamente todos los datos introducidos y así evita que se borren accidentalmente informaciones valiosas. | database/bank <br> I'm very happy with my database because it automatically saves all the data introduced and thus prevents accidentally erasing valuable data. |
| **guardar** | to keep; save |
| **borrar** | erase |
| **accidentalmente** | accidentally |
| **valioso (a)** | valuable |

el **paquete integrado**

integrated program package; integrated software package

Para su oficina, un paquete integrado es más que suficiente, contiene un programa de tratamiento de textos, uno de edición de imágenes, un programa de gráficas y una hoja de cálculo.

For your office, an integrated software package is more than adequate; it contains a word processing program, an image processing program, a graphics program and a spreadsheet.

el **programa de tratamiento de textos**

word processing program

el **programa de edición de imágenes**

image processing program

el **programa de gráficas**

graphics program

la **hoja de cálculo**

electronic spreadsheet

el **medio de almacenaje**

storage medium

Para llevar los ficheros al taller de filmación y también como medio de almacenaje de las aplicaciones multimedia, hemos comprado un lector magneto-óptico para cartuchos de 230 megas.

For taking the data files to the photo exposure service and also as a storage medium for our multimedia applications, we have purchased a magnetic-visual drive for 230-MB cassettes.

el **taller de filmación**

photo exposure service

la **aplicación multimedia**

multi-media application

el **lector magneto-óptico**

magnetic-visual drive

el **cartucho**

cartridge; cassette

**almacenar**

to store; warehouse

el **sistema operativo**

operating system

Nos hemos decantado por este sistema operativo, porque ya trae incorporada la capacidad de trabajar en red, la tarjeta de sonido y la de video.

We finally decided on this operating system because it has a built in networking capacity, and sound and video cards.

la **capacidad de trabajar en red**

networking capacity

la **red**

network

la **tarjeta**

card

la **impresora**

printer

Después de conectar la impresora a la red, fue necesario una ampliación de RAM para que el servidor no se quedara colgado cada dos por tres.

After connecting the printer to the network, a RAM upgrade was necessary so that the server wouldn't keep getting stuck every few minutes.

| | |
|---|---|
| **conectar** | to connect |
| la **ampliación de RAM** | RAM upgrading |
| el **servidor** | server; user |
| **quedarse colgado (a)** | to get stuck |
| **cada dos por tres** | every five/few minutes |
| **imprimir** | to print |
| la **impresión** | print out |
| el **ordenador portátil**<br>Con mi ordenador portátil, un módem y un programa de correo electrónico, trabajo independientemente y, no obstante, puedo contactar con la oficina en cualquier momento. | portable/laptop computer<br>With my portable computer, a modem and an E-mail program, I work on my own, but I can still get in touch with the office anytime. |
| el **módem** | modem |
| el **programa de correo electrónico** | E-mail program |
| **contactar** | to contact; get in touch with |
| la **protección de datos**<br>Aunque es molesto introducir cada vez la clave de acceso, la protección de datos para mí es primordial. | data protection<br>Although it's a nuisance to have to insert the password every time, data protection is all-important to me. |
| **molesto (a)** | annoying |
| la **clave de acceso** | password |
| **primordial** | all-important |

## ■■ Form and Construction of a Business Letter ■■

la **correspondencia**
Han contratado una nueva secretaria que se encargará de llevar toda la correspondencia diaria y la correspondencia comercial con los países de habla española.

correspondence
They have hired a new secretary who will take care of all daily correspondence and commercial correspondence with Spanish-speaking countries.

la **correspondencia comercial**
commercial correspondence

**llevar la correspondencia**
take care of correspondence

los **países de habla español**
Spanish-speaking countries

la **correspondencia de entrada**
first mail collection/pickup

la **correspondencia de salida**
last mail collection/pickup

la **carta comercial**
Una carta comercial se compone básicamente del encabezamiento, cuerpo con el contenido de la carta y la fórmula de cortesía.

commercial letter
Essentially, a commercial letter consists of a salutation, the body of the letter, and the complimentary close.

el **encabezamiento**
El encabezamiento lo constituyen el grupo de palabras o fórmulas con que se empieza una carta, como por ejemplo: estimados sres., etc.

salutation
The salutation includes those words or standard formulas with which one begins a letter, such as, e.g. Dear Sirs:, etc.

**Estimados Señores (Sres.)**
Dear Sirs:

**Muy Señor mío, Muy Señor nuestro**
Dear Sir:

**Estimado Sr. X, Estimada Sra. X**
Dear Mr. X; Dear Mrs./Ms. X

la **fórmula de cortesía**
politeness formula; complimentary close

el **papel de carta**
Todo el papel de carta con membrete está en el tercer cajón del escritorio.

letter stationery
All the letterhead stationery is in the third desk drawer.

el **sobre con ventana**

La ventaja de un sobre con ventana es que no hay que escribir de nuevo en el sobre la dirección del destinatario.

envelope with window; window envelope
The window envelope has the advantage of making it unnessary to rewrite the address of the person for whom the letter is intended.

el **destinatario,** la **destinataria** — addressee; person for whom a letter is intended

el, la **remitente** — sender

la **referencia** — reference; file notice

En las cartas comerciales, la referencia se escribe debajo de la fecha y consta de las iniciales de la persona que dicta la carta y de la que la mecanografía, separadas por una barra o guión. — In commercial letters the reference is written beneath the date and consists of the initial of the person who dictated the letter and of the person who typed it, separated by a slant or a dash.

**n/ref. (nuestra referencia)** — our reference

**s/ref. (su referencia)** — your reference

la **inicial** — initial

**mecanografiar** — to type

la **barra** — dash

el **guión** — hyphen

el **asunto** — matter; re; in re; reference

El asunto se escribe antes del contenido de la carta y describe, en pocas palabras, el tema que se trata en la misma. — "Re" is written before the body of the letter and summarizes briefly what the letter is in reference to.

**a la atención de** — attention

Se escribe a la atención del Sr./Sra. X, cuando la carta va dirigida a una persona en concreto de la empresa. — One writes "Attention: Mr./Ms. X" when the letter is directed to a specific person in the firm.

**confidencial** — confidential

El director de la empresa en Sevilla ha recibido una carta estrictamente confidencial de la casa central en Madrid. — The managing director in Seville has received a strictly confidential letter from company headquarters in Madrid.

**muy atentamente** — very sincerely/truly yours

"Sin más por el momento, se despide muy atentamente" es una fórmula de despedida muy empleada en la correspondencia comercial. — "With nothing more to add for the moment I remain yours sincerely" is a frequently used complimentary close in commercial correspondence.

**un cordial saludo** — cordially

Escribir al final de una carta comercial "reciba un cordial saludo" supone un nivel estilístico menos formal. — Writing "cordially" at the end of a business letter indicates a less formal style.

el **nivel estilístico** — level of style

| | |
|---|---|
| **formal** | formal |
| el **anexo** | enclosure |

**el registro de entrada**
A todas las cartas que llegan a la empresa se les pone un sello de registro de entrada que indica la fecha en que han sido recibidas.

receipt docket
All incoming letters to the company are docketed to indicate the date received.

**el registro de salida** — record of mailing

**el sello de registro de salida** — mailing docket

**el membrete**
En el membrete de una carta comercial figuran normalmente impreso, entre otros el nombre y logotipo de la empresa, número de identificación fiscal, dirección, teléfono y fax.

letterhead
A company's letterhead, usually printed, shows the firm name and logo, tax identification number, address, and telephone and fax numbers.

la **fórmula de despedida** — complimentary close

**el formato de una carta**
Todas las cartas redactadas en la empresa deben responder a un formato homogéneo ya prefijado que determina los márgenes, el interlineado a un espacio o a doble espacio, etc.

format of the letter
All letters sent by a company should be standardized by corresponding to a set format that has established margins, single or double spacing, etc.

| | |
|---|---|
| **homogéneo (a)** | homogenous; standard |
| **prefijar** | to preset |
| el **margen** | margin |
| el **interlineado** | spacing |
| **a un espacio** | single spaced |
| **a doble espacio** | double spaced |
| la **antefirma** | title; designation of position (put before the signature) |

La antefirma es el sello de la empresa que se pone exclusivamente junto a una firma al pie de una carta cuando el remitente es una persona jurídica.

The designation of office is the firm seal which is placed next to a signature at the foot of a letter only when the sender is a juristic person.

**por poder (p.p.)**

by power of attorney; by authority granted; by procuration; (p.o.a.)

Cuando la persona que firma una carta tiene poderes otorgados por la empresa para tal fin, se pondrán las iniciales p.p. debajo del nombre de la razón social y delante de la firma en sí.

When the person who signs a letter has authority granted by the company for that purpose, the initials p.o.a. are placed below the firm name and before the signature itself.

**por orden (p.o.)**
Si la persona que firma una carta tan sólo tiene orden de firmar, entonces se escribirán las iniciales p.o. debajo del nombre de la razón social y delante de la firma.

signed for by; on behalf of
If the person who signs a letter written in Spanish is authorized only to sign it, then the initials p.o. are written under the firm name and in front of the signature.

la **postdata (P.D.)**

postscript

el **post scriptum (P.S.)**
La posdata o post scriptum es una nota a pie de página que se escribe siempre detrás de la firma.

postscriptum
The postscript is a footnote which always appears after the signature.

la **nota a pie de página**

footnote

## Formulas and Phrases

**adjuntar**
Según lo convenido, le adjuntamos nuestra nueva lista de precios vigentes a partir de marzo y hasta finales de junio.

to enclose
As promised, we are enclosing our new list with prices valid from March to the end of June.

**según lo convenido**

as agreed upon/promised

**vigente**

valid

**a partir de**

from; beginning

**(a) finales de**

till the end of

**(a) principios de**

at the beginning of

**(a) mediados de**

in the middle of

**adjunto**
Adjunto le enviamos nuestro prospecto, donde encontrará información más detallada sobre nuestro programa de producción.

enclosed
Enclosed we're sending you our prospectus in which you will find more detailed information on our production program.

**a vuelta de correo**
A vuelta de correo le enviaremos nuestra oferta para los artículos solicitados por Ustedes.

by return of mail
By return of mail we will send you our offer for the articles you asked for.

**por correo aparte**
Por correo aparte les remitimos algunas muestras de nuestros diferentes modelos y acabados.

under separate cover
Under separate cover we're sending you some samples of our different models and finishes.

**a la mayor brevedad posible**
Teniendo en cuenta que nuestra oferta sólo es válida hasta finales del mes corriente, les rogamos ordenen su pedido a la mayor brevedad posible.

as soon as possible
Bearing in mind that our offer is valid only until the end of the current month, we ask you to please place your order as soon as possible.

**para mayor brevedad**

for the sake of brevity

**tener en cuenta**

to bear in mind

el **mes corriente**

current month

**ordenar un pedido**

to place an order

**en tales circunstancias**
En tales circunstancias, lamentamos tener que retirar nuestra oferta como consecuencia de la demora de su pedido.

in such circumstances
In such circumstances, we regret that we must withdraw our offer because your order arrived too late.

**en respuesta a**
En respuesta a su solicitud de información le enviamos en el anexo nuestras tarifas actuales, así como las condiciones de entrega y pago.

in reply to
In reply to your request for information we are sending you in the enclosure a list of our currently valid prices, as well as terms of delivery and payment.

**hasta la fecha**

up to now/the present date; as of now

Lamentamos comunicarles que hasta la fecha no se ha producido el pago de las tres últimas facturas que aún tienen pendientes con nosotros. Por eso, rogamos se pongan en contacto con nuestro departamento financiero lo antes posible.

We must regretfully inform you that as of now you are in arrears for the three outstanding bills you still have not paid us. Therefore, we ask you to please get in touch with our accounting deparment as soon as possible.

**ponerse en contacto con**

to get in touch with; contact

**lo antes posible**

as soon as possible

**tener pendiente**

to be outstanding/payable/unpaid

**en espera de**
En espera de sus noticias, aprovechamos la ocasión para saludarles muy atentamente.

in expectation of
Waiting to hear from you, we take advantage of this occasion to send you our best regards.

**aprovechar la ocasión**

to take the opportunity to

**complacerse**
De acuerdo con nuestra conversación telefónica, nos complace comunicarle que su solicitud ha sido aceptada por nuestra dirección.

to be pleased; take the liberty of
In confirmation of our telephone conversation, we are pleased to inform you that your request has been granted by our management.

**de acuerdo con** | in accord with

**estimar oportuno (a)**
La dirección de la empresa ha estimado oportuno reconsiderar su oferta, por lo que en breve recibirá noticias nuestras.

to consider opportune/suitable
The firm's management has thought it opportune to reconsider your offer which means that you will be hearing from us shortly.

**en breve** | shortly

**reconsiderar** | to reconsider

**con el objeto de**
Con el objeto de agilizar nuestras relaciones comerciales, nos complace comunicarle nuestro nuevo servicio telefónico que le atenderá las 24 horas del día.

for the purpose of
For the purpose of making our business relations easier, we are pleased to tell you about our new telephone service which will receive your calls 24 hours a day.

la **contestación**
Después de haber transcurrido un mes sin recibir contestación a nuestro escrito de fecha 12 de febrero de 1995, deducimos que nuestra oferta no ha sido de su interés.

reply
Since a month has passed and we have received no reply to our letter of February 12, 1995, we must conclude that our offer does not interest you.

**transcurrir** | to pass

el **escrito** | letter; document

**ser de interés** | to be of interest

**sírvanse enviar**
Sírvanse enviarnos a la mayor brevedad posible su nuevo catálogo y lista de precios para la próxima temporada.

please send
Please send us as soon as possible, your new catalogue and price list for the coming season.

**mencionar**
Tal y como le mencionamos en nuestra última carta, la documentación que Usted solicita de nosotros no obra ya en nuestro poder, por lo que rogamos aclaren internamente este supuesto malentendido.

to mention
As we already mentioned in our last letter, the documentation you ask for from us is no longer in our possession, therefore we ask you to please clear up this supposed misunderstanding within the firm.

**tal y como** | as already

**aclarar un malentendido** | to clear up a misunderstanding

**obrar en poder de** | to be in possession of

**supuesto (a)**

supposed

**salvo aviso en contrario**

Salvo aviso en contrario, su pedido
será entregado el jueves a última hora
de la tarde.

save an order to the contrary;
unless otherwise notified
Unless you are otherwise notified,
your order will be delivered late
Thursday afternoon.

**a última hora**

just before close of business; late;
last minute

**a petición de**
A petición de nuestro representante,
el mencionado contrato se modificará
en los puntos 2 y 10, de lo que se
desprende que el tipo de comisión se
verá incrementado entre un 2 y un
5%, lamentando los trastornos que
esto le haya podido ocasionar.

at the request of
At the request of our agent the
contract mentioned will be
changed in points 2 and 10, which
means that the commission will
increase between 2 and 5%; we
regret any inconvenience this may
have caused you.

**desprenderse de**

to gather/gain from; result in

**ocasionar trastornos**

to cause inconvenience

**encarecidamente**

Rogamos encarecidamente liquiden
la cuenta que tienen con nosotros
antes de final de mes.

urgently; intensely; insistently;
earnestly
We urge you earnestly to pay
the delinquent account you have
with us before the end of the
month.

**llamar la atención**
Permítanos llamar su atención sobre la
necesidad de saldar todas sus cuentas
con nosotros antes de poder atender
su nuevo pedido.

to call attention to
Allow us to call your attention to
the necessity of your settling all
your accounts with us before we
can accept your new order.

**pertinente**
Con el objeto de agilizar nuestro
envío, recomendamos solucionan
todos los trámites con las autoridades
pertinentes ya que se trata de un
asunto de máxima prioridad.

pertinent
In order to speed up our shipment,
we recommend that you take care
of any formalities with the pertinent
authorities, since it is a top priority
matter.

**de máxima prioridad**

top priority

| **pormenorizar** | go into detail; give a detailed account/breakdown |
|---|---|

**pormenorizado (a)**

En el anexo le enviamos un informe pormenorizado de todas nuestras actividades comerciales en América Central desde el pasado año.

broken down in detail
In the enclosure we're sending you a detailed breakdown of all our business activities in Central America since last year.

| **Most Common Address Abbreviations** | | | |
|---|---|---|---|
| C/ | calle | Ctra. oder crta. | carretera |
| Av. (Avda.) | avenida | entlo. | entresuelo |
| P° | paseo | izq. | izquierda |
| Pza. | plaza | dcha. | derecha |
| Pje. | pasaje | n° | número |

*Sample address:*

Sr. D. Antonio Gómez Mendoza
Director de Ventas
VECA S.A.
C/Doctor Esquerdo, n° 20, 3° dcha.
28028 Madrid

━━━━━━━━━━ **Mail** ━━━━━━━━━━

el **correo**
No me envie la documentación por
correo, la necesito hoy mismo, así
que mándemela por fax.

mail
Don't send me the papers by mail;
I need them today, therefore send
them to me by fax.

los **Correos y Telégrafos**

Correos y Telégrafos sufre hoy la
competencia de empresas privadas
de distribución domiciliaria y de
empresas de mensajería y paquetería.

Post and Telegraph Office
(corresponds to the US Postal
Service)
The Spanish postal system is
today suffering from competition
from private companies that make
home deliveries and from messenger and parcel delivery services.

**domiciliario (a)**

home; residence

la **empresa de mensajería y
paquetería**

messenger and package delivery
company

la **oficina de Correos**
Para mandar un paquete no hace falta
dirigirse a la central, puede hacerlo
desde cualquier oficina de Correos.

post office
To send a package you don't have
to go to the main post office; you
can do it in any post office.

el **apartado de Correos**
Como a mi casa no llega el correo
porque vivo en el campo, tengo un
apartado de Correos en el pueblo
más próximo.

post office box
Because there are no mail deliveries
to my house in the country, I have
a post office box in the nearest
town.

el **código postal**
Para facilitar la labor de clasificación
y distribución, escriba siempre el
código postal junto al nombre del
municipio.

zip code
To make sorting and delivery
easier, always write the zip code
along with the town.

el **municipio**

municipality; place; town

el **correo ordinario**
Las cartas entre particulares se suelen
mandar por correo ordinario.

ordinary mail
Letters between private parties are
usually sent by ordinary mail.

el **correo urgente**
En el correo urgente todo el trabajo
tiene que salir a diario.

express mail; special delivery
Mail must be dispatched daily for
express mail.

el **servicio postal express**
Correos se ha fijado como objetivo
un incremento mínimo del 50%
anual en el servicio postal express a
nivel nacional.

express mail delivery
The Spanish postal system has set
a minimum goal of 50% annual
increase of domestic express mail
deliveries.

**fijarse como objetivo**

to set a goal; plan

**por correo certificado**
Para poder demostrar que se ha
realizado el envío, lo mejor es
hacerlo por correo certificado.

by certified/registered mail
To prove that you sent it, the best
thing is to send it by certified mail.

**contra reembolso**

COD

**por avión**
No olvides poner en el sobre "por
avión" si es que quieres que la carta
le llegue pronto a tu amiga en Nueva
Zelanda.

by air mail
Don't forget to put "by air mail"
on the envelope if you want your
girl friend in New Zealand to get
the letter promptly.

**lista de correos**

general delivery

el **franqueo**
Ya hay incluso empresas que se
dedican a recoger el correo de otras
empresas para su franqueo y posterior
entrega en las oficinas de Correos.

postage
There already exist firms specialized
in collecting and putting postage
on other companies' mail, and
then taking it to the post office for
mailing.

**franquear**

to put postage on

los **gastos de franqueo,** la **tarifa
postal**
Los gastos de franqueo para cartas
son diferentes según se trate de
sobres normalizados o no.

postage expenses

Postage costs vary depending on
whether the envelope is normal
size or not.

el **sobre normalizado**
El sobre normalizado es aquel que se
ajusta a unas medidas estándars homo-
logadas por Correos y Telégrafos.

standard/normal size envelope
The standard size envelope conforms
to the norms approved by the
Spanish postal service.

**homologado (a)**

approved; set

el **paquete postal**

postal package; parcel post

el **matasellos**
En el matasellos figura siempre la
fecha y el lugar desde donde se ha
realizado el envío.

postal cancellation
The postal cancellation always
shows the date and place of the
mailing.

|  |  |
|---|---|
| el **envío** | shipment; mailing |
| el **estándar** | standard |
| la **carta certificada** | certified/registered letter |
| Las cartas certificadas tienen la ventaja de que las posibilidades de que se extravíen son prácticamente nulas. Para certificar una carta hay que rellenar un impreso. | Registered letters have the advantage that the chances of their getting lost are practically non-existent. To register a letter it is necessary to fill out a form. |
| el **impreso para certificar** | form for registered mail |
| **extraviarse** | to get lost |
| **nulo (a)** | nil; non-existent |
| el **envío con valor declarado** | insured mail; sending/mailing with a declared value |
| El envío con valor declarado se recomienda siempre que se trate de documentos u objetos de elevado valor. | Sending it with a declared value is always advisable for documents or objects of great value. |
| **elevado (a)** | elevated; great |
| el **impreso publicitario** | advertising printed matter; junk mail |
| Los mailings son un sistema muy extendido y por ello, un ciudadano medio recibe al año más impresos publicitarios que cartas de un particular. | Advertising mass mailings are very widespread, therefore the average person receives more advertising mail than letters from people. |
| el **ciudadano medio,** la **ciudadana media** | average citizen/person |
| **no doblar** | do not fold |
| Al enviar revistas por correo conviene poner en el sobre "no doblar". | When sending periodicals by mail it is advisable to put "Do not fold" on the envelope. |
| el **giro postal** | postal money order |
| No me envíes el dinero por giro postal sino por giro telegráfico que, aunque es más caro, me llega de un día para otro. | Instead of sending me the money by postal money order, have it telegraphed; even though it's more expensive I'll get it by the next day. |
| el **formulario para giro postal** | postal money order form |
| el **giro telegráfico** | telegraphic money order; sending money by telegraph |
| **de un día para otro** | by the next day |
| **abierto (a) para inspección postal** | may be opened for postal inspection |
| Hay sobres especiales donde figura "abierto para inspección postal" que ante todo se emplean para impresos comerciales ahorrándose, así, bastante dinero en el franqueo. | There are special envelopes printed "open for postal inspection" which are primarily used for commercial printed matter and which cut down considerably on postage costs. |

| | |
|---|---|
| el **impreso comercial** | commercial printed matter |
| el **motivo de la devolución**<br>Sr. Cartero, marque el motivo de la devolución:<br>[ ] ausente de su domicilio<br>[ ] rehusado<br>[ ] desconocido. | reason for non-delivery/return<br>Dear Mr./Ms. Mailcarrier please check the reason for non-delivery:<br>[ ] not at home<br>[ ] refused<br>[ ] unknown. |
| **marcar** | to mark; check; dial |
| **ausente** | not at home |
| **rehusado (a)** | refused |
| **reexpedir**<br>¡Reexpídase a manos del destinatario! | to forward<br>Please forward to the addressee! |
| la **clasificación** | sorting |
| la **distribución** | delivery |

# Telecommunication

el **abonado,** la **abonada**
Este abonado ha cambiado de número, por favor, marque el 003.

telephone subscriber/customer
This customer has changed his/her number; please dial 003.

el **servicio de información telefónica**

(telephone) information

Desde que me he enterado de que el servicio de información telefónica cobra ocho pasos, es decir, 52,48 pesetas para averiguar un número en España y el doble para uno en el extranjero, prefiero consultar la guía telefónica.

Ever since I found out that asking for information costs eight units, i.e. 52.48 pesetas for a number in Spain and double that for a foreign number, I prefer to look the number up in the telephone book myself.

el **paso**

unit

la **guía telefónica**

telephone book

las **páginas amarillas**

yellow pages

la **Telefónica**

Spanish National Telephone Company

Telefónica se ha comprometido a regalar el aparato de teléfono en caso de que tarde más de cuatro semanas en instalar la línea.

The telephone company has promised not to charge for the telephone if it doesn't connect it within four weeks.

**instalar la línea**

to install the line; connect the telephone

la **conexión**
¿Cuánto tiempo tarda en efectuar la conexión de la línea?

connection
How much time will it take for the line to be connected?

la **tarjeta telefónica**
La proliferación de las tarjetas telefónicas no sólo es una medida efectiva para prevenir robos en las cabinas, sino que también ofrece mayor comodidad al usuario a la hora de efectuar una llamada.

telephone card
The widespread use of telephone cards is not only an effective way of preventing telephone booths from being burgled, but it also provides more convenience to the user when making a call.

la **proliferación**

proliferation

la **cabina telefónica**

telephone booth

la **comodidad**

convenience

el **usuario,** la **usuaria**

user

**marcar el número**
Para hacer una llamada, descuelgue el auricular y marque el número.

to dial the number
To make a call, lift the receiver and dial the number.

**efectuar una llamada, hacer una llamada**

to make a call

la **conversación telefónica**
No es muy amante de las conversaciones telefónicas, siempre ha preferido escribir cartas.

telephone conversation
She doesn't like talking on the telephone and has always preferred to write letters.

**amante de**

fond of; partial to

la **conferencia (telefónica)**

long-distance call

la **llamada sin recargo**
Si tiene algún problema técnico, marque el 900 282 282; tratándose de una llamada sin recargo, no le supondrá ningún coste adicional.

toll-free call
If you have any technical problem, dial 900 282 282; since it's a toll-free call, you will not have to pay any additional charge.

el **coste adicional**

additional charge/expenses

el **teléfono público**
Los destrozos realizados por gamberros en los teléfonos públicos están causando un importante daño económico a Telefónica.

public telephone
Damage done by vandals to public telephones is causing substantial economic damage to the Spanish Telephone Company.

la **señal**
Estoy intentando llamar a Ricardo, pero no da señal, únicamente un tono contínuo.

dial tone
I'm trying to call Ricardo, but I don't get a dial tone, just a continuous buzz.

el **tono contínuo**

constant/continuous tone/buzz

**cortar la línea**
¡Será que le habrán cortado la línea otra vez por impago de la factura!

to cut off telephone service
They've probably cut off his telephone service again because he hasn't paid the bill.

el **impago**

non-payment

la **señal de ocupado**

busy signal

las **telecomunicaciones**
Las innovaciones tecnológicas en telecomunicaciones han marcado directamente los distintos períodos económicos: desde el invento del teléfono hasta la comunicación digital por cable y satélite.

telecommunications
Technological innovations in telecommunications have had a direct influence on economic periods; from the invention of the telephone to digital communications via cable and satellite.

**marcar**

to mark; characterize

los **medios de comunicación**
El mayor incremento en la creación de nuevos puestos de trabajo se producirá, previsiblemente, en el sector de los medios de comunicación.

communications media
The largest increase in the creation of new jobs will probably take place in the communications media sector.

la **creación**

creation

**previsiblemente**

foreseeably; probably

el **teléfono móvil**

mobile telephone

el **auricular**

receiver

**descolgar**
He descolgado el teléfono porque no quiero que me molesten a estas horas.

to lift the receiver
I lifted the receiver because I don't want to be annoyed at this time of day/evening.

el **teléfono inalámbrico**

cordless telephone

el **contestador automático**

answering machine

**conmutar**
Estoy hasta las narices de tener que conmutar constantemente entre el teléfono y el fax, voy a solicitar una línea separada para el fax.

to switch over/back and forth
I'm sick and tired of having to switch back and forth constantly between the telephone and the fax; I'm going to ask for a separate fax line.

el **videotex**
Las ventajas del videotex son el acceso directo a la información deseada y el hecho de ser disponible a cualquier hora.

videotex; view data
Videotex's advantages are direct access to the desired information and the fact that it's always available.

la **autopista de la información**
Las grandes empresas con intereses en el sector multimedia e incluso numerosos gobiernos ven en las autopistas de la información el negocio del siglo.

information highway
Large companies with interests in the multimedia sector and even numerous governments regard the information highways as the business opportunity of the century.

## ■■■ Phrases Used on the Telephone ■■■

**estar comunicando**
El día de tu cumpleaños te llamé varias veces para felicitarte, pero desgraciadamente siempre estaba comunicando.

to be busy (line)
I tried to call you several times on your birthday to offer my congratulations, but unfortunately the line was always busy.

**llamar a alguien al teléfono**
Sr. Antón, le llaman al teléfono, creo que es una conferencia.

to be wanted on the telephone
Mr. Antón, you're wanted on the telephone; I think it's a long distance call.

**quisiera hablar con, me gustaría hablar con**
Quisiera hablar con el Sr. Moreno, por favor.

I'd like to speak with

I'd like to speak with Mr. Moreno, please.

**en estos momentos**

Lo siento, pero en estos momentos no puede ponerse, tiene una visita.

for the moment; at present; right now
I'm sorry, but he can't come to the phone right now; he's with someone.

**no poder ponerse**

to not be able to come to the phone

**tener una visita, estar con una visita**

to have a visitor; be with someone

**dejar un recado**
¿Quiere que le deje algún recado?

to leave a message
Is there any message you want me to leave for him?

**volver a llamar**
No, gracias, volveré a llamar más tarde.

to call back
No, thank you, I'll call back later.

**esperar al aparato**
Si es tan amable de esperar un momento al aparato, la Sra. Servera viene en seguida.

to hold the line
Please hold the line a moment, Ms. Servera will be right with you.

**si es tan amable**

if you would be so kind; please

**cortarse**
Siento volver a molestarle, pero estaba hablando con el Sr. Reynaldo y se ha cortado la línea.

to be/get cut off
I'm sorry to trouble you again, but I was talking with Mr. Reynaldo and we were cut off.

**dejar en espera**
Mira, con el botón rojo puedes dejar una llamada en espera y el de la izquierda es para rellamada, es decir, marca automáticamente el último número marcado.

to put a call on hold
Look, with the red button you can put a call on hold and this button on the left is for redialing, i.e. it automatically redials the last number called.

la **rellamada**

redial

**por la otra línea**
Lo siento, ahora mismo no se puede poner porque está hablando por la otra línea.

on the other line
I'm sorry, she can't take your call right now because she's talking on the other line.

**localizar**
La próxima semana, como estamos haciendo reformas en el despacho, si no me puede localizar en mi número habitual, pida que le pongan con la extensión 341.

to reach/get hold of on the phone
If you can't reach me at my usual number next week because of renovations going on in the office, ask to be connected with extension 341.

**poner con**

to be connected with

la **extensión**

extension

**pasar una llamada**
Durante las próximas dos horas no me pase ninguna llamada porque tengo una reunión con el director general.

to put through a call
Don't put through any calls for me during the next two hours because I'll be in conference with the managing director.

**equivocarse de número**
Perdone las molestias, creo que me he vuelto a equivocar de número.

to dial the wrong number
Excuse my disturbing you, but I think I've dialed a wrong number again.

**perdonar las molestias**

to excuse for being disturbed/ annoyed

la **interferencia**
Apenas entiendo lo que me dices, hay bastantes interferencias. Así que te volveré a llamar.

interference; static
I can hardly hear what you're saying, there's so much static. Therefore I'll call you back.

la **central**
Por favor, póngame con la central.

main switchboard
Please connect me with the main switchboard.

| Spelling Alphabet | |
|---|---|
| A | Antonio |
| B | Barcelona |
| C | Carmen |
| Ch | Chocolate |
| D | Dolores |
| E | Enrique |
| F | Francia |
| G | Gerona |
| H | Historia |
| I | Inés |
| J | José |
| K | Kilo |
| L | Lorenzo |
| Ll | Llobregat |
| M | Madrid |
| N | Navarra |
| Ñ | Ñoño |
| O | Oviedo |
| P | París |
| Q | Querido |
| R | Ramón |
| S | Sábado |
| T | Tarragona |
| U | Ulises |
| V | Valencia |
| W | Washington |
| X | Xiquena |
| Y | Yagüe |
| Z | Zaragoza |

## Highway Transport

| | |
|---|---|
| el **transporte** | transport; shipping |
| el **medio de transporte** | means of shipping |
| A pesar de sus efectos negativos sobre el medio ambiente, el camión sigue siendo un medio de transporte absolutamente necesario en el terrestre. | Despite its deleterious effects on the environment the truck continues to be an indispensable means of surface transportation. |
| el **transporte terrestre** | surface transportation; overland shipping |
| el **camionero** | truck driver |
| Los conflictos entre camioneros franceses y españoles han provocado grandes atascos en la frontera entre ambos países. | The conflicts between French and Spanish truck drivers have caused huge traffic jams at the frontier between the two countries. |
| el **atasco** | traffic jam/backup |
| la **camioneta** | van; delivery wagon |
| Debido a las estrechas calles en el madrileño barrio de Lavapiés, el transporte de mercancías ha sido limitado en lo que respecta a la carga máxima de las camionetas. | Due to the narrow streets in the Lavapiés section of Madrid, the maximum load of goods carried by commercial vans has been limited. |
| la **carga máxima** | maximum load |
| la **carga útil** | maximum permitted load; payload; carrying capacity |
| El término "carga útil" se refiere al porcentaje de carga de un medio de transporte que no es necesario para su locomoción. | The term "payload" refers to that portion of the load of a means of transportation which is not necessary for its moving. |
| la **locomoción** | locomotion; operation; moving forward |
| **trasladar** | to reload |
| Vamos a llevar la carga hasta nuestra agencia de transportes ubicada en el lugar de entrega y allí tendremos que trasladarla a las camionetas. | We're going to take the shipment to our haulage firm located at the delivery site and once there, we'll have to reload it into vans. |
| **ubicado (a)** | located |
| el **lugar de entrega** | delivery site |

**cargar**
Antes de cargar o descargar los camiones, diríjanse a la oficina.

to load
Before loading or unloading the trucks, report to the office.

**descargar**

to unload

la **carga**

load; shipment

la **agencia de transportes**

haulage firm; shipping agency; forwarding agency

el, la **agente de transportes**

shipping agent; carrier; forwarding agent

**transportar**

to transport; ship

el **ramo de transportes**
En el ramo de transportes se puede observar una creciente tendencia a las concentraciones.

shipping business
One can observe an increasing tendency to mergers in the shipping business.

el, la **transportista**

transporter; carrier; freight forwarder/manager

El transportista se dedica de forma profesional al transporte de mercancías, basándose su actividad en las condiciones estipuladas en un contrato de transporte.

The freight forwarder is concerned professionally with the shipment of goods on the basis of the conditions stipulated in a shipping contract.

el **contrato de transporte**

shipping contract

la **carta de porte**

bill of lading; consignment note; waybill

el **duplicado de la carta de porte**
El duplicado de la carta de porte ofrece una cierta seguridad contra falsificaciones, puesto que es muy difícil modificar el original y el duplicado a la vez.

duplicate copy of the bill of lading
The duplicate of the bill of lading offers some protection against forging, since it is very difficult to change both the original and the duplicate.

**modificar**

to modify; change

**a la vez**

simultaneously; at the same time

el **certificado de recepción del transitorio**
El certificado de recepción del transitorio es un acreditivo de haber recibido una mercancía para su posterior expedición.

freight forwarder's attestation of receipt
The freight forwarder's receipt is a proof of his having received goods for subsequent forwarding.

el **acreditivo**

proof; supporting document

**posterior**

later; subsequent

el **tráfico de mercancías sueltas**

trade in loose/unit goods

las **mercancías perecederas**
En la prensa se han publicado artículos sobre una agencia de transporte
en Gerona que hizo apagar la instalación de refrigeración de sus camiones
frigoríficos para ahorrar gasolina, con
el resultado de que las mercancías
perecederas transportadas llegaron
en mal estado.

perishable goods
The press published articles about
a carrier in Gerona who had the air
conditioners in their refrigerated
trucks shut off in order to save
fuel; as a result the perishable
goods they were carrying arrived
in poor condition.

la **instalación de refrigeración**

air conditioning; refrigeration

el **camión frigorífico**

refrigerated truck

los **derechos de tránsito**
Cada vez son más los países europeos
que exigen el pago de derechos de
tránsito a los camiones extranjeros en
concepto de uso de sus autopistas.

road tolls; road use fees
More and more European countries
are charging foreign trucks transit
fees for using their highways.

## Rail Transport

el **transporte ferroviario**

rail transport; shipping by rail

el **transporte por ferrocarril**
El movimiento ecologista insiste en
fomentar el transporte ferroviario ya
que, ecológicamente, perjudica mucho
menos que el transporte por carretera.

shipping by rail
The ecological movement insists
on the promotion of rail transport,
since it is far less harmful to the
environment than highway transport.

**ferroviario (a)**

rail

el **AVE (Tren de Alta Velocidad)**
El AVE que cubre el trayecto Madrid—
Sevilla en menos de tres horas ha
conseguido una muy buena aceptación
entre los viajeros, que queda reflejada
en el alto grado de ocupación y en
unos pingües beneficios para RENFE.

Spanish high speed train
The AVE, which runs from Madrid
to Seville in less than three hours
has been very well received by
travellers, which is reflected in
most seats being filled and fat
profits for RENFE.

la **RENFE (Red Nacional de los
Ferrocarriles Españoles)**

Spanish National Rail

la **ocupación**

occupation; capacity

**pingüe**

abundant

el **auto-expreso**
En España, el auto-expreso es muy
popular debido a que conecta las grandes urbes con las regiones costeras y,
además, tiene unas tarifas módicas.

auto train; Motorail train
In Spain, the auto train is very
popular because it connects big
cities with coastal areas, and in
addition, offers low rates.

| | |
|---|---|
| **popular** | popular |
| la **región costera** | coastal area |
| la **gran urbe** | big city |

| | |
|---|---|
| el **tren de mercancías**<br>En el transporte de productos a granel en vagones de gran capacidad, los trenes de mercancías no tienen competencia. | freight train<br>Nothing can compete with freight trains for transporting bulk goods in large capacity freight cars. |
| los **productos a granel** | bulk/quantity goods |
| el **vagón de gran capacidad** | large capacity freight car |
| el **tren de largo recorrido** | long-distance train |
| el **vagón cisterna** | tanker |
| el **vagón frigorífico** | refrigerated railroad car |
| las **mercancías pesadas**<br>Rogamos nos proporcione un vagón cubierto para mercancías sueltas y dos vagones descubiertos para mercancías pesadas. | heavy goods<br>Please make available to us a covered freight car for unit goods and two open cars for heavy goods. |
| las **mercancías sueltas** | loose/unit goods |
| el **vagón cubierto** | closed/covered freight car |
| el **vagón abierto,** el **vagón plataforma** | open freight car |
| la **estación expedidora** | dispatch/shipping station |
| la **estación de destino**<br>En la estación de destino, nuestro representante se encargará de todos los trámites necesarios. | station of final destination<br>At the final destination station our agent will deal with all necessary formalities. |
| el **enlace ferroviario**<br>Para grandes empresas con un considerable movimiento de mercancías vale la pena instalar un enlace ferroviario propio. | railroad connection/hook up<br>For big companies with a large turnover of goods, it's worth the trouble of arranging for a rail connection of their own. |
| el **movimiento de mercancías** | merchandise turnover |
| el **talón de transporte ferroviario,** el **talón ferrocarril**<br>El talón de transporte ferroviario sirve de documento justificativo y no se puede transmitir por endoso. | rail bill of lading<br>The rail bill of lading serves as a supporting document and cannot be transferred by endorsement. |
| el **documento justificativo** | proof; supporting document |

# Maritime Transport

la **navegación**
Ya desde la Edad Media, la navegación —y especialmente la navegación de alta mar—ha determinado el papel de España como nación bélica y comerciante.

seafaring
Ever since the Middle Ages, seafaring—especially on the high seas—has determined Spain's role as a war waging and commercial nation.

la **navegación de alta mar**

seafaring/travel on the high seas

**bélico (a)**

belligerent; war waging

la **navegación fluvial**

river traffic

la **navegación interior**
El ocaso de la industria del carbón y del acero ha repercutido negativamente en la situación de la navegación fluvial.

navigation on domestic waters
The deep decline in the coal and steel industries has had a negative effect on river traffic.

el **ocaso**

setting; decline

la **navegación costera**

navigation in coastal waters

el **puerto interior**
Con el paso del tiempo, los puertos interiores de España han perdido importancia, debido al desarrollo de otros medios de comunicación.

inland port
With the passing of time, Spanish inland ports have declined in importance thanks to the development of other means of transportation.

el **puerto franco**
Un puerto franco es un puerto donde las mercancías pueden ser importadas sin el previo pago de los derechos aduaneros correspondientes.

free port
A free port is a port through which goods can be imported without customs duties having previously been paid on them.

**previo (a)**

previous

la **marina mercante**
Al igual que en otros países, muchos barcos pertenecientes a la marina mercante española han sido registrados bajo banderas de conveniencia con el único fin de obtener ventajas fiscales y de ajustarse a una legislación laboral menos estricta.

merchant marine
As is the case with other countries, many ships belonging to the Spanish merchant marine have been registered under flags of convenience, for the sole purpose of securing tax advantages and of being subject to less strict labor regulations.

la **bandera de conveniencia**

flag of convenience

el **buque**

ship

| | |
|---|---|
| la **compañía naviera** | shipping company/line |
| el **buque de vapor** | steamship |
| el **buque frigorífico** | refrigerator ship |

el **petrolero**
Debido a las últimas catástrofes ecológicas causadas por petroleros, se han disparado las primas para asegurarles.

oil tanker
Because of the latest ecological catastrophes caused by oil tankers, their insurance premiums have gone sky high.

el **buque-cisterna** — tanker

el **armador**
Los armadores españoles están reclamando un mayor apoyo del Estado para defender sus navieras frente a la competencia extranjera.

ship owner
Spanish ship owners are demanding more government support to help their firms meet foreign competition.

la **naviera** — shipping firm

la **navegación sin ruta fija**
La particularidad de la navegación sin ruta fija reside en que la compañía naviera decide, en el mismo puerto de descarga, cual será el siguiente puerto de destino.

tramp steamer traffic
The special characteristic of tramp steamers is that the shipping company decides, in the very port it's being unloaded, what its next port of call will be.

la **particularidad** — particularity; special characteristic

el **puerto de embarque** — port of embarkation/loading

el **puerto de descarga** — port where cargo is unloaded

el **puerto de destino** — port of destination

**descargar** — to unload

el **servicio regular marítimo** — scheduled/regular sea run/service

el **fletamento** — charter; chartering

el **contrato de fletamento**
El objeto de un contrato de fletamento, concluido entre el fletador y el fletante, es la explotación de un barco ajeno contra pago del precio convenido.

charter contract/agreement
The purpose of a charter agreement, contracted between the lessor and the lessee, is the use of someone else's ship upon payment of the agreed upon price.

el **fletador** — person chartering/renting the ship from; lessee

el, la **fletante** — person renting the ship to; lessor

**fletar**
Muchos pescadores que, hoy en día,
ya no pueden vivir de la pesca, fletan
sus barcos con turistas.

to rent/charter a ship
Many fishermen who nowadays
are no longer able to earn their
living by fishing, rent their boats
to tourists.

**el flete**
El flete es el importe pagado por el
fletador al fletante en concepto de
alquiler de un buque.
Muchos barcos que transportaban
plata de América del Sur al Reino
de España se hundieron y con ellos
su valioso flete.

freight; ship's cargo
The freight charge is the sum paid
by the person chartering the ship
to the lessor for the renting of a ship.
Many ships carrying silver from
South America to the Kingdom of
Spain sank and with them their
valuable cargo.

**hundirse**

to sink

**el conocimiento de embarque**
En el conocimiento de embarque el
transportista certifica la recepción de
una mercancía con la obligación
contraída de transportarla al lugar
indicado.

bill of lading
On the bill of lading the carrier
certifies receipt of a cargo as well
as the contractual obligation to
forward it to the place indicated.

**el conocimiento de embarque
limpio**
El conocimiento de embarque limpio
no contiene ninguna cláusula de
reserva respecto al estado de la mercancía o del embalaje.

clean bill of lading

A clean bill of lading contains no
clause making any reservation
concerning the condition of the
merchandise or its packaging.

**la cláusula de reserva**

reserve clause

**el conocimiento de embarque
sucio**
En un conocimiento de embarque
sucio se expresan reservas sobre el
estado del flete transportado.

foul bill of lading

In a foul bill of lading, reservations
are made about the condition of
the freight transported.

**certificar**

to certify; confirm

**el consignatario de buques,** la
**consignataria de buques**
El consignatario de buques gestiona
los trámites necesarios para la entrada
del buque en el puerto de destino.

shipping agent; sea route carrier

The shipping agent takes care of the
necessary formalities for the ship's
arrival at the port of destination.

**el manifiesto del buque**
El manifiesto del buque, a presentar
en aduana, es un listado de la mercancía que transporta el buque.

ship's manifest
The ship's manifest, which has to
be presented at customs, is a listing
of the ship's cargo.

| | |
|---|---|
| el **listado** | list |
| la **recepción** | receipt |
| **contraer** | to contract |

## ■ Air Transport ■

**a bordo**
El capitán Guitierrez y su tripulación les dan la bienvenida a bordo de nuestro Airbus A 320 con destino a Francfort.

on board
Our captain Guitierrez and his crew welcome you on board our Airbus A 320 with destination Frankfurt.

el **capitán**
captain

la **tripulación**
crew

**dar la bienvenida**
to welcome

la **línea aérea**
airline

la **compañía aerea**
airline company

la **escala**
Después de una breve escala en Barcelona serviremos la comida, empezando por la clase preferente.

stopover
After a short stopover in Barcelona, a meal will be served starting with first class.

la **clase turista**
tourist class

la **clase preferente**
first class

el **exceso de equipaje**
Lo siento, pero tendrá que pagar un suplemento por exceso de equipaje.

excess baggage
I'm sorry but you'll have to pay an excess baggage supplement.

el **bulto**
Vamos a facturar dos bultos cada uno, el ordenador portátil voy a llevarlo como equipaje de mano.

piece of luggage
Each of us will check two pieces of luggage; I'll take the portable computer with me as carry on luggage.

el **equipaje de mano**
carry on luggage

la **puerta**
Una vez facturado el equipaje, diríjanse a la puerta 73 y esperen hasta que anuncien su vuelo por altavoz.

gate
Once your luggage has been checked, please go to gate 73 and wait until they announce your flight on the loudspeaker.

**facturar el equipaje**
to check luggage

**dirigirse a**
to go to

la **terminal**
¿Salidas internacionales? – Pase primero por la terminal de vuelos nacionales y antes de llegar a la terminal de carga ya verá un indicador.

terminal
International departures? First go through the domestic flights terminal and before coming to the air freight terminal you'll see a sign pointing the way.

la **terminal de carga**

air freight terminal

el **indicador**

sign

el **tráfico de transporte aéreo**
El tráfico de transporte aéreo es recomendable en el caso de mercancías de reducido tamaño y de gran valor, además de todas aquellas, que se deban entregar con rapidez.

air freight traffic/shipment
Shipping by air freight is advisable for small, very valuable merchandise, as well as for all merchandise intended for speedy delivery.

**recomendable**

advisable

la **compañía de fletamento aéreo**
Las grandes líneas aéreas suelen tener como filial una compañía de fletamento aéreo, puesto que ambas, en la mayoría de los casos, se complementan perfectamente.

charter airline

Major airlines usually have a charter airline subsidiary, since in most cases, they complement each other perfectly.

**complementarse**

to complement

**fletar**
Para trasladar los objetos de la exposición hemos fletado un avión, ya que el riesgo es menor.

to charter
For transporting the exhibition items, we've chartered a plane, since the risk is less.

la **carta de porte aéreo,** el **conocimiento de embarque aéreo**
En la carta de porte aéreo, cuyo contenido y formato están determinados por la IATA, se detallan informaciones respecto al aeropuerto y de salidas y destino, datos exactos sobre la mercancía, etc.

air bill of lading

In the air bill of lading, the content and format of which are determined by the IATA, information is given respecting the airport of departure and the airport of arrival, exact data concerning the merchandise, etc.

**detallar**

to list in detail

el **contenido**

content

la **IATA (Asociación de Transporte Aéreo Internacional)**

International Airlines Association

el **aeropuerto destinatario**

airport of destination

el **aeropuerto de salida**

departure airport

## Types of Insurance

| | |
|---|---|
| la **compañía de seguros,** la **entidad aseguradora** | insurance company |

Mediante adquisiciones y absorciones de entidades aseguradoras españolas, las grandes compañías multinacionales se han hecho fuertes en el mercado español de seguros.

By takeovers and buy outs of Spanish insurance companies, the big multinational companies have achieved a strong position on the Spanish insurance market.

| | |
|---|---|
| **hacerse fuerte** | to grow/become strong |
| el **mercado de seguros** | insurance market |
| el **seguro obligatorio** | compulsory liability insurance; legally required insurance |

Se debe diferenciar entre el seguro obligatorio, como, p. ej., el seguro de responsabilidad civil de suscripción obligatoria para el automóvil o el seguro contra incendios que se debe contratar al comprar una casa y seguros voluntarios, como, p. ej., el seguro de hogar.

One must distinguish between legally required insurance, as e.g. motor vehicle liability insurance, or the fire insurance that should be taken out when buying a house, and voluntary insurance, like e.g. household insurance.

| | |
|---|---|
| el **seguro de responsabilidad civil de suscripción obligatoria del automóvil** | motor vehicle personal liability insurance |
| el **seguro voluntario,** el **seguro facultativo** | voluntary insurance |
| el **seguro del hogar** | household/home contents insurance |
| el **seguro de automóvil a todo riesgo** | full-coverage insurance; fully comprehensive insurance |
| el **seguro a riesgo parcial** | partial-coverage insurance |

Ningún asegurador español ofrece un seguro a riesgo parcial para una moto de gran cilindrada que cubra la sustracción de la misma.

No Spanish underwriter will offer a partial coverage insurance policy that will cover theft of a high cylinder motorcycle.

| | |
|---|---|
| la **cilindrada** | large cyclinder capacity; cubic capacity; piston displacement |
| la **sustracción** | theft |
| el **seguro contra rotura de cristales** | insurance against breakage of glass |

el **seguro contra incendios**
El seguro contra incendios que, normalmente, incluye un seguro contra la caída del rayo, cubre los daños materiales originados tanto por caso fortuito como por malquerencia de extraños.

fire insurance
Fire insurance, which normally includes lightning insurance, covers material damages, whether caused by chance or by another's malicious intent.

**cubrir**

to cover

el **seguro contra la caída del rayo**

lightning insurance

los **daños materiales**

material damages

el **caso fortuito imprevisto**

unforeseen chance circumstance

la **malquerencia de extraños**

malicious intent of another

el **seguro de responsabilidad civil**
El seguro de responsabilidad civil indemniza por daños infligidos a otros por parte del tomador de la póliza.

personal liability insurance
Personal liability insurance makes good on claims for damages done to others by the policyholder.

**infligir**

to inflict on; do

**indemnizar**

to indemnify; make good on a claim; compensate

el **tomador de la póliza**

policyholder

el **seguro de vida**
El seguro de vida, mediante la participación en los beneficios, se está convirtiendo cada vez más en un instrumento de formación de capital.

life insurance
Profit-sharing life insurance is more and more becoming an instrument for building capital.

la **formación de capital**

capital building/accumulation

la **participación en los beneficios**

profit-sharing

el **seguro de vida para caso de supervivencia**

endowment insurance

el **seguro en caso de muerte**

insurance in the event of death

el **seguro de transporte marítimo**
Con el seguro de transporte marítimo puede asegurarse el buque y el cargamento.

maritime transport insurance
With maritime transport insurance you can insure the ship and its cargo.

el **cargamento**

cargo

el **seguro de fletes**

freight insurance

| | |
|---|---|
| la **compañía aseguradora** | underwriting/insuring company |
| el **seguro contra accidentes del trabajo**<br>El seguro contra accidentes en el trabajo es contratado por la empresa y asegura al empleado contra percances en el ejercicio de su trabajo y durante el camino al centro de trabajo y a la salida. | workers' compensation insurance<br><br>Workers' compensation insurance is contracted for by the company and insures the employee against mishaps while on the job as well as on the way to and from the work site. |
| **asegurar** | to insure |
| el **percance** | mishap |
| el **ejercicio** | performance |
| el **seguro combinado** | combined insurance |
| el **seguro médico privado**<br>Aunque los hospitales y médicos de la Seguridad Social garantizan un buen servicio médico, son muchos los que contratan un seguro médico privado. | private health insurance<br>Although hospitals and doctors participating in Social Security guarantee good medical care, there are many who have private health insurance policies. |
| el **seguro de protección jurídica**<br>El seguro de protección jurídica que hasta hace poco sólo se ofrecía como seguro adicional a otras pólizas está ganando terreno dentro del ramo asegurador español. | insurance for legal costs<br>Insurance for legal costs, which until recently was offered only as a supplement to other policies, is gaining ground within the Spanish insurance industry. |
| el **seguro adicional** | extra insurance |
| **ganar terreno** | to gain ground |
| el **ramo asegurador** | insurance field/sector/branch/industry |
| el **seguro de crédito a la exportación**<br>El seguro de crédito a la exportación tiene su finalidad en la cobertura de riesgos a las cuales están sometidas las exportaciones de bienes y servicios españoles. Estas pólizas son emitidas por la CESCE. | export credit insurance<br><br>Export credit insurance is intended for coverage of the risks to which the export of Spanish goods and services are exposed. These policies are issued by the CESCE. |
| la **CESCE (Compañía Española de Seguros de Créditos a la Exportación)** | Spanish Export Credit Company |
| el **seguro de transporte de mercancías** | insurance of goods in transit |

241

| | |
|---|---|
| la **DGS (Dirección General de Seguros)** | Uniform Insurance Regulatory Board |
| Las aseguradoras españolas podrán actuar en toda la UE con el control único de la DGS. | Spanish insurers will be able to operate in all the countries of the European Union under the sole control of the Uniform Insurance Regulatory Board. |
| el **reaseguro** | reinsurance |
| El reaseguro cubre el riesgo asumido por un asegurador para evitar que se produzca la quiebra del mismo por no poder hacer frente a las indemnizaciones a desembolsar. | Reinsurance covers the risk assumed by an insurer to avoid his going bankrupt because of inability to meet compensation claims for damages. |
| **asumir un riesgo** | to assume a risk |
| el **reasegurador** | reinsurer |
| **desembolsar** | to pay out |

## ▬▬▬ Insurance Activities ▬▬▬

el **seguro**
Un seguro se puede definir como la asunción de un determinado riesgo por parte de un asegurador contra pago de una prima de seguro.

insurance
An insurance can be defined as the assumption of a determined risk on the part of an insurer in return for payment of an insurance policy premium.

el **riesgo**
risk

la **asunción**
assumption

el **asegurador,** la **aseguradora**
insurer; underwriter

la **prima de seguro**
insurance premium

**asegurado (a)**
Durante el transporte la mercancía está asegurada contra pérdida.

insured
During transport, the merchandise is insured against loss.

**a todo riesgo**
La mercancía debe ser asegurada a todo riesgo.

against all risks
The merchandise is insured against all risks.

el **asegurado,** la **asegurada**
El tomador del seguro es la persona que contrata el seguro y que se compromete al pago de las primas convenidas, mientras que el asegurado tiene el derecho de hacer uso del seguro suscrito.

(person) insured
The person who takes out the insurance signs the contract and promises to pay the premiums agreed upon, while the person insured has the right to make claims on the policy contracted for.

el **tomador del seguro,** el, la **contratante del seguro**

person who takes out an insurance policy

**contratar un seguro, suscribir un seguro**

to contract for/take out insurance; to sign up for insurance

**convenido (a)**

agreed upon

el **coasegurado,** la **coasegurada**

(person) co-insured

la **póliza de seguro**
Suscribir una póliza de seguro con una compañía de seguros directos es una medida eficaz para bajar los costes, si bien se debe renunciar al asesoramiento de un agente de seguros.

insurance policy
To take out an insurance policy with a direct insurer is an effective way to lower costs, even if it means doing without the advice of an insurance agent.

la **compañía de seguros directos**

direct insurance company

**renunciar a**

to do without

el **asesoramiento**

counselling; advice

el, la **agente de seguros**

insurance agent

el **corredor de seguros,** la **corredora de seguros**

insurance broker

el **objeto del seguro**

thing/item insured

el **objeto asegurado**
La cobertura cubre todos los objetos asegurados hasta un valor de 400.000 pesetas. Los objetos cuya valoración sobrepasa este límite deben ser indicados aparte.

object insured
Coverage extends to all the items insured up to a value of 400,000 pesetas. Items whose value exceeds that limit should be listed separately.

la **valoración**

(estimate of) value; appraisal

el **límite**

limit

**indicar**

to indicate; list

el **sobreseguro**

over-insurance

el **infraseguro**
Le recomendamos una revaloración de sus objetos de valor, ya que el infraseguro impedirá que Ud. pueda reclamar la cobertura total en caso de que se produzca un siniestro.

under-insurance
We recommend that you have your valuable items reappraised, since under-insurance will prevent you from making a claim for complete coverage in the event that a loss should occur.

la **revaloración**

reappraisal; reassessment

| | |
|---|---|
| el **objeto de valor** | valuable object/item |
| la **cobertura** | coverage |
| Rogamos establezcan un seguro, que ofrezca cobertura total a nuestra mercancía. | We ask you to please contract for insurance that offers complete coverage of our merchandise. |
| la **suma asegurada** | the sum insured |
| las **Cláusulas del Instituto para Mercancías** | Institute Cargo Clauses |
| Rogamos extender una póliza de seguros con arreglo a las Cláusulas del Instituto para Mercancías. | Please make out an insurance policy according to the Institute Cargo Clauses. |
| la **póliza flotante** | floater; policy that protects against loss |
| Dado que tenemos embarques regulares a Lima, estamos interesados en una póliza flotante. | Since we have regular departures to Lima, we're interested in a floater. |
| la **cláusula de exclusión** | exclusion clause |
| Todo contrato de seguro de vida contiene una cláusula de exclusión para casos de suicidio. | Every life insurance policy contains an exclusion clause in case of suicide. |
| el **suicidio** | suicide |
| la **acumulación de riesgos** | accumulation of risks |
| Algunas compañías de seguros de coches excluyen, por acumulación de riesgos, a personas menores de 25 años con un vehículo, cuyo motor tenga una razón motor-cilindrada que invite a una conducción arriesgada, como, p. ej., los GTI. | Some automobile insurance companies exclude, because of accumulation of risks, persons under 25 with a vehicle whose motor-cylinder ratio lends itself to risky driving, like, e.g. the GTI's. |
| la **razón** | ratio |
| la **conducción** | driving |
| **arriesgado (a)** | risky |
| la **bonificación por no siniestralidad** | reduction in premium for not having filed a claim |
| Me llevé una sorpresa desagradable al descubrir que mi entidad aseguradora española me reconocía sólo el 15% de mi bonificación por no siniestralidad adquirida en Alemania. | I got a nasty surprise when I found out that my Spanish insurance company would allow me only 15% of the bonus I earned in Germany for not having made any claims. |
| la **franquicia** | deductible |
| la **franquicia obligatoria** | obligatory deductible |
| Los seguros de los coches de alquiler tienen una franquicia obligatoria relativamente alta. | Insurance contracts for rented cars have a relatively high deductible. |

la **clasificación de primas**
Le vamos a mandar las condiciones generales de seguro y, además, la clasificación de primas.

scale of premiums
We're going to send you the general conditions for insurance and also the scale of premiums.

las **condiciones generales de seguro**

general insurance conditions

la **nota de cobertura provisional**
En cuanto hayamos recibido firmado el formulario de solicitud de seguro, le haremos llegar la nota de cobertura provisional.

notice of provisional coverage
As soon as we've received your signed insurance application form, we'll send a notice of provisional coverage.

el **formulario de solicitud de seguro**

insurance application form

## Insurance Cases

el **siniestro**
Lloyds tiene pendientes derechos de pago de indemnizaciones de siniestros ocurridos en el último lustro por valor de 9.000 millones de libras.

damage; loss
Lloyds has outstanding payment obligations of 9 billion pounds for damage claims filed within the last five years.

los **derechos de pago de indemnizaciones**

compensation; claims for damages

la **indemnización**

indemnification; compensation; payment of damages

el **lustro**

period of five years

la **contingencia asegurada**

event giving rise to an insurance claim

el **aviso de siniestro**

report of damage; filing of an insurance claim

Con este aviso de siniestro quiero poner en su conocimiento un daño causado por agua. Les ruego manden un perito para evaluar los daños producidos.

With this report of damage I wish to inform you of water damage that occurred. Please send an expert to evalute the damage done.

**poner u/c en conocimiento de alguien**

to inform someone of something

el **daño causado por agua**

water damage

la **pérdida**

loss

la **avería**

transport damage; average; breakdown

el **perito**

expert

245

| | |
|---|---|
| **evaluar** | to evaluate |
| el **daño** | damage(s) |
| el **resarcimiento por daños y perjuicios** | compensation for damage and loss |

El resarcimiento por daños y perjuicios reclamado por Ud. no se corresponde con la determinación de los daños efectuada por nuestro perito, por lo tanto consideramos desmesuradas sus pretensiones.

The compensation claims for damage and loss made by you do not correspond to the determination of damage made by our expert, therefore we consider your claims (to be) excessive.

| | |
|---|---|
| **corresponderse con** | to correspond to; agree with |
| la **determinación de los daños** | determination of damage |
| **desmesurado (a)** | excessive |
| la **avería gruesa,** la **avería común** | general average |
| la **compensación** | compensation; claim |

Como Ud. se ha negado a observar nuestras recomendaciones sobre disminuición de riesgo y no ha instalado un sistema de alarma, no podemos reconocer, en su totalidad, la compensación exigida.

Since you failed to implement our recommendations for limitation of risk and you didn't install an alarm system, we cannot accept the full amount of your claim for damages.

| | |
|---|---|
| la **disminuición de riesgo** | limiting of risks |
| el **sistema de alarma** | alarm system |
| **en su totalidad** | completely; totally |
| la **agravación del riesgo** | aggravation of risk |
| la **prevención de siniestros** | prevention of damages |
| el **informe pericial,** el **peritaje** | expert report |

Para la liquidación del siniestro necesitamos el informe pericial de un perito independiente.

For the settlement of your claim for damages we need the report of an independent expert.

| | |
|---|---|
| la **liquidación del siniestro** | settlement/liquidation of a claim for damages |

# General Information

la **ley**
El control de cambios está regulado
por ley.

law
Surveillance of exchange rates is
regulated by law.

**regulado (a)**

regulated

la **entrada en vigor**
La entrada en vigor de las leyes se
produce, de manera general, un mes
después de su publicación.

taking effect
In general, laws take effect one
month after their promulgation.

la **legislación**
La legislación sobre las telecomunicaciones es cada día mas compleja.

legislation
Legislation concerning telecom-
munication grows more complex
every day.

**legal**

legal

**ilegal**
El tráfico de drogas es ilegal.

illegal
Drug traffic is illegal.

el **abogado,** la **abogada**
El abogado defiende los derechos e
intereses de sus clientes.

lawyer
Lawyers defend the rights and
interests of their clients.

el **bufete**
Los grandes bufetes suelen contar con
la colaboración de algún Catedrático
de Universidad prestigioso.

law firm
Major law firms generally rely on
the collaboration of a well-known
university professor.

**prestigioso (a)**

prestigious; well-known

el **notario,** la **notaria**
El notario da fé de los actos jurídicos
que se realizan ante él.

notary
The notary certifies legal transactions done in his presence.

**dar fé**

to certify

la **acción**
Las acciones deben ser ejercitadas
en tiempo y forma debidos.

legal action; complaint
Legal actions must be brought
within the statutory time period
and in due form.

**ejercer una acción**

to bring an action

la **demanda**
En la demanda se contiene el petitum del demandante.

charge; complaint
The plaintiff's complaint is contained in the petition.

el, la **demandante**

plaintiff

el **petitum**

petition

el **demandado,** la **demandada**

accused person

**demandado (a)**
El empresario puede ser demandado por el trabajador si no recibe su salario.

legally charged
The entrepreneur can be legally charged by an employee, if he/she does not receive his/her wages.

la **garantía**
Con frecuencia las garantías consisten en un deposito en metálico.

guarantee; bail
Often a cash deposit constitutes bail.

el **fiador,** la **fiadora**
El fiador es la persona que avala con sus bienes el cumplimiento de las obligaciones de un tercero.

guarantor
The guarantor is someone who pledges his own property as a guarantee of the obligations of a third party.

**avalar**

guarantee

el **escrito de acusación**
El escrito de acusación es redactado por el Fiscal, y a veces, también por la acusación particular.

indictment
The indictment is drawn up by the district attorney's office and sometimes also by the accessory prosecutor.

la **acusación particular**

accessory prosecutor

el **juez,** la **jueza**

judge

el **Fiscal**

district attorney's office; the prosecution

el **juicio**

judgment

el **acta de juicio**

legal proceeding; record of the proceeding

En el acta del juicio deben quedar recogidas las declaraciones de los testigos.

Statements made by witnesses should be contained in the record.

la **acusación**

indictment; accusation

la **cédula de citación**
El juez cita a testigos y peritos mediante la cédula de citación.

summons
The judge invites witnesses and experts by issuing summonses.

la **declaración de los testigos**

witness statements

los **hechos probados**
Los hechos probados son aquellos que el juez o tribunal, admite como suficientemente acreditados en la sentencia.

proven facts
Proven facts are those which the judge or the court considers sufficiently believable in a verdict.

**acreditado (a)** — believable; proved

la **sentencia** — sentence; verdict

el **arbitraje** — arbitration
El arbitraje es medio para la solución de controversias cada vez más utilizado.
Arbitration is an increasingly popular means for resolving disputes.

la **personalidad jurídica** — legal personality
Sin personalidad jurídica no se puede contratar.
Without legal personality no contract can be made.

**contratar** — to contract; enter into/make a contract
Para poder contratar validamente es condición indispensable ser mayor de edad o estar emancipado.
To make a legally valid contract it is indispensable that one be of age or legally responsible.

la **extinción** — expiration
Con la extinción de un contrato no se acaban sus efectos jurídicos.
When a contract expires its legal repercussions do not cease.

**jurídico (a)** — legal; juridical

el **incumplimiento del contrato** — non-compliance with the contract; violation of contract
Una parte puede demandar a la otra ante el juez por incumplimiento del contrato.
One contract party may bring a legal complaint against another for violation of contract.

**demandar** — to bring an action; lodge a complaint

la **facultad** — capacity; authority
La ley y los estatutos propios regulan las facultades del Consejo de Administración de una sociedad.
The law and its own statutes regulate the authority of a corporate Executive Board.

la **fuerza mayor** — act of God
En los casos de fuerza mayor no hay responsabilidad penal ni civil.
In act of God cases there is neither penal nor civil legal responsibility.

el **marco legal** — legal framework
El delito de difamación no está contemplado en nuestro marco legal.
The crime of defamation does not exist in the framework of our laws.

el **negocio jurídico** — legal transaction
Dentro de la categoría de negocios jurídicos, quizá sea la compraventa el más común y frecuente.
In the category of legal transactions, perhaps the most frequent and the most common is buying-selling.

el **precepto**
Los preceptos legales pueden ser injustos.

precept; rule and regulation
Legal rules and regulations can be unjust.

el **acto jurídico**
El acto jurídico es aquel hecho que tiene relevancia para el mundo del Derecho.

legal transaction
A legal transaction is that action which is of significance for the world of the law.

el **fuero**

El conjunto de fueros que afecta a una determinada región constituye el Derecho Foral.

special law in a certain region or city; local laws
The ensemble of local laws which affect a specific region is contained in local statutes.

el **reglamento**

regulation

**emancipado (a)**

legally responsible

**otorgar poder**
Para otorgar poder se acude a la Notaría.

to grant power-of-attorney
To grant power-of-attorney one goes to the notary's office.

la **notaría**

notary's office

el **poder general para pleitos**

El abogado suele recibir de su cliente un poder general para pleitos.

general power-of-attorney in legal proceedings
The lawyer usually receives a general power-of-attorney in legal proceedings from his client.

el **representante legal**
Un representante legal está facultado para llevar a cabo actos jurídicos en nombre de otro.

legal representative
A legal representative is authorized to carry out legal transactions in the name of another.

la **parte alícuota**
Las herencias se dividen con frecuencia en partes alícuotas.

pro-rata; equal parts
Estates are frequently divided into equal parts.

la **herencia**
La herencia está constituida por el conjunto de derechos y obligaciones que deja una persona al fallecer.

estate; inheritance
The estate consists of the totality of rights and obligations left by a decedent.

el **enriquecimiento injusto**
El enriquecimiento injusto no debe ser favorecido por el Derecho.

unjustified enrichment
Unjustified enrichment should not be encouraged by the law.

la **imprudencia**

imprudence; negligence

la **difamación**

defamation

**indemnizado (a)**
En caso de accidente con daños, los asegurados y perjudicados son indemnizados.

compensated; indemnified
In the event of an accident with damages, the insured and damaged parties are compensated.

| | |
|---|---|
| el **perjudicado,** la **perjudicada** | damaged party |
| el **incidente** | incident |
| El juez consideró el incidente como suficiente para suspender el juicio. | The judge considered the incident sufficiently important to stop the proceedings. |
| **suspender el juicio** | to break off; suspend; stop |
| la **instancia** | jurisdiction |
| Cuando el delito es de terrorismo, en España la instancia que debe juzgar es la Audiencia Nacional. | When the crime is terrorism, the Spanish National Court (Supreme Court) is the court of original jurisdiction. |
| la **Audiencia Nacional** | National Tribunal (Spanish Supreme Court) |
| **juzgar** | to judge |
| En España, la función de juzgar sólo la llevan a cabo Jueces y Magistrados. | In Spain, the exercise of judging is the sole province of judges and magistrates. |
| el **magistrado,** la **magistrada** | magistrate |
| el **móvil** | motive; cause |
| El móvil es el motivo de un delito. | The cause of a crime is its motive. |
| la **novación** | novation (substitution of a new obligation for an old one) |
| El contrato sufrió la novación de temporal a indefinido. | The contract underwent novation from temporary to indefinite duration. |
| la **omisión** | omission |
| la **notificación** | official notification/notice |
| La notificación del desahucio debe recibirse antes de que se produzca. | The eviction order should be received before it is implemented. |
| el **desahucio** | eviction |

## Civil Law

| | |
|---|---|
| el **Código Civil** | Civil Code |
| Ante un vacío legal determinado, se ha de acudir siempre al Código Civil como derecho supletorio. | In the case of a specific gap in the law, one must always have recourse to the Civil Code as additional law. |
| **supletorio (a)** | completing; supplementary; additional |

el **estado civil**
El matrimonio cambia el estado civil de una persona.

civil/marital status
Marriage changes an individual's marital status.

**adoptar**
Muchas parejas infértiles adoptan niños provenientes de otros continentes.

to adopt
Many childless couples adopt children from other continents.

**suceder**
Suceder al Rey de España significa adquirir la condición de Jefe de Estado.

succeed to
To succeed the King of Spain means to assume the rank of Chief of State.

**enviudar**
En la Guerra Civil enviudaron muchas mujeres.

to be/become widowed
In the Civil War many women were widowed.

la **propiedad**
La usucapción es un medio de adquisición de la propiedad proveniente del Derecho Romano.

property
Obtaining property by prescription is a method of acquisition that originates in Roman Law.

la **posesión**
Se debe entender la posesión como el poder de hecho sobre una determinada cosa.

possession
Possession should be understood as power of disposition over a specific thing.

**arrendado (a)**
La ventaja de tener una vivienda arrendada es que el precio del alquiler se desgrava en la declaración de la renta.

rented
The advantage of renting one's residence is that the rent is tax deductible.

**hipotecado (a)**
El comprador siempre debe informarse de si el bien que pretende adquirir está hipotecado o no.

mortgaged
The buyer should always find out whether the property he plans to acquire is mortgaged or not.

**subastado (a)**
Los bienes subastados se adjudican al mejor postor.

auctioned
Auctioned property is knocked down to the highest bidder.

el **postor**

bidder

**vendido (a)**
Un bien vendido ha cambiado de propietario.

sold
Property that is sold has changed hands.

**asegurado (a)**
Los bienes asegurados incrementan por ello su valor.

insured
That fact that they are insured, increases the value of insured goods.

**testar**
Morir sin testar ocasiona perjuicios
a los herederos.

to make a will
To die intestate results in disad-
vantages for the heirs.

**el usufructo**
El usufructo permite usar y disfrutar
de una cosa aunque no se sea propietario de ella.

usufruct; use and enjoyment
The right of usufruct permits the
use and enjoyment of something
even though someone else owns it.

**la usucapción**

usucaption; obtaining by prescription

**la usura**
En los tiempos de la usura el dinero
era un bien muy escaso.

usury
In ages when usury flourished,
money was in short supply.

**el grado de parentesco**

degree of kinship

**la patria potestad**
Tras un proceso de separación matrimonial, la patria potestad puede
corresponder al padre o a la madre.

custody rights
After a divorce, custody rights can
be granted either to the father or
the mother.

**el proceso de separación
matrimonial**

divorce proceedings

**el vacío legal**

gap in the law

# The Contract

**el contrato**
Un contrato es todo acuerdo o pacto
de voluntades entre dos o más personas dirigido a crear obligaciones entre
ellas.

contract
A contract is any agreement or
voluntary accord between two or
more persons designed to create
obligations between them.

**la parte**
El Tratado de Roma fue firmado en
1957 por las Altas Partes Contratantes.

party
The Treaty of Rome was signed
in 1957 by the High Contracting
Parties.

**contratante**

contracting

**el contenido del contrato**
El contenido del contrato está formado
por el conjunto de derechos y obligaciones a que da origen.

content of the contract
The content of the contract consists
of the totality of the rights and
obligations which it establishes.

**la obligación**
La obligación es el vínculo legal que
impone una acción o una omisión.

obligation
The obligation is the legally binding contract point which can give
rise to an action or an omission.

la **prestación**
El contenido de una obligación está constituido por una o varias prestaciones.

service
The content of an obligation consists of one or more services.

la **contraprestación**
La contraprestación es la prestación realizada por una parte en pago de la prestación de la otra parte.

consideration; service in return
Consideration is the service of one party as payment for the services of the other party.

la **relación contractual**
La relación contractual se rige por las cláusulas contractuales y, subsidiariamente, por la ley.

contractual relationship
The contractual relationship is determined by clauses in the contract, or subsidiarily, by law.

**contractual**

contractual

la **cláusula**
El contrato está integrado por una serie de cláusulas que recogen los diferentes aspectos del acuerdo alcanzado por las partes.

clause
The contract consists of a series of clauses, which express the different aspects of the agreement to which the parties have come.

la **cláusula penal**
Un contrato puede contener una cláusula penal para el caso de incumplimiento.

penal clause; liquidated damages
A contract can contain a penal clause in the case that the contract is not fulfilled.

**celebrar un contrato**
Un contrato puede celebrarse en el domicilio de una de las partes contratantes.

to sign a contract
A contract can be signed in the home of one of the contracting parties.

**válido (a)**
Un contrato es válido cuando reúne tres requisitos: el consentimiento de las partes, la certitud del objeto contractual y la causa de la obligación contractual.

valid
A contract is valid if it fulfills three requisites: the consent of the parties; the determination of the object of the contract; and the subject of the contractual obligation.

**nulo (a)**
Un contrato es nulo cuando no es válido.

null; invalid
A contract is null and void when it's invalid.

el **objeto del contrato**

object of the contract

el **objeto contractual**
Pueden ser objeto de un contrato los bienes enajenables y los servicios lícitos.

contractual object
Goods which can be sold and legally admissible services can be the object of a contract.

la **causa del contrato**
La causa de un contrato es para cada parte contratante la contraprestación de la otra parte.

subject of the contract
For each contracting party the subject of the contract is the consideration of the other party.

**cumplir**
Las partes deben cumplir sus obligaciones contractuales realizando las prestaciones que integran estas obligaciones.

to fulfill
The parties should fulfill their contractual obligations and perform the services which appertain to these obligations.

el **tiempo de pago**

pay period

el **lugar del pago**
El lugar del pago es el pactado por las partes y en su defecto el previsto por la ley.

place of payment
The place of payment is agreed on by the parties and when not specified, it is the place foreseen by the law.

**exigir**
El acreedor sólo puede exigir al deudor el cumplimiento de las obligaciones que estén ya vencidas.

to require; demand
The creditor can demand only that the debtor comply with the obligations that are already due.

la **mora**
Habitualmente, si se incurre en mora, han de pagarse altos intereses.

delay
Usually, if one falls behind, high interest charges will be incurred.

**resolver**
Las partes pueden resolver el contrato de mutuo acuerdo.

to dissolve
The parties can dissolve the contract by mutual agreement.

la **condición**

condition

**vencer**
Cuando las partes establecen condiciones y término, las obligaciones vencen y son por tanto exigibles.

to be/become due
When the parties set conditions and objective, the obligations become due and are therefore payable on demand.

la **obligación accesoria**
La obligación accesoria depende de una obligación principal, cuyos efectos tiende a asegurar o a completar.

additional/contingent obligation
A contingent obligation is dependent on the principal obligation, whose effects it tends to insure or complete.

la **obligación pecuniaria**
La obligación pecuniaria consiste en entregar una suma de dinero.

monetary/pecuniary obligation
A monetary obligation consists in handing over a sum of money.

**compensar**
Sólo las obligaciones pecuniarias, vencidas, líquidas y exigibles pueden compensarse mutuamente.

to compensate
Only those monetary obligations which are due, liquid and payable on demand can be mutually compensated.

la **cláusula arbitral**
Las partes introducen en el contrato una cláusula arbitral para dirimir eventuales divergencias por la vía extrajudicial.

arbitration clause
The parties include an arbitration clause in the contract to provide for settling any possible future differences of opinion out of court.

**dirimir** — to decide; settle; end

**por la vía extrajudicial** — out of court

**subcontratar** — to subcontract
Para cumplir las obligaciones contractuales, puede subcontratarse la realización de las prestaciones con un tercero. — To fulfill your contractual obligations, you can conclude a subcontract with a third party for the performance of services.

la **capacidad contractual** — legally of age to enter into a contract
Un menor de edad no tiene capacidad contractual. — A minor is not legally of age for making a contract.

la **certitud** — certainty

**anulable** — annulable; rescindable; cancellable; voidable
Las partes pueden impugnar un contrato que, por adolecer de algún defecto, resulte anulable. — The parties can challenge a contract that can be voided because it suffers from some defect.

**impugnar** — to challenge

el **consentimiento** — consent; agreement
Otorgando su consentimiento, las partes hacen patente su voluntad de celebrar el contrato. — By giving their consent, the parties have made clear their wish to enter into a contract.

**enajenable** — sellable

**lícito (a)** — licit

el **contrato eficaz** — effective contract
Un contrato válido no es necesariamente eficaz si las obligaciones contractuales están sujetas a condición o a término. — A valid contract is not necessarily effective if the contractual obligations are dependent on any condition or objective.

la **forma del contrato** — contract form

la **extinción de las obligaciones** — cancelling of the obligations
La forma más importante de extinción de las obligaciones contractuales es el pago o cumplimiento voluntario. — The most important form in which contract obligations are cancelled is payment or voluntary fulfillment.

la **moratoria** — moratorium
La moratoria consiste en el aplazamiento del momento de cumplimiento de las obligaciones contractuales. — The moratorium is the deferment of the time when contract obligations are due to be fulfilled.

la **responsabilidad contractual** — contract liability
La responsabilidad contractual puede ser debida a dolo, culpa o negligencia o morosidad. — Contract liability can be incurred due to intention, guilt, negligence, or delay.

| | |
|---|---|
| el **dolo** | intention |
| la **negligencia** | negligence |
| la **morosidad** | delay; tardiness |
| la **indemnización de daños y perjuicios** | compensation for damages and losses |
| La parte que incurra en responsabilidad contractual queda sujeta a la indemnización de los daños y perjuicios causados a la otra parte. | The party held contractually responsible, is obligated to compensate the other party for damages or losses it caused the other party to suffer. |
| **incurrir en responsabilidad** | to be held liable |
| el **término** | term |
| El término es la fecha o evento cierto fijado por las partes para la plena eficacia del contrato. | The term is the date or definite event designated by the parties for the full taking effect of the contract. |
| la **eficacia** | efficacy; taking effect |

## Types of Contracts

el **precontrato**

pre-contract

Precontrato es el contrato mediante el cual las partes se comprometen a celebrar en el futuro otro contrato que actualmente no pueden o no quieren concluir.

The pre-contract is the contract by which the parties promise to conclude a contract in the future which at present they are unable or unwilling to sign.

el **contrato verbal**

verbal contract

Contrato verbal es aquél que no está formalizado por escrito.

A verbal contract is one that is not in written form.

el **contrato típico**

standard contract

Contrato típico es aquél cuyos elementos fundamentales están regulados por ley.

A standard contract is one whose basic elements are regulated by law.

el **contrato de exclusividad**

exclusive contract

el **contrato de compraventa**

purchase-sales contract

el **contrato de arrendamiento**

leasing/rental contract; leasing agreement

Contrato de arrendamiento es aquél por el cual un arrendador se obliga a proporcionar a un arrendatario el goce o uso de una cosa o derecho determinados durante un tiempo determinado a cambio de un precio cierto.

In a rental contract a lessor pledges to grant a lessee the use and enjoyment of something specific or of a specific right for a set period of time and at a certain price.

|  |  |
|---|---|
| el **arrendador,** la **arrendadora** | lessor; person who rents to |
| el **arrendatario,** la **arrendataria** | lessee; person who rents from |
| el **contrato colectivo**<br>El sindicato firmó este año un contrato colectivo muy favorable para sus intereses. | collective bargaining contract<br>This year the union signed a collective bargaining contract very favorable to its interests. |
| el **contrato de transporte**<br>Contrato de transporte es aquél por el cual una parte se obliga a cambio de un precio a trasladar de un lugar a otro un bien o a una persona determinados. | transportation/freight contract<br>In a transportation contract one party pledges, for a consideration, to transport specified merchandise or a specific person or persons from one place to another. |
| el **contrato de fletamento**<br>Contrato de fletamento es el contrato de arrendamiento de un buque para el transporte de mercancías o personas. | affreightment contract/charter<br>An affreightment contract arranges for the renting of a ship for the transport of merchandise or persons. |
| el **contrato de representación**<br>Contrato de representación es aquél por el cual un representante se obliga a actuar en nombre y por cuenta del representado. | agent contract<br>In an agent contract, an agent promises to act in the name of and for the account of the person for whom he is acting as agent. |
| el **representado,** la **representada** | person represented by an agent |
| el **contrato de préstamo**<br>Contrato de préstamo es aquél por el cual el prestamista entrega al prestatario dinero a cambio de un interés. | loan contract<br>In a loan contract the lender lends money to the borrower at a rate of interest. |
| el, la **prestamista** | lender |
| el **prestatario,** la **prestataria** | borrower |
| el **contrato de seguro** | insurance contract |
| el **contrato unilateral**<br>Un contrato es unilateral porque crea obligaciones para una sola de las partes implicadas. | unilateral contract<br>A contract is unilateral because it creates obligations for only one of the parties concerned. |
| el **contrato bilateral**<br>Un contrato es bilateral cuando crea obligaciones recíprocas para las partes implicadas. | bilateral contract<br>A contract is bilateral when it creates mutual obligations for the parties concerned. |
| el **contrato de subarriendo**<br>Contrato de subarriendo es aquél por el cual el arrendatario de una cosa o derecho se obliga a proporcionar a un tercero el goce o uso de dicha cosa. | subleasing contract<br>In a subleasing contract, the lessee of a thing or right promises to grant the use and enjoyment of said thing or right to a third party. |

el **goce** — enjoyment; usufruct

el **contrato de distribución** — distribution contract
Ejemplos de contratos de distribución son los contratos de suministro y de abastecimiento. — Examples of distribution contracts are supply and delivery contracts.

el **contrato de suministro** — supplier contract
Contrato de suministro es aquél por el cual un fabricante se obliga a vender sus productos a un distribuidor para su reventa al público. — In a supplier contract a manufacturer pledges to sell his products to a distributor for resale to the public.

la **reventa** — resale

el **contrato de abastecimiento** — delivery/provisioning contract

el **contrato de reaseguro** — reinsurance contract
El objeto de contrato de reaseguro es cubrir el riesgo de tener que abonar la indemnización pactada con su tomador. — The purpose of the reinsurance contract is to cover the risk of having to pay the policyholder's agreed upon compensation claim.

el **contrato de sociedad** — corporate contract
Contrato de sociedad es aquél por el cual dos o más personas se obligan a poner en común bienes o industria para su explotación. — In a corporate contract two or more persons pledge to pool equity or labor in order to make a profit.

## Trial Law

el **tribunal** — tribunal; court
(En España,) el Tribunal Supremo esta integrado por cinco Salas; de lo Civil, de lo Penal, de lo Contencioso-Administrativo, de lo Social y de lo Militar. — (In Spain,) the Supreme Court consists of five courts; a civil, penal, administrative, social, and a military court.

la **sala** — court

el **inculpado,** la **inculpada** — accused person

el **actor,** la **actora** — plaintiff
El actor puede comparecer ante juicio sin abogado en ciertos casos. — In certain cases the plaintiff can appear in court without a lawyer.

| | |
|---|---|
| la **defensa** | defense |
| La defensa defiende los intereses de su cliente. | The defense defends the interests of its client. |
| el, la **cliente** | client |
| el **proceso** | trial |
| el **plazo** | term |
| la **parte en un proceso** | participant in a trial |
| el **perito** | expert |
| El médico, el arquitecto o cualquier otro profesional, están facultados para ser peritos en un proceso. | Doctors, architects or any other professionals, are authorized to appear as expert witnesses in a trial. |
| **probar** | to prove |
| el **medio de prueba** | method of proving |
| Un medio de prueba puede ser la declaración de testigos. | One method of proving can be the statements of witnesses. |
| **citar a juicio** | to issue a summons to; summon |
| Los testigos son citados a juicio. | The witnesses are summoned to court. |
| **testificar** | to testify |
| El cometer falso testimonio al testificar se castiga con pena de prisión. | Committing perjury on the witness stand is punished with a prison term. |
| el **testimonio** | testimony |
| **falso (a)** | false |
| **confesar** | to confess |
| Confesar significa reconocer la culpa propia y comunicar toda la verdad. | To confess means to acknowledge one's guilt and to tell the whole truth. |
| **dictar sentencia** | to render a verdict; pass sentence |
| **ejecutar la sentencia** | to carry out the sentence |
| Una vez dictada, las partes pueden solicitar que sea ejecutada la sentencia. | Once sentence is passed, the parties may ask that it be carried out. |
| la **conciliación** | reconciliation; settlement |
| En la conciliación ambas partes pueden alcanzar un acuerdo satisfactorio. | Settlement means that both parties can come to a satisfactory agreement. |
| la **avenencia** | agreement |
| Cuando hay avenencia en la conciliación, no se llega a celebrar el juicio. | When there is agreement in the settlement, no judicial proceeding takes place. |

el, la **insolvente**
Los insolventes tienen derecho a un
abogado de oficio.

insolvent person
Insolvent persons are entitled to a
public defender.

el **abogado de oficio,** la
**abogada de oficio**

public defender

**embargado (a)**
Cuando no se pagan las multas, se
corre el riesgo de ser embargado.

seized; confiscated; sequestrated
Failure to pay fines can result in a
levy.

el **órgano jurisdiccional**
El Tribunal Supremo es un órgano
jurisdiccional colegiado.

judicial organ
The Supreme Court is a collective
judicial organ.

la **competencia**
La Audiencia Nacional tiene competencia sobre los delitos de terrorismo.

competence
The Spanish Supreme Court is
competent to try terrorist crimes.

el **juzgado**
El juzgado es la sede material de un
órgano jurisdiccional.

court
The court is the physical site of a
judicial organ.

**consignar la fianza**
Las fianzas se consignan en el juzgado.

to put up/pay bail
Bail is paid in jail.

el **litisconsorcio**

associates in a lawsuit; joint
litigants

**acumular acciones**
Se pueden acumular las acciones
cuando los pedimentos de las partes
son idénticos.

consolidate legal actions
Legal actions can be consolidated
when the suits of the parties are
identical.

el **pedimento**

claim; suit; petition

la **pretensión**
La pretensión de una parte es el objetivo que ésta quiere conseguir.

petition
A petition describes the goals a
petitioner wishes to attain.

la **capacidad de las partes**

legal capacity of the parties in a
judicial process

Para poder litigar es necesario inicialmente analizar la capacidad de las
partes y la naturaleza de lo pedido.

In order to litigate it is first necessary to examine the legal capacity
of the parties and the nature of the
petition.

el **edicto**
La autoridad judicial puede citar por
edictos cuando no da con el paradero
del citado.

decree; edict
The court can issue decrees to
summon when the whereabouts of
the person summoned are unknown.

el **paradero**

whereabouts

| | |
|---|---|
| **el objeto del proceso** <br> La custodia del hijo puede ser objeto de un proceso. | object of the suit <br> Child custody can be the object of a suit. |
| **la prueba documental** <br> Un contrato de compraventa puede ser prueba documental. | documentary proof <br> A purchase-sales contract can be documentary proof. |
| **motivado (a)** <br> Las resoluciones judiciales siempre deberán de ser motivadas. | motivated; well-grounded <br> Judicial decisions must always be well-grounded. |
| **reconvenir** <br> Reconvenir consiste en la reclamación que hace el propio demandado al contestar a la demanda. | to file a counter suit <br> To file a counter suit means the accused makes a legal complaint when responding to the charge against him. |
| **el recurso** | recourse |
| **recusar** <br> El juez puede ser recusado por una de las partes. | to recuse; reject for prejudice <br> The judge can be recused by one of the parties. |
| **las alegaciones** <br> Las alegaciones son realizadas por los abogados de las partes. | objections <br> Objections are made by the parties' lawyers. |
| **abstener** <br> Un perito puede abstenerse del procedimiento si es amigo de una de las partes. | to abstain; stay away from <br> An expert can abstain from the proceedings if he is a friend of one of the parties. |

## Criminal Law

| | |
|---|---|
| **el delito** <br> Ultimamente se ha generalizado entre los Estados la tipificación del delito ecológico. | crime <br> Recently, environmental crimes have been recognized among states. |
| **el imputado, la imputada** | person accused |
| **la tentativa** <br> Existe la tentativa cuando el sujeto da principio a la ejecución de un delito pero no la termina por causa o accidente que no sean su propio y voluntario desistimiento. | attempt <br> One speaks of an attempt when the accused starts to commit a criminal act but does not complete it because of an accident or some other reason not due to his own voluntary cessation of criminal activity. |

los **atenuantes**
Los atenuantes sirven para rebajar la condena.

extenuating circumstances
Extenuating circumstances serve to reduce the sentence.

la **culpa**

guilt

la **condena**

punishment

**calumniar**

Calumniar es imputar falsamente un delito, siendo especialmente grave si se hace por escrito y con publicidad.

to calumniate; slander; accuse falsely
To calumniate is to impute a crime erroneously to someone, a particularly aggravated act when it is done publicly in writing.

la **corrupción**
La corrupción política es uno de los principales problemas con que tienen que enfrentarse los gobiernos en la actualidad.

corruption
Political corruption is one of the chief problems governments have to deal with nowadays.

el **fraude**

fraud

la **quiebra fraudulenta**

fraudulent bankruptcy

el **robo**
El robo es el más grave de los delitos contra la propiedad.

theft
The most serious crime against property is theft.

el **contrabando**
Entre España y Francia es frecuente el contrabando de ganado.

smuggling; contraband
There is much cattle smuggling between Spain and France.

**falsificado (a)**
Llevar un pasaporte falsificado puede ocasionar a su portador serios problemas.

falsified; false
Carrying a false passport can give rise to serious problems for the bearer.

la **pena**

punishment

la **prisión**

prison

**detener**

to arrest

**interrogar**
Tras interrogar la Policía al sospechoso durante mas de una hora, éste confesó haber sido el autor del crimen.

to interrogate
After the police interrogated the suspect for more than an hour, he confessed to having committed the crime.

las **fuerzas de seguridad**
De las fuerzas de seguridad españolas, la más conocida internacionalmente es la Guardia Civil.

security forces
The Guardia Civil is the best known internationally of Spain's security forces.

**declarar**
Tras declarar ante el juez, se hallaron indicios de criminalidad suficientes como para decretar su ingreso en prisión.

to declare; testify
After testifying to the judge, sufficient evidence of criminal intent was found to put him in prison.

la **víctima**

victim

**reincidir**
Reincidir en un delito agrava la pena.

to relapse;
Recidivism, relapsing into the same crime, increases the sentence.

la **acción popular**
La acción popular es la acción penal que ejercitan, junto con el Ministerio Fiscal, aquellos ciudadanos que hayan visto sus derechos especialmente vulnerados por un delito.

accessory action; class action suit
A class action suit, brought in conjuction with the prosecution, is a judicial action brought by citizens who perceive their rights as having been particularly violated by a crime.

**vulnerado (a)**

violated

**agravante**
La reincidencia siempre se considera como agravante.

aggravating
Recidivism is always considered an aggravating circumstance.

la **reincidencia**

recidivism; relapse into crime

la **alevosía**
La nocturnidad junto con la alevosía pueden calificar el homicidio como asesinato.

malice; treachery; premeditation
The cover of darkness and premeditation can result in homicide being declared murder.

el **homicidio**

homicide

el **asesinato**

murder

**indultar**
Indultar consiste en revisar total o parcialmente una pena, pero a diferencia de la amnistía, no borra totalmente los efectos del delito.

to pardon
Granting a pardon can mean totally or partially remitting a sentence, but in contradistinction to amnesty it does not totally wipe out the effects of the crime.

la **amnistía**

amnesty

**prevaricar**

Un Juez puede prevaricar cuando dicta a sabiendas una sentencia injusta.

to violate one's official duty; bend the law
A judge can violate his official duty when he knowingly renders an unjust verdict.

la **libertad condicional**
El decretar la libertad condicional es una prerrogativa del juez.

release on parole
Releasing on parole is a judge's prerogative.

la **apropiación indebida**
La apropiación indebida es el delito por el cual un sujeto se apropia de un bien que previamente le fue entregado con obligación de devolverlo.

misappropriation
Misappropriation is the crime of taking possession of a property previously entrusted to him with the obligation of returning it.

**apropiarse**

to take possession of

la **evasión de capitales**

flight of capital

el **blanqueo de dinero**
Con frecuencia se invierte en propiedades en la Costa del Sol para de esta manera llevar a cabo el blanqueo del dinero procedente de las drogas.

money laundering; whitewashing
Investments in property on the Costa del Sol are frequently made in order to whitewash money from drug trafficking.

CIVITAS
Biblioteca de Legislación

CODIGO
DE COMERCIO
Y
LEYES
COMPLEMENTARIAS

DECIMOSEPTIMA EDICION
ACTUALIZADA A SEPTIEMBRE DE 1993

EDITORIAL CIVITAS

# Banking

la **banca**
En los últimos años la banca española se ha vuelto mucho más competitiva.

banking system
In recent years the Spanish banking system has become much more competitive.

la **banca privada**
Dentro de la banca privada española, el BBV y el Banco Central Hispano son las instituciones de crédito más importantes.

private banking sector
In the private bank sector, the BBV and the Banco Central Hispano are the most important credit institutions.

la **caja de ahorros**
Las cajas de ahorros se dedican sobre todo a captar dinero de particulares para prestárselo también a particulares.

savings bank
Savings banks are primarily devoted to getting money from private individuals in order to lend it to private individuals.

la **Caja Postal de Ahorros**
La integración de la Caja Postal de Ahorros en el Grupo Argentaria permite la ampliación de los servicios prestados al cliente.

Postal Savings Association
The entry of the Postal Savings Association into the Argentaria group has permitted the expansion of customer services.

**bancario (a)**
Francfort como sede del Banco Central Europeo ocupa un lugar destacado en el sistema bancario mundial.

banking
As the seat of the European Central Bank, Frankfurt occupies an important place in world banking.

el **banquero,** la **banquera**
Algunos de los más conocidos banqueros españoles han trabajado anteriormente en grandes empresas públicas.

banker
Some of the best known Spanish bankers previously worked in large state owned enterprises.

la **clientela**
La clientela la componen todas las personas que hacen uso de los servicios del banco.

clientele
All persons who make use of a bank's services constitute its clientele.

el **sistema bancario**
En este país el sistema bancario ha experimentado profundos cambios, tanto en la banca privada como en la pública.

banking system
In this country the banking system has undergone profound changes, as much in the private as in the national or federal reserve banking sector.

**en círculos bancarios**
En círculos bancarios reina cierta preocupación por el alto porcentaje de deudores morosos.

in banking circles
In banking circles a certain unease prevails concerning the high percentage of debtors in arrears.

#### el **Banco de España**

Bank of Spain

#### **fijar**

to fix; establish

El Banco de España fija el tipo de interés que han de seguir todas las entidades bancarias.

The Bank of Spain establishes the interest rate which is to be followed by all credit institutions.

#### **garantizar**

to guarantee

El Banco de España garantiza el funcionamiento del sistema bancario.

The Bank of Spain guarantees the functioning of the banking system.

#### el **Banco Hipotecario**

Mortgage Bank (Name of the official Spanish Building Fund)

Muchos españoles se han comprado una casa con la ayuda de un préstamo concedido por el Banco Hipotecario.

Many Spaniards have bought a house with the help of a loan granted by the Banco Hipotecario.

#### la **institución de crédito**

credit institution

#### la **entidad bancaria**

banking corporation

El Banco de España ha pedido a las instituciones de crédito que apliquen a sus clientes las bajadas de los tipos de interés.

The Bank of Spain has asked credit institutions to pass on interest rate reductions to their customers.

#### el **banco corresponsal**

correspondence bank

Si una institución de crédito no está representada en una ciudad o país, puede actuar allí a través de un banco corresponsal con el que tiene una relación permanente.

If a credit institution is not represented in a city or country, it can do business through a corresponding bank with which it maintains permanent business relations.

#### el **banco comercial**

commercial bank

#### las **operaciones bancarias**

banking operations

Muchos bancos amplian sus operaciones bancarias a otros campos tales como seguros de vida y enfermedad.

Many banks are expanding their banking operations into other fields such as life and health insurance.

#### la **transacción**

transaction

El acuerdo entre VW y SEAT de efectuar sus transacciones comerciales en marcos alemanes ha causado pérdidas muy elevadas a la empresa española.

The agreement between VW and SEAT to carry out their business transactions in German marks has caused heavy losses for the Spanish company.

#### el **horario de atención al público**

banking hours

Ultimamente, muchos bancos y cajas de ahorros han ampliado su horario de atención al público.

Recently many banks, savings banks, and savings and loan associations have extended their hours.

la **caja de seguridad**
Se recomienda a los clientes que
vayan a salir de vacaciones que dejen
sus objetos de valor en una caja de
seguridad de su banco.

safe(ty) deposit box
It is recommended to customers
going on vacation that they leave
any objects of value in a safe
deposit box in their bank.

el **código bancario**
Cada banco tiene asignado por el
Banco de España un número de identificación que recibe el nombre de
código bancario.

bank code (number)
The Bank of Spain assigns every
bank an identification number
which is called its bank code.

el **código cuenta cliente**
Para evitar equivocaciones, a cada
cliente se le asigna un código de
cuenta cliente (sucursal + dígito de
control + número de cuenta).

customer identification number
To avoid mistakes, every customer
is assigned a customer identification
number (branch + control number
+ account number).

el **secreto bancario**
Los bancos están obligados a guardar
secreto bancario, es decir, que no
deben comunicar datos sobre el estado
de cuenta de sus clientes, solvencia,
etc.

bank secrecy
The banks are obligated to maintain banking secrecy, i.e. they
should not disclose information
concerning the state of their customers' accounts, credit rating, etc.

el **encaje bancario**
El encaje bancario está constituido
por las reservas de dinero legal que
los bancos han de mantener en su
caja y en el banco central para
atender la demanda de efectivo por
parte de sus depositantes.

bank reserves
Bank reserves consist of the reserves
of legal tender the banks must
maintain in their vaults and in the
central bank to be able to meet any
demands for payment made by
their depositors.

las **operaciones activas**

Entre las operaciones activas de un
banco figuran la concesión de créditos
e hipotecas, así como el descuento de
letras.

lending and investment activities;
asset operations
Among the asset operations of a
bank are the granting of credit and
mortgages, as well as the discounting of bills.

las **operaciones pasivas**
Las operaciones pasivas sirven, sobre
todo, para la obtención de recursos
ajenos.

liability operations
Liability operations are concerned
primarily with the acquiring of
outside equity.

las **operaciones en divisas**
Las operaciones en divisas de la clientela se efectúan en los departamentos
internacionales de los respectivos
bancos.

dealing in foreign currencies
Transactions in foreign currencies
on behalf of customers take place
in the international departments of
the respective banks.

las **operaciones de compensación**
En las operaciones de compensación,
el banco negocia las órdenes de compra y venta de títulos-valores por
parte de sus clientes según una determinada cotización en bolsa.

compensation transactions

In compensation transactions for
its customers the bank executes
orders for the purchase and sale of
securities according to the prices
quoted on the stock exchange.

**la cámara de compensación**
Las letras se presentan a la cámara de compensación dos días hábiles antes de su vencimiento para el cobro.

clearinghouse
At the clearinghouse bills are presented for collection two business days before they are due.

**la administración patrimonial**
En la administración patrimonial, el banco se hace cargo de los bienes patrimoniales y depósitos de sus clientes.

estate/financial/equity management
In financial management the bank looks after the investments and deposits of its customers.

**la emisión de billetes**
La emisión de billetes es competencia exclusiva del Banco de España.

issue of banknotes
The issue of banknotes is the sole prerogative of the Bank of Spain.

**el apoderado, la apoderada**
El apoderado puede firmar en representación del banco todo aquello a lo que dicha institución de crédito le haya autorizado.

authorized representative/signatory
The authorized signatory can sign everything for the bank which the credit institution in question has authorized him to sign.

**el interventor, la interventora**
El interventor efectúa periódicamente controles sobre los distintos departamentos'del banco con el fin de comprobar si los trabajos se están realizando correctamente.

comptroller; auditor
The comptroller carries out periodic checks on the bank's various departments in order to ascertain whether banking operations are being performed properly.

**la cartera de valores**
La cartera de valores abarca los títulos-valores administrados por el banco.

investment portfolio
The investment portfolio contains the securities managed by the bank.

**la autocartera**
El Banco de España ha limitado el porcentaje de la autocartera para controlar operaciones especulativas.

securities belonging to the bank
The Bank of Spain has limited the percentage of securities banks can own in order to control speculative transactions.

**el coeficiente de caja**

Mediante el coeficiente de caja, el Banco de España limita la liquidez de los bancos obligándoles a cubrir un porcentaje que varía según el mercado.

minimum reserves; obligatory reserves
Through minimum reserves, the Bank of Spain limits the liquidity of banks by compelling them to maintain a percentage of their reserves which varies according to market fluctuations.

**el mercado de capitales**
El mercado de capitales es el mercado para dinero a medio y largo plazo.

capital market
The capital market is the middle and long term money market.

el **mercado monetario**
En el mercado monetario se negocian los medios financieros a corto plazo.

the money market
Short term capital is transacted on the money market.

el **título-valor**

security

el **empréstito**
El empréstito es el préstamo que toma unas empresas a cambio de la emisión de títulos-valores.

loan
The capital loan is the sum of borrowed obligations a company assumes when it issues stocks or bonds.

la **obligación**
La obligación es remunerada por un interés determinado.

bond; debenture
Bonds bear a set rate of interest.

el **movimiento electrónico de pagos**
Los bancos están realizando inversiones considerables para optimizar el movimiento electrónico de pagos.

electronic transfer of funds

The banks are investing considerable sums for the improvement of the system of electronic transfer of funds.

la **banca electrónica**

electronic banking

la **transmisión de datos en soporte magnético**
Hasta el día 20 del mes siguiente, los bancos tienen que entregar al Banco de España las informaciones respecto al balance y a las cuentas de pérdidas y ganancias en soporte magnético.

data transmission via magnetic tape carrier
Via magnetic tape, the banks must provide the Bank of Spain with information concerning balances and profit and loss accounting before the 20th of next month.

---

# Money and Currency

el **dinero en metálico**
Las tarjetas de crédito son una alternativa para no llevar encima grandes cantidades de dinero en metálico.

cash; money in specie
Credit cards represent an alternative to carrying large amounts in cash.

la **tarjeta de crédito**

credit card

los **fondos**
El gobierno español todavía debe aumentar los fondos destinados a apoyar la creación de nuevas empresas.

means; funds
The Spanish government still needs to increase the funds it makes available for encouraging the creation of new businesses.

la **moneda base**
Desde la conferencia de Bretton-Woods (1944), el dólar americano es la moneda base internacional.

base/key currency
Ever since the Bretton-Woods conference in 1944, the American dollar is the international base currency.

la **moneda fuerte**
Al ser el marco alemán la moneda más fuerte del Sistema Monetario Europeo (SME), se ha convertido en la moneda base europea.

strong currency
Since the German mark is the strongest currency in the European Monetary System, it has become the European key currency.

la **moneda débil**

weak currency

la **cotización**
La cotización del dólar ha caído en las últimas semanas.

exchange rate; price quotation
In the last few weeks the exchange rate for the dollar has fallen.

el **tipo de cambio**
A partir de 1972, el tipo de cambio de las monedas comenzó a regularse en Europa según la oferta y la demanda.

currency exchange rate
Beginning in 1972, the currency exchange rate in Europe has been dependent on supply and demand.

la **unidad de cuenta**
Desde 1979, el ECU es la unidad de cuenta europea.

unit of account
Since 1979, the ECU has been the European unit of accounting.

el **Sistema Monetario Europeo (SME)**
En 1979 se creó el Sistema Monetario Europeo.

European Monetary System

In 1979 the European Monetary system was created.

la **reforma monetaria**

monetary reform

la **política monetaria**
La política monetaria, controlada por el banco emisor de cada país, es el conjunto de medidas que garantiza el desarrollo óptimo de su moneda.

monetary policy
Monetary policy, determined by the national bank of each country, is the ensemble of measures that guarantee the optimal development of each currency.

la **devaluación**
Durante 1993, la peseta ha sufrido repetidas devaluaciones favoreciendo, así, a las exportaciones españolas.

devaluation
During 1993, the peseta suffered several devaluations, thus encouraging Spanish exports.

la **revaluación**
El encarecimiento de las exportaciones y el abaratamiento de las importaciones son consecuencia de la revaluación de una moneda.

revaluation; valuing up
Revaluation of a currency results in exports becoming more expensive and imports becoming cheaper.

el **control de divisas**
Con el control de divisas se pretende llevar un registro de las entradas y salidas de moneda extranjera.

currency control/regulation
Through currency regulation an attempt is being made to keep a list of the foreign currency entering and leaving the country.

la **reserva de divisas**
Para mantener a la peseta dentro de su banda de fluctuación, el Banco de España tuvo que hacer uso de sus reservas de divisas.

reserves of foreign currency
To keep the peseta within its range of fluctuation, the Bank of Spain had to make use of its reserves of foreign currency.

la **falsificación de billetes**
Con la introducción de las fotocopiadoras a color se abrieron nuevas posibilidades en la falsificación de billetes.

counterfeiting of banknotes
With the introduction of color photocopiers, new possibilities for counterfeiting banknotes have opened.

el **dinero negro**

money not declared for taxes

el **dinero caliente**

hot money

el **blanqueo de dinero**

money laundering

la **moneda de curso legal**
La peseta es la moneda de curso legal en España.

legal tender
The peseta is legal tender in Spain.

el **derecho de acuñación**
Unicamente la Casa de Moneda y Timbre ostenta, en España, el derecho de acuñación.

coining privilege/prerogative
Only the Spanish National Mint has the right of coinage.

**ostentar**

to possess; exercise

la **Casa de Moneda y Timbre**

Spanish National Mint

**poner en circulación**
En 1993, el Banco de España ha puesto en circulación los nuevos billetes de 2.000 pesetas.

to put into circulation
In 1993, the Bank of Spain put into circulation the new 2,000 peseta notes.

**retirar de la circulación**
Los bancos emisores dan un plazo de tiempo relativamente amplio para retirar de la circulación las monedas o billetes que han de ser sustituídos por los nuevos.

withdraw from circulation
The national banks allow a relatively long period of time for withdrawal from circulation of notes and coins which are to be substituted by new ones.

la **masa monetaria**
La limitación de la masa monetaria es uno de los objetivos principales de la política económica de la mayoría de los países.

amount of money; money supply
Limitation of the money supply is one of the chief economic policy objectives in most countries.

las **disposiciones legales sobre divisas**
Dentro de la Comunidad Económica Europea, las disposiciones legales sobre divisas van siendo cada vez menos severas.

legal regulations concerning foreign currencies
Within the European Economic Community, foreign currency regulations are becoming less and less strict.

| | |
|---|---|
| **la banda de fluctuación**<br>La banda de fluctuación indica el valor máximo y mínimo entre los que puede oscilar el tipo de cambio de una moneda. | range of fluctuation<br>The range of fluctuation indicates the upper and lower limits within which the rate of exchange for a particular currency can vary. |
| **oscilar** | to oscillate; fluctuate; vary |
| **las fluctuaciones de divisas** | currency fluctuations |
| **las oscilaciones de divisas** | changes in currency exchange rates |
| **la paridad de monedas** | parity of currencies |
| **la paridad monetaria**<br>En un sistema de tipos de cambios fijos, la paridad de monedas refleja la relación de una moneda respecto a la moneda base. | monetary parity<br>In a system of fixed exchange rates, currency parity reflects a currency ratio to the base currency. |
| **el patrón monetario**<br>El marco alemán actúa como patrón monetario entre el dólar y las restantes monedas del Sistema Monetario Europeo. | anchor currency; model currency<br>The German mark serves as an anchor currency between the dollar and the other currencies of the European Monetary System. |
| **la depreciación**<br>Con el paso del tiempo se produce una inevitable depreciación del dinero. | depreciation; devaluation<br>With the passage of time, currency devaluation is inevitable. |
| **el debilitamiento**<br>El debilitamiento del dólar supuso un fortalecimiento del yen japonés y del marco alemán. | weakening; decline<br>The decline in the dollar led to a strengthening of the Japanese yen and the German mark. |
| **el fortalecimiento** | strengthening |
| **el riesgo monetario** | monetary risk |
| **la cobertura de moneda extranjera**<br>Gracias a la entrada de turistas, el Banco de España dispone de una buena cobertura de moneda extranjera. | foreign currency cushion<br>Thanks to the flow of tourists, the Bank of Spain is well cushioned with foreign currency. |
| **apoyar**<br>Para evitar un mayor debilitamiento del franco francés, el Bundesbank apoyó en varias ocasiones a la moneda francesa. | to support<br>To avoid a further weakening of the French franc, the German National Bank supported the French franc on several occasions. |
| **la convertibilidad** | convertibility |

**convertible**

Hasta 1914, gran número de monedas se podían convertir en oro o en libras esterlinas convertibles en oro.

convertible

Up to 1914, a great number of currencies could be converted to gold or to pounds sterling convertible into gold.

## Keeping an Account

el **número de cuenta**
Si alguien no recuerda el número de su cuenta, en el banco lo pueden averiguar a través de su N.I.F. (Número de Identificación Fiscal).

account number
If someone doesn't remember her/his account number, the bank will be able to find it through the customer's N.I.F. (Tax Identification Number).

el **estado de una cuenta,** el **saldo de una cuenta**
También los cajeros automáticos le informan del saldo de una cuenta.

bank (account) balance

Automatic teller machines will also let you know how much is in your account.

**poner al día**
Como el titular de una libreta de ahorros no recibe extractos, debe dirigirse al banco para poder ponerla al día.

to bring up to date
Since the possessor of a savings account passbook receives no bank statements, he must ask the bank to bring it up to date.

**proporcionar**
¿Me podría proporcionar un nuevo talonario de cheques?

to provide; get; give
Can you give me a new check book?

**figurar**
En los extractos de cuentas figuran los últimos movimientos que se han efectuado.

to appear; show
Bank statements show the latest transactions made in the account.

**cancelar**
Se necesitan las firmas de todos los titulares para poder cancelar la cuenta.

to cancel; close out
The signature of all the account holders is necessary to close out an account.

la **cuenta corriente**
Las cuentas corrientes ofrecen una gran versatilidad, pero intereses muy bajos.

current account
Current accounts are very flexible but they pay very low interest.

la **versatilidad**

versatility; flexibility

la **cuenta de ahorro**
Para poder abrir una cuenta de ahorro necesitamos su N.I.F. (Número de Identificación Fiscal).

savings account
In order to open a savings account we need your N.I.F. (Tax Identification Number).

el **beneficiario,** la **beneficiaria**
¡No olvide escribir el nombre del beneficiario de la transferencia!

receiver; payee
Don't forget to write the name of the receiver of the transfer.

la **transferencia**

transfer

**con cargo a**
Quisiera realizar una transferencia
con cargo a mi cuenta.

debited to
I want to have a transfer made, to
be debited to my account.

**a favor de**

in favor of

la **comisión**
Cuando compres pesetas tienes que
contar con la comisión de cambio
que se lleva el banco.

commission; brokerage fee
When you buy pesetas you have
to take into account the bank's
commission.

la **liquidación**
Cada tres meses el banco realiza la
liquidación de intereses de las cuentas
de sus clientes.

liquidation; account balancing
Every three months the bank
calculates the interest on its
customers' accounts.

**efectuar**
Cada vez más bancos ofrecen la posibilidad de efectuar operaciones bancarias por teléfono.

to do; execute
More and more banks are offering
the possibility of doing banking
by telephone.

**girar dinero**
Una manera rápida y segura de girar
dinero a una cuenta en el extranjero
es haciéndolo por télex.

to transfer money
A fast and safe way to transfer
money to a foreign account is to
do it by telex.

**ingresar**
No me gusta que tengas tanto dinero
en casa, ¿por qué no lo ingresas en
tu cuenta?

to deposit
I don't like your having so much
money in the house; why don't
you deposit it into your account?

el **ingreso en cuenta**

depositing to an account

**retirar**
Sólo el titular o las personas autoriza-
das por él pueden retirar dinero de
una cuenta.

to withdraw
Only the account holder or persons
authorized by him/her can withdraw
money from an account.

el **reintegro**
En el formulario de reintegro deben
figurar, entre otros, el número de
cuenta y el importe que se desea
retirar.

withdrawal
On a withdrawal slip there should
appear, among other things, the
account number and the sum one
wishes to withdraw.

**cargar en cuenta, adeudar**
El mes que viene me cargan en cuenta
los pagos efectuados con la tarjeta de
crédito.

to debit an account
Next month my account will be
debited for the credit card payments
I made.

el **asiento**
Todo movimiento de la cuenta bancaria
genera un asiento contable.

bookkeeping
Every transaction in a bank account
is accompanied by a bookkeeping
activity.

el **movimiento de cuenta**

account activity/transaction

la **comisión de mantenimiento**
Las altas comisiones de mantenimiento de algunos bancos han provocado la protesta de muchos clientes.

banking charges
Some banks' high banking charges have caused many customers to protest.

**sobregirar una cuenta, tener la cuenta al descubierto**
Sobregirar una cuenta representa tener que pagar intereses desproporcionados.

to overdraw an account

When people overdraw their account they have to pay exorbitant interest.

**saldar una cuenta**
Antes de tomar medidas más drásticas, le rogamos por última vez proceda a saldar su cuenta.

to balance/settle an account
Before we take more drastic measures, we're asking you for the last time to please proceed with the settling of your account.

**domiciliar la nómina**

Al domiciliar la nómina, muchos bancos ofrecen a sus clientes ventajas a la hora de solicitar un préstamo.

to have one's salary transferred automatically
Many banks offer favorable credit terms to customers who have a salary account.

la **orden de pago**
Le transmitiré la orden de pago a mi banco para que le transfiera el importe a su cuenta.

order to pay
I will send the payment order to my bank so that the sum can be transferred to your account.

la **transferencia de orden permanente**
A través de una transferencia de orden permanente, todos los meses le mando dinero a mi hija que estudia en Berlín.

standing order

By standing order, I send money every month to my daughter studying in Berlin.

el **procedimiento de nota de cargo**
Mientras que en la transferencia de orden permanente el importe de la transferencia es siempre el mismo, en el procedimiento de nota de cargo éste puede variar.

debiting procedure

In a standing order the amount of money to be transferred remains constant, whereas in a debiting transaction the amount can vary.

la **domiciliación de recibos**

payment by standing order

**domiciliar un recibo**

to debit directly

el, la **mandante**
El importe de la transferencia se adeuda en la cuenta del mandante y se abona en la del beneficiario.

client; customer
The amount of the transfer is debited from the customer's account, and credited to the payee's account.

**abonar**

to credit

el **extracto de cuenta**
Por razones de seguridad, la empresa
prefiere recoger los extractos de
cuenta en el banco.

bank statement
For security reasons, the company
prefers to pick up bank statements
at the bank.

la **notificación de abono**
Hoy he recibido la notificación de
abono del dinero que me mandaste.

notice of crediting
Today I received the notification
of crediting to my account of the
money you sent me.

la **notificación de adeudo**
Aún no hemos recibido la notificación
de adeudo del último plazo del televi-
sor.

notice of debiting
We still haven't received the
notice of debiting of the last
payment for the television set.

los **clientes preferentes**
A pesar de la nueva bajada de los tipos
de interés, sólo los clientes preferentes
de los bancos se beneficiaron de esta
medida.

preferred clients
Despite the new lowering of interest rates, only the bank's preferred
clients could take advantage of
them.

la **cuenta en moneda extranjera**
Muchos alemanes residentes en
España tienen una cuenta en moneda
extranjera, en este caso concreto, en
marcos alemanes.

foreign currency account
Many Germans who live in Spain
have a foreign currency account,
in their specific case, in German
marks.

**residente**

resident

la **cuenta en divisas**
Desde principios de 1993, cualquier
ciudadano de un país de la CEE
puede abrir una cuenta en divisas.

foreign currency account
Beginning in early 1993, any
citizen of a country in the EEC
can have a foreign currency
account.

la **cuenta en pesetas convertibles**
Según las nuevas normas españolas,
tanto los residentes como los no residentes pueden ser titulares de cuentas
en pesetas convertibles.

account in convertible pesetas

According to the new Spanish
regulations, residents as well as
non-residents can have an account
in convertible pesetas.

**no residente**

non-resident

la **cuenta-vivienda**
Una cuenta-vivienda ofrece la ventaja
de tener una elevada desgravación
fiscal.

building society account
An account with a savings and
loan association offers considerable tax advantages.

la **cuenta a plazo**
Las cuentas a plazo suponen no poder
disponer del dinero durante un período
de tiempo determinado, pero como
compensación se obtiene un tipo de
interés más alto.

time deposit account
Time deposit accounts are blocked
for a specific period of time, but to
compensate for that, one gets a
higher interest rate.

| | |
|---|---|
| **disponer de** | to have access to; use; be available |
| los **capitales a plazo** | time deposits |
| los **depósitos a término** | term deposits |
| Los capitales a plazo tienen el inconveniente de una disponibilidad limitada, es decir, se debe observar un plazo de preaviso previamente pactado. | Time deposits have the disadvantage of limited availability, i.e. one must respect a set period of time previously negotiated. |
| el **plazo de preaviso** | period of notice |
| **pactar** | to agree; negotiate |
| **observar un plazo** | to respect a term |

# ▬▬ Check and Bill of Exchange Transactions ▬▬

**cobrar un cheque**
Para cobrar un cheque, si éste es nominativo, el banco tiene la obligación de comprobar la identidad de la persona que lo presenta.

to cash a check
To cash a check made out to an individual, the bank is obliged to verify the identity of the person presenting the check.

**extender un cheque**
¿Prefiere que le abone el importe por transferencia o que le extienda un cheque a su nombre?

to make out/draw a check
Shall I have the money transferred to you or would you like me to make out a check to you personally?

**ingresar un cheque para abonar en cuenta**
La persona que extiende un cheque puede evitar su pago en efectivo escribiendo en el mismo "para abonar en cuenta."

to deposit a check for crediting to an account
A person who makes out a check can block its payment in cash by writing on it "for deposit only."

el **día hábil**
El cheque se abona en cuenta con valor dos días hábiles después de su entrega.

business/work day
The check is credited to an account two business days after its deposit.

**bloquear un cheque**
En caso de robo o pérdida de un cheque, se debe comunicar este hecho inmediatamente al banco por escrito para que sea bloqueado.

to stop payment on a check
If a check is stolen or lost, the bank should be informed immediately in writing so that payment on it can be stopped.

el **cheque al portador**

El cheque al portador tiene la desventaja de que, en caso de pérdida, cualquier persona lo puede cobrar ya que no figura ningún nombre en concreto.

bearer check; check made out to cash
The disadvantage of a check made out to cash is that, if lost, anyone can cash it, since no specific name appears on it.

280

el **cheque sin fondo**

not covered check; bad/rubber check; check for which there are insufficient funds

Muchos comercios no aceptan cheques de particulares por miedo a que sean cheques sin fondo.

Many businesses don't accept personal checks because they're afraid they'll bounce.

la **letra de cambio**
La letra de cambio es tanto un instrumento de crédito como de pago.

bill of exchange; bank draft
The bill of exchange is as much an instrument of credit as of payment.

la **letra de cambio aceptada**

acceptance/bill of agreement/exchange

La letra de cambio aceptada es una letra aceptada por el girado en la que estampa su firma comprometiéndose así a su pago.

An acceptance bill is a bill accepted by the drawee who signs it and thus accepts responsibility for its payment.

**estampar una firma**

to sign

el **librador**
Con el libramiento de una letra, el librador concede un crédito al librado, pues éste no paga inmediadamente sino al vencimiento de la letra.

issuer/ drawer of a bill
With the issuing of a bill of exchange the drawer grants a credit to the drawee, since the drawee does not pay immediately but upon the day the bill falls due.

el **librado,** el **girado**
El librado es la persona obligada a pagar si la letra de cambio ha sido previamente aceptada.

drawee
The drawee is the person obliged to pay if the bill of exchange has been previously accepted by him.

el **tenedor de una letra,** el **tomador de una letra**
El tenedor de una letra es la persona a la que se ha de pagar.

payee

The payee of a bill of exchange is the person to whom payment is to be made.

el **vencimiento**
El librador y el librado fijan de mutuo acuerdo, si es posible, el vencimiento de la letra.

due date
The drawer and the drawee determine by mutual accord, if possible, the due date of the bill.

**vencer**

to become due

**extender una letra, girar una letra, librar una letra**

to make out a bill of exchange

**aceptar una letra**
Al aceptar la letra, el librado se obliga a su pago.

to accept a bill of exchange
Upon acceptance, the drawee promises to pay it.

**pagadero a la vista**
Si no viene indicado el vencimiento de la letra, se considera que es pagadero a la vista.

payable on sight
If the due date of the bill is not indicated, it is assumed that the bill is payable on sight.

el, la **endosante**
El endosante es la persona que transmite el documento a otra persona, el endosatario, que ahora pasa a adquirir todos los derechos de la letra.

endorser; former creditor of the bill
The endorser is the person who transfers the document to that other person, the endorsee, who then acquires all rights to the bill.

el **endosatario,** la **endosataria**

endorsee; transferee; new creditor of the bill

el **endoso de una letra**

endorsement of a bill

el **protesto de una letra**
El protesto de una letra debe realizarse dentro de los cinco días hábiles siguientes a la fecha de vencimiento de la letra.

protesting of a bill
The protesting of a bill should be done within five business days after the bill's due date.

el **cheque bancario**
Un cheque bancario es extendido por el banco, el cual garantiza su pago.

bank check
A bank check is drawn by the bank which guarantees its payment

el **cheque al contado,** el **cheque de ventanilla**
El cheque de ventanilla lo emplea el propio otorgante para retirar dinero al contado de su cuenta.

check made out to cash

A check made out to cash is used by the drawer to withdraw money from her/his own account.

el, la **otorgante**

drawer

el **cheque conformado**
Con un cheque conformado se garantiza al tenedor del mismo que existen fondos suficientes en la cuenta del librador para pagar el importe del cheque.

certified check
A certified check assures its payee that sufficient funds exist in the drawer's account to pay the amount of the check.

el **tenedor,** la **tenedora**

bearer; holder; possessor; payee

el **cheque cruzado**

crossed check; deposit only check; non-negotiable check

El importe de un cheque cruzado no puede ser pagado en efectivo, sino que ha de ser abonado en cuenta.

The amount of a crossed check cannot be paid out in cash but must be credited to an account.

el **cheque en blanco**

blank check

el **cheque nominativo**
Al cobrar un cheque nominativo, el banco exige la presentación del D.N.I. (Documento Nacional de Identidad).

check made out to an individual
When cashing a check made out to an individual, the bank insists on identification.

la **letra al cobro**
El banco se encarga de la gestión de las letras al cobro, abonando al tenedor el valor nominal de las mismas descontadas las comisiones.

collection bill
The bank undertakes the processing of bills of collection, crediting their face value to the bearer after deducting commissions.

## la **letra al descuento**

Letras al descuento son las letras que el banco compra a sus clientes antes del vencimiento de las mismas.

discount bills

Discount bills are those bills that a bank buys from its customers before their due date.

## la **letra a la vista**

En la letra a la vista no figura el vencimiento para cobrarla. Se puede presentar dentro del plazo de un año desde su emisión.

sight draft/bill

Sight bills do not show a due date. They can be presented within a term of one year after their issue.

## la **letra girada a la propia orden**

En una letra girada a la propia orden, el librador es al mismo tiempo el librado.

bill drawn to one's own order

In a bill drawn to one's own order, the drawer and the drawee are identical.

## el **valor nominal**

El valor nominal es el importe que figura en la letra.

face/par/nominal value

The face value is the amount shown on the bill.

## el **descuento de letras**

Mediante el descuento de letras, el tenedor dispone de liquidez antes del vencimiento de las mismas, ya que el banco le anticipa el importe a cobrar deduciendo los gastos.

discounting of bills of exchange

Through the discounting of a bill, the bearer has financial means at his disposal before the bill's due date, since the bank advances to him the money to be collected after deducting its own commission.

## el **tipo de descuento**

El tipo de descuento de letras depende del tipo de descuento fijado por el Banco de España.

discount rate

The discount rate on bills depends on the discount rate set by the Bank of Spain.

## el **acreedor cambiario**, la **acreedora cambiaria**

Cuando el tenedor de una letra la endosa a un banco, éste se convierte en el nuevo acreedor cambiario.

creditor of a bill of exchange

When the payee of a bill endorses it over to a bank, the bank becomes the new creditor of the bill.

## la **prórroga de una letra de cambio**

La prórroga de una letra de cambio significa ampliar el período de vencimiento extendiendo una nueva letra de cambio.

extension of a bill

Extending a bill means postponing its due date by issuing a new bill of exchange.

## el **efecto a cobrar**

Los efectos a cobrar figuran en el activo del balance.

collectible bill; demand bill

Collectible bills are shown as assets on the balance sheet.

## el **efecto a pagar**

Los efectos a pagar figuran en el pasivo del balance, ya que suponen una obligación de pago.

debit bill; payable bill

Payable bills are shown as liabilities on the balance sheet, since they are obligations to pay.

# Credits and Loans

| | |
|---|---|
| el **crédito** | credit |
| **pedir un crédito** | to ask for credit |
| Voy a tener que pedir un crédito para poder pagar el coche. | I'm going to have to ask for credit to be able to pay for the car. |
| **solicitar un préstamo** | to apply for a loan |
| **otorgar un crédito, conceder un crédito** | to grant credit |
| Antes de conceder un crédito, los bancos estudian, entre otros, la solvencia del cliente. | Before granting credit, the banks investigate, among other things, the customer's credit rating. |
| **tramitar** | to formalize; work out; process |
| Al no tener Juan todos los documentos necesarios, no pudo tramitar su solicitud de crédito hipotecario. | Since Juan didn't have all the necessary papers with him, his application for mortgage credit couldn't be processed. |
| la **tramitación de un crédito** | processing of an application for credit |
| Normalmente la tramitación de un crédito no supera los tres días. | Usually the processing of a credit application doesn't take more than three days. |
| la **apertura de un crédito** | opening of (a line of) credit; granting credit |
| El banco cobra una comisión por la apertura de un crédito. | When granting credit, the bank charges a commission. |
| el **contrato de crédito** | credit agreement/contract |
| En un contrato de crédito conviene leer con atención la letra pequeña. | In a contract for credit it is advisable to read the small print carefully. |
| la **duración de un préstamo** | term of the loan |
| Los expertos opinan que la duración de un préstamo no debería ser superior a 12 años para no pagar tanto en concepto de intereses. | In the opinion of the experts, a loan's term should not exceed 12 years to avoid paying excessive interest. |
| **a corto plazo** | short term |
| **a largo plazo** | long term |
| **financiar** | to finance |
| Para poder financiar sus inversiones, muchas empresas tienen que hacer uso de un crédito. | Many companies have to seek credit in order to finance their investments. |

las **facilidades de pago**
Desde que han disminuído las ventas de apartamentos en la costa, las constructoras ofrecen enormes facilidades de pago.

easy payment terms
Ever since the decline in the sale of apartments on the coast, the builders have been offering very easy payment terms.

**determinar**
En el contrato de crédito se determinan las condiciones según las cuales el banco presta dinero a un cliente.

to set; establish; fix
In a credit agreement the conditions are established under which the bank will lend money to a customer.

el **tipo de interés,** la **tasa de interés**

rate of interest

**hipotecar**
Para poder comprar una casa en el campo tuvo que hipotecar el apartamento que tenía en Madrid.

to mortgage; take out a mortgage
To be able to buy a house in the country, she had to take out a mortgage on her apartment in Madrid.

la **solvencia**
La solvencia de un cliente viene determinada, entre otras cosas, por sus ingresos.

solvency; credit rating/standing
A customer's credit rating depends, among other things, on his income.

el **aval**
Manuel no pudo obtener el crédito que necesitaba para abrir el bar porque no disponía de un aval.

security; collateral
Manuel couldn't get the credit he needed to open a bar because he had no collateral.

el, la **avalista**
Para que una persona se pueda convertir en avalista de otra necesita tener cierta solvencia.

guarantor
For a person to serve as guarantor of another person, a rather good credit standing is necessary.

el **monte de piedad**
Hoy en día, los montes de piedad son frecuentados también por personas acomodadas.

pawn shop
Nowadays even the affluent patronize pawn shops.

**acomodado (a)**

well-off; affluent

el **factoring**
En el factoring, una empresa cede sus cobros pendientes a una sociedad financiera que, contra pago de una comisión por el riesgo asumido, adelanta el importe a la empresa y se hace cargo de su cobro.

factoring
In factoring, a company hands over its accounts receivable to a financing corporation, which in return for a commission for the risk it assumes, advances the money to the company and proceeds to collect the bills.

**ceder**

to yield; hand over

285

la **sociedad financiera**

financial corporation

**adelantar un importe**

to advance a sum

las **operaciones de leasing**
En las operaciones de leasing se
distingue entre el leasing financiero
y leasing operativo.

leasing operations/transactions
In leasing transactions a distinction
is made between financial leasing
and operational leasing.

el **leasing financiero**
El leasing financiero es un arrendamiento de bienes duraderos con
opción de compra que trae consigo
numerosas ventajas fiscales para el
arrendatario, y que se ha extendido
en los últimos años al sector de los
bienes de consumo.

finance leasing
Finance leasing, the leasing of
durable goods with a purchase
option, carries with it numerous
tax advantages for the lessee. In
recent years it has become quite
widespread in the consumer goods
sector.

el **arrendatario**

lessee

el **leasing operativo**
El leasing operativo es una forma
tradicional de arrendamiento de bienes
para un plazo determinado, pero con
la ventaja adicional de un servicio
gratuito de mantenimiento.

operative leasing
Operative leasing is a traditional
form of goods rental for a determined period, but with the additional advantage of a cost free
maintenance service.

el **crédito hipotecario**
Si no se cumple con las condiciones
de pago del crédito hipotecario, existe
la posibilidad de que el banco se quede
con la propiedad inmobiliaria.

mortgage credit
If mortgage payments are not met,
the possibility of the bank fore-
closing on the property exists.

el **crédito por descubierto**
El límite máximo de un crédito por
descubierto es, normalmente, el
importe de dos sueldos.

overdraft facility
The upper limit of an overdraft
facility is usually two months
salary.

el **crédito en cuenta corriente**
El crédito en cuenta corriente es un
crédito flexible cuantitativa y temporalmente que se adapta a las necesidades de liquidez de las empresas.

current account credit
The amount and term of current
account credit varies according
to the liquidity requirements of
companies.

**flexible**

flexible

**cuantitativamente**

quantitatively

el **tomador del préstamo**
Para convertirse en tomador de un
préstamo hay que cumplir ciertas
condiciones, tales como tener ingresos
regulares.

borrower; receiver of credit
In order to get credit it is necessary
to fulfill certain conditions, such
as having a regular income.

| | |
|---|---|
| el **límite de crédito** | limit on credit; credit line |
| el **techo de crédito** | credit ceiling |
| el **límite del crédito**<br>El límite del crédito queda siempre muy por debajo del valor real del objeto empeñado. | lending limit<br>The lending limit is always much lower than the real value of the object pawned. |
| **empeñar** | to pawn |
| el **préstamo a interés fijo**<br>En determinados tipos de créditos, los bancos ofrecen la posibilidad de elegir entre préstamo a interés fijo o variable. | fixed interest loan<br>In certain types of credit, the banks offer the possibility of selecting a loan with a fixed or a variable rate of interest. |
| el **préstamo a interés variable** | variable interest rate loan |
| el **préstamo hipotecario**<br>Antes de solicitar un préstamo hipotecario conviene tener cierta cantidad de dinero ahorrado en una cuenta-vivienda. | mortgage loan<br>Before applying for a mortgage loan, it is advisable to have saved enough for a down payment in a savings account. |
| el **deudor moroso**<br>En España, hay agencias de cobro especializadas en cobrar a los deudores morosos, como por ejemplo "El cobrador del Frac". | dilatory debtor; delinquent debtor<br>In Spain, there are collection agencies, such as e.g. "The Collector in Tails," that specialize in the collection of dilatory debts. |
| la **agencia de cobro** | collection agency |
| **no estar al corriente de los pagos**<br>Quien durante dos meses no esté al corriente de los pagos contraídos con el banco, es considerado deudor moroso. | not to be up to date in payments; be in arrears<br>Whoever is two months in arrears on contractually obligatory payments to a bank, is considered a dilatory debtor. |
| la **cuota de amortización**<br>La cuota de amortización se adeuda en cuenta el día que vence. | amortization rate<br>The amortization rate is debited from the account on the day it is due. |
| el **período de amortización**<br>El período de amortización lo fija el banco de mutuo acuerdo con su cliente. | amortization period/term<br>The term of amortization is fixed by the bank in mutual agreement with the customer. |
| el **interés compuesto**<br>El interés compuesto se produce cuando los intereses devengan a su vez nuevos intereses. | compound interest<br>Compound interest is generated when interest itself earns new interest. |

287

| los **intereses acreedores** | interest on deposits |
| los **intereses deudores** | interest on debit balance |
| el **crédito pignoraticio** | credit on securities/pledges; Lombard credit |

El crédito pignoraticio es un tipo de crédito que el banco central concede a los bancos comerciales que ofrecen como garantía acciones o títulos-valores.

Lombard credit is a type of credit which the central bank grants to commercial banks which pledge stocks or securities as security.

el **tipo de pignoración**

bank rate for loans on securities; Lombard rate

El tipo de pignoración se aplica a los créditos pignoraticios y viene fijado por el banco central siendo generalmente un poco más alto que el tipo de descuento.

The Lombard rate is applied to Lombard credits and is set by the central bank; it is usually a little higher than the discount rate.

el **tipo de interés interbancario**

interbank interest rate

El tipo de interés interbancario se aplica a los préstamos efectuados entre bancos.

The interbank rate is the interest rate applied to interbank loans.

## Exchange Transactions

la **Bolsa**
La Bolsa de Madrid, la más antigua de España, está ubicada en un edificio impresionante cerca del museo del Prado.

stock exchange
Madrid's Stock Exchange, Spain's oldest, is located in an impressive building near the Prado Museum.

la **bolsa**

stock market

la **bolsa de valores (títulos)**
Según los bienes fungibles negociados, la Bolsa se clasifica en bolsa de títulos-valores, bolsa de mercancías y mercado de divisas.

securities exchange
Depending on the nature of the fungible goods traded, the exchange is classified as a securities, commodities, or currency exchange.

los **bienes fungibles**

fungible goods

**clasificar**

to classify

la **bolsa de mercancías,** la **bolsa de contratación**

commodities exchange

el **mercado de divisas,** la **bolsa de cambios**

currency exchange

la **plaza bursátil**
España cuenta con cuatro plazas bursátiles: Madrid, Barcelona, Bilbao y Valencia.

stock exchange sites
In Spain, stock exchanges are found in Madrid, Barcelona, Bilbao, and Valencia.

**bursátil**

stock exchange related

el, la **agente de cambio y Bolsa**

broker

**especular**
Ha comprado un paquete importante de acciones para poder especular a corto plazo en el mercado.

to speculate
She/He bought a large block of stocks in order to engage in short term speculation on the market.

la **sesión bursátil,** la **jornada bursátil**
En la sesión del miércoles, el índice IBEX-35 perdió 8,75 puntos y tocó fondo en el 286,56%, arrastrando a las demás Bolsas españolas.

stock exchange trading session

In Wednesday's trading, the IBEX-35 index lost 8.75 points and sank to 286.56%, taking down with it the other Spanish exchanges.

**tocar fondo**

to touch bottom; bottom out; sink

**el índice bursátil**

market index

Los vaivenes del índice bursatil no son necesariamente un fiel reflejo del desarrollo de la economía que a veces, incluso, se manifiesta de forma contraria.

The ups and downs of the market index are not necessarily a faithful reflection of economic development, which sometimes can be at odds with market behavior.

**el vaivén**

ups and downs; vagaries

**la cotización**

price quotation

La primera cotización de un valor durante una jornada bursátil se denomina cotización de apertura.

The first price quotation of a security during a day's trading is called the opening quotation.

**el valor**

security

**la cotización de apertura**

opening quote/quotation/price/ notation

**cotizar**

to quote; list

No todas las empresas cumplen los requisitos necesarios para que sus acciones coticen en bolsa.

Not all companies fulfill the necessary requirements for having their stocks listed on the exchange.

**la acción**

stock

**la cotización de cierre,** el **precio de cierre**

closing quote/price/notation

**concertar operaciones bursátiles**

to engage in market trading

Debido a la incertidumbre política, se han concertado pocas operaciones bursátiles y las cotizaciones han marcado niveles mínimos del ejercicio.

Due to political uncertainty, few market transactions were made and prices fell to their year's low.

**la incertidumbre**

uncertainty; instability

**el nivel mínimo del año ejercicio**

year's low

**el volumen de contratación**

volume of trading

**la contratación de valores**

securities market; secondary market

**la contratación bursátil**

trading on the exchange; market transactions

La contratación bursátil antes de la apertura lleva el nombre de bolsín de la mañana; los valores ahí negociados se consideran de cotización oficiosa.

Market trading before the opening of the exchange is called the morning outside market; securities traded there are considered semi-official.

**el bolsín de la mañana**

morning outside market

**las operaciones antes de la apertura de la bolsa**

market trading before the opening of the exchange

| | |
|---|---|
| los **valores negociados** | traded securities |
| **oficioso (a)** | semiofficial |
| de **cotización extraoficial** | unofficial premarket opening quotation |
| la **cotización oficial** | official quotation |
| las **operaciones después del cierre de la bolsa** | after market closing transactions |
| el **mercado extraoficial** | unofficial market; behind the scenes market |

En el mercado extraoficial que forma parte del mercado secundario predomina el comercio por cuenta propia, por ej., entre bancos que así se aprovechan de las variaciones en los cambios.

On the behind the scenes market, which is a part of the secondary market, private trading predominates, e.g. between banks that take advantage of price fluctuations.

| | |
|---|---|
| el **comercio por cuenta propia** | private trading; trading for one's own account |
| **predominar** | to predominate |
| el **fondo de inversión** | investment fund |

Los fondos de inversión son, en la actualidad, los activos financieros de mayor rentabilidad.

At present, investment funds are the most profitable types of investment.

| | |
|---|---|
| la **recuperación de las cotizaciones** | market (quotations) recovery |

El empujón dado por los inversores institucionales y los retoques de última hora, condujeron a una leve recuperación de las cotizaciones, mejorando así los precios de cierre.

The upward trend started by institutional investors and last minute corrections led to a small recovery of prices, thus improving closing quotations.

| | |
|---|---|
| el **inversor institucional** | institutional investor |
| el **empujón** | impetus; push |
| el **retoque** | correction; adjustment |
| la **recogida de beneficios,** la **realización de plusvalías** | profit taking |

Se espera que hoy sea una jornada de recogida de beneficios, después del continuado camino alcista de las últimas semanas.

After the steady upward movement of the last few weeks there will probably be profit taking today.

| | |
|---|---|
| el **camino alcista** | upward course/trend/movement; bull market |
| la **variación en los cambios** | price fluctuations |

la **tendencia bajista**
Al no producirse la esperada reducción del tipo de interés por parte del Bundesbank alemán se ha acentuado la ya existente tendencia bajista en las bolsas españolas.

downward trend
When the German Bundesbank failed to lower interest rates, as had been expected, the already existent downward trend on Spanish exchanges was intensified.

**acentuar**

to accentuate; intensify

la **tendencia alcista**
La última semana, la bolsa de México ha experimentado una tendencia alcista en sus cotizaciones.

upward trend; bull market
Last week, prices on the Mexican stock exchange were bullish.

**continuado (a)**

steady; continuing

---

■■■■■ **Securities and the Capital Market** ■■■■■

el **mercado de valores**
En España, la negociación en el mercado de valores se lleva a cabo en el así llamado "mercado contínuo": un sistema de contratación bursátil asistido por ordenador bajo el control de la Comisión Nacional del Mercado de Valores.

securities market
In Spain, trading on the securities market is carried out on the so-called "continuing market," a computer based market trading system regulated by the National Securities Exchange Commission.

el **mercado contínuo**

continuing market (computer based market trading system)

**asistido (a) por ordenador**

computer based

la **Comisión Nacional del Mercado de Valores (CNMV)**

National Securities Exchange Commission

la **negociación bursátil**

market trading

el **mercado financiero**
Los mercados financieros se pueden subdividir en: mercado monetario para operaciones de crédito a corto plazo y mercado de capitales para operaciones de crédito a largo plazo.

financial market
Financial markets can be subdivided into: the money market for short term credit transactions and the capital market for long term credit transactions.

**subdividir**

to subdivide

las **operaciones de crédito**

credit operations/transactions

el **euromercado**
El euromercado es un mercado monetario y de capitales para créditos y operaciones de emisiones negociados fuera del país donde está domiciliado el agente económico que está por detrás de las operaciones.

Euromarket
The Euromarket is a money and capital market both for credits and issuing transactions undertaken outside the country of residence of the economic agent responsible for those transactions.

| las **operaciones de emisiones** | issuing operations/transactions |

**estar domiciliado (a)** — to be resident in

el **euromercado de capitales** — European capital market
El euromercado de capitales es el mercado para empréstitos internacionales. — The European capital market is the market for international loans.

el **empréstito internacional** — international loan

el **empréstito público** — government bond

el **euromercado de créditos** — European credit market

el **euromercado del dinero** — European money market

el **mercado primario de valores** — primary market

el **mercado de emisiones** — issuing market
El mercado primario es el mercado para la primera colocación de acciones, obligaciones y títulos de deuda del Estado emitidos por primera vez. — The primary market is the market for the initial placing of stocks, bonds, and government paper issued for the first time.

la **colocación** — placing; offering

los **títulos de deuda del Estado** — government paper/debentures/bonds

los **fondos públicos** — public funds

la **obligación** — bond

el **mercado secundario de valores** — securities secondary market
El mercado secundario de valores es el mercado para títulos que ya han sido previamente vendido en el mercado primario. — The secondary securities market is the market for securities that have been previously sold in the primary market.

los **valores de renta fija** — fixed rate securities
Las obligaciones son títulos de renta fija. El titular tiene derecho a recibir un interés fijo y puede reivindicar el reembolso del valor a su valor nominal. — Bonds are fixed rate securities. The bearer is entitled to receive a fixed rate of interest and can cash them in at their face value.

el, la **titular** — bearer

**reivindicar** — to demand; claim

el **reembolso** — cashing in; buying back

los **títulos de renta variable** — dividend paying securities
Los títulos se pueden subdividir en títulos de renta variable y de renta fija. — Securities can be subdivided into variable and fixed rate securities.

**la opción**
Una opción concede, contra pago de una prima, el derecho a adquirir (opción de compra) o vender (opción de venta) en un plazo determinado un cierto número de acciones a un precio fijado con antelación.

option
For the payment of a premium, an option grants the right to buy (purchase option) or sell (sales option) a determined number of stocks at a previously established price within a set period of time.

**la opción de compra**

purchase option; put

**la opción de venta**

sale option; call

**el mercado español de futuros financieros**
Los instrumentos financieros empleados en el mercado español de futuros financieros (MEFF) son: deuda pública, bonos del Tesoro y letras de Tesoro.

Spanish forward and futures market
The financial instruments employed in the Spanish futures market are: public debt; treasury bonds and treasury notes.

**el instrumento financiero**

financial instrument

**la deuda pública**

public debt

**el bono del Tesoro**

three year treasury bond

**la letra del Tesoro**

three month treasury note

## ■ General Information ■

el, la **contribuyente**
Los contribuyentes tienen una cita anual con el fisco en el mes de junio.

taxpayer
Taxpayers are called upon to file a tax return with the authorities once a year in June.

el **fisco**

official taxation authority (Internal Revenue Service in the USA)

(la) **Hacienda**

treasury; exchequer; ministry of finance; taxing authority

el **impuesto**
A diferencia de la tasa, en el impuesto el contribuyente no recibe contraprestación directa alguna por parte de la Administración.

tax
In contradistinction to the fee, the taxpayer receives no direct service whatever from the taxing authority.

la **tasa**
La comunidad de Madrid cobra tasas por la prestación de servicios sanitarios.

fee
The municipality of Madrid charges fees for the performance of public health services.

los **tributos**

taxes

la **liquidación del impuesto**

Si la liquidación del impuesto le sale negativa, haga una cruz en la casilla correspondiente según sea a devolver o compensar y presente el impreso en su delegación de Hacienda.

tax assessment/calculation/ estimation
If your calculation of estimated taxes shows that you have overpaid, then make a cross in the appropriate box to indicate whether you prefer a refund or a tax credit and submit the form to your local tax office.

la **casilla**

box

**compensar**

to be compensated/credited

la **delegación de Hacienda**

La delegación de Hacienda es una unidad administrativa de carácter provincial dependiente del Ministerio de Hacienda.

local tax office; branch of taxing authority
The tax office is an administrative entity on the provincial level and is a part of the Ministry of the Treasury.

**pagar impuestos**

to pay taxes

el **sistema tributario**
El presidente del grupo mayoritario de la oposición ha anunciado una importante reforma del sistema tributario si es que gana las próximas elecciones.

taxation system
The head of the largest opposition party promised a major overhaul of the taxation system if he won the next election.

**tributario (a)** — taxing

**mayoritario (a)** — majority

el **Impuesto de Actividades Económicas (IAE)** — Tax on Economic Activities; trade tax; tax on businesses

Antes de ejercer cualquier actividad profesional es necesario darse de alta en Hacienda en el Impuesto de Actividades Económicas para la actividad a desempeñar. — Before engaging in any freelance professional activity it is necessary to register as a taxpayer with the taxing authority before engaging in the intended activity.

**darse de alta en Hacienda** — to get on the tax roles; register with the tax authority

el **fraude fiscal** — fiscal fraud; cheating on taxes

Hacienda ha ido adoptando medidas cada vez más eficaces para evitar el fraude fiscal. — The taxing authority has taken more and more effective measures against tax cheats.

**adoptar medidas** — to take measures/steps

**eficaz** — effective

el **cruce de datos** — comparative balancing of data

La Administración tributaria realiza un cruce de datos que permite cotejar los datos de que dispone con los que aporta el contribuyente y comprobar así su veracidad. — The tax authorities undertake a comparative balancing of data which enables them to contrast the information they have with what the taxpayer has supplied and thus compare their accuracy.

la **Administración tributaria** — taxing administration

**cotejar datos** — compare and contrast data

la **veracidad** — accuracy; truth

la **obligación tributaria** — obligation to pay taxes

La Ley General Tributaria quiere impulsar el cumplimiento voluntario de las obligaciones tributarias aunque sea fuera de plazo. Para ello se han reducido los actuales recargos de demora. — The General Tax Law tries to encourage voluntary compliance with the obligation to pay taxes, even after the deadline. To that end the then valid late payment penalties were lowered.

la **Ley General Tributaria** — General Tax Law

**impulsar** — to stimulate; encourage

el **cumplimiento** — compliance

**fuera de plazo** — after the deadline; after due date

el **recargo de demora** — late payment penalty

la **evasión de impuestos**
Hacienda ha propuesto que no sólo la evasión de impuestos, sino también eludir el pago de los mismos sea considerado delito fiscal.

**eludir**

el **delito fiscal**

tax evasion
The tax authorities have suggested that not only tax evasion but also tax avoidance be considered criminal actions.

to avoid

fiscal crime; criminal non-payment of taxes

el **impuesto directo**
Los impuestos directos gravan los ingresos del trabajo y de las actividades profesionales.

**gravar**

las **actividades profesionales**

el **impuesto indirecto**
Los impuestos indirectos gravan el consumo y gasto destacando: el IVA, el impuesto de lujo y los impuestos sobre hidrocarburos.

direct tax
Direct taxes are levied on salaried persons as well as free-lance professionals.

to levy; tax

(free-lance) professional activities

indirect tax
Indirect taxes are levied on consumption and expenses, of which the most important are the Value Added Tax, the luxury tax, and the tax on hydrocarburants (petroleum).

el **impuesto de lujo**

el **impuesto sobre hidrocarburos**

el **recaudador,** la **recaudadora**

el **Impuesto sobre el Valor Añadido (IVA)**
El tipo de IVA en España asciende en la actualidad al 16%.

luxury tax

petroleum tax

tax collector

Value Added Tax (VAT)

The Spanish Value Added Tax is currently 16%.

el **tipo reducido de IVA**
Existen tipos reducidos de IVA, como el que se aplica a los libros que asciende al 3%.

reduced Value Added Tax
There are also reduced VAT's such as the 3% VAT collected on books.

el **pago a cuenta**

el **pago fraccionario**
Los pagos a cuenta del Impuesto sobre la Renta de las Personas Físicas es una obligación fiscal de toda empresa y profesional.

estimated/advanced tax payment

partial payment
Estimated tax payments on income earned is a fiscal obligation of all companies and free-lance professionals.

**trimestral**
Tienen carácter trimestral y se han de efectuar entre los días 1 y 20 de los meses de enero, abril, julio y octubre de cada año.

quarterly
They are due quarterly and are payable, respectively, between the 1st and 20th of the months of January, April, July, and October of each year.

la **deuda tributaria**

El cálculo de la deuda tributaria en el impuesto sobre sociedades presenta numerosas dificultades.

amount of taxes to be paid; tax debt; tax due
Calculating the tax due in corporate tax returns presents many difficulties.

el **impuesto sobre el tabaco**

tax on tobacco

el **impuesto sobre el alcohol y las bebidas derivadas**

tax on alcohol and related beverages

el **impuesto de circulación**

motor vehicles tax

el **impuesto sobre bienes inmuebles (IBI)**

El impuesto sobre bienes inmuebles (IBI), hasta 1992 denominado contribución territorial, es el que tienen que tributar las propiedades rústicas y urbanas.

property/real estate tax

The property tax, called "contribución territorial" until 1992, is the tax levied on rural and urban properties.

**tributar**

to pay taxes; be taxed

la **contribución territorial**

property tax (until 1992)

la **propiedad rústica**

rural property

la **propiedad urbana**

urban property

el **convenio de doble imposición**

Entre los países europeos existe un convenio de doble imposición que se aplica cuando una inversión o prestación de servicio se realiza en un país diferente del país residencia del sujeto pasivo, teniendo la finalidad de evitar la aplicación de dos tasas fiscales sobre el mismo objeto.

double taxation agreement

There is a double taxation agreement between European countries, which is applied when an investment or performance of services is performed in a country other than the one in which the taxpayer is resident; this is intended to avoid the taxpayer being taxed twice.

la **tasa fiscal**

tax rate/scale

el **país residencia**

country of residence

el **sujeto pasivo**

taxpayer; person liable to pay taxes

la **aplicación**

application

# The Tax Return

el **Impuesto sobre la Renta de las Personas Físicas (IRPF)**

Income Tax On Natural Persons

El Impuesto sobre la Renta de las Personas Físicas grava con carácter general todas las rentas procedentes de los rendimientos del trabajo y de las actividades profesionales y artísticas, así como del capital mobiliario e inmobiliario y de los incrementos de patrimonio.

In general, income tax is levied on income from employment, on free-lance and artistic activities, as well as on capital, renting, leasing, and increases in equity.

**artístico (a)**

artistic

la **renta**

revenue; income

los **rendimientos de las actividades profesionales y artísticas**

income from free-lance professional and artistic activities

los **rendimientos del capital mobiliario**

income from capital

los **rendimientos del capital inmobiliario**

income from renting and leasing

el **incremento del patrimonio**

increase in assets/equity

los **rendimientos del trabajo**

income from work for others; salaried employment

Se consideran rendimientos del trabajo todas aquellas retribuciones dinerarias o en especie que se deriven directa o indirectamente del trabajo personal.

All income, in money or in kind, originating directly or indirectly from personal work, is considered income from employment.

las **retribuciones dinerarias**

payment in money

las **retribuciones en especie**

payment in kind

el **Impuesto sobre Sociedades (IS)**

taxes on corporations

Las personas jurídicas cumplen con la obligación de tributar a través del Impuesto sobre Sociedades.

Legal persons comply with their obligation to pay taxes by paying corporate taxes.

la **declaración de la renta**

income tax return

Necesito de la empresa un certificado de retenciones que debo adjuntar con mi declaración de la renta que me ha salido positiva.

I need a withholding statement from the company showing withholdings made, so that I can enclose it with my tax return, which indicates that I have to pay taxes.

el **certificado de retenciones**

withholding statement

la **declaración positiva**

tax return showing that taxes are owed

la **declaración negativa**

tax return showing overpayment

la **declaración a devolver**

tax return showing a refund is due

**presentar la declaración**

to file a tax return

Antes de presentar la declaración no olvide pegar las etiquetas identificativas y recuerde que el plazo para la presentación de las declaraciones positivas finaliza el 20 de junio y el de las negativas hasta el 30 de junio.

Before filing the return don't forget to affix the identifying labels and remember that the deadline for filing returns on which taxes are owed is June 20, and June 30 for returns on which a refund is due.

la **etiqueta identificativa**

identifying label; sticker with information on the taxpayer

En las etiquetas identificativas figuran nombre y apellidos del declarante así como el número de identificación fiscal o NIF.

On the identifying label are found the first and last names of the person filing the return as well as her/his tax identification number.

el, la **declarante**

taxpayer

el **número de identificación fiscal (N.I.F.)**

personal tax identification number

El N.I.F. de todo ciudadano español se compone del número del documento nacional de identidad o DNI más una letra del alfabeto.

A Spanish citizen's tax identification number is composed of the number on her/his national identity document in addition to a letter of the alphabet.

el **código de identificación fiscal (CIF)**

corporate tax identification number

Las comunidades de bienes y las sociedades mercantiles tienen adjudicados un Código de Identificación Fiscal.

Property communities and trading companies are assigned a tax identification number.

**deducir**

to deduct

En la declaración de la renta se pueden deducir, entre otros, los gastos médicos y las cuotas satisfechas a los sindicatos.

Among other things, medical expenses and union dues can be deducted on an income tax return.

**satisfacer**

to pay

la **cuota**

quota; sum; dues

**gastos excepcionales, gastos deducibles**

exceptional expenses; deductible expenses

el **importe exento de impuestos**    non-taxable amount

la **Agencia Tributaria (AEAT)**    State Information Office For
Questions About Taxes
La Agencia Tributaria entró en funcio-    The "Agencia Tributaria" came
namiento el 1 de enero de 1992 con    into being January 1, 1992 for the
el fin de minimizar los costes adminis-    purpose of lowering administrative
trativos que soportan los ciudadanos    costs borne by citizens when deal-
en sus relaciones con la Hacienda    ing with the taxing authority.
Pública.

**soportar**    to bear

los **datos fiscales**    tax data/information
A veces, los datos fiscales recogidos    Sometimes tax information gathered
por Hacienda han ido a parar a empre-    by the taxing authority winds up
sas privadas que comercializan bases    in the hands of private firms that
de datos, haciéndose uso indebido de    sell data banks; this constitutes an
los mismos.    improper use of such information.

**hacer uso indebido**    to make improper/unauthorized
use of

las **rentas exentas del impuesto**    tax-free income
Remuneraciones como las derivadas    Cash benefits such as those stem-
de la incapacidad permanente se    ming from personal disability are
incluyen dentro de las rentas exentas    classified as tax-free income.
del impuesto.

la **incapacidad permanente**    permanent disability

el **período impositivo**    tax period
El período impositivo del Impuesto    The tax period for corporate taxes
sobre Sociedades coincide con el    coincides with each company's
ejercicio económico de cada entidad    fiscal year, which in turn, may or
que puede, a su vez, ser coincidente    may not coincide with the calendar
o no con el año natural.    year.

el **ejercicio económico**    fiscal/accounting year

el **año natural**    calendar year

**ser coincidente con**    to be coincidental with

**cumplimentar**    to fill out
La entidad declarante deberá cumpli-    The company filing the tax return
mentar las nueve primeras páginas    must fill out the first nine pages of
del impreso.    the tax form.

**declarante**    filing a return

el **impreso**    printed tax form

la **base imponible**
La base imponible para la liquidación del Impuesto sobre Sociedades se obtiene a partir del resultado contable de la entidad declarante.

taxable base; taxable income
The taxable base for corporate tax is obtained from the bookkeeping records of the corporation filing.

la **tributación**

taxation

la **forma de tributación**
Desde 1991, los matrimonios y unidades familiares pueden optar entre dos formas de tributación del IRPF: tributación individual y tributación conjunta.

form of taxation
Since 1991, married couples and households can choose between two kinds of tax assessment and can file either a single or a joint return.

la **unidad familiar**

family unit; household

la **tributación individual**

individual/separate taxation

la **tributación conjunta**

joint taxation

la **declaración conjunta**

joint tax return

la **declaración simplificada**

short form tax return; simplified return (for lower and average income brackets)

La diferencia básica entre la declaración simplificada y la ordinaria consiste en que en la simplificada sólo se recogen los supuestos más comunes que son los que menos complicaciones representan a la hora de hacer la declaración.

The basic difference between the simplified return and the standard one is that in the simplified one only the most common, least complicated data are considered when the return is filed.

el **supuesto**

(tax) information supplied

la **complicación**

complication

la **declaración ordinaria**

standard form (for higher income brackets)

la **estimación directa**
En la nueva Ley del IRPF son dos los regímenes en virtud de los cuales el empresario puede declarar los rendimientos obtenidos: estimación directa y estimación objetiva.

direct/individual estimation of tax
In the new income tax law there are two systems by which the entrepreneur can declare profits earned: the direct and the standard form.

| el **régimen** | regimen; system; mode |
| **en virtud de** | according to; by |
| la **estimación objetiva (EO)** | standard tax form |
| el **beneficio fiscal**<br>Los beneficios fiscales que el Estado otorga a las empresas vienen anualmente especificados en la Ley de Presupuestos Generales. (España) | tax advantage<br>Tax advantages granted to business by the government are specified in the Annual Budget Law. (Spain) |

# 23 | The National Economy: Economics

━━━━━━━━ **General Information** ━━━━━━━━

la **economía**
Los tratadistas neoclásicos fueron los primeros en elevar la economía a la categoría de ciencia.

economics
Neoclassical scholars were the first to raise economics to the status of a science.

**económico (a)**
México ha mejorado mucho su situación económica gracias al Tratado de Libre Comercio.

economic
Thanks to the Free Trade Agreement, Mexico has considerably improved its economic position.

la **producción nacional**
La producción nacional de cereales se redujo a consecuencia de la sequía.

national production
Due to the drought, national grain production declined.

la **capacidad económica**

economic capacity

el **Producto Nacional Bruto**
El Producto Nacional Bruto es la suma del valor de todos los bienes y servicios producidos por un país en un año.

Gross National Product
The Gross National Product is the sum total of the value of all goods and services produced by a country in one year.

el **Producto Interior Bruto**
El Producto Interior Bruto recoge la producción de bienes y servicios, valorada a precios de mercado, de las unidades productivas residentes en un país durante un período determinado.

Gross Domestic Product
The Gross Domestic Product expresses the production of goods and services, valued at their market price, of producing entities located in a country during a specific period.

la **tasa de crecimiento**
Si el Producto Interior Bruto alcanza la tasa de crecimiento prevista el paro podría reducirse.

growth rate
If the Gross Domestic Product attains the projected growth rate, unemployment could decline.

el **consumo**
El consumo es una de las magnitudes constitutivas de la demanda agregada.

consumption; consuming
Consumption is one of the essential orders of magnitude in total demand.

**restringir**
El Ministerio de Sanidad pretende restringir el consumo de tabaco y bebidas alcohólicas porque son perjudiciales para la salud.

to restrict; limit
The Ministry of Health tries to limit the consumption of tobacco and alcoholic beverages because they are harmful to health.

la **contabilidad nacional**
La contabilidad nacional recoge las transacciones efectuadas entre los diferentes sectores de un país.

total national economic accounting
Total national economic accounting consists of transactions made between the different sectors of a country.

la **renta nacional**
La renta nacional está creciendo en Venezuela año tras año.

national income
Every year, Venezuela's national income is increasing.

el **endeudamiento**
El endeudamiento de los países subdesarrollados obstaculiza su despegue económico.

endebtment
The national debt of underdeveloped countries is an obstacle to their economic advancement.

**impedir**
Las barreras arancelarias impiden la libre circulación de mercancías entre los países.

to impede; prevent
Tariff barriers limit the free circulation of goods between countries.

la **demanda de dinero**

demand for money; money needs

la **depresión monetaria**
La reducción del gasto público ha provocado una depresión monetaria.

monetary depression
The reduction of public expenditures has led to a monetary depression.

las **relaciones comerciales**

trade/commercial relations

la **balanza comercial**
La balanza comercial ha sido crónicamente deficitaria en España.

balance of trade
Spain's balance of trade has shown chronic deficits.

la **balanza de mercancías y servicios**
La devaluación de la peseta ha saneado considerablemente el saldo de la balanza de mercancías y servicios.

balance of goods and services

The devaluation of the peseta has gone a long way to reestablish a better balance of goods and services.

la **balanza de comercio exterior**
Una balanza de comercio exterior con saldo positivo es muy importante para la salud de una nación.

balance of foreign trade
A favorable balance of foreign trade is very important for the health of a country's economy.

la **balanza de pagos**
La balanza de pagos de un país está compuesta por la balanza por cuenta corriente y la balanza por cuenta de capitales.

balance of payments
A country's balance of payments is composed of its balance of trade and its capital balance.

el **desequilibrio**
La economía guatemalteca viene padeciendo importantes desequilibrios estructurales.

imbalance
Guatemala's economy suffers from significant structural imbalances.

el, la **economista**
Según mi opinión Keynes ha sido el economista más significativo de nuestro siglo.

economist
In my opinion, Keynes was the most important economist of our century.

la **macroeconomía**
La macroeconomía es la parte de la teoría económica que estudia el comportamiento de los agentes económicos en terminos de demanda, oferta etc.

macroeconomics
Macroeconomics is that part of economic theory which examines the behavior of participants in the economy in terms of supply, demand, etc.

**macroeconómico (a)**

macroeconomic

el **cuadro macroeconómico**

macroeconomic scene

el **indicador económico**
El estudio de los indicadores económicos sirve para diagnosticar el estado de la economía.

economic indicator
The examination of economic indicators is used for diagnosing the state of the economy.

el **agente económico**
La economía política es la ciencia que estudia el comportamiento de los agentes económicos.

factor/participant in the economy
Political economics is the science that examines the behavior of economic factors.

la **demanda agregada**
La demanda agregada representa la cantidad demandada de bienes y servicios por una economía durante un período determinado.

aggregate/total demand
Total demand represents the demanded quantity of an economy's goods and services in a specific period.

la **microeconomía**
La microeconomía es la parte de la economía que estudia el comportamiento individual de los agentes económicos.

microeconomics
Microeconomics is that part of economics that examines the individual behavior of participants in the economy.

la **balanza de capitales**
El aumento de los tipos de interés ha arrojado un saldo muy favorable de la balanza de capitales.

capital account
The increase in interest rates has led to a very favorable balance in capital account.

la **balanza por cuenta corriente**

balance of trade

**deficitario (a)**

in deficit; negative

**capitalizar**
En el cálculo de la deuda se han capitalizado los intereses.

to capitalize
When calculating the degree of debt, they capitalized the interest.

la **cifra de importaciones**
La cifra de importaciones se ha triplicado como consecuencia de la revaluación de la peseta.

sum (derived from) imports
The sum of imports has tripled as a result of the upvaluing of the peseta.

| | |
|---|---|
| la **evolución de la balanza de pagos**<br>La evolución de la balanza de pagos ha mejorado gracias a las sucesivas devaluaciones de la peseta. | development of the balance of payments<br>The development of the balance of payments has improved thanks to repeated devaluations of the peseta. |
| el **superávit**<br>La balanza de pagos de operaciones corrientes arrojará superávit el próximo ejercicio económico. | surplus<br>The balance of payments in current business operations will show a surplus in the next fiscal year. |
| el **superávit en la balanza comercial,** el **excedente en la balanza comercial** | surplus in the balance of trade |
| el **déficit en la balanza comercial** | deficit in the balance of trade |

# Population

| | |
|---|---|
| el **capital humano**<br>El capital humano es el factor productivo fundamental en cualquier organización. | human capital<br>Human capital is the fundamental productive factor in all organizations. |
| el **bienestar** | well being; prosperity |
| el **coste de vida** | cost of living |
| **elevar el nivel de vida**<br>En los años 60 el desarrollo económico elevó el nivel de vida de los españoles. | to raise the standard of living<br>In the 60's economic development raised the standard of living of the Spanish people. |
| la **renta per cápita**<br>La renta per cápita resulta de dividir la renta nacional por la población total. | per capita income<br>Per capita income is obtained by dividing the national income by the total population. |
| la **renta disponible**<br>El incremento de los impuestos reduce la renta disponible. | disposable/spendable income<br>Tax increases reduce disposable income. |
| el **movimiento migratorio**<br>Las guerras y las catástrofes naturales provocan movimientos migratorios de la población. | migratory movement<br>Wars and natural disasters cause migratory movements of the population. |
| la **emigración**<br>La emigración provoca en muchas personas problemas sociales, culturales y familiares. | emigration<br>Emigration causes social, cultural, and family problems for many people. |

**evaluar**
Antes de tomar una decisión es conveniente evaluar las diferentes alternativas.

to evaluate; ponder
Before making a decision it is advisable to evaluate the various alternatives.

la **demografía**
La demografía es la ciencia que se dedica al estudio de las colectividades humanas desde el punto de vista estadístico.

demographics
Demographics is the science devoted to the study of human groupings from a statistical perspective.

**demográfico (a)**
Se ha efectuado un estudio demográfico para determinar el grado de envejecimiento de la población.

demographic
A demographic study has been done to determine the degree of aging of the population.

la **densidad**
La densidad de población es relativamente baja en España.

density
Population density is relatively low in Spain.

el **censo**
Siendo Cirino emperador se mandó realizar el censo del mundo entero.

census
When Cirino was emperor, he ordered that a census of the whole world be undertaken.

el **descenso de la natalidad**
El descenso de la natalidad experimentado por España en los últimos años, la coloca entre los países de más baja natalidad del mundo.

decline in the birthrate
The decline in the birthrate registered in Spain in recent years, makes Spain one of the countries with the lowest birthrate in the world.

**omitir**
En el informe se omitieron datos de absoluto interés.

to issue
The report omitted information of major interest.

**generar**
La renta genera riqueza.

to generate; create
Income generates wealth.

## Economic Development

el **desarrollo económico**
Numerosos países industrializados participaron en la conferencia para el desarrollo económico del tercer mundo.

economic development
Many industrial countries took part in the conference for third world economic development.

**encontrarse**
La economía chilena se encuentra en fase de recuperación y crecimiento.

to meet
The Chilean economy is in a recovery and growth phase.

la **fase**

la **coyuntura**

El sector del automóvil se halla en una coyuntura mundial expansiva.

**coyuntural**

el **ciclo económico**
La economía norteamericana se halla en un ciclo económico expansivo.

**expansivo (a)**

el **ciclo coyuntural**
El mismo ciclo coyuntural se repite cada año por esta época.

el **auge de la economía**
La política económica del Gobierno producirá un auge de la economía que se traducirá en un aumento del bienestar de los ciudadanos.

el **experimentar auge**
El sector de las telecomunicaciones ha experimentado un gran auge gracias a los recientes avances tecnológicos.

el **crecimiento económico**
La consecución del pleno empleo pasa por un crecimiento económico sostenido.

la **consecución**

el **crecimiento real**
Para el cálculo del crecimiento real se deducen los incrementos correspondientes a la depreciación de los equipos productivos.

la **recesión**
La recesión a nivel mundial ha supuesto una traba más al proceso de transición al capitalismo de las economías del Este.

el **receso económico**
El receso económico sufrido en los últimos años hará que la economía española no alcance los objetivos de crecimiento previstos para este año.

phase

current state of being; economic circumstance
The automobile sector is in a worldwide state of economic expansion.

pertaining to the economy

economic cycle
North America's economy is in a cycle of economic expansion.

expansive

economic cycle
The same economic cycle is repeated every year at this time.

economic upturn
The government's economic policies will produce an economic upturn which will be translated into an increase in prosperity for all citizens.

to experience an economic upturn
The telecommunications sector has seen a great economic upturn thanks to recent technological advances.

economic growth
Achieving full employment depends on continuing greater economic growth.

achievement

real growth
To calculate real growth one deducts increases which effect the depreciation of the means of production.

recession
The worldwide recession has been an additional hinderance to the economies of former Eastern Bloc countries in the process of their transition to capitalism.

economic recession
The economic recession suffered in recent years will be responsible for the Spanish economy's failure to achieve the growth levels projected for this year.

el **deterioro**

deterioration

la **inflación**
La inflación es un fenómeno económico que se manifiesta por una subida generalizada del nivel de precios.

inflation
Inflation is an economic phenomenon that is reflected in an across the board rise in prices.

el **incremento**
Carlos A. Menem ha conseguido reducir drásticamente el ritmo de incremento de la inflación que Argentina venía sufriendo.

rise
Carlos A. Menem has succeeded in drastically reducing the inflationary spiral from which Argentina long suffered.

**paulatinamente**
La economía americana se recupera paulatinamente de su última recesión.

slowly
The American economy is slowly recovering from its last recession.

**recuperarse**

to recover; recuperate

la **inestabilidad**
La inestabilidad económica retrae la inversión extranjera.

instability
Economic instability discourages foreign investment.

**retraer**

to retract; contract; retard

la **depresión económica**
América Latina sufre una depresión económica por motivos estructurales.

economic depression
For structural reasons, Latin America is undergoing an economic depression.

la **crisis económica**
El sistema capitalista sufre periódicamente crisis económicas.

economic crisis
The capitalist system suffers from periodic economic crises.

la **estabilización**
El Plan de Estabilización de 1959 supuso para España el primer reajuste de liberalización económica.

stabilization
The 1959 Stabilization Plan prompted Spain's first shift towards economic liberalization.

el **ciclo**
La economía evoluciona mediante ciclos alternantes.

cycle
The economy progresses by means of alternating cycles.

**alternante**

alternating

la **recuperación**

recovery

el **crecimiento**

growth

**acelerado (a)**

accelerating

el **ritmo de crecimiento**

El ritmo de crecimiento de la economía mundial se ha ralentizado en los últimos tiempos.

growth rate/rhythm

Recently, the rate of growth in the global economy has slowed.

**ralentizarse**

to slow down

el **auge coyuntural**

Los meses de verano producen un auge coyuntural en el sector turístico español.

upswing in economic conditions

The summer months bring with them an upswing in the tourist sector in Spain.

el **pleno empleo**

full employment

la **oscilación de la coyuntura**

fluctuation in economic conditions

la **depresión cíclica**

Todas las economías sufren depresiones cíclicas.

cyclical decline/depression

All national economies undergo cyclical depressions.

**decreciente**

falling

**inflacionista**

Las tendencias inflacionistas, bajo determinados supuestos, pueden constituirse en motores de desarrollo económico.

inflationary

Under certain conditions, inflationary tendencies can become factors that drive the economy forward.

la **tasa de inflación**

La tasa de inflación en España es todavía elevada si la comparamos con el resto de países de la Unión Europea.

rate of inflation

The inflation rate in Spain is still high in comparison to the other countries in the European Union.

la **deflación**

La deflación se caracteriza por una caída del nivel general de precios.

deflation

Deflation is characterized by a general falling off of prices.

la **tasa de deflación**

rate of deflation

el **diferencial**

El diferencial de inflación de España respecto a los países de la OCDE es todavía muy significativo.

differential; difference

Spain's rate of inflation, compared to the rate prevalent in OECD countries, is still quite significant.

**inherente**

La elevación de precios es inherente a la inflación.

inherant

Price rises always accompany inflation.

el **programa coyuntural**

Para la consecución de objetivos a corto plazo se han establecido programas coyunturales cuyo horizonte temporal es de un año.

economic program

To achieve short term objectives, economic programs of one year's duration have been instituted.

# The Economy and the Market

el **mercado**
En ocasiones las empresas realizan operaciones de dumping para acaparar cuotas de mercado.

market
Sometimes companies engage in price dumping operations to gain market shares.

la **cuota del mercado**
Las grandes superficies aumentan su cuota de mercado en el sector de la alimentación.

market share
Shopping centers are increasing their market share in the food industry.

los **bienes**

goods

los **servicios**

services

la **oferta**
El precio es la variable que relaciona la oferta y la demanda.

supply
The price is the variable which connects supply and demand.

la **demanda**
La demanda de fondos de inversión ha aumentado en los últimos años.

demand
In the last few years the demand for investment funds has increased.

**creciente**
La demanda de teléfonos móviles es creciente en nuestro país.

growing
The demand for portable telephones is growing in our country.

el **índice de precio**
En el índice de precios las magnitudes que se relacionan son precios.

price index
In the price index, the orders of magnitude that are in ratio to each other, are prices.

el **Indice de Precios al Consumo (IPC)**
El Indice de Precios al Consumo (IPC) se elabora mensualmente.

Consumer Price Index

The Consumer Price Index is compiled monthly.

el **aumento de los precios**

price increase

la **elevación de precios**
El aumento de los precios ha quedado por debajo de las expectativas de inflación.

raise in prices
Price increases have remained lower than those projected because of the rate of inflation.

el **encarecimiento**
El encarecimiento del coste de la vida reduce en términos reales la renta disponible.

rise
The rise in the cost of living reduces real disposable income.

**elevar**
El incremento de la demanda eleva los precios.

to raise
Increase in demand causes prices to rise.

la **estabilización de precios**

price stabilization

la **fijación de precios**
En la economía dirigida la fijación de precios la realiza el Estado.

price fixing
In a planned economy, the state fixes price levels.

la **depresión**
La caída de la demanda ha producido una depresión en los precios.

depression; drop
The decline in demand caused prices to drop.

**decrecer**
El consumo de electrodomésticos ha decrecido en los últimos años.

to sink; decline
In recent years the use of household appliances has declined.

**descender**
El consumo de tabaco entre los adolescentes ha descendido en España.

to decline; drop
Tobacco consumption among adolescents in Spain has declined.

la **competencia**
La competencia entre las empresas es una de las claves del sistema capitalista.

competition
Competition between firms is one of the keystones of the capitalist system.

**sufrir la competencia**

to be subject to competition

**competir**
Por el control del mercado de bebidas de cola compiten varias empresas norteamericanas.

to compete
Various North American companies are in competition for control of the cola market.

la **competitividad**
La racionalización de los costes mejora la competitividad de las empresas.

competitiveness
Streamlining operating costs improves the competitiveness of companies.

**consumir**
Los medios de comunicación, en determinadas ocasiones, incitan a consumir a los ciudadanos.

to consume
The communications media, at certain times, stimulate people to consume more.

**gastar**
Las economías domésticas gastan la mayor parte de su renta en bienes de consumo.

to spend
Private households spend most of their income on consumer goods.

los **gastos**

expenses

el **mercado interior**
Si la demanda no queda satisfecha en el mercado interior hay que recurrir a las importaciones.

domestic market
If the domestic market cannot meet the demand, then it must be met by imports.

el **mercado exterior**
Las economías cerradas prácticamente no existen, hoy en día todos los países realizan intercambios comerciales con el mercado exterior.

foreign market
There are practically no closed economies; nowadays all countries maintain trade relations with foreign markets.

el **bien económico**
Se entiende por bien económico todo aquello que suministra a su poseedor alguna utilidad o beneficio.

economic asset
By economic asset is meant everything which provides its possessor some utility or profit.

el **bien duradero**
Bienes duraderos son aquellos que permanecen de modo permanente al patrimonio de las personas.

durable goods
Durable goods are those which figure permanently in an individual's assets.

**desplegar**
Se desplegaron importantes redes comerciales por parte de las grandes compañías aseguradoras.

to construct
Important distribution networks were constructed by the big insurance companies.

el **coeficiente**
Ha aumentado el coeficiente que relaciona la demanda con el precio.

coefficient
The coefficient that connects demand and price, has risen.

**alterado (a)**
Los mercados bursátiles están muy alterados debido a las fluctuaciones de los tipos de interés.

upset; disturbed
Securities markets are very disturbed because of interest rate fluctuations.

la **elevación**
La elevación de los precios determinó, finalmente, la quiebra del sector.

raise; increase
Price increases finally led to the sector's collapse.

el **dumping**
El dumping consiste en vender productos a un precio inusualmente barato o incluso por debajo del coste.

dumping
Dumping is selling products at an extraordinarily low price, or even selling them below cost.

el **monopolio**
El monopolio es un tipo de mercado que se caracteriza por tener un solo oferente que aprovecha su situación de dominio para imponer el precio.

monopoly
Monopoly is a kind of market in which a single supplier takes advantage of his dominant position to impose his own price.

el **fallo del mercado**

Los fallos del mercado son consecuencia de una ineficaz asignación de los recursos.

market insufficiency; market defects
Market insufficiency is the result of an inefficient allotment of means.

**ineficaz**

inefficient

el **excedente**
La Unión Europea almacena los excedentes lácteos para evitar la caída de los precios.

surplus
The European Union warehouses milk surpluses to keep prices from falling.

**el equilibrio**
Se da equilibrio en un mercado cuando la oferta y la demanda coinciden.

balance
One can speak of a balanced market when supply and demand coincide.

**la disparidad de precios**
Hay una gran disparidad de precios entre los hoteles de Madrid.

price gap/disparity
There are great differences in hotel prices in Madrid.

**el reajuste de los precios**
La entrada de nuevos competidores al mercado ha producido un reajuste de los precios.

price readjustment
The appearance of new competitors on the market has led to a readjustment in prices.

**el mercado negro**
En el mercado negro se producen transacciones de ciertos bienes a un precio distinto del de mercado legal y al margen de la fiscalidad.

black market
On the black market certain goods are traded at a price different from the regular market price and such transactions are marginally illegal.

**el rédito**
Los réditos de capital siguen siendo muy altos en Argentina.

return on capital
Returns on capital continue to be very high in Argentina.

**la competición**
Hubo una dura competición entre los acreedores para hacerse con el control de la empresa.

competition
There was stiff competition among the creditors for control of the company.

**el competidor, la competidora**
En el mercado del hardware hay muchos competidores.

competitor
There are many competitors on the hardware market.

**superfluo (a)**
Para reducir el nivel de gasto las economías domésticas tienen que controlar el consumo de bienes superfluos.

superfluous
To reduce expenses, private households have to keep close watch on the consumption of non-essential items.

**el flujo**
El flujo de inversiones es cada vez mayor.

flow
The flow of investments is continuously increasing.

**repatriar**
Los disturbios obligaron a los inversores extranjeros a repatriar sus capitales.

to repatriate; withdraw
The unrest forced foreign investors to withdraw their capital.

**el índice**
El índice es una relación entre dos magnitudes.

index
The index is the ratio between two orders of magnitude.

**la magnitud**

(order of) magnitude

# Economic Systems

la **economía capitalista**
En Chile hay un sistema de economía capitalista.

capitalist(ic) economy
In Chile there is a capitalistic economic system.

la **economía de mercado**
La economía de mercado ha propiciado el crecimiento acelerado de los países industrializados.

market economy
The market economy has caused the accelerated growth of the industrialized countries.

la **liberalización**

liberalization

la **economía planificada**

planned economy

la **economía dirigida**
La economía planificada, como sistema, propone la propiedad colectiva de los medios de producción.

directed economy
A system of planned economy provides for the collectivization of the means of production.

el **plan económico**

economic plan

**nacionalizar**

to nationalize

la **transición**

transition

la **economía mixta**
La economía mixta se caracteriza por un gran peso específico de las empresas públicas.

mixed economy
In a mixed economy, state owned enterprises play a preponderant role.

la **autarquía**

autarchy

**autoabastecerse**
Si no existiesen las relaciones comerciales las comunidades tendrían que autoabastecerse.

to be self-sufficient
If trade relations did not exist, communities would have to be self-sufficient.

la **economía keynesiana**
Una situación de pleno empleo fomentada por la inversión pública es la nota predominante de la economía keynesiana.

Keynesian economics
A condition of full employment, encouraged by government investment, is the primary characteristic of Keynesian economics.

la **economía cerrada**
Se considera que una economía es cerrada cuando no efectúa intercambios comerciales con el resto del mundo.

closed economy
An economy is considered closed when it carries on no trade relations with the rest of the world.

el **autoabastecimiento**
El autoabastecimiento supone renunciar a cualquier clase de intercambio comercial.

self-sufficiency
Self-sufficiency means the rejection of any kind of trade relations.

## la **economía informal**
La economía informal se encuentra, sobre todo, en los países en vías de desarrollo.

informal economy
The informal economy is found primarily in the developing countries.

## la **economía de plantación**
Localizada en las zonas tropicales, la economía de plantación se basa en la explotación de la barata mano de obra local.

plantation economy
Found in tropical regions, the plantation economy is based on the exploitation of the cheap local labor supply.

## la **economía concentrada**
El sistema económico en que el Estado y las empresas colaboran en la elaboración de planes económicos es el que se denomina economía concentrada.

concentrated economy
The economic system in which the state and private companies work together in economic plans is what is called a concentrated economy.

## el **plan quinquenal**
Los planes quinquenales fueron instaurados por Stalin en la URSS, y básicamente eran una planificación de las metas económicas a alcanzar cada cinco años.

five year plan
The five year plans were instituted by Stalin in the Soviet Union and essentially, they were a setting of economic goals to be attained every five years.

## **nacionalizado (a)**
La banca no está nacionalizada en España.

nationalized
Banks are not nationalized in Spain.

la **región**
La Constitución Española reconoce el derecho a la autonomía de las nacionalidades y regiones que integran el Estado español.

region
The Spanish Constitution recognizes the right to autonomy of the nationalities and regions that constitute the Spanish state.

la **autonomía**

autonomy

el **ente**

entity; corporation

la **propiedad estatal**
Algunas empresas públicas son de exclusiva propiedad estatal.

state-owned property
Some public companies are exclusively owned by the state.

la **propiedad pública**
Los bienes de propiedad pública están constituidos por los bienes reservados al sector público, los bienes de dominio público, los comunales y los que integran el Patrimonio Nacional y los bienes patrimoniales de las empresas públicas.

public property
Public property goods are composed of those goods reserved to the public sector, publicly and communally owned goods, those which constitute the National Heritage, and those that are part of the assets of publicly owned enterprises.

**público (a)**
Radio Televisión Española es un Ente de derecho público.

public
Spanish Radio and Television is a publicly owned corporation.

━━━━━━ Economic Policy ━━━━━━

la **política económica**
La política económica es el principal instrumento con que cuenta el Estado para actuar sobre la economia.

economic policy
Economic policy is the chief means the state relies on to influence the economy.

la **medida**

measure

la **promoción industrial**

El Instituto Nacional de Industria es encargado de la promoción industrial en España.

promotion/encouragement of industry
The National Institute of Industry is responsible for promoting industry in Spain.

la **convergencia económica**
El Fondo de Compensación Interterritorial pretende propiciar la convergencia económica entre las diferentes regiones que constituyen el Estado español.

economic convergence/coordination
The Interterritorial Compensation Fund is trying to encourage economic coordination between the different regions that make up the Spanish state.

**propiciar**

to favor; encourage; to support

**ayudar**
El Fondo Social Europeo ayuda a las zonas más deprimidas a incrementar su nivel de renta.

to help
The European Social Fund helps the most depressed areas to raise their income level.

el **incentivo**

incentive

la **ayuda financiera**

financial aid

el **apoyo financiero**
Algunas empresas necesitan apoyo financiero del Estado para subsistir.

financial support/help
Some companies need financial support from the government in order to survive.

la **subvención**

subvention; subsidy

la **política agraria**
El Estado coordina su política agraria con la de la Unión Europea.

agricultural/farm policy
The state coordinates its agricultural policy with the European Union's policy.

la **política de rentas**
La política de rentas es un instrumento de política económica destinada fundamentalmente a contener las rentas salariales para controlar la inflación.

wage policy
Wage policy is an instrument of political economics conceived primarily to hold down wages and bring inflation under control.

**congelar precios y salarios**
El Gobierno pretende congelar precios y salarios como única medida para controlar la inflación.

to freeze prices and wages
The government is trying to freeze prices and wages as the only measure to control inflation.

el **fomento**
El Estado tiene encomendado el fomento y desarrollo de los diferentes sectores que integran la economía.

support; encouragement
The state is entrusted with the support and development of the different sectors that constitute the economy.

el **fomento del empleo**
El Ministro de Trabajo debe proponer nuevas medidas de fomento de empleo.

encouragement of employment
The Department of Labor should propose new measures to stimulate employment.

la **restricción**
En momentos de crisis las restricciones son necesarias.

restriction
In times of crisis restrictions are necessary.

la **eliminación**
La eliminación total de fronteras en Europa es un proyecto en vías de desarrollo.

elimination
The total elimination of frontiers in Europe is a project that is being developed.

la **política monetaria**
La política monetaria es un instrumento de política económica que actúa sobre la economía a través de la oferta monetaria.

monetary policy
Monetary policy is an instrument of political economics which effects the economy through the money supply.

las **disponibilidades líquidas**
El gobierno ha tomado medidas para reducir las disponibilidades líquidas en manos del público, y así controlar la inflación.

liquid cash assets
The government has taken measures to reduce the liquid cash assets in the hands of the public, and thus to control inflation.

la **depreciación de la moneda**

money devaluation

la **depreciación monetaria**
La depreciación de la moneda es un instrumento de la política económica de los Gobiernos.

currency devaluation
The devaluation of the currency is an instrument of the economic policy of governments.

la **política fiscal**
La política fiscal es un elemento de política económica que utiliza la demanda agregada como medio de actuación sobre la economía.

taxation policy
Taxation policy is an element of political economics which uses total demand as an instrument for economic taxation.

## The National Budget

el **presupuesto**
El presupuesto siempre se presenta formalmente equilibrado.

budget
Every budget submitted is formally balanced.

el **Presupuesto General del Estado**
El Presupuesto General del Estado ha sido congelado este año.

National Budget

The National Budget was frozen this year.

el **gasto público**
El gasto público es un instrumento de política económica típicamente keynesiano.

public expenses; government outlays
Public expenses are a typically Keynesian instrument of economic policy.

el **déficit**
Para este año se pretende corregir el déficit público y el de la balanza de pagos.

deficit
Attempts are being made this year to correct the public deficit and the balance of payments.

el **déficit presupuestario (a)**

budget deficit

la **Deuda del Estado**
La Deuda del Estado es un instrumento para contener el déficit.

government debt
Government debt is a means for limiting the deficit.

**presupuestario (a)**
Ciertas medidas presupuestarias son necesarias.

budget
Certain budgetary measures are necessary.

**equilibrado (a)**

balanced

la **Ley General Presupuestaria**
La Ley General Presupuestaria (España) contiene los principios generales referentes a la actuación del Gobierno y la Administración respecto a los derechos y obligaciones de naturaleza económica del Estado y del sector público.

General Budget Law
The General Budget Law (Spain) contains the general principles pertaining to government and administrative measures with respect to the rights and obligations of an economic nature on the part of the state and the public sector.

los **Pagarés del Tesoro**
Con la emisión de pagarés del tesoro se pretendía en principio cubrir los desfases de tesorería del Tesoro Público.

treasury paper (bills/notes/bonds)
The issuance of treasury paper was basically intended to cover the gaps in the Public Treasury's reserves.

el **Tribunal de Cuentas**

National Audit Office (corresponds to the Committee on Public Accounts in the US)

El Tribunal de Cuentas es el supremo órgano fiscalizador de las cuentas y de la gestión económica del Estado, así como del sector público.

The National Audit Office is the supreme regulatory organ for surveillance of government and public sector accounting activities.

la **Deuda Pública**
La Deuda Pública es un medio para obtener recursos financieros empleado por el Estado y las Comunidades Autónomas.

Public Debt
Public debt is a means employed by the government and the autonomous regions for the procurement of financial means.

## Economic Institutions

el **Instituto Nacional de Empleo (INEM)**
Una de las principales atribuciones del Instituto Nacional de Empleo (INEM) (España) es la gestión y el pago de las prestaciones por desempleo.

National Labor Institute

One of the chief functions of the National Labor Institute (Spain) is the administration and payment of unemployment insurance.

el **Instituto Nacional de Industria**

National Institute of Industry

la **Cámara de Industria y Comercio**

Las Cámaras de Industria y Comercio (España) tienen como objetivo prioritario fomentar y afianzar las relaciones comerciales nacionales e internacionales.

Chamber of Commerce and Industry

The first priority of Chambers of Commerce and Industry (Spain) is to encourage and build up national and international trade relations.

**afianzar**

to strengthen; guarantee; build up

la **Cámara de Comercio Internacional**

La Cámara de Comercio Internacional (España) tiene encomendada la tarea de poner los medios necesarios para la normalización de las relaciones comerciales internacionales.

International Chamber of Commerce

The International Chamber of Commerce (Spain) is entrusted with the task of providing the necessary means for the normalization of international trade relations.

el **Ministerio de Hacienda**

El Ministerio de Hacienda desarrolla toda la política recaudatoria y tributaria en España.

Ministry of Finance; Treasury Department

The Treasury Department sets all tax collecting and taxation criteria in Spain.

**centralizar**

La Consejería de Hacienda centraliza todos los pagos de la Junta de Andalucía.

to centralize

The regional tax administration office centralizes all payments of the Andalusian Provincial Government.

**encomendar**

to entrust; order; put in charge of

**encargado (a)**

ordered; in charge; responsible for

el **MOPTMA (Ministerio de Obras Públicas, Transportes y Medio Ambiente)**

Ministry for Public Works, Transportation, and Environment

el **Instituto Nacional de Estadística (INE)**

National Statistical Institute

la **Consejería de Hacienda**

regional financial administrative offices

el **Tribunal de Defensa de la Competencia**

El Tribunal de Defensa de la Competencia es presidido por D. Miguel Angel Fernández Ordoñez.

Anti-Trust Bureau

The President of the Anti-Trust Bureau is Don Miguel Angel Fernández Ordoñez.

## Environmental Dangers and Environmental Protection

| | |
|---|---|
| la **contaminación del medio ambiente,** la **contaminación medioambiental** | environmental contamination/ pollution |
| La contaminación medioambiental y la reducción progresiva de la capa de ozono son algunos de los grandes problemas a los que se enfrentan los países industrializados. | Environmental pollution and the continuing reduction in the ozone layer are some of the major problems industrialized countries are facing. |
| la **capa de ozono** | ozone layer |
| **enfrentarse** | to be faced/confronted with |
| la **polución** | pollution |
| A la polución del aire y a las emisiones contaminantes procedentes de los hidrocarburos se les atribuye la responsabilidad del efecto invernadero. | Air pollution and toxic emissions of hydrocarbons are thought to be responsible for the greenhouse effect. |
| la **contaminación atmosférica** | atmospheric contamination; air pollution |
| el **hidrocarburo** | hydrocarbon |
| **atribuir a** | to attribute to |
| el **efecto invernadero** | greenhouse effect |
| El efecto invernadero provoca un calentamiento paulatino de la tierra y es responsable del cambio climático y de otras consecuencias desastrosas. | The greenhouse effect causes gradual global warming and is responsible for climate changes and other disastrous consequences. |
| **provocar** | to cause; provoke |
| el **calentamiento de la tierra** | global warming |
| **paulatino (a)** | gradual |
| el **cambio climático** | change in climate |
| **desastroso (a)** | disastrous |
| el **destrozo** | catastrophe; destruction; damage |
| la **emisión** | emission |

las **emisiones contaminantes**
En la Cumbre sobre el clima, cele-
brada en Berlín (abril 1995), no se ha
llegado a ningún acuerdo para reducir
las emisiones contaminantes de dióxido de carbono, de las que, en un
75%, son responsables los países
industrializados.

toxic emissions
At the April 1995 Summit Conference on the Climate, no agreement
was reached on the reduction of
toxic carbon dioxide emissions,
for 75% of which the industrial
countries are responsible.

el **dióxido de carbono (CO$_2$)**

carbon dioxide

el **equilibrio ecológico**
Con demasiada frecuencia, el frágil
equilibrio ecológico se ve alterado por
catástrofes ecológicas tales como las
mareas negras, poniendo en peligro la
supervivencia económica de las personas que viven del mar.

ecological balance
All too often the delicate ecological
balance is disturbed by ecological
catastrophes such as the oil polluted
black tides which endanger the
economic survival of people who
live from the sea.

la **marea negra**

black tide; oil slick

la **supervivencia económica**

economic survival

la **lluvia ácida**
La lluvia ácida, causada por el dióxido
de azufre, provoca una acidificación
del suelo y, con ello, la destrucción
del equilibrio biológico.

acid rain
Acid rain, caused by sulfur dioxide,
leads to soil acidification, and
thereby, the destruction of the
biological balance.

el **dióxido de azufre**

sulfur dioxide

la **acidificación**

acidification

la **erosión**
La erosión, con la consiguiente degradación de la superficie cultivable de la
tierra, está teniendo consecuencias
nefastas sobre la agricultura.

erosion
Erosion, and the lower yields on
arable lands which it causes, is
having a disastrous effect on
agriculture.

**consiguiente**

consequent; resulting

la **degradación**

deterioration; break down

la **superficie cultivable**

area of arable land

**nefasto (a)**

disastrous

el **incendio forestal**
A pesar de los cada vez más sofisticados sistemas de prevención, los frecuentes incendios forestales están
mermando considerablemente la
capacidad de regeneración de los
bosques.

forest fire
Despite increasingly sophisticated
prevention systems, frequent forest fires are considerably depleting
the regenerative capacities of the
woods.

| | |
|---|---|
| el **sistema de prevención** | prevention system |
| **mermar** | to deplete; cut back; reduce |
| la **capacidad de regeneración** | capacity for regenerating |
| el **acuífero** | aquifer |
| Las extracciones de aguas de los acuíferos de zonas húmedas protegidas que se destinan al riego de cultivos están provocando su progresiva desecación. | Tapping aquifers in protected wet areas for the irrigation of cultivated lands is causing their progressive desiccation. |
| la **zona húmeda** | wet area |
| la **desecación** | desiccation; drying up |
| la **salinización** | salinization |
| En muchas regiones costeras se está comprobando una paulatina salinización de las aguas subterráneas debido a la explotación masiva y a las infiltraciones de agua del mar. | A gradual salinization of ground water due to abusive exploitation and sea water infiltrations has been observed in many coastal regions. |
| **comprobarse** | to be confirmed/observed |
| las **aguas subterráneas** | ground water |
| la **explotación masiva** | abusive exploitation; overexploitation |
| la **infiltración** | infiltration |
| la **desertización** | desertification |
| Los países mediterráneos se enfrentan a una desertización progresiva de consecuencias dramáticas que se pondrán de manifiesto el próximo siglo. | Mediterranean countries are threatened by progressive desertification with dramatic consequences which will become apparent in the next century. |
| **dramático (a)** | dramatic |

## ■■■■ The Waste Industry; Waste Disposal ■■■■

| | |
|---|---|
| **deteriorar** | to deteriorate |
| Los residuos de las fábricas contaminan y deterioran el medio ambiente. | Factory wastes pollute and damage the environment. |
| los **residuos sólidos urbanos** | solid household wastes |
| Para favorecer la recogida selectiva de los residuos sólidos urbanos se han instalado puntos verdes de recogida con contenedores especiales para cada producto. | To encourage the collection of pre-sorted solid household wastes, collection centers marked with a green point have been set up with special containers for each product. |

| | |
|---|---|
| **favorecer** | to encourage |
| la **recogida selectiva de residuos** | collection of separated/sorted garbage |
| el **punto verde** | green point (collection center with special containers) |
| el **contenedor** | container |
| el **vertedero** | garbage dump; landfill |

A pesar de las facilidades existentes, la actitud incívica de muchos ciudadanos ha contribuído a la aparición de vertederos incontrolados de negativo impacto medioambiental.

Despite the existing facilities, the selfish attitude of many citizens has helped give rise to unauthorized garbage dumps which have a negative impact on the environment.

| | |
|---|---|
| **incívico (a)** | uncivic; anti-social; selfish |
| la **aparición** | appearance |
| **incontrolado (a)** | uncontrolled; unauthorized |
| el **impacto medioambiental** | environmental impact |
| el **reciclaje** | recycling |

El reciclaje, o recuperación de materiales suceptibles de ser reutilizados, permite reducir considerablemente el empleo de materias primas y energía.

Recycling, or the recovery of material capable of being reused, makes possible substantial reductions in the use of raw material and energy.

| | |
|---|---|
| la **recuperación** | recovery |
| **suceptible** | susceptible; capable of |
| **reutilizar** | to reuse |
| **reciclado (a)** | recycled |
| el **compostaje** | composting |

Con la puesta en funcionamiento de la primera planta de compost, Menorca ha apostado por el compostaje para una eliminación y un aprovechamiento más racional de los desperdicios biológicos.

With the setting up of the first composting facilities, Menorca has chosen composting as a more efficient method for the disposing and recycling of biodegradable wastes.

| | |
|---|---|
| la **planta de compost** | composting facility |
| la **eliminación de residuos** | waste disposal |
| el **aprovechamiento de desperdicios** | solid waste recycling |

| | |
|---|---|
| los **desperdicios biológicos** | biodegradable waste |
| la **depuradora** | water purification plant |
| Con las depuradoras se pretende el aprovechamiento máximo de los limitados recursos hídricos, ya que las aguas residuales convertidas en aguas depuradas pueden ser reutilizadas para el riego agrícola, de zonas verdes, etc. | Water purification plants are designed to make maximum use of limited water reserves, since the purified water obtained from waste waters can be reused for the irrigation of cultivated fields, green zones, etc. |
| los **recursos hídricos** | water reserves/resources |
| las **aguas residuales** | waste waters |
| las **aguas depuradas** | purified waters |
| el **riego agrícola** | irrigation of land under cultivation |
| las **zonas verdes** | green zones |
| la **incineración de residuos** | waste incineration |
| Las incineradoras no encuentran aceptación porque durante la incineración de residuos, y en concreto en la quema de plásticos, se liberan grandes cantidades de dioxina y de otros metales pesados. | Incinerators are not popular because during the incineration process, especially of synthetic materials, large amounts of residual dioxin and other heavy metals are released. |
| la **incineradora** | incinerator |
| la **quema** | burning |
| **liberar** | to liberate; release |
| la **dioxina** | dioxin |
| el **plástico** | plastic; synthetic material |
| el **metal pesado** | heavy metal |
| el **cementerio nuclear** | terminal/permanent atomic waste disposal site |
| El almacenamiento de residuos radioactivos en los llamados cementerios nucleares sigue siendo un punto de discordia entre los intereses de la población civil y los intereses político-económicos. | The storing of radioactive materials in so-called atomic "cemeteries" continues to be a source of controversy between the civilian population and politico-economic interests. |
| los **residuos radioactivos** | atomic residues; atomic waste |
| la **discordia** | discord; controversy |
| la **población civil** | civilian population |

# Environmental Protection

la **conservación de la naturaleza**
Organizaciones ecologistas como
Greenpeace tienen una importante
función social apelando la conciencia
ciudadana en temas como la conservación de la naturaleza y protección del
medio ambiente, aún cuando en la
mayoría de los casos choquen con los
intereses económicos de las grandes
potencias.

conservation of nature
Ecological organizations, like
Greenpeace, have an important
societal function by appealing to
social consciousness when dealing
with themes like nature conservation and environmental protection,
even though in most instances they
clash with the economic interests
of the great powers.

la **organización ecologista**

ecological organization

el, la **ecologista**

ecologist

la **conciencia ciudadana**

civic/social consciousness

la **protección del medio
ambiente**

environmental protection

los **fluorclorocarbonados (FCC)**
Nuestro propio futuro y el de nuestros
hijos depende en gran medida de una
drástica reducción del empleo de
fluorclorocabonados y de las emisiones contaminantes.

chlorofluorocarbons (CFCs)
Our own and our children's future
depends to a large degree on a
drastic reduction in the use of
chlorofluorocarbons and toxic
emissions.

**biodegradable**
La gama de productos ecológicos con
una composición biodegradable casi
al 100% es cada vez más amplia.

biodegradable
The range of ecological products
that are almost 100% biodegradable
is becoming larger and larger.

**ecológico (a)**

ecological

la **composición**

composition

el **papel reciclado**
Si se generalizara totalmente el uso de
papel reciclado, muchas talas indiscri-
minadas de árboles se harían innece-
sarias.

recycled paper
If the use of recycled paper came
into widespread general use, much
indiscriminate cutting down of
trees would become unnecessary.

la **tala**

cutting down

**innecesario (a)**

unnecessary

la **gasolina sin plomo**
Cada vez es mayor el número de automóviles y motorcicletas que llevan
incorporados un catalizador que les
permite emplear gasolina sin plomo,
reduciendo así, las emisiones de ese
metal pesado tan nocivo.

lead free gasoline
More and more automobiles and
motorcycles are now equipped
with a catalytic converter which
makes possible the use of lead
free gasoline, thus reducing that
metal's very toxic emissions.

el **catalizador**

catalytic converter

**nocivo (a)**

toxic; harmful

el **Parque Natural**
España cuenta ya con 17 Parques
Naturales.

Natural/Nature Park
Spain already has 17 Natural
Parks.

la **catalogación**
A través de la catalogación de Parque
Natural de zonas de gran importancia
ecológica se garantiza la protección y
conservación de su fauna y flora.

cataloguing; classification
The protection and conservation
of the flora and fauna in areas of
great ecological importance are
guaranteed by their being classified as natural parks.

la **infracción**
Desgraciadamente, las infracciones
cometidas en materia medioambiental
en muchos casos aún no son sanciona-
das tan contundentemente como se
merecerían.

infraction; crime; offense
Unfortunately, environmental
crimes in many cases are still not
treated with the severity they
deserve.

**medioambiental**

environmental

**contundentemente**

bluntly; severely

**derrochar**
Muchas personas no concienciadas
ecológicamente derrochan agua y
energía eléctrica como si se tratase
de recursos naturales infinitos.

to squander; waste
Many people lacking in environmental awareness waste water and
electrical energy as if they were
natural resources in infinite supply.

**no concienciado (a) ecológica-
mente**

not environmentally aware

**concienciado (a) ecológica-
mente**

environmentally aware

los **recursos naturales**

natural resources

**infinito (a)**

infinite

el **derroche**

squandering; waste

## ■■■■■■■ Institution and Organization ■■■■■■■

la **Comunidad Europea (CE)**
Los miembros fundadores de la Comunidad Europea fueron Bélgica, Francia, Italia, Luxemburgo, los Países Bajos y la República Federal de Alemania.

European Community
The founding members of the European Community were Belgium, France, Italy, Luxembourg, the Netherlands, and the Federal Republic of Germany.

el **miembro fundador**

founding member

la **Comunidad Económica Europea (CEE)**

European Economic Community

el **Tratado de Roma**
En el Tratado de Roma se sentaron las bases para la Comunidad Europea y el Euratom, su primera modificación importante fue la entrada en vigor del Acta Unica Europea el 1.7.1987.

Treaty of Rome
In the Treaty of Rome the foundations for the European Community and Euratom were created. Its first important modification was the taking effect of the Act of European Union on July 7, 1987.

**sentar las bases**

to lay the groundwork/foundations for

la **Comunidad Europea de la Energía Atómica (Euratom)**

European Atomic Energy Community

la **modificación**

modification

el **Acta Unica Europea**

Act of European Union

**comunitario (a)**
En una rueda de prensa, el comisario europeo responsable de la política de desarrollo y pesca se quejó de que siempre fuera el mismo país el que hiciera prevalecer sus propios intereses nacionales sobre los comunitarios.

In a press conference, the European commissioner in charge of development and fishing complained that it was always the same country that put its own national interests above the interests of the community.

la **rueda de prensa**

press conference

el **comisario europeo,** la **comisaria europea**

European commissioner

la **política de desarrollo**

development policy

**hacer prevalecer** — to impose

**la minoría de bloqueo** — blocking minority
Echando leña al fuego en el conflicto sobre pesca y minoría de bloqueo, España amenazó con impedir la ampliación de la UE si ignoraban sus peticiones. — Spain fanned the flames of the conflict around fish quotas and the blocking minority by threatening to prevent the expansion of the EU, if her demands were not met.

**echar leña al fuego** — to fan the flames

**ignorar** — to ignore

**la petición** — petition; demand

**la Unión Europea (UE)** — European Union
La Unión Europea, que hasta el 11 de noviembre de 1993 se llamaba Comunidad Europea, se ha puesto, en una declaración solemne, como propósito final la creación de los "Estados Unidos de Europa". — In a solemn declaration, the European Union, known as the European Community until November 11, 1993, has set itself the ultimate goal of creating a "United States of Europe."

**la declaración** — declaration

**el propósito final** — ultimate/final goal

**el Tratado de la Unión Europea (TUE)** — Treaty of European Union

**el Tratado de Maastricht** — Treaty of Maastricht
El Tratado de la Unión Europea, rubricado en Maastricht el día 7 de febrero de 1992, recoge el principio de subsidiariedad que regula la delimitación de competencias entre los países miembros y la Comunidad. — The Treaty of European Union, signed in Maastricht on February 7, 1992, takes up the principle of subsidiarity which regulates the spheres of competence and authority between the member nations and the Community.

**rubricar** — to sign

**recoger** — to take up; summarize

**la delimitación** — delimitation

**el principio de subsidiariedad** — subsidiarity principle

**la Conferencia Europea Intergubernamental** — European Intergovernmental Conference
El Tratado de Maastricht prevé para 1996 la convocatoria de una Conferencia Europea Intergubernamental para completar o revisar algunos aspectos del mismo. — The Treaty of Maastricht makes provision for the convening of a European Intergovernmental Conference for the complementation or revision of some aspects of the treaty.

| | |
|---|---|
| la **convocatoria** | convening; calling |
| **completar** | to complete; complement |
| **revisar** | to revise |
| el **Consejo Europeo** | European Council |
| El Consejo Europeo está compuesto por los Jefes de Estado de los Estados miembros, así como por el Presidente de la Comisión y se reúne dos veces al año. | The European Council is composed of the heads of state of the member states, along with the President of the European Commission; it meets twice a year. |
| el **Jefe de Estado** | head of state |
| el **Estado miembro** | member state |
| la **Comisión** | Commission |
| La comisión es el órgano ejecutivo, le corresponde velar por los intereses de la Comunidad y asegurar la aplicación y el cumplimiento de los tratados. | The commission is the executive organ responsible for looking out for the Community's interests and ensuring the application of treaties and compliance with them. |
| el **órgano ejecutivo** | executive organ |
| **velar** | to look out for |
| el **Parlamento Europeo** | European Parliament |
| Los 518 diputados del Parlamento Europeo, elegidos por sufragio universal directo, no se agrupan por Estados sino por grupos políticos. | The 518 deputies to the European Parliament, elected by direct universal suffrage, are classified according to political parties, not countries. |
| el **sufragio universal directo** | direct universal suffrage |
| el **grupo político** | political group/party |
| el **Tribunal de Cuentas** | Audit Office |
| Los doce miembros del Tribunal de Cuentas, creado en 1975, examinan la buena gestión del presupuesto. | The twelve members of the Audit Office, created in 1975, check on the correct administration of the budget. |
| el **Comité Económico y Social** | Economic and Social Committee |
| El Comité Económico y Social es un órgano de obligada consulta en determinadas materias y está compuesto por representantes de los diferentes sectores económicos y sociales. | The Economic and Social Committee is a body that must be consulted in certain matters and is composed of representatives of the different economic and social sectors. |
| la **consulta** | consultation |

| | |
|---|---|
| el **Tribunal de Justicia Europeo** | European Court |
| el **convenio de Schengen** | Schengen Agreement (of 1991) |
| El convenio de Schengen, cuyos artífices son los estados del Benelux, Alemania y Francia, tiene como objetivo la abolición de los controles fronterizos para personas y mercancías. | The Schengen Agreement, conceived by the Benelux countries, Germany, and France, aims for the abolition of border controls for people and merchandise. |
| el, la **artífice** | author; originator |
| la **abolición** | abolition |

## Economic Policy of the EU

el **Mercado Unico Europeo,** el **Mercado Interior Europeo**
En el Acta Unica Europea, el Mercado Unico Europeo se dibuja como un verdadero Mercado Común sin fronteras aduaneras, eliminando las trabas existentes entre las economías nacionales.

Single/Domestic European Market

In the Act of European Union, the European domestic market is portrayed as a truly common market with no customs duties, and in which existing trade barriers between national economies will be eliminated.

| | |
|---|---|
| **dibujarse** | to be portrayed |
| el **Mercado Común** | Common Market |
| **eliminar** | to eliminate |
| la **traba** | barrier |
| la **economía nacional** | national economy |
| la **eliminación de aranceles** | elimination of customs duties/tariffs |

la **Unión Aduanera**
La Unión Aduanera, prevista ya en el Tratado de Roma, significa la supresión total del pago de derechos de aduana y de las restricciones cuantitativas en los intercambios comerciales.

Customs Union
The Customs Union, already provided for in the Treaty of Rome, means the complete doing away with customs duties and quantitive limits on commercial trading.

la **Asociación Europea de Libre Cambio**
El 1 de enero de 1994, los Estados miembros de la Unión Europea y de la Asociación Europea de Libre Cambio se han asociado creando el Espacio Económico Europeo.

European Free Trade Association

On January 1, 1994, the member states of the European Union and of the European Free Trade Association joined together to create the European Economic Sphere.

| | |
|---|---|
| el **Espacio Económico Europeo** | European Economic Sphere |
| la **Unión Económica y Monetaria** | Economic and Currency Union |
| Casi ningún país de los que aspiran a acceder a la fase final de la Unión Económica y Monetaria cumple las condiciones exigidas: disciplina presupuestaria, estabilidad de precios y mantenimiento durante dos años en los márgenes normales de fluctuación. | Almost no country seeking access to the final stage of the Economic and Currency Union fulfills the required conditions; budgetary discipline, price stability and remaining for two years within the normal fluctuation margins. |
| **aspirar** | to aspire; seek |
| la **disciplina presupuestaria** | budgetary discipline/restraint |
| la **estabilidad de precios** | price stability |
| el **mantenimiento** | maintenance; staying |
| la **convergencia** | convergence; adaptation; rapprochment |
| En la primera fase de la Unión Económica y Monetaria, los Estados miembros presentaron programas de convergencia económica. | In the first stage of the Economic and Currency Union, the member states presented economic convergence programs. |
| la **moneda única** | single currency |
| la **moneda nacional** | national currency |
| la **libre circulación de personas, bienes, servicios y capitales** | free circulation of persons, goods, services, and capital |
| La libre circulación de personas, bienes, servicios y capitales es uno de los requisitos imprescindibles para el desarrollo continuo de la UE. | The free circulation of persons, goods, and capital is one of the indispensable requirements for the continued development of the EU. |
| el **Sistema Eurcpeo de Bancos Centrales** | European Central Banking System |
| El Sistema Europeo de Bancos Centrales será el responsable exclusivo de la política monetaria, delegando algunas funciones en los Bancos Centrales nacionales. | The European Central Banking system will have sole responsibility for monetary policy, with some functions delegated to the central banks of member nations. |
| **delegar** | to delegate |
| la **función** | function |
| el **Banco Central Europeo** | Central European Bank |
| el **Banco Europeo de Inversiones (BEI)** | European Investment Bank (EIB) |
| El Banco Europeo de Inversiones concede préstamos y garantías para favorecer el desarrollo regional. | The European Investment Bank grants loans and guarantees to encourage regional development. |

| | |
|---|---|
| el **Fondo Europeo de Desarrollo Regional (FEDER)**<br>El Fondo Europeo de Desarrollo Regional (FEDER), el Fondo Social Europeo (FSE) y el Fondo Europeo de Orientación y Garantía Agrícola (FEOGA) son los Fondos Estructurales para fomentar la cohesión económica y social. | European Fund for Regional Development (EFRD)<br>The European Fund for Regional Development, the European Social Fund, the European Agricultural and Guarantee Fund are structural funds for the promotion of economic and social cohesion. |
| el **Fondo Social Europeo (FSE)** | European Social Fund (ESF) |
| el **Fondo Europeo de Orientación y Garantía Agrícola (FEOGA)** | European Agricultural Orientation and Guarantee Fund (EAOGF) |
| la **cohesión** | cohesion |
| la **subvención**<br>Ya han surgido las primeras empresas que ofrecen servicios de asesoramiento sobre la mejor forma de conseguir subvenciones otorgadas por la Unión Europea. | subsidy; subvention<br>Firms have already appeared that offer consulting services on how best to get hold of subventions granted by the European Union. |
| **surgir** | to rise; appear |
| los **sanciones económicas**<br>La Comisión Europea ha impuesto sanciones económicas de 105 millones de ecus a 16 empresas por haberse repartido el mercado de vigas de acero. | economic sanctions<br>The European Commission has imposed economic sanctions totaling 105 million ecus on 16 companies for having divided up the steel girder market among themselves. |
| **repartirse el mercado** | to divide up the market |
| la **viga de acero** | steel girder |

335

━━━━━━━━━ **General Information** ━━━━━━━━━

la **economía mundial**
USA, la Unión Europea y Japón son los líderes de la economía mundial.

global economy
The USA, the European Union, and Japan are the leaders in the global economy.

la **superación**
Los dos grandes retos a los que se enfrenta la economía mundial son la superación de la crisis de endeudamiento y la depauperación que afecta a la mayor parte del Tercer Mundo.

overcoming
The two greatest challenges facing the global economy are the settling of the deep debt crisis and the impoverishment affecting the greater part of the third world.

la **crisis de endeudamiento**

debt crisis

la **depauperación**

pauperization; impoverishment

el **desequilibrio económico**
Hay un gran desequilibrio económico entre países ricos y países pobres.

economic imbalance
There is a great economic imbalance between rich and poor countries.

el **Tercer Mundo**

third world

el **país subdesarrollado**
Muchos países subdesarrollados estiman que el GATT se inclina más hacia los intereses de los países industrializados a costa de los menos desarrollados.

underdeveloped countries
Many underdeveloped countries think that GATT is more oriented to the interests of the industrialized countries at the expense of the less developed ones.

**estimar**

to think; estimate

**a costa de**

at the expense of

el **país en vías de desarrollo**
Los países en vías de desarrollo son aquellos cuyo nivel de desarrollo se ha quedado descolgado respecto del resto de los países.

developing country
Developing countries are countries whose degree of development has lagged behind the level in other countries.

el **nivel de desarrollo**

state/degree/level of development

**quedarse descolgado (a)**

to have lagged behind

el **país en vías de industrialización**
Los países en vías de industrialización están en el umbral de la industrialización y ya tienen una fuerte proyección exportadora, como, p. ej., algunas naciones en el sureste asiático.

country beginning to industrialize

Countries beginning to industrialize are on the threshold of industrialization and already have a strong export orientation, such as, e.g. some nations of Southeast Asia.

| | |
|---|---|
| el **umbral** | threshold |
| el **país industrializado** | industrialized country |
| el **sureste asiático** | Southeast Asia |
| la **ayuda al desarrollo** | development assistance |
| la **ayuda exterior** | outside help |

En España, ha surgido un movimiento que pide que se destine el 0,7% del PIB a la ayuda exterior.

In Spain, a movement has appeared which advocates that 0.7% of the Gross Domestic Product be ear-marked for aid to developing countries.

| | |
|---|---|
| el **movimiento** | movement |
| el **conflicto Norte-Sur** | North-South conflict |

El conflicto Norte-Sur no es sólo un conflicto entre los intereses opuestos de los países acreedores y deudores, sino un problema que determinará el futuro de nuestro planeta en el milenio próximo.

The North-South conflict is not only a conflict of opposing interests between creditor and debtor nations, but also a problem which will determine the future of our planet in the next millenium.

| | |
|---|---|
| **opuesto (a)** | opposing |
| el **país acreedor** | creditor nation |
| el **país deudor** | debtor nation |
| el **diálogo Norte-Sur** | North-South dialogue |
| las **grandes potencias** | great powers |

## International Economic Policy

el **mercado mundial**
world/global market

Los acuerdos del GATT afectan a la mayoría de las transacciones comerciales efectuadas en el mercado mundial.

The GATT agreements affect most business transactions on the world market.

la **guerra comercial**
trade war

Lo que ha motivado a EE UU a amenazar a Japón con una guerra comercial sin precedentes ha sido la negativa japonesa a rectificar su trato discriminatorio hacia los productos americanos, produciéndose así un gigantesco superávit en la balanza comercial japonesa.

What motivated the USA to threaten Japan with an unprecedented trade war was the Japanese refusal to correct its discriminatory treatment of American products, thus producing a giant surplus in Japan's balance of trade.

**motivar**
to motivate

| | |
|---|---|
| **sin precedentes** | unprecedented |
| **rectificar** | to correct |
| el **trato discriminatorio** | discriminatory treatment |
| **gigantesco (a)** | giant |
| las **represalias comerciales** | commercial/trade reprisals |

Las amenazas de EE UU de tomar represalias comerciales inquietan a Japón que, no obstante, está dando largas a una apertura de sus mercados.

US threats to take commercial reprisals disturb Japan; nevertheless Japan has dragged its feet on the issue of opening its markets.

| | |
|---|---|
| **inquietar** | to upset/disturb |
| **dar largas** | to prolong; postpone; drag out |
| la **apertura** | opening |
| el **proteccionismo** | protectionism |

Muchos socios comerciales de EE UU se quejan del proteccionismo que todavía ejerce Washington en el sector textil.

Many US trade partners complain of the protectionist policies Washington still practices in the textiles sector.

| | |
|---|---|
| el **socio comercial,** la **socia comercial** | trade partner |
| **presionar** | to put pressure on; pressure |

Después de presionar a los europeos durante la reanudación de las negociaciones sobre el futuro del sector audiovisual, los americanos han adoptado una actitud más conciliadora para alejarse del punto muerto.

After putting pressure on the Europeans when negotiations on the future of the audio visual sector were resumed, the Americans later adopted a more conciliatory attitude to break the deadlock.

| | |
|---|---|
| la **reanudación** | resumption |
| **adoptar una actitud** | to take/adopt an attitude |
| **conciliador (ora)** | conciliatory |
| **alejarse de** | to move away from |
| el **punto muerto** | deadlock; impasse; stalemate |
| la **claúsula de la nación más favorecida** | most favored nation clause |

Uno de los pilares del GATT es la cláusula de la nación más favorecida, según la cual un país debe conceder las ventajas arancelarias acordadas con una nación a todos los demás países con quienes existen convenios de nación más favorecida.

One of the pillars of the GATT agreements is the most favored nation clause which provides that a country which has been granted tariff advantages must in turn grant them to all other countries with which most favored nation agreements exist.

| | |
|---|---|
| el **pilar** | pillar |
| la **ventaja arancelaria** | tariff/customs advantage |
| el **convenio de la nación más favorecida** | most favored nation agreement |
| los **derechos especiales de giro (DEG)** | special bill drawing rights; special transfer rights |
| Los derechos especiales de giro son unidades de cuenta que sirven como activo financiero de reserva y medio de pago permitiendo incrementar la liquidez internacional. | Special bill drawing rights are accounting units which serve as financial reserve assets and instruments of payment that make possible growth in international liquidity. |
| **servir de** | serve as |
| el **activo financiero** | financial assets |

## ▬▬▬ International Organizations and Mergers ▬▬▬

| | |
|---|---|
| el **Banco Mundial** | World Bank |
| El capital privado desplazará al Banco Mundial en la financiación de Latinoamérica y Asia, mientras la institución financiera aumentará su presencia como asesor de programas de desarrollo. | Private capital will replace the World Bank in the financing of South America and Asia, although financial institutions will play a more prominent role as consultants for development programs. |
| **desplazar** | to displace; replace |
| la **presencia** | presence |
| el **programa de desarrollo** | development program |
| el **Banco Internacional de Pagos (BIP)** | International Payments Bank |
| el **Fondo Monetario Internacional (FMI)** | International Monetary Fund |
| El Fondo Monetario Internacional ha propuesto un ajuste estructural a través de un conjunto de medidas destinadas a resolver los desequilibrios macroeconómicos. | The International Monetary Fund has proposed a structural adjustment package with measures for the stabilization of macroeconomic imbalances. |
| el **ajuste estructural** | structural adjustment |
| el **conjunto de medidas** | series/package/ensemble of measures |

el **Club de los Diez**

Club of Ten

El Club de los Diez reúne a los gobernadores de los bancos centrales de los diez países occidentales de mayor peso económico.

The Club of Ten brings together the presidents of the central banks of the 10 economically most important Western countries.

el **gobernador,** la **gobernadora**

governor; director; chairperson; president

el **peso**

weight

la **Organización de Cooperación y Desarrollo Económico (OCDE)**

Organization for Cooperation and Economic Development (OCED)

La Organización de Cooperación y Desarrollo Económico es, hoy en día, un importante foro internacional de debate y cada año se publica un informe sobre la actual situación económica de sus 24 estados miembros.

Nowadays the Organization for Cooperation and Economic Development is an important international discussion forum and every year it publishes a report on the current economic situation of its 24 member states.

el **foro**

forum

el **debate**

debate

el **Acuerdo General sobre Aranceles y Comercio**

General Agreement on Tariffs and Trade (GATT)

Los objetivos del GATT, que a finales de 1993 tenía 115 miembros de pleno derecho, son la eliminación de los aranceles, de la discriminación comercial, de la contingentación de importaciones y de las distorsiones de competencia.

The goals set by GATT, which had 115 full-fledged members at the end of 1993, are the elimination of tariffs, trade discrimination, import restrictions, as well as unfair competition.

el **miembro de pleno derecho**

full-fledged member

la **discriminación**

discrimination

la **contingentación de importaciones**

import limitations

las **distorsiones de competencia**

unfair competition

el **bloque comercial**

trade block/group

Los más importantes bloques comerciales americanos son el Tratado de Libre Comercio entre EE UU, Canadá y Méjico, MERCOSUR y el Pacto Andino.

The most important American trade blocks are the Free Trade Treaty between the USA, Canada, and Mexico, MERCOSUR and the Andean Pact.

el **Tratado de Libre Comercio**

Free Trade Treaty (member nations, USA, Canada, Mexico)

el **Mercado Común Centro-americano**

Central American Common Market

el **MERCOSUR**

MERCOSUR es la asociación de los países Argentina, Brasil, Uruguay y Paraguay con el fín de crear un mercado interior y suprimir todo lo que pueda obstaculizar su progreso económico.

MERCOSUR

MERCOSUR is the association of the countries Argentina, Brazil, Uruguay, and Paraguay for the purpose of creating a domestic market and the elimination of anything that might stand in the way of economic progress.

**obstaculizar**

to block; impede; stand in the way of

el **Pacto Andino**

El Pacto Andino, fundado en 1969, abarca Bolivia, Ecuador, Colombia y Venezuela y tiene como objetivo coordinar la política económica de sus países miembros. El día 1.1.1992, fueron eliminados sus aranceles interiores.

Andean Pact

The purpose of the Andean Pact, founded in 1969, is the coordination of the economic policies of its member nations, Bolivia, Ecuador, Colombia, and Venezuela. On January 1, 1992 its member states abolished tariff barriers with each other.

**coordinar**

to coordinate

la **política económica**

economic policy

el **Banco Interamericano de Desarrollo**

El Banco Interamericano de Desarrollo, fundado en 1959 dentro de la OEA y ubicado en Washington, ha financiado ya numerosos programas de desarrollo.

Interamerican Bank for Development

The Interamerican Bank for Development, founded in 1959 within the framework of the OAS and located in Washington, has already financed numerous development programs.

la **OEA (Organización de Estados Americanos)**

OSA (Organization of American States)

el **programa de desarrollo**

development program

la **Conferencia de las Naciones Unidas sobre el Comercio y el Desarrollo (UNCTAD)**

La Conferencia de las Naciones Unidas sobre el Comercio y el Desarrollo es una conferencia económica mundial, siendo uno de sus objetivos primordiales la estabilización de los precios en favor de los países suministradores de materias primas.

United Nations Conference on Trade and Development (UNCTAD)

The United Nations Conference on Trade and Development is a world economic conference; one of its fundamental goals is price stabilization to help the countries that supply raw materials.

| | |
|---|---|
| la **conferencia económica mundial** | world economic conference |
| la **estabilización** | stabilization |
| el **país suministrador** | supplier nation |
| la **Organización de los Países Exportadores de Petróleo (OPEP)** | Organization of Petroleum Exporting Countries (OPEC) |
| la **Organización Internacional del Trabajo** | International Labor Organization |

# ▮▮▮ **Abbreviations of Spanish Business Terms** ▮▮▮

| | |
|---|---|
| **acpt.** | aceptación |
| **admón.** | administración |
| **AEAT** | Agencia Tributaria |
| **AEEDE** | Asociación Española de Dirección de Empresas |
| **apdo.** | apartado |
| **art.** | artículo |
| **atte.** | atentamente |
| **Av., Avda.** | avenida |
| **AVE** | Tren de Alta Velocidad |
| **Bco.** | Banco |
| **BEI** | Banco Europeo de Inversiones |
| **BIP** | Banco Internacional de Pagos |
| **b.°** | beneficio |
| **B.O.E.** | Boletín Oficial del Estado |
| **C/:** | calle |
| **c/c** | cuenta corriente |
| **CCOO** | Comisiones Obreras |
| **CE** | Comunidad Europea |
| **CEE** | Comunidad Económica Europea |
| **CEOE** | Confederación Española de Organizaciones Empresariales |
| **CESCE** | Compañía Española de Seguros de Créditos a la Exportación |
| **C&F** | coste y flete |
| **cgo.** | cargo |
| **Cía.** | compañía |
| **cje.** | corretaje |
| **CIF** | coste, seguro y flete |
| **CIF** | código de identificación fiscal |
| **CNMV** | Comisión Nacional del Mercado de Valores |
| **c°** | cambio |
| **C.O.U.** | Curso de Orientación Universitaria |
| **cta.** | cuenta |
| **cte.** | corriente |
| **Ctra.** | carretera |
| **D.** | don |
| **Dª** | doña |
| **D/A** | documentos contra aceptación |
| **dcha.** | derecha |
| **DDP** | entregada, derechos pagados |
| **DEG** | derechos especiales de giro |
| **DEQ** | entregada en muelle |
| **DES** | entregada sobre buque |
| **d/f** | días fecha |
| **DGS** | Dirección General de Seguros |
| **DGTE** | Dirección General de Transacciones Exteriores |
| **D.N.I.** | Documento Nacional de Identidad |
| **d/p** | documentos contra pago |
| **dpto.** | departamento |
| **EE.UU.** | Estados Unidos |
| **entlo.** | entresuelo |

| | |
|---|---|
| **EO** | estimación objetiva |
| **EPA** | Encuesta sobre Población Activa |
| **Euratom** | Comunidad Europea de la Energía Atómica |
| **FAS** | franco al costado del buque |
| **F.C.** | ferrocarril |
| **FCA** | franco transportista |
| **FCC** | fluorclorocarbonado |
| **FEDER** | Fondo Europeo de Desarrollo Regional |
| **FEOGA** | Fondo Europeo de Orientación y Garantía Agrícola |
| **FITUR** | Feria Internacional del Turismo |
| **FMI** | Fondo Monetario Internacional |
| **FOB** | franco a bordo |
| **F.P.** | Formación Profesional |
| **FSE** | Fondo Social Europeo |
| **G/** | giro |
| **G.P.** | giro postal |
| **GRE** | garantía de riesgo a la exportación |
| **G.V.** | gran velocidad |
| **Hnos.** | hermanos |
| **IAE** | Impuesto de Actividades Económicas |
| **IATA** | Asociación de Transporte Aéreo Internacional |
| **IBI** | impuesto sobre bienes inmuebles |
| **ICAC** | Instituto de Contabilidad y Auditoría de Cuentas |
| **ICEX** | Instituto (Español) de Comercio Exterior |
| **I+D** | Investigación y Desarrollo |
| **id.** | idem |
| **I.L.T.** | incapacidad laboral transitoria |
| **impte.** | importe |
| **INE** | Instituto Nacional de Estadística |
| **INEM** | Instituto Nacional de Empleo |
| **Ing°** | ingeniero |
| **IPC** | Indice de Precios al Consumo |
| **IRPF** | Impuesto sobre la Renta de las Personas Físicas |
| **IS** | Impuesto sobre Sociedades |
| **IVA** | Impuesto sobre el Valor Añadido |
| **izq.** | izquierda |
| **J.D.** | junta directiva |
| **J. de G.** | junta de gobierno |
| **J.G.** | junta general |
| **L/** | letra de cambio |
| **liq.** | líquido |
| **m/a** | mi aceptación |
| **m/cgo.** | mi cargo |
| **m/cta.** | mi cuenta |
| **M.E.C.** | Ministerio de Educación y Ciencia |
| **MEFF** | mercado español de futuros financieros |
| **m/f.** | mi favor |
| **m/fra.** | mi factura |
| **m/g.** | mi giro |
| **m/l.** | mi letra |
| **m/o.** | mi orden |
| **MOPTMA** | Ministerio de Obras Públicas, Transportes y Medio Ambiente |

345

| | |
|---|---|
| **m/r.** | mi remesa |
| **m/ref.** | mi referencia |
| **m/t.** | mi talón |
| **N.B.** | nota bene |
| **n/cta.** | nuestra cuenta |
| **n/cgo.** | nuestro cargo |
| **n/f.** | nuestro favor |
| **n/fra.** | nuestra factura |
| **n/g.** | nuestro giro |
| **N.I.F** | número de identificación fiscal |
| **n/l.** | nuestra letra |
| **n°** | número |
| **n/o.** | nuestra orden |
| **n/r.** | nuestra remesa |
| **n/ref.** | nuestra referencia |
| **n/t.** | nuestro talón |
| **ntro./a.** | nuestro/a |
| **O/** | orden |
| **OCDE** | Organización de Cooperación y Desarrollo Económico |
| **OEA** | Organización de Estados Americanos |
| **OJD** | Oficina de Justificación de la Difusión |
| **OPA** | oferta pública de adquisición de acciones |
| **OPEP** | Organización de los Países Exportadores de Petróleo |
| **P/** | pagaré |
| **P.A.** | por autorización |
| **pág.** | página |
| **p.b.** | peso bruto |
| **P/d.** | porte debido |
| **P.D.** | postdata |
| **p.e., p.ej.** | por ejemplo |
| **PER** | Plan de Empleo Rural |
| **P.G.C.** | Plan General de Contabilidad |
| **PHN** | Plan Hidrológico Nacional |
| **P.N.** | peso neto |
| **p°** | paseo |
| **Pje.** | pasaje |
| **p.o.** | por orden |
| **p.p.** | por poder |
| **P.p.** | porte pagado |
| **p.pdo.** | próximo pasado |
| **pral.** | principal |
| **pról.** | prólogo |
| **prov.** | provincia |
| **P.S.** | post scriptum |
| **pts.** | pesetas |
| **PVP** | precio de venta al público |
| **Pza.** | plaza |
| **Rbí.** | recibí |
| **Rbla.** | rambla |
| **RENFE** | Red Nacional de los Ferrocarriles Españoles |
| **SA** | sociedad anónima |
| **S.E u O.** | salvo error u omisión |

| | |
|---|---|
| **Sgte(s).** | siguiente(s) |
| **SIMO** | Feria de Material Informático |
| **SL** | sociedad de responsabilidad limitada |
| **SME** | Sistema Monetario Europeo |
| **S.M.I.** | Salario Mínimo Interprofesional |
| **s/n** | sin número |
| **Sr.** | señor |
| **Sra.** | señora |
| **Srta.** | señorita |
| **s/ref.** | su referencia |
| **Sres.** | señores |
| **S.R.L.** | Sociedad de responsabilidad limitada |
| **Suc.** | sucursal |
| **tfno.** | teléfono |
| **tlx.** | télex |
| **TUE** | Tratado de la Unión Europea |
| **UC** | Unión de Consumidores |
| **Ud.** | usted |
| **Uds.** | ustedes |
| **UE** | Unión Europea |
| **UGT** | Unión General de Trabajadores |
| **UNCTAD** | Conferencia de las Naciones Unidas sobre el Comercio y el Desarrollo |
| **V° B°** | visto bueno |
| **Vd.** | usted |
| **Vds.** | ustedes |
| **v/d** | valor declarado |
| **VIAPRO** | viaje de prospección de mercados |
| **vt°** | vencimiento |

## Spanish Speaking Countries, Capitals, and Currencies

| PAÍS | CAPITAL | MONEDA |
|---|---|---|
| Argentina | Buenos Aires | el austral |
| Bolivia | La Paz | el peso |
| Chile | Santiago | el peso |
| Colombia | Bogotá | el peso |
| Costa Rica | San José | el colón |
| Cuba | La Habana | el peso |
| Ecuador | Quito | el sucre |
| El Salvador | San Salvador | el colón |
| España | Madrid | la peseta |
| Guatemala | Ciudad de Guatemala | el quetzal |
| Honduras | Tegucigalpa | el lempira |
| México | México D.F. | el peso |
| Nicaragua | Managua | el córdoba |
| Panamá | Ciudad de Panamá | el dólar |
| Paraguay | Asunción | el guaraní |
| Perú | Lima | el inti/nuevo sol |
| Puerto Rico | San Juan | el dólar |
| República Dominicana | Santo Domingo | el peso |
| Uruguay | Montevideo | el peso |
| Venezuela | Caracas | el bolívar |

# Index

All the basic vocabulary words appear as **boldfaced entries**, whereas all the continuing vocabulary entries are in lightface.

## Ch

## D

importador, -ora 165
importar 165
importe 199
importe exento de impuestos 301
importe neto de la cifra de negocios 103
importe total 194
imprenta 202
**imprescindible** 24
**impresión** 212
**impreso** 301
**impreso comercial** 224
**impreso para certificar** 223
**impreso publicitario** 223
**impresora** 211
**imprevistos** 86
**imprimir** 212
**imprudencia** 250
impuesto 295
Impuesto de Actividades Económicas 296
**impuesto de circulación** 298
**impuesto de lujo** 297
**impuesto directo** 297
**impuesto indirecto** 297
**impuesto sobre bienes inmuebles** 298
**impuesto sobre el alcohol y las bebidas derivadas** 298
**impuesto sobre el tabaco** 298
Impuesto sobre el Valor Añadido 134, 297
**impuesto sobre hidrocarburos** 297
Impuesto sobre la Renta de las Personas Físicas 299
Impuesto sobre Sociedades 299
**impugnar** 256
impulsar 296
imputado, imputada 262
inalcanzable 117
inasequible 188
**inauguración** 109
**inaugurar** 144

incansable 165
**incapacidad laboral transitoria** 30
**incapacidad permanente** 301
**incautación** 167
**incautarse** 176
**incendio forestal** 324
incentivar 89
incentivo 319
incertidumbre 290
incidente 197
**incidente** 251
incidir en 98
**incierto, a** 37
**incineración de residuos** 327
**incineradora** 327
incitar a la compra 162
incívico, a 326
inclinarse por 146
**incluir en el orden del día** 208
**inclusión** 186
**incompatible** 27
incontrolado, a 326
**incorporación** 17
incoterms 177
**incrementar** 117
incremento 115, 310
incremento del patrimonio 299
inculpado, inculpada 259
**incumplimiento de contrato** 172
incumplimiento del contrato 249
incumplir las obligaciones de pago 199
**incurrir en** 85
**incurrir en responsabilidad** 257
indemnización 35, 245
**indemnización de daños y perjuicios** 257
**indemnizado, a** 250
indemnizar 240
independientemente 123
indicación 175
indicador 238

**indicador económico** 133, 306
indicar 243
**índice** 315
índice bursátil 290
**índice de audiencia** 149
índice de precio 312
Indice de Precios al Consumo 312
**índice obtenido por muestreo** 140
indispensable 19
índole 197
inducir 135
**indultar** 264
industria 44
industria alimentaria 45
industria clave 45
**industria conservera** 46
industria del calzado 44
industria del carbón y del acero 44
**industria del ocio** 48
**industria electrónica** 46
**industria farmacéutica** 46
industria química 45
**INE** 322
**INEM** 14
INEM 321
**ineficaz** 314
inestabilidad 310
**inestabilidad laboral** 12
**infiltración** 325
**infinito, a** 329
inflación 310
**inflacionista** 311
infligir 240
influenciar 145
informe financiero 78
**informe pericial** 246
**infracción** 329
**infracción de un contrato** 187
**infraseguro** 243
**infrautilización** 109
infructuoso, a 196
**ingresar** 17, 277

# P

**perfeccionamiento** 24
**perfilarse** 133
**perfil del candidato** 16
**período de amortiza-
ción** 287
**período de circulación**
118
**período de prueba** 37
**período impositivo** 301
**peritaje** 246
perito 245, 260
**perjudicado, perjudi-
cada** 251
**perjuicio** 135
permanecer 72
permiso de trabajo 12
persona de contacto 18
personalidad jurídica
249
**personalizado, a** 159
personarse 16
persuadir 146
perteneciente a 155
**pertinente** 219
pesca de altura 40
pesca de bajura 40
peso 341
peso bruto 125
pesquero, a 40
petición 142, 331
**peticionario, a** 86
**peticionario, peticiona-
ria** 86
petición de oferta 180
petitum 248
petrolero 235
petroquímico, a 45
**P.G.C.** 95
pieza de recambio 109
pieza de repuesto 109
pignorable 120
**pilar** 340
pillar 174
pingüe 232
**piquete de huelga** 33
**pisapapeles** 203
**piscifactoría** 42
plan de inversiones 87
**plan de viabilidad** 65,
90
plan económico 316
plan financiero 76

**Plan General de Con-
tabilidad** 95
planificación 112
**planificación de medios
publicitarios** 152
**plan quinquenal** 317
planta 107
**planta de compost** 326
**planta siderúrgica** 45
**plantearse** 114
plantilla 73
**plástico** 327
plaza bursátil 289
plazo 260
**plazo de almacenaje**
121
plazo de entrega 192
plazo de garantía 124
**plazo de preaviso** 36,
280
plazo de suministro 192
pleno, a 47
**pleno, a** 109
**pleno empleo** 311
**pliego de condiciones**
86, 182
**pluriempleo** 15
plus 35
**p.o.** 216
**población activa** 15
**población civil** 327
poder adquisitivo 131
**poder general para
pleitos** 250
poder para concluir con-
tratos 160
polígono industrial 107
política agraria 319
política de desarrollo
330
política de la compañía
116
política de rentas 319
política económica 318,
342
política fiscal 320
política monetaria 271,
320
póliza de seguro 243
**póliza flotante** 244
polo de desarrollo 319
polución 323

**ponencia** 24
poner a disposición 72
**poner a la venta** 164
poner al día 276
poner al servicio de 116
**poner con** 228
**poner de manifiesto**
106
**poner en circulación**
274
**poner en entredicho**
85
poner en marcha 112
poner en peligro 122
**ponerse de acuerdo** 32
ponerse en contacto con
217
poner u/c en conoci-
miento de alguien 245
poner un anuncio 148
popular 233
**popularidad** 167
por avión 222
por correo aparte 216
por correo certificado
222
**por cuenta ajena** 14
**por cuenta de** 195
**por cuenta propia** 14
por desapercibido 174
por duplicado 206
**por equivocación** 197
**por la otra línea** 228
por la presente 192
**por la vía extrajudicial**
256
**pormenorizado, a** 220
**pormenorizar** 220
**por orden** 216
por orden alfabético 205
**por poder** 215
por principio 192
**por procedimiento
judicial** 173
**por término medio** 140
por todo lo alto 152
por triplicado 206
por valor de 152
**por vía judicial** 200
posesión 252
posibilitar 111
**posición clave** 70